MONSTER MANUAL II

ED BONNY, JEFF GRUBB, RICH REDMAN, SKIP WILLIAMS, STEVE WINTER

ADDITIONAL DESIGN
DAVID ECKELBERRY, JAMES JACOBS

EDITORS
DALE DONOVAN, PENNY WILLIAMS

MANAGING EDITOR
KIM MOHAN

CREATIVE DIRECTOR
RICHARD BAKER

RPG CATEGORY MANAGER
ANTHONY VALTERRA

VICE PRESIDENT OF RPG R&D
BILL SLAVICSEK

VICE PRESIDENT OF PUBLISHING
MARY KIRCHOFF

PROJECT MANAGER
MARTIN DURHAM

PRODUCTION MANAGER
CHAS DELONG

ART DIRECTOR
DAWN MURIN

COVER ARTIST
HENRY HIGGINBOTHAM

INTERIOR ARTISTS
GLEN ANGUS, DAREN BADER, THOMAS BAXA, MATT CAVOTTA, DENNIS CRAMER, DAVID DAY, BRIAN DESPAIN, TONY DITERLIZZI, MICHAEL DUTTON, JEFF EASLEY, EMILY FIEGENSCHUH, DONATO GIANCOLA, LARS GRANT-WEST, REBECCA GUAY, QUINTON HOOVER, JEREMY JARVIS, ALTON LAWSON, TODD LOCKWOOD, RAVEN MIMURA, MATT MITCHELL, VINOD RAMS, WAYNE REYNOLDS, DAVID ROACH, SCOTT ROLLER, RICHARD SARDINHA, MARC SASSO, BRIAN SNODDY, ANTHONY WATERS, SAM WOOD

GRAPHIC DESIGNERS
CYNTHIA FLIEGE, SHERRY FLOYD, SEAN GLENN

GRAPHIC PRODUCTION SPECIALIST
ERIN DORRIES

PLAYTESTERS: Oscar Aird, Aaron Alberg, Bill E. Anderson, Matthew Avery, Greg Bartholomew, Paul Bender, Alfonso Betencourt, Ed Bonny, Alan T. Bonnin, Constance M. Bonnin, Aaron J. Borio, Sarah Bruner, Scott Buchan, Ed Cheng, David Christ, Tod Chubucos, Tom Clark, Jennifer Clarke Wilkes, Mike Colasante, Andy Collins, Dan Cooper, Rex Crossley, Predrag Djukic, Martin Durham, David Eckelberry, Phil R. Edwards, Troy D. Ellis, Robert N. Emerson, Lon A. Faulkner III, George Fields, Kurschon Finch, Donald J. Fisher, John Ford, Chris Frizzell, Benjamin J. Gehrke, Ed Gibson, Garry Griffith, Jr., Gregory D. Gutke, Robert Gutschera, Michael C. Harris, Michelle Harris, Matt Hartwell-Herrero, Darrin Harvey, William H. Hezeltine, Patrick W. Higgins, David M. Hirst, Paula Horton, Tyler T. Hurst, Brian R. James, Charles James, Farrah James, Michael Johnson, Rafe Kaplan, Robert Kelly, Christopher M. Kiraly, Bradley Kuiper, Jabe Lawdonski, Michael Lawdonski, Mikhael D. Lombard, Todd Meyer, Ernest E. Morahan, Brian Moseley, Chad J. Mowry, Tammy R. Overstreet, Rasmus Pechuel, Jon Pickens, Chris Picone, Alan Plechaty, David K. Poole, Zack Powers, Leonard F. Radcliff, Mark B. Randol, Sean K Reynolds, Joe Rick, Noel J. Rousseau, Brad Ruby, Dima Rutgos, John Ruys, Charles Ryan, Jeremy W. Sands, Dan Savelli, Chris Shepard, Jacque Shepard, Ken Shepard, Ryan Schindler, Mike Selinker, Monica Shellman, Gus Sirakis, Ed Stark, Douglas Steves, Melissa Thom, David Thomas, Dara C. Tressler, Jeff Tressler, Christine Tromba, Keith Tyra, Rydia Q. Vielehr, Clint E. Wagoner, Frank Waldon, Michael S. Webster, Ira White, Jeff Wilkes, Penny Williams, Skip Williams, Johnny Wilson, Alex Winter, Steve Winter.

RESOURCES: Monsters for this book were developed from many sources, including the *Monstrous Compendium* series, *Masters of the Wild*, adventures such as *Heart of Nightfang Spire* by Bruce Cordell and *Deep Horizon* by Skip Williams, and articles from DRAGON® Magazine and DUNGEON® Magazine. The razor boar is based on material created by Jeff Holt. The scorpionfolk is based on material created by Benjamin Monk.

Based on the original DUNGEONS & DRAGONS® rules created by E. Gary Gygax and Dave Arneson, and the new DUNGEONS & DRAGONS game designed by Jonathan Tweet, Monte Cook, Skip Williams, Richard Baker, and Peter Adkison.

Dedication by cover artist Henry Higginbotham: To my father, James L. Higginbotham. Without his world travels and knack for collecting exotic artifacts, I wouldn't have the imagination I have today. Thanks, Dad.

U.S., CANADA, ASIA, PACIFIC, & LATIN AMERICA
Wizards of the Coast, Inc.
P.O. Box 707
Renton WA 98057-0707
Questions? 1-800-324-6496

ISBN-10: 0-7869-2873-5

EUROPEAN HEADQUARTERS
Hasbro UK, Ltd
Caswell Way
Newport, Gwent NP9 0YH
GREAT BRITAIN
Please keep this address for your records

620-88268000-001-EN
9 8 7 6 5 4
First Printing: September 2002

ISBN-13: 978-0-7869-2873-6

MONSTERS BY TYPE (AND SUBTYPE)

Aberration: avolakia, catoblepas, darktentacles, fihyrs, grell, hook horror, ixitxachitls, julajimus, meenlock, moonbeast, morkoth, neogis, psurlons, windghost, wyste.

(Air): air weird, breathdrinker, crystal dragon, emerald dragon, immoth, sylph.

Animal: desmodu bats, dire animals, grizzly mastodon, legendary animals, titanic creature, warbeast.

(Aquatic): cryptoclidus, kopru, legendary shark, leviathan, megalodon, morkoth, ocean giant, ocean strider, sirine.

Beast: dinosaurs, forest sloth, megalodon, rampager, razor boar, warbeast.

(Cold): frost salamander, immoth, ocean giant.

Construct: automatons, bogun, bronze serpent, captured one, chain golem, clockwork horrors, dread guard, golems, half-golems, juggernaut, nimblewright, raggamoffyns, rogue eidolon, runic guardian.

Dragon: dragons, felldrakes, hellfire wyrm, linnorms.

(Earth): amethyst dragon, dune stalker, earth weird , galeb duhr, gravecrawler, mountain giant, rukarazyll, sapphire dragon, stone spike.

Elemental (Air): air weird, breathdrinker, immoth, tempest.

Elemental (Earth): earth weird, galeb duhr, stone spike, tempest.

Elemental (Fire): fire bat, fire weird, tempest.

Elemental (Water): immoth, tempest, water weird.

(Evil): breathdrinker.

Fey: jermlaine, ocean strider, sirine, spirit of the land.

(Fire): ash rat, effigy, fire bat, sun giant, hellfire wyrm, fire weird.

Giant: firbolg, fomorian, giants.

Humanoid: captured one.

(Incorporeal): banshee, crimson death, effigy, glimmerskin, jahi, spirit of the land.

Magical Beast: ash rat, asperi, blood ape, chaos roc, chimeric creature, cloaked ape, cloud ray, corollax, fiendwurm, frost salamander, gambol, gravorg, leviathan, mooncalf, moonrat, mudmaw, nethersight mastiff, nightmare beast, phase wasp, phoenix, shadow spider, spellgaunt, swamplight lynx.

Monstrous Humanoid: abeils, boggle, braxat, desmodu, kopru, loxo, ormyrr, scorpionfolk, spell weaver, tauric creature, thri-kreen, yak folk.

Ooze: bone ooze, flesh jelly, reason stealer, teratomorph.

Outsider: bladeling, chaond, dune stalker, ether scarab, glimmerskin, monster of legend, zenythri.

Outsider (Air): sylph.

Outsider (Chaotic, Evil): abyssal maw, abyssal ravager, abyssal skulker, ethereal slayer, jarilith, jovoc, kelvezu, palrethee, zovvut.

Outsider (Evil): dune stalker, rukarazyll, vaporighu, yugoloths.

Outsider (Evil, Lawful): advespa, amnizu, durzagon, malebranche, marrash.

Outsider (Good): cervidal, lupinal.

Plant: greenvise, myconids, needlefolk, orcwort, red sundew, twig blight.

Shapechanger: ethereal doppelganger, grimalkin.

Undead: banshee, bone naga, corpse gatherer, crimson death, death knight, deathbringer, effigy, famine spirit, gravecrawler, jahi, ragewind, spawn of Kyuss, spellstitched creature.

Vermin: great old master neogi, leechwalker, megapede, titanic creature, warbeast.

(Water): topaz dragon, water weird.

INTRODUCTION

This book contains entries for more than 250 creatures, both hostile and benign, for use in DUNGEONS & DRAGONS® adventures. These creatures offer a wide range of challenges for player characters.

This introduction explains how to read a creature's write-up. All the information necessary to run the creature is presented in an easy-to-read format.

Entries for creatures are presented alphabetically by name. Some creatures, such as demons, are presented in groups, with the individual varieties ordered from weakest to strongest within the entry.

The appendix describes a number of different creatures that are created by adding a "template" to an existing creature. An example of this is the tauric creature, which adds the "tauric" template to a range of eligible creatures.

At the end of the book is a list of the monsters organized by Challenge Rating. This makes it easy for the Dungeon Master to tailor encounters to the party level of the player characters (see Challenge Rating, later in the introduction).

Each monster entry is organized in the same general format, as described below. The information is presented in a condensed form. For complete information on the characteristics of monsters, consult the Player's Handbook or the Dungeon Master's Guide.

MAIN STATISTICS BLOCK

This text contains basic game information on the creature, organized as follows.

NAME

This is the name by which the creature is generally known. The descriptive text (following the main statistics block and the secondary statistics block) may give other names.

SIZE AND TYPE

This line begins with the creature's size (Huge, for example). The eight size categories are briefly described in the Creature Sizes table below.

Size modifiers apply to the creature's Armor Class (AC) and attack bonus, its Hide checks, and its grapple checks. A creature's size also determines how far it can reach to make a melee attack and how much space it occupies in a fight (see Face/Reach, below, and also Big and Little Creatures in Combat, in Chapter 8 of the *Player's Handbook*). The size and type line continues with the creature's type (giant, for example). Type determines how magic affects a creature. For example, the *hold animal* spell affects only creatures of the animal type. Type also determines many of the creature's characteristics and abilities, as described in the next section.

Type Characteristics

The Typical Creature Statistics by Type table, beginning on the following page, provides a variety of statistics that vary according to creature type and size. The first three columns give suggested ranges of values for physical ability scores (Strength, Dexterity, and Constitution). The next two columns give the minimum and maximum number of Hit Dice the creature may have. A "—" in the maximum column means that there is no upper limit to the Hit Dice a creature may have at a given size. The final four columns give the suggested base damage for four common natural attack forms (slam, bite, claw, and gore). This information provides a useful guideline for creating your own monsters.

A creature's type also determines its Hit Die size, base attack bonus, good saving throws, number of skill points, and number of feats, as well as certain other characteristics. These characteristics are detailed in the type descriptions that follow the table.

Type Descriptions

The formulas for calculating a monster's skill points and

CREATURE SIZES

Size	Examples	AC/Attack Modifier	Hide Modifier	Special Size Modifier (Grapple)	Dimension*	Weight**
Fine	Housefly	+8	+16	−16	6 in. or less	1/8 lb. or less
Diminutive	Toad	+4	+12	−12	6 in.–1 ft.	1/8 lb.–1 lb.
Tiny	Bogun, jermlaine	+2	+8	−8	1 ft.–2 ft.	1 lb.–8 lb.
Small	Fire bat	+1	+4	−4	2 ft.–4 ft.	8 lb.–60 lb.
Medium-size	Human, needlefolk	+0	+0	+0	4 ft.–8 ft.	60 lb.–500 lb.
Large	Desmodu, immoth	−1	−4	+4	8 ft.–16 ft.	500 lb.–4,000 lb.
Huge	Moonbeast	−2	−8	+8	16 ft.–32 ft.	4,000 lb.–32,000 lb.
Gargantuan	Megalodon	−4	−12	+12	32 ft.–64 ft.	32,000 lb.–250,000 lb.
Colossal	Chaos roc	−8	−16	+16	64 ft. or more	250,000 lb. or more

*Biped's height, quadruped's body length (nose to base of tail).
**Assumes that the creature is roughly as dense as a regular animal. A creature made of stone will weigh considerably more. A gaseous creature will weigh much less.

Typical Creature Statistics by Type

	Str	Dex	Con	Minimum Hit Dice	Maximum Hit Dice	Slam	Bite	Claw	Gore
ABERRATION									
Fine	1	22–23	10–11	1/16 d8	—	—	1d2	—	1
Diminutive	1	20–21	10–11	1/8 d8	—	—	1d3	1	1d2
Tiny	2–3	18–19	10–11	1/4 d8	—	1	1d4	1d2	1d3
Small	6–7	16–17	10–11	1/2 d8	—	1d2	1d6	1d3	1d4
Medium-size	10–11	14–15	12–13	1d8	—	1d3	1d8	1d4	1d6
Large	18–19	12–13	16–17	2d8	—	1d4	2d6	1d6	1d8
Huge	26–27	12–13	20–21	4d8	—	1d6	2d8	1d8	2d6
Gargantuan	34–35	10–11	24–25	16d8	—	1d8	4d6	2d6	2d8
Colossal	42–43	10–11	28–29	32d8	—	2d6	4d8	2d8	4d6
ANIMAL									
Fine	1	22–23	10–11	1/16 d8	1/8 d8	—	1	—	1
Diminutive	1	20–21	10–11	1/8 d8	1/4 d8	—	1d2	1	1d2
Tiny	2–3	18–19	10–11	1/4 d8	1/2 d8	1	1d3	1d2	1d3
Small	6–7	16–17	10–11	1/2 d8	1d8	1d2	1d4	1d3	1d4
Medium-size	10–11	14–15	12–13	1d8	2d8	1d3	1d6	1d4	1d6
Large	18–19	12–13	16–17	2d8	4d8	1d4	1d8	1d6	1d8
Huge	26–27	12–13	20–21	4d8	16d8	1d6	2d6	1d8	2d6
Gargantuan	34–35	10–11	24–25	16d8	32d8	1d8	2d8	2d6	2d8
Colossal	42–43	10–11	28–29	32d8	—	2d6	4d6	2d8	4d6
BEAST									
Fine	1	22–23	10–11	1/16 d10	1/8 d10	—	1	—	1
Diminutive	1	20–21	10–11	1/8 d10	1/4 d10	—	1d2	1	1d2
Tiny	2–3	18–19	10–11	1/4 d10	1/2 d10	1	1d3	1d2	1d3
Small	6–7	16–17	10–11	1/2 d10	1d10	1d2	1d4	1d3	1d4
Medium-size	10–11	14–15	12–13	1d10	2d10	1d3	1d6	1d4	1d6
Large	18–19	12–13	16–17	2d10	4d10	1d4	1d8	1d6	1d8
Huge	26–27	12–13	20–21	4d10	16d10	1d6	2d6	1d8	2d6
Gargantuan	34–35	10–11	24–25	16d10	32d10	1d8	2d8	2d6	2d8
Colossal	42–43	10–11	28–29	32d10	—	2d6	4d6	2d8	4d6
CONSTRUCT									
Fine	4–5	18–19	—	1/16 d10	1/8 d10	1	—	—	1
Diminutive	6–7	16–17	—	1/8 d10	1/4 d10	1d2	—	1	1d2
Tiny	8–9	14–15	—	1/4 d10	1/2 d10	1d3	1	1d2	1d3
Small	10–11	12–13	—	1/2 d10	1d10	1d4	1d2	1d3	1d4
Medium-size	12–13	10–11	—	1d10	2d10	1d6	1d3	1d4	1d6
Large	20–21	10–11	—	2d10	4d10	1d8	1d4	1d6	1d8
Huge	28–29	8–9	—	4d10	16d10	2d6	1d6	1d8	2d6
Gargantuan	32–33	6–7	—	16d10	32d10	2d8	1d8	2d6	2d8
Colossal	36–37	4–5	—	32d10	—	4d6	2d6	2d8	4d6
DRAGON									
Fine	2–3	14–15	10–11	1/2 d12	1d12	—	1d2	1	1
Diminutive	6–7	12–13	10–11	1d12	3d12	—	1d3	1d2	1d2
Tiny	10–11	10–11	12–13	3d12	6d12	—	1d4	1d3	1d3
Small	12–13	10–11	12–13	4d12	9d12	—	1d6	1d4	1d4
Medium-size	14–15	10–11	14–15	7d12	13d12	1d4	1d8	1d6	1d6
Large	18–19	10–11	16–17	10d12	21d12	1d6	2d6	1d8	1d8
Huge	26–27	10–11	20–21	19d12	33d12	1d8	2d8	2d6	2d6
Gargantuan	34–35	10–11	24–25	27d12	38d12	2d6	4d6	2d8	2d8
Colossal	42–43	10–11	28–29	38d12	—	2d8	4d8	4d6	4d6
ELEMENTAL									
Fine	4–5	18–19	10–11	1/8 d8	—	1	1	—	—
Diminutive	6–7	16–17	10–11	1/4 d8	—	1d2	1d2	1	—
Tiny	8–9	14–15	10–11	1/2 d8	—	1d3	1d3	1d2	1
Small	10–11	12–13	10–11	1d8	—	1d4	1d4	1d3	1d2
Medium-size	12–13	10–11	12–13	2d8	—	1d6	1d6	1d4	1d3
Large	20–21	10–11	16–17	4d8	—	1d8	1d8	1d6	1d4
Huge	24–25	8–9	20–21	8d8	—	2d6	2d6	1d8	1d6
Gargantuan	28–29	6–7	24–25	16d8	—	2d8	2d8	2d6	1d8
Colossal	32–33	4–5	28–29	32d8	—	4d6	4d6	2d8	2d6

	Str	Dex	Con	Minimum Hit Dice	Maximum Hit Dice	Slam	Bite	Claw	Gore
FEY									
Fine	1	22–23	10–11	1/16 d6	1/8 d6	—	—	—	1
Diminutive	1	20–21	10–11	1/8 d6	1/4 d6	—	1	1	1d2
Tiny	2–3	18–19	10–11	1/4 d6	1/2 d6	1	1d2	1d2	1d3
Small	6–7	16–17	10–11	1/2 d6	1d6	1d2	1d3	1d3	1d4
Medium-size	10–11	12–13	10–11	1d6	2d6	1d3	1d4	1d4	1d6
Large	14–15	12–13	12–13	2d4	4d6	1d4	1d6	1d6	1d8
Huge	18–19	12–13	14–15	4d6	16d6	1d6	1d8	1d8	2d6
Gargantuan	22–23	10–11	16–17	16d6	32d6	1d8	2d6	2d6	2d8
Colossal	26–27	10–11	18–19	32d6	—	2d6	2d8	2d8	4d6
GIANT									
Fine	1	12–13	10–11	1/16 d8	1/8 d8	—	—	—	1
Diminutive	1	12–13	10–11	1/8 d8	1/4 d8	—	1	1	1d2
Tiny	2–3	10–11	10–11	1/4 d8	1/2 d8	1	1d2	1d2	1d3
Small	6–7	10–11	10–11	1/2 d8	1d8	1d2	1d3	1d3	1d4
Medium-size	14–15	10–11	12–13	1d8	2d8	1d3	1d4	1d4	1d6
Large	20–21	8–9	14–15	2d8	4d8	1d4	1d6	1d6	1d8
Huge	24–25	8–9	18–19	4d8	16d8	1d6	1d8	1d8	2d6
Gargantuan	28–29	8–9	22–23	16d8	32d8	1d8	2d6	2d6	2d8
Colossal	32–33	6–7	26–27	32d8	—	2d6	2d8	2d8	4d6
HUMANOID									
Fine	1	12–13	10–11	1/16 d8	1/8 d8	—	—	—	1
Diminutive	1	12–13	10–11	1/8 d8	1/4 d8	—	1	1	1d2
Tiny	2–3	10–11	10–11	1/4 d8	1/2 d8	1	1d2	1d2	1d3
Small	6–7	10–11	10–11	1/2 d8	1d8	1d2	1d3	1d3	1d4
Medium-size	10–11	10–11	10–11	1d8	2d8	1d3	1d4	1d4	1d6
Large	14–15	8–9	14–15	2d8	4d8	1d4	1d6	1d6	1d8
Huge	18–19	8–9	18–19	4d8	16d8	1d6	1d8	1d8	2d6
Gargantuan	22–23	6–7	22–23	16d8	32d8	1d8	2d6	2d6	2d8
Colossal	26–27	4–5	26–27	32d8	—	2d6	2d8	2d8	4d6
MAGICAL BEAST									
Fine	1	22–23	10–11	1/16 d10	—	—	1	—	1
Diminutive	1	20–21	10–11	1/8 d10	—	—	1d2	1	1d2
Tiny	2–3	18–19	10–11	1/4 d10	—	1	1d3	1d2	1d3
Small	6–7	16–17	10–11	1/2 d10	—	1d2	1d4	1d3	1d4
Medium-size	10–11	14–15	12–13	1d10	—	1d3	1d6	1d4	1d6
Large	18–19	12–13	16–17	2d10	—	1d4	1d8	1d6	1d8
Huge	26–27	12–13	20–21	4d10	—	1d6	2d6	1d8	2d6
Gargantuan	34–35	10–11	24–25	16d10	—	1d8	2d8	2d6	2d8
Colossal	42–43	10–11	28–29	32d10	—	2d6	4d6	2d8	4d6
MONSTROUS HUMANOID									
Fine	1	22–23	10–11	1/16 d8	—	—	—	—	1
Diminutive	1	20–21	10–11	1/8 d8	—	—	1	1	1d2
Tiny	2–3	18–19	10–11	1/4 d8	—	1	1d2	1d2	1d3
Small	6–7	16–17	10–11	1/2 d8	—	1d2	1d3	1d3	1d4
Medium-size	10–11	12–13	10–11	1d8	—	1d3	1d4	1d4	1d6
Large	18–19	12–13	12–13	2d8	—	1d4	1d6	1d6	1d8
Huge	26–27	12–13	14–15	4d8	—	1d6	1d8	1d8	2d6
Gargantuan	34–35	10–11	16–17	16d8	—	1d8	2d6	2d6	2d8
Colossal	42–43	10–11	18–19	32d8	—	2d6	2d8	2d8	4d6
OOZE									
Fine	4–5	18–19	10–11	1/16 d10	—	1	1	—	—
Diminutive	6–7	16–17	10–11	1/8 d10	—	1d2	1d2	1	—
Tiny	8–9	14–15	10–11	1/4 d10	—	1d3	1d3	1d2	1
Small	10–11	12–13	10–11	1/2 d10	—	1d4	1d4	1d3	1d2
Medium-size	12–13	10–11	10–11	1d10	—	1d6	1d6	1d4	1d3
Large	20–21	10–11	14–15	2d10	—	1d8	1d8	1d6	1d4
Huge	28–29	8–9	18–19	4d10	—	2d6	2d6	1d8	1d6
Gargantuan	32–33	6–7	22–23	16d10	—	2d8	2d8	2d6	1d8
Colossal	36–37	4–5	26–27	32d10	—	4d6	4d6	2d8	2d6

	Str	Dex	Con	Minimum Hit Dice	Maximum Hit Dice	Slam	Bite	Claw	Gore
OUTSIDER									
Fine	4–5	18–19	10–11	1/16 d8	—	1	1	—	—
Diminutive	6–7	16–17	10–11	1/8 d8	—	1d2	1d2	1	—
Tiny	8–9	14–15	10–11	1/4 d8	—	1d3	1d3	1d2	1
Small	10–11	12–13	10–11	1/2 d8	—	1d4	1d4	1d3	1d2
Medium-size	12–13	10–11	12–13	1d8	—	1d6	1d6	1d4	1d3
Large	20–21	10–11	16–17	2d8	—	1d8	1d8	1d6	1d4
Huge	28–29	8–9	20–21	4d8	—	2d6	2d6	1d8	1d6
Gargantuan	32–33	6–7	24–25	16d8	—	2d8	2d8	2d6	1d8
Colossal	36–37	4–5	28–29	32d8	—	4d6	4d6	2d8	2d6
PLANT									
Fine	4–5	18–19	10–11	1/16 d8	1/8 d8	1	—	—	1
Diminutive	6–7	16–17	10–11	1/8 d8	1/4 d8	1d2	—	1	1d2
Tiny	8–9	14–15	10–11	1/4 d8	1/2 d8	1d3	1	1d2	1d3
Small	10–11	12–13	10–11	1/2 d8	1d8	1d4	1d2	1d3	1d4
Medium-size	12–13	10–11	12–13	1d8	2d8	1d6	1d3	1d4	1d6
Large	20–21	10–11	16–17	2d8	4d8	1d8	1d4	1d6	1d8
Huge	28–29	8–9	20–21	4d8	16d8	2d6	1d6	1d8	2d6
Gargantuan	32–33	6–7	24–25	16d8	32d8	2d8	1d8	2d6	2d8
Colossal	36–37	4–5	28–29	32d8	—	4d6	2d6	2d8	4d6
SHAPECHANGER									
Fine	4–5	18–19	10–11	1/16 d8	1/8 d8	1	1	—	—
Diminutive	6–7	16–17	10–11	1/8 d8	1/4 d8	1d2	1d2	1	—
Tiny	8–9	14–15	10–11	1/4 d8	1/2 d8	1d3	1d3	1d2	1
Small	10–11	12–13	10–11	1/2 d8	1d8	1d4	1d4	1d3	1d2
Medium-size	12–13	10–11	12–13	1d8	2d8	1d6	1d6	1d4	1d3
Large	20–21	10–11	16–17	2d8	4d8	1d8	1d8	1d6	1d4
Huge	28–29	8–9	20–21	4d8	16d8	2d6	2d6	1d8	1d6
Gargantuan	32–33	6–7	24–25	16d8	32d8	2d8	2d8	2d6	1d8
Colossal	36–37	4–5	28–29	32d8	—	4d6	4d6	2d8	2d6
UNDEAD									
Fine	4–5	18–19	—	1/16 d12	—	1	1	—	—
Diminutive	6–7	16–17	—	1/8 d12	—	1d2	1d2	1	—
Tiny	8–9	14–15	—	1/4 d12	—	1d3	1d3	1d2	1
Small	10–11	12–13	—	1/2 d12	—	1d4	1d4	1d3	1d2
Medium-size	12–13	10–11	—	1d12	—	1d6	1d6	1d4	1d3
Large	20–21	10–11	—	2d12	—	1d8	1d8	1d6	1d4
Huge	28–29	8–9	—	4d12	—	2d6	2d6	1d8	1d6
Gargantuan	32–33	6–7	—	16d12	—	2d8	2d8	2d6	1d8
Colossal	36–37	4–5	—	32d12	—	4d6	4d6	2d8	2d6
VERMIN									
Fine	1	12–13	10–11	1/16 d8	—	—	1	—	1
Diminutive	1	12–13	10–11	1/8 d8	—	—	1d2	1	1d2
Tiny	2–3	10–11	10–11	1/4 d8	—	1	1d3	1d2	1d3
Small	6–7	10–11	10–11	1/2 d8	—	1d2	1d4	1d3	1d4
Medium-size	10–11	10–11	10–11	1d8	—	1d3	1d6	1d4	1d6
Large	18–19	8–9	14–15	2d8	—	1d4	1d8	1d6	1d8
Huge	26–27	8–9	18–19	4d8	—	1d6	2d6	1d8	2d6
Gargantuan	34–35	6–7	22–23	16d8	—	1d8	2d8	2d6	2d8
Colossal	42–43	6–7	26–27	32d8	—	2d6	4d6	2d8	4d6

feats often use the term "extra Hit Dice" (abbreviated "EHD"). To determine a monster's EHD, subtract the minimum Hit Dice value for that monster's size and type (as given on the Typical Creature Statistics by Type table) from its actual Hit Dice, as given in its entry.

If a formula specifies "Int bonus," use the creature's Intelligence modifier only if it is a positive number; otherwise use +0. If a formula specifies "Int modifier," use the creature's Intelligence modifier, whether it is bonus or a penalty.

Each monster is proficient with any weapons, armor, or shield mentioned in its entry, as well as with all armor that is lighter than what it wears. Creatures not specified as wearing armor or carrying shields are not proficient with those items, but some creatures have additional weapon proficiencies by virtue of their type, as given below.

Aberration: An aberration has a bizarre anatomy, strange abilities, an alien mindset, or any combination of the three.

Hit Die: d8.

Base Attack Bonus: As cleric (3/4 HD, rounded down).

Good Saving Throw: Will.

Skill Points: (2 × Int score) + (2 × EHD).

Feats: Int bonus + 1 per 4 EHD.

Example: Catoblepas.

Notes: Unless otherwise noted, an aberration has darkvision with a range of 60 feet.

Animal: An animal is a nonhumanoid creature, usually a vertebrate. All the animals included in this book lived on the planet Earth in historical times, or are larger versions of such creatures.

Hit Die: d8.

Base Attack Bonus: As cleric (3/4 HD, rounded down).

Good Saving Throws: Usually Fortitude and Reflex, but varies by specific creature.

Skill Points: 10 to 15.

Feats: None.

Example: Dire horse.

Notes: An animal has an Intelligence score of 1 or 2. (A predatory animal usually has an Intelligence score of 2, which reflects its cunning.) Unless otherwise noted, animals also have low-light vision.

Beast: A beast is a nonhistorical, vertebrate creature with a reasonably normal anatomy and no magical or unusual abilities.

Hit Die: d10.

Base Attack Bonus: As cleric (3/4 HD, rounded down).

Good Saving Throws: Fortitude and Reflex.

Skill Points: 10 to 15.

Feats: None.

Example: Rampager.

Notes: A beast has an Intelligence score of 1 or 2. Unless otherwise noted, it also has darkvision with a range of 60 feet and low-light vision.

Construct: A construct is an animated object or artificially constructed creature.

Hit Die: d10.

Base Attack Bonus: As cleric (3/4 HD, rounded down).

Good Saving Throws: None.

Skill Points: None.

Feats: None.

Example: Bronze serpent.

Notes: A construct usually has no Intelligence score and never has a Constitution score. Unless otherwise noted, it has darkvision with a range of 60 feet.

A construct is immune to mind-affecting effects (charms, compulsions, phantasms, patterns, and morale effects), poison, *sleep*, paralysis, stunning, disease, death effects, necromantic effects, and any effect that requires a Fortitude save unless it also works on objects. It is not subject to critical hits, subdual damage, ability damage, ability drain, or energy drain. A construct is not at risk of death from massive damage (see Injury and Death in Chapter 8 of the *Player's Handbook*), but when reduced to 0 or fewer hit points, it is immediately destroyed. Since it was never alive, a construct cannot be raised or resurrected.

A construct cannot heal damage, though it can be healed through repair in the same way an object can. The fast healing special quality works for those constructs that have it, despite their lack of Constitution.

Dragon: A dragon is a reptilian creature, usually winged, with magical or unusual abilities.

Hit Die: d12.

Base Attack Bonus: As fighter (equal to HD).

Good Saving Throws: Fortitude, Reflex, Will.

Skill Points: (6 + Int modifier) × HD.

Feats: 1 + 1 per 4 HD.

Example: Sapphire dragon.

Notes: Dragons are immune to *sleep* and paralysis effects, and unless otherwise noted, they have both darkvision (with a range of at least 60 feet) and low-light vision.

Elemental: An elemental is a creature composed of one of the four classical elements: air, earth, fire, or water.

Hit Die: d8.

Base Attack Bonus: As cleric (3/4 HD, rounded down).

Good Saving Throws: Reflex (air, fire) or Fortitude (earth, water).

Skill Points: (2 × Int score) + (2 × EHD).

Feats: Int bonus + 1 per 4 EHD.

Example: Water weird.

Notes: An elemental is immune to poison, *sleep*, paralysis, and stunning. Since it has no clear front or back, it is not subject to critical hits or flanking. Unless otherwise noted, an elemental has darkvision with a range of 60 feet. A slain elemental cannot be raised or resurrected, although a *wish* or *miracle* spell can restore it to life.

Fey: This type of creature has supernatural abilities and connections to nature or to some other force or place. Most fey are human-shaped.

Hit Die: d6.

Base Attack Bonus: As wizard (1/2 HD, rounded down).

Good Saving Throws: Reflex and Will.

Skill Points: (3 × Int score) + (2 × EHD).

Feats: 1 + Int bonus + 1 per 4 EHD.

Example: Jermlaine.

Notes: A fey is proficient with all simple weapons and, unless otherwise noted, has low-light vision.

Giant: A giant is a creature of humanoid shape and great strength. Most giants are at least Large in size.

Hit Die: d8.

Base Attack Bonus: As cleric (3/4 HD, rounded down).

Good Saving Throw: Fortitude.

Skill Points: 6 + Int modifier + EHD.

Feats: 1 + 1 per 4 EHD.

Example Firbolg.

Notes: A giant is proficient with all simple weapons and, unless otherwise noted, has darkvision with a range of 60 feet.

Humanoid: A humanoid usually has two arms, two legs, and one head, or a humanlike torso, arms, and head.

Humanoids are usually Small or Medium-size, with few or no supernatural or extraordinary abilities. A humanoid is proficient with all simple weapons.

Hit Die: d8.

Base Attack Bonus: As cleric (3/4 HD, rounded down).

Good Saving Throw: Usually Reflex, but varies by specific creature.

Skill Points: 6 + Int modifier + EHD.

Feats: 1 + 1 per 4 EHD.

Example Goblin (see *Monster Manual*).

Notes: Every humanoid has a type modifier (see the next section), often the name of a race or racial type. For instance, goblins and bugbears are both of the type humanoid (goblinoid).

Magical Beast: A creature of this type is similar to a beast but can have an Intelligence score higher than 2. Magical beasts usually have supernatural or extraordinary abilities.

Hit Die: d10.

Base Attack Bonus: As fighter (equal to HD).

Good Saving Throws: Fortitude and Reflex.

Skill Points: (2 × Int score) + EHD.

Feats: 1 + Int bonus + 1 per 4 EHD.

Example: Corollax.

Notes: Unless otherwise noted, a magical beast has dark-vision with a range of 60 feet and low-light vision.

Monstrous Humanoid: A monstrous humanoid has some humanoid and some monstrous or animalistic features. It often has supernatural abilities as well.

Hit Die: d8.

Base Attack Bonus: As fighter (equal to HD).

Good Saving Throws: Reflex and Will.

Skill Points: (2 × Int score) + (2 × EHD).

Feats: 1 + Int bonus + 1 per 4 EHD.

Example: Braxat.

Notes: A monstrous humanoid is proficient with all simple weapons. Unless otherwise noted, it has darkvision with a range of 60 feet.

Ooze: An ooze is an amorphous or mutable creature.

Hit Die: d10.

Base Attack Bonus: As cleric (3/4 HD, rounded down).

Good Saving Throws: None.

Skill Points: None.

Feats: None.

Example: Flesh jelly.

Notes: An ooze is immune to poison, *sleep*, paralysis, stunning, and polymorphing. Since it has no clear front or back, it is not subject to critical hits or flanking. An ooze has no Intelligence score and is therefore immune to all mind-affecting effects (charms, compulsions, phantasms, patterns, and morale effects).

Oozes are blind but have the blindsight special quality. A creature of this type has no natural armor bonus, but it is nevertheless difficult to kill because its body is composed primarily of simple protoplasm. This phenomenon is reflected by bonus hit points (in addition to those from Hit Dice and Constitution score) that an ooze receives, according to the creature's size, as shown on the table below.

Ooze Size	Bonus Hit Points
Fine	—
Diminutive	—
Tiny	—
Small	5
Medium-size	10
Large	15
Huge	20
Gargantuan	30
Colossal	40

Outsider: An outsider is a nonelemental creature that comes from another dimension, reality, or plane, has an ancestor from such a place, or undergoes a change that makes it similar to such creatures.

Hit Die: d8.

Base Attack Bonus: As fighter (equal to HD).

Good Saving Throws: Fortitude, Reflex, Will.

Skill Points: (8 + Int modifier) × HD.

Feats: 1 + 1 per 4 HD.

Example: Abyssal ravager.

Notes: An outsider is proficient with all simple weapons. If its Intelligence score is 6 or higher, it is also proficient with all martial weapons. A slain outsider cannot be raised or resurrected, although a *wish* or *miracle* spell can restore it to life. Unless otherwise noted, outsiders have darkvision with a range of 60 feet.

Plant: This type encompasses all vegetable creatures, including both normal plants and plant creatures.

Hit Die: d8.

Base Attack Bonus: As cleric (3/4 HD, rounded down).

Good Saving Throw: Fortitude.

Skill Points: None.

Feats: None.

Example: Greenvise.

Notes: A plant is immune to poison, *sleep*, paralysis, stunning, and polymorphing and is not subject to critical hits or mind-affecting effects (charms, compulsions, phantasms, patterns, and morale effects). Unless otherwise noted, a creature of this type has low-light vision.

Shapechanger: This type of creature has a stable body but can assume other forms.

Hit Die: d8.

Base Attack Bonus: As cleric (3/4 HD, rounded down).

Good Saving Throws: Fortitude, Reflex, and Will.

Skill Points: (2 × Int score) + EHD.

Feats: 1 + Int bonus + 1 per 4 EHD.

Example: Grimalkin.

Notes: Unless otherwise noted, a shapechanger has darkvision with a range of 60 feet.

Undead: Undead are once-living creatures animated by spiritual or supernatural forces.

Hit Die: d12.

Base Attack Bonus: As wizard (1/2 HD, rounded down).

Good Saving Throw: Will.

Skill Points: $(3 \times$ Int score$) + (2 \times$ EHD$)$.

Feats: 1 + Int bonus + 1 per 4 EHD.

Example: Banshee.

Notes: An undead has no Constitution score. It is immune to mind-affecting effects (charms, compulsions, phantasms, patterns, and morale effects), poison, *sleep*, paralysis, stunning, disease, death effects, necromantic effects, and any effect that requires a Fortitude save unless it also works on objects. The creature is not subject to critical hits, subdual damage, ability damage, ability drain, or energy drain.

An undead with no Intelligence score cannot heal damage, though it can be healed. (An intelligent undead heals damage normally, despite its lack of Constitution.) Negative energy (such as an *inflict* spell) heals any undead creature. The fast healing special quality works for those undead that have it regardless of their lack of Constitution.

An undead is not at risk of death from massive damage (see Injury and Death in Chapter 8 of the *Player's Handbook*), but when reduced to 0 or fewer hit points, it is destroyed. It cannot be raised, and although *resurrection* can affect it, such attempts almost always fail because most undead are unwilling to be brought back to life (see Bringing Back the Dead in Chapter 10 of the *Player's Handbook*).

An undead spellcaster uses its Constitution modifier (+0) or its Charisma modifier, whichever is higher, when making Concentration checks. Unless otherwise noted, an undead has darkvision with a range of 60 feet.

Vermin: This type includes insects, arachnids, arthropods, worms, and similar invertebrates.

Hit Die: d8.

Base Attack Bonus: As cleric (3/4 HD, rounded down).

Good Saving Throw: Fortitude.

Skill Points: 10 to 15.

Feats: None.

Example: Leechwalker.

Notes: A vermin has no Intelligence score and is therefore immune to all mind-affecting effects (charms, compulsions, phantasms, patterns and morale effects). Unless otherwise noted, it has darkvision with a range of 60 feet. A poisonous vermin of at least Medium-size gets a bonus to the save DC for its poison based on its size, as shown on the accompanying table.

Vermin Size	Poison Save DC Bonus
Medium-size	+2
Large	+4
Huge	+6
Gargantuan	+8
Colossal	+10

Type Modifiers

Type modifiers appear as parenthetical notes following the creature type. This notation indicates that the creature is associated with an environment (aquatic, for example), a subtype of creature (goblinoid), a form of energy (fire), a state of being (incorporeal), or the like.

A type modifier can identify a subtype within a larger type, such as undead (incorporeal), or link creatures that share characteristics, such as humanoid (goblinoid), or connect members of different types that share an attribute. For example, frost salamanders and immoths belong to the magical beast and elemental types, respectively, but both are also of the cold subtype.

Some common type modifiers that affect a creature's abilities are described below.

Cold: A cold creature is immune to cold damage. It takes double damage from fire unless a saving throw for half damage is allowed, in which case it takes half damage on a success or double damage on a failure.

Fire: A fire creature is immune to fire damage. It takes double damage from cold unless a saving throw for half damage is allowed, in which case it takes half damage on a success or double damage on a failure.

Incorporeal: An incorporeal creature has no physical body. It can be harmed only by other incorporeal creatures, +1 or better magic weapons, spells, spell-like abilities, and supernatural abilities. It is immune to all nonmagical attack forms. Even when hit by spells or magic weapons, it has a 50% chance to ignore any damage from a corporeal source (except force effects, such as *magic missile*, or attacks made with ghost touch weapons). An incorporeal creature has no natural armor bonus, but it does have a deflection bonus equal to its Charisma modifier (minimum +1, even if the creature's Charisma score would not normally provide a bonus).

An incorporeal creature can pass through solid objects, but not force effects, at will. Its attacks pass through (ignore) natural armor, armor, and shields, although deflection bonuses and force effects (such as *mage armor*) work normally against them. An incorporeal creature moves silently and cannot be heard with Listen checks if it doesn't wish to be. It has no Strength score, so it uses either its Strength modifier (+0) or its Dexterity modifier, whichever is higher, for its melee attacks.

HIT DICE

This line gives the number and size of Hit Dice the creature has, plus any bonus hit points. A parenthetical note provides the average hit points for a typical specimen. A creature's Hit Dice total is also its level for the purpose of determining how spells affect it, its rate of natural healing, and its maximum ranks in a skill.

INITIATIVE

This line gives the creature's modifier to initiative rolls. This value is the sum of the creature's Dexterity modifier and +4 for the Improved Initiative feat, if applicable.

SPEED

Unless stated otherwise, the first entry on this line gives the creature's tactical speed on land (the amount of distance it can

cover in one move action). If the creature has other modes of movement, these are given after the main entry. Unless otherwise noted, modes of movement are natural, not magical. The other possible modes of movement are detailed below.

Burrow: The creature can tunnel through dirt, but not through rock unless the descriptive text says otherwise. A creature cannot run while burrowing.

Climb: A creature with a climb speed has Climb as a class skill and gains a +8 racial bonus on Climb checks (included in the creature's Climb modifier). The creature must make a Climb check to climb any wall or slope with a DC higher than 0, but it always can choose to take 10 (see Checks without Rolls in Chapter 4 of the *Player's Handbook*), even if rushed or threatened. The creature moves at the given speed while climbing. If it chooses an accelerated climb (see Climb in Chapter 4 of the *Player's Handbook*), it moves at double the given climb speed (or its normal land speed, whichever is lower) and makes a single Climb check at a –5 penalty. A creature cannot run while climbing. It retains its Dexterity bonus to Armor Class (if any) while climbing, and an opponent gets no special bonus on his or her attacks against it while it climbs.

Fly: The creature can fly at the given speed if carrying no more than a light load (see Carrying Capacity, in Chapter 9 of the *Player's Handbook*, and Strength, below). All fly speeds include a parenthetical note indicating maneuverability, as follows.

Perfect: The creature can perform almost any aerial maneuver it wishes. It moves through the air as well as a human does over smooth ground.

Good: The creature is very agile in the air and can fly as well as a housefly or hummingbird, but it cannot change direction as readily as those with perfect maneuverability.

Average: The creature can fly as adroitly as a small bird.

Poor: The creature flies as well as a very large bird.

Clumsy: The creature can barely fly at all.

Creatures that fly can make dive attacks. This type of attack works just like a charge, but the diving creature must move a minimum of 30 feet. It can make only claw attacks, but these deal double damage. A creature can use the run action while flying, provided it flies in a straight line.

For more information, see Tactical Aerial Movement in Chapter 3 of the DUNGEON MASTER'S *Guide*.

Swim: A creature with a swim speed can move through water at the given speed without making Swim checks. It gains a +8 racial bonus on any Swim check (included in its Swim modifier) to perform some special action or avoid a hazard. The creature always can choose to take 10, even if rushed or threatened when swimming. A creature can use the run action while swimming, provided it swims in a straight line.

ARMOR CLASS

The Armor Class line gives the creature's AC for normal combat and includes a parenthetical mention of the modifiers contributing to it (usually size, Dexterity, and natural armor). The creature's AC against touch attacks and its AC when flat-footed are also provided.

The amount of a creature's natural armor bonus corresponds to the material that covers its body. The skin of a creature such as a human, dwarf, or elf provides no natural armor bonus. A creature with thick skin or fur has a natural armor bonus ranging from +1 (the grimalkin, for instance) to +3 (the blood ape). A creature with an exceptionally tough hide has a natural armor bonus of +4 (the loxo) or higher. Some creatures, such as the hook horror, have a high natural armor bonus (+10 in this case) because of a strong, rigid exoskeleton. With other creatures, such as the vaporighu, a high natural armor bonus (+11, in this case) indicates a malleable, amorphous body that is difficult to strike effectively.

The scales of a dragon provide it with a natural armor bonus that usually starts out at +5 or +6 for a wyrmling and can be as high as +38 or +39 for a great wyrm. See the dragon entries in this book for more details.

Attacks

This line gives all the creature's physical attacks, whether with natural or manufactured weapons. If the creature is capable of multiple attacks (either more than one attack with a certain attack form, or more than one attack using different attack forms), all its attack bonuses are given here. The given attack bonuses include all applicable modifiers.

Attack Routine: Many creatures can attack in more than one way or with different combinations of weapons. In such a case, the creature's Attacks entry gives an attack routine for each mode of attack. Multiple attack routines in an Attacks entry are separated by commas.

For example, the entry for the chaos roc reads "2 claws +41 melee and bite +36 melee, or 2 wings +41 melee." The claw attacks and the bite are one attack routine, and the two wing attacks are another attack routine. A creature with multiple attack routines cannot use more than one of those routines in a given round.

An attack routine can include an attack with a manufactured weapon as well as a natural weapon attack.

Natural Weapons: These include teeth, claws, tentacles, and the like. The entry gives the number of attacks along with the type of weapon (2 claws, for example), attack bonus, and form of attack (melee or ranged). The first listing is for the creature's primary weapon, and it includes an attack bonus that incorporates applicable modifiers for size, Strength, Dexterity, the Weapon Focus feat, and anything else that affects this value.

The remaining weapons mentioned (if any) are secondary. Each of these attacks has a –5 penalty on the attack roll, no matter how many secondary attacks there are. Creatures with the Multiattack feat (see the Creature Feats sidebar, later in the introduction) take only a –2 penalty on secondary attacks.

All of the foregoing assumes that the creature makes a full attack (see Attack Actions in Chapter 8 of the *Player's Handbook*) and employs all its natural weapons. If a creature

instead chooses the attack option (and thus makes only a single attack), it uses its primary attack bonus.

Unless otherwise noted, a natural weapon threatens a critical hit on a natural attack roll of 20.

Manufactured Weapons: Creatures that use swords, bows, spears, and the like follow the same rules as characters do.

Sometimes a creature may follow up a manufactured weapon attack with one or more of its natural weapon attacks. All natural attacks used in combination with a weapon attack are secondary attacks, regardless of whether they were primary or secondary in the creature's natural attack sequence.

DAMAGE

This line provides the damage each of the creature's attacks deals.

Natural Weapons: A creature's primary attack damage includes its full Strength modifier (1 1/2 × its Strength bonus if it is the creature's sole attack, or 1 × its Strength bonus if it has multiple natural weapons or multiple attacks with the same natural weapon). Secondary attacks add only 1/2 × the creature's Strength bonus. If any attacks also cause some special effect other than normal hit point damage (poison, disease, energy drain, paralysis, or the like), that information is given here. Unless otherwise noted, a creature deals double damage with a natural weapon on a critical hit.

Natural weapons have types just as other weapons do (see Weapon Qualities in Chapter 7 of the *Player's Handbook*). The most common of these are summarized below.

Bite: The creature attacks with its mouth, dealing piercing, slashing, and bludgeoning damage.

Claw or *Rake:* The creature rips with a sharp appendage, dealing piercing and slashing damage.

Gore: The creature spears the opponent with an antler, horn, or similar appendage, dealing piercing damage.

Slam or *Tail Slap:* The creature batters opponents with an appendage, dealing bludgeoning damage.

Sting: The creature stabs with a stinger, dealing piercing damage. Stingers are usually poisoned.

Manufactured Weapons: Creatures that use swords, bows, spears, and the like follow the same rules as characters do. Regardless of how many hands (or other appendages capable of wielding a weapon) a creature may have, only one of them is primary. The rest count as off hands. The damage bonus for a melee weapon attack depends on the hand or hands that wield the weapons, as shown on the table below. Apply the given multiplier to the creature's Strength bonus (if it has one) and add the result to the damage rolled.

| | | | Weapon Held In | |
Type of Weapon	Primary Hand	Off Hand	Primary plus Off Hand	Two Off Hands
Not light	×1	×1/2	×1 1/2	×1
Light	×1	×1/2	×1	×1/2

No standard weapon can be wielded with more than two hands. (A custom version of a weapon may be able to be wielded with more than two hands; in such a case, the additional damage bonus would apply for each off hand used.)

A Strength penalty applies to the damage of any weapon at 1 × its value, regardless of which hand or how many hands are used to wield it. This penalty does not accumulate when an additional hand is used to grasp a weapon.

If a monster has the superior two-weapon fighting or superior multiweapon fighting special quality, all of its hands are considered primary for the purpose of damage bonuses.

FACE/REACH

This line describes how much space the creature needs to fight effectively and how close it has to be to threaten an opponent. This information is written in the format "x ft. by y ft./z ft." The numbers before the slash show the creature's fighting space (width first, length second). The number after the slash is the monster's natural reach.

If the creature has exceptional reach because of a weapon, tentacle, or the like, the extended reach and its source are noted in parentheses. A natural weapon that provides exceptional reach (such as the cloud ray's tail or the moon-calf's tentacle rake) may be used against foes that are adjacent to the creature.

A creature's Face/Reach entry depends on its size and anatomy, as outlined in the table below:

FACE/REACH BY CREATURE SIZE

Size	Example Creature	Face*	Natural Reach
Fine	Housefly	1/2 ft. by 1/2 ft.	0 ft.
Diminutive	Toad	1 ft. by 1 ft.	0 ft.
Tiny	Meenlock	2 1/2 ft. by 2 1/2 ft.	0 ft.
Small	Ixitxachitl	5 ft. by 5 ft.	5 ft.
Medium-size	Human	5 ft. by 5 ft.	5 ft.
Large (tall)**	Runic guardian	5 ft. by 5 ft.	10 ft.
Large (long)†	Gravorg	5 ft. by 10 ft.	5 ft.
Huge (tall)**	Moonbeast	10 ft. by 10 ft.	15 ft.
Huge (long)†	Bronze serpent	10 ft. by 20 ft.	10 ft.
	Shadow spider	15 ft. by 15 ft.	10 ft.
Gargantuan (tall)**	Corpse gatherer	20 ft. by 20 ft.	20 ft.
Gargantuan (long)†	Fiendwurm	10 ft. by 40 ft.	10 ft.
	Megalodon	20 ft. by 40 ft.	10 ft.
Colossal (tall)**	Mountain giant	40 ft. by 40 ft.	25 ft.
Colossal (long)†	Leviathan	50 ft. by 200 ft.	15 ft.

*Listed width by length.
**Tall creatures are those that are taller than they are long or wide. Long creatures are as long or longer, or as wide or wider, than they are tall.
†Big, long creatures may be of several shapes. A Gargantuan corpse gatherer fills a 20-foot-square area, while a Gargantuan fiendwurm fills a space 40 feet long and 10 feet wide. (If the fiendwurm coiled itself into a circle, it would take up a 20-foot-by-20-foot space.)

SPECIAL ABILITIES

Many creatures have unusual abilities, which can include special attack forms, resistance or vulnerability to certain types of damage, and enhanced senses, among others. A monster entry breaks these abilities into Special Attacks and Special Qualities. The latter category includes defenses, vulnerabilities, and other special abilities that are not modes of attack.

A special ability can be designated as extraordinary, spell-like, or supernatural, or it may have no designator (in which case the ability is considered natural). The designators are defined below.

Extraordinary (Ex): Extraordinary abilities are non-magical, don't go away in an antimagic field, and are not subject to any effect that disrupts magic. Using an extraordinary ability is a free action unless otherwise noted.

Spell-Like (Sp): Spell-like abilities are magical and work just like spells, though they are not spells and thus have no verbal, somatic, material, focus, or XP components. These effects go away in an antimagic field and are subject to spell resistance. There is usually a limit on the number of times a spell-like ability can be used, but one that is designated as "always active" or "at will" has no usage limit.

A creature with spell-like abilities has an effective caster level, which sets the difficulty of dispelling that creature's spell-like abilities and defines any level-dependent variables (such as range and duration) that might apply. The creature's effective caster level never affects which spell-like abilities it can have; sometimes the given caster level is lower than the level a spellcasting character would have to be in order to cast the spell of the same name. Likewise, it's not necessary for a creature to have levels in a particular spellcasting class in order to use a spell-like ability that resembles one of that class's spells. The saving throw (if any) to resist or negate the effect of a spell-like ability has a DC of 10 + the level of the spell the ability resembles or duplicates (the lowest possible level, where this differs by class) + the creature's Charisma modifier.

Using a spell-like ability is a standard action unless otherwise noted, and doing so while threatened provokes an attack of opportunity. A spell-like ability can be disrupted just as a spell can be. Spell-like abilities cannot be used to counterspell, nor can they be counterspelled, but they can be used defensively just as spells can (see the Concentration skill description in Chapter 4 of the *Player's Handbook*).

Supernatural: Supernatural abilities are magical and go away in an antimagic field but are not subject to spell resistance. Using a supernatural ability is a standard action unless otherwise noted. Such an ability may have a use limit or be usable at will, just like a spell-like ability. However, supernatural abilities do not provoke attacks of opportunity and never require Concentration checks.

SPECIAL ATTACKS

This line identifies the creature's special attacks. (If it has none, this line is absent.) Details of the most common types of special attacks are given below. Where specific values are given for save DCs against special attacks, they are for a creature with the HD and ability scores given in the main statistics block. Additional information can be found in the creature's descriptive text.

Ability Score Loss (Su): Some attacks reduce the opponent's score in one or more abilities. This loss can be permanent or temporary (see Ability Score Loss in Chapter 3 of the *Dungeon Master's Guide*).

Ability Drain: This effect permanently reduces a living opponent's ability score when the creature hits with a melee attack. The creature's descriptive text gives the affected ability and the number of ability score points drained. If an attack that causes ability drain scores a critical hit, it drains twice the given amount. (If the damage is expressed as a die range, roll double the usual number of dice.) A draining creature heals 5 points of damage it has taken (10 on a critical hit) whenever it drains an ability score, no matter how many points it drains. If the amount of healing is more than the damage the creature has taken, it gains any excess as temporary hit points, which last a maximum of 1 hour.

Some ability drain attacks allow a Fortitude save with a DC of 10 + 1/2 draining creature's HD + draining creature's Charisma modifier. If no saving throw is mentioned, none is allowed.

Ability Damage: This attack temporarily reduces an opponent's ability score. The creature's descriptive text gives the ability and the amount of damage. If an attack that causes ability damage scores a critical hit, it deals twice the given amount. (If the damage is expressed as a die range, roll double the usual number of dice.) Temporary ability damage heals naturally at the rate of 1 point per day for each affected ability.

Breath Weapon (Su): A breath weapon attack usually deals damage and is often based on some type of energy (such as fire). It allows a Reflex save for half damage with a DC of 10 + 1/2 breathing creature's HD + breathing creature's Constitution modifier. A creature is immune to its own breath weapon and to the breath weapons of others of its kind unless otherwise noted.

Constrict (Ex): This special attack crushes an opponent, dealing bludgeoning damage, after the creature makes a successful grapple check (see Grapple in Chapter 8 of the *Player's Handbook*). The amount of damage is given in the creature's entry. If the creature also has the improved grab ability (see below), it deals constrict damage in addition to the damage dealt by the weapon it used to grab.

Energy Drain (Su): This attack saps a living opponent's vital energy and happens automatically when the creature's melee or ranged attack hits. Each successful energy drain bestows one or more negative levels (the descriptive text specifies how many). See Energy Drain in Chapter 3 of the *Dungeon Master's Guide* for details. If an attack that includes an energy drain scores a critical hit, it drains twice the given amount. For each negative level bestowed on an opponent, the draining creature heals 5 points of damage it has taken. If the amount of healing is more than the damage the creature has taken, it gains any excess as temporary hit points, which last a maximum of 1 hour.

The affected opponent takes a –1 penalty on all skill and ability checks, attack rolls, and saving throws, and loses 1 effective level or Hit Die (whenever level is used in a die

roll or a calculation) for each negative level. A spellcaster loses one spell slot of the highest level he or she can cast and (if applicable) one prepared spell of that level; this loss persists until the negative level is removed.

If they are not removed with a spell, such as *restoration*, negative levels remain until 24 hours have passed. At that time, the afflicted opponent must attempt a Fortitude save with a DC of 10 + 1/2 draining creature's HD + draining creature's Charisma modifier. On a success, the negative level goes away with no harm to the opponent. On a failure, the negative level goes away, but the opponent's level (or HD) is also reduced by one. A separate saving throw is required for each negative level.

Fear (Su or Sp): There are several types of attacks that magically induce fear in an opponent.

Fear Aura (Su): This ability either operates continuously or can be used at will. In either case, using it is a free action. A fear aura can immobilize an opponent (for example, the moonbeast's aura) or function similarly to the *fear* spell (for example, the aura of a malebranche). Other specific effects are also possible.

If a fear effect allows a saving throw, it is a Will save with a DC of 10 + 1/2 fearsome creature's HD + fearsome creature's Charisma modifier.

Frightful Presence (Ex): This ability makes a creature's very presence unsettling to foes. It takes effect automatically when the creature performs some sort of dramatic action (such as charging, attacking, or snarling). Opponents within range that witness the action may become panicked, frightened, or shaken (see Condition Summary in Chapter 3 of the *Dungeon Master's Guide*).

Actions required to trigger the ability are given in the creature's descriptive text. The range is usually 30 feet, but the entry gives any exceptions. The duration is usually 5d6 rounds.

This ability affects only opponents with fewer Hit Dice and/or levels than the creature has. An affected opponent can resist the effects with a successful Will save (DC 10 + 1/2 frightful creature's HD + frightful creature's Charisma modifier). An opponent that succeeds at the saving throw is immune to that creature's frightful presence for 24 hours.

Gaze (Su): A gaze attack takes effect when opponents look at the creature's eyes (see Gaze Attacks in Chapter 3 of the *Dungeon Master's Guide*). The attack can have almost any sort of effect: petrification, death, energy drain, charm, fear, and so on. The typical range is 30 feet. Most gaze attacks operate continuously as long as the creature is conscious and has its eyes open.

The type of saving throw against a gaze attack varies, but it is usually a Will or Fortitude save (DC 10 + 1/2 gazing creature's HD + gazing creature's Charisma modifier). A successful saving throw negates the effect.

Every opponent within range of a gaze attack must attempt a saving throw each round at the beginning of its turn in the initiative order. An opponent is vulnerable only if looking directly at the creature. An opponent can avoid having to make the saving throw by not looking at the creature, which can be done by averting one's eyes or by using a barrier to sight.

Averting One's Eyes: The opponent avoids looking at the creature's face and instead looks at its body, watches its shadow, tracks it in a reflective surface, or the like. Each round, the opponent has a 50% chance to avoid needing to make a saving throw against the gaze attack. The creature with the gaze attack, however, gains one-half concealment against that opponent.

Barrier to Sight: An opponent that cannot see the creature at all cannot be affected by its gaze attack. This can be accomplished by turning one's back on the creature, shutting one's eyes, or wearing a blindfold or head covering that prevents sight. The creature with the gaze attack gains total concealment against the opponent.

A creature with a gaze attack can actively gaze as an attack action by choosing a target within range. That opponent must attempt a saving throw unless successful at avoiding the gaze as described above. Thus, it is possible for an opponent to have to save against a creature's gaze attack twice during the same round, once before the opponent's action and once during the creature's turn.

Gaze attacks can affect ethereal opponents. Unless otherwise noted, a creature is immune to its own gaze attack and to those of others of its own kind.

Improved Grab (Ex): If the creature hits with a melee weapon (usually a claw or bite attack), it deals normal damage and attempts to start a grapple as a free action without provoking an attack of opportunity (see Grapple in Chapter 8 of the *Player's Handbook*). No initial touch attack is required, and a Tiny or Small creature does not have a special size penalty; instead it uses its regular size modifier for attacks. Unless otherwise noted, improved grab works only against opponents at least one size category smaller than the creature.

The creature can conduct the grapple normally, or it can simply use the part of its body it used in the improved grab attack to hold the opponent. If it chooses to do the latter, it takes a –20 penalty on grapple checks until its next turn (at which point it can choose to continue taking the –20 penalty, or decide not to continue taking it), but it is also not considered grappled during that time. The creature does not lose its Dexterity bonus to Armor Class, it still threatens an area, and it can use its remaining attacks normally.

Unlike a regular grapple, a successful hold does not deal any additional damage beyond that dealt by the weapon in the initial round, unless otherwise noted (for example, the constrict ability deals its damage the same round). If the creature does have an ability that allows extra damage, each successful grapple check it makes during successive rounds deals the damage given for the attack that established the hold. Otherwise, it deals damage from all applicable special attacks as well (the amount is given in the creature's descriptive text).

Whenever a creature gets a hold after an improved grab attack, it pulls the opponent into its space. This act does not provoke attacks of opportunity. If it chooses to take a −20 penalty on its grapple check, it can move (possibly carrying away the opponent), provided it can drag the latter's weight.

Poison (Ex): A poison attack deals its initial damage, usually in the form of ability damage, to the opponent on a failed Fortitude save. Unless otherwise noted, another saving throw is required 1 minute later (regardless of the first save's result) to avoid the poison's secondary damage. The creature's descriptive text provides the details.

The Fortitude save against poison has a DC of 10 + 1/2 poisoning creature's HD + poisoning creature's Constitution modifier. A successful save avoids the damage.

Psionics (Sp): Psionic abilities are generated with the power of a creature's mind. As a general rule, psionics are treated as spell-like abilities; the use of one is a standard action, and it can be used a certain number of times per day (or at will), as specified in the creature's descriptive text.

If your campaign uses the *Psionics Handbook,* substitute the psionic power of the same name for each of these abilities. With the *Psionics Handbook* it's also possible for the psionic creatures in this book (the braxat, the gem dragons, and the thri-kreen) to be fully fleshed out with psionic attack and defense modes and class equivalents for manifesting powers, which are provided for each psionic creature in the Attack/Defense Modes paragraph of the psionics entry. Parenthetical notes elsewhere in each psionic creature's descriptive text indicate other adjustments that need to be made when the *Psionics Handbook* is used.

Ray (Su or Sp): A ray behaves like a ranged attack (see Aiming a Spell in Chapter 10 of the *Player's Handbook*). It requires a ranged touch attack roll, ignoring armor and shield (the opponent's touch AC applies) and using the creature's ranged attack bonus. Ray attacks are always made as if at short range (no range increment penalty applies). The creature's descriptive text specifies the maximum range, effects, and any applicable saving throw.

Spells: Some creatures can cast arcane or divine spells just as members of a spellcasting class can (and can activate magic items accordingly). These creatures are subject to the same spellcasting rules as characters are. Spells per day and spells known are given for a creature with the ability scores noted in the main statistics block.

A spellcasting creature is not actually a member of a class unless its entries says so, and it does not gain any class abilities or features. For example, a creature that casts arcane spells as a sorcerer cannot acquire a familiar. Unless otherwise noted, a creature with access to cleric spells that does not actually have levels as a cleric must prepare the spells in the normal manner and receives no extra slots for domain spells, though it may be able to choose spells from particular domains. In any case, such a creature does not have access to a domain's granted powers.

Swallow Whole (Ex): If the creature begins its turn with an opponent held in its mouth (see Improved Grab, above), it can attempt a new grapple check, as though attempting to pin the opponent. If it succeeds, it swallows its prey and the opponent takes bite damage.

Being swallowed has various additional consequences, depending on the creature doing the swallowing, but a swallowed creature is considered grappled, while the creature that did the swallowing is not. A swallowed creature can try to cut its way free with any light piercing or slashing weapon (the amount of cutting damage required to get free is noted in the creature description), or it can just try to escape the grapple. If the swallowed creature chooses the latter course, success puts it back in the attacker's mouth, where it may be bitten or swallowed again.

The creature's descriptive text specifies what size opponents it can swallow. The creature's stomach or gullet can hold either one or two opponents of the largest size category it can swallow, or a certain number of creatures of smaller size, as specified in the creature's descriptive text.

Trample (Ex): As a standard action during its turn each round, the creature can trample opponents at least one size category smaller than itself, unless otherwise noted. The creature merely has to move over the opponents. The trample deals bludgeoning damage (the descriptive text gives the amount).

A trampled opponent may attempt an attack of opportunity with a −4 penalty on the attack roll. An opponent that chooses not to make an attack of opportunity may instead attempt a Reflex save for half damage. The save DC is 10 + 1/2 trampling creature's HD + trampling creature's Strength modifier.

SPECIAL QUALITIES

This line identifies the creature's special qualities. (If it has no special qualities, this line is absent.) Details of the most common special qualities are given below. Additional information can be found in the creature's descriptive text.

Blindsight (Ex): Using nonvisual senses, such as sensitivity to vibrations, scent, acute hearing, or echolocation, the creature maneuvers and fights normally without vision. Invisibility and darkness are irrelevant, though the creature still can't discern ethereal beings. The ability's range is specified in the creature's descriptive text. The creature usually does not need to make Spot or Listen checks to notice creatures within range of its blindsight ability.

Damage Reduction (Su): Most weapons (natural or manufactured) that hit the creature deal less damage than they ordinarily do. (The creature's wounds heal immediately, or the hit turns into a glancing blow; in either case, the opponent knows the attack was ineffective.) The creature takes normal damage from energy attacks (even nonmagical ones), spells, spell-like abilities, and supernatural abilities. A magic weapon or a creature with its own damage reduction (DR) can sometimes damage the creature normally, as noted below.

The creature's entry indicates the amount of damage ignored (usually 5 to 25 points) and the type of weapon that overcomes the ability. For example, the boggle's entry reads "DR 5/+1." Each time a foe hits a boggle with a weapon, the damage dealt by that attack is reduced by 5 points (to a minimum of 0). However, a +1 weapon deals full damage.

Any weapon more powerful than the type given in the creature's DR statistic also overcomes the ability. (See Table 3–13: Damage Reduction Rankings in the DUNGEON MASTER's Guide.) For example, a boggle (DR 5/+1) takes normal damage from weapons with +2 or better bonuses from magic, but not from nonmagical weapons. Nonmagical enhancement bonuses (such as those of masterwork or adamantine weapons) do not enable a weapon to overcome damage reduction.

For purposes of harming other creatures with damage reduction, a creature's natural weapons count as the type that overcomes its own innate damage reduction. However, damage reduction from spells, such as *stoneskin*, does not confer this ability. The amount of damage reduction is irrelevant. For example, a bronze serpent (DR 10/+1) deals full damage to a boggle, as if the bronze serpent's bite attack were made with a +1 weapon.

Darkvision (Ex): This ability enables a creature to see in lightless conditions, out to a range specified in the creature's descriptive text. Darkvision is black and white only (no colors can be detected), and it does not allow a creature to see something it could not see in lighted conditions, such as an invisible creature. A creature with darkvision is vulnerable to gaze attacks, just as a creature without darkvision would be in lighted conditions.

Fast Healing (Ex): The creature regains hit points at an exceptionally fast rate, usually 1 or more hit points per round, as given in the entry. (For example, an ethereal doppelganger has fast healing 8.) Fast healing is like natural healing (see Chapter 8 of the *Player's Handbook*), except that it does not restore hit points lost from starvation, thirst, or suffocation. Fast healing only works on a creature that is alive. Unless otherwise noted, the ability does not allow lost body parts to be reattached.

Immunity: Many creatures are immune to various harmful effects. For example, creatures with fire immunity take no damage from fire.

In some cases, an attack can deal several kinds of damage at once, and in these cases the immunity might negate all, some, or none of the damage. Some attacks combine smaller amounts of damage in discrete parts. For example, an *ice storm* spell deals 3d6 points of bludgeoning damage plus 2d6 points of cold damage. A creature that has cold immunity suffers only the bludgeoning damage from an *ice storm* spell. A creature that is immune to bludgeoning damage suffers only the cold damage from an *ice storm* spell.

Other forms of attack deal multiple kinds of damage simultaneously. For example, a creature's bite attack deals piercing, slashing, and bludgeoning damage, but that damage is not divided into separate parts. In these cases, a creature vulnerable to any one of the types of damage delivered takes the attack's full damage. For example, a creature immune to slashing damage still suffers full damage from a bite.

Low-Light Vision (Ex): This ability is possessed by creatures whose eyes are extraordinarily sensitive to light, so that they can see twice as far as normal in dim light. See Table 9–7: Light Sources and the Vision and Light section in Chapter 9 of the *Player's Handbook*; also see Low-Light Vision in Chapter 3 of the DUNGEON MASTER's Guide.

Regeneration (Ex): Creatures with this ability are difficult to kill. Damage dealt to the creature is treated as subdual damage—and the creature automatically heals this subdual damage at a fixed rate per round, as given in the entry. (For example, an elemental weird has regeneration 10.) Certain attack forms, typically fire and acid, deal normal damage to the creature. The creature's descriptive text contains these details.

A creature with regeneration that has been rendered unconscious through subdual damage can be killed with a coup de grace (see Helpless Defenders in Chapter 8 of the *Player's Handbook*) if the type of attack used for the coup de grace deals normal damage to the creature.

Attack forms that don't deal hit point damage (for example, a *disintegrate* effect and most poisons) ignore regeneration. Regeneration also does not restore hit points lost from starvation, thirst, or suffocation.

Body Part Regeneration: Some creatures have a special form of regeneration that enables them to regrow lost portions of their bodies or reattach severed limbs or body parts; details are given in the creature's entry. (For instance, both the darktentacles and the grell have tentacle regeneration.)

Resistance to Energy (Ex): The creature disregards some amount of damage of the given type each round (commonly acid, cold, fire, or electricity). The entry indicates the amount and type of damage ignored. For example, a gem dragon has fire resistance 30, so it disregards the first 30 points of fire damage dealt to it each round.

Scent (Ex): This ability allows the creature to detect approaching enemies, sniff out hidden foes, and track by sense of smell. Creatures with the scent ability can identify familiar odors just as humans can identify familiar sights with their eyes.

A creature with the scent ability can detect opponents within 30 feet by sense of smell. If the opponent is upwind, the range increases to 60 feet; if downwind, it drops to 15 feet. Strong scents, such as smoke or rotting garbage, can be detected at twice the ranges noted above. Overpowering scents, such as skunk musk or troglodyte stench, can be detected at triple normal range.

When a creature detects a scent, the exact location is not revealed—only its presence somewhere within range. The creature can take a partial action to note the direction of

the scent. If it moves to within 5 feet of the source, the creature can pinpoint that source.

A creature with the scent ability can follow tracks by smell, making a Wisdom check to find or follow a track. The typical DC for a fresh trail is 10 (no matter what kind of surface holds the scent). This DC increases or decreases depending on how strong the quarry's odor is, the number of creatures in the tracked group, and the age of the trail. For each hour that the trail is cold, the DC increases by 2. The ability otherwise follows the rules for the Track feat (see Chapter 4 of the *Player's Handbook*). Creatures tracking by scent ignore the effects of surface conditions and poor visibility.

Spell Resistance (Ex): The creature can avoid the effects of spells, spell-like abilities, and magic items that directly affect it. The entry includes a numerical rating. To determine if a spell or spell-like ability works, the spellcaster makes a caster level check (roll 1d20 + caster level). If the result equals or exceeds the creature's spell resistance (SR) rating, the spell works normally, although the creature is still allowed a saving throw (if applicable). See Spell Resistance in Chapter 3 of the DUNGEON MASTER'S *Guide* for details.

Turn Resistance (Ex): The creature (usually an undead) is less easily affected by clerics or paladins (see Turn and Rebuke Undead in Chapter 8 of the *Player's Handbook*) than it would be otherwise. When resolving a turn, rebuke, command, or bolster attempt, add the given bonus to the creature's Hit Dice total. For example, a spawn of Kyuss has turn resistance +2 and 4 HD. Attempts to turn, rebuke, command, or bolster treat the spawn as if it had 6 HD, though it is a 4-HD creature for any other purpose.

SAVES

This line gives the creature's Fortitude, Reflex, and Will save modifiers, which take into account its type, ability score modifiers, and any special qualities.

ABILITIES

This line lists all six of the creature's ability scores, in order: Str, Dex, Con, Int, Wis, Cha. These values are average for the creature's kind. Most abilities work as described in Chapter 1 of the *Player's Handbook*, with the exceptions noted below.

Strength: Quadrupeds can carry heavier loads than characters can. To determine a quadruped's carrying capacity, use Table 9–1: Carrying Capacity in the *Player's Handbook*, multiplying by the appropriate modifier for the creature's size: Fine 1/4, Diminutive 1/2, Tiny 3/4, Small 1, Medium 1 1/2, Large 3, Huge 6, Gargantuan 12, and Colossal 24.

Intelligence: A creature can speak all the languages mentioned in its descriptive text, plus one additional language per point of Intelligence bonus. Any creature with an Intelligence score of 3 or higher understands at least one language (Common, unless otherwise noted).

Nonabilities: Some creatures lack certain ability scores. Such a creature does not have an ability score of 0—it lacks the ability altogether. The modifier for a nonability is +0. Other details of nonabilities are as follows.

Strength: Any creature that can physically manipulate objects has at least 1 point of Strength.

A creature with no Strength score can't exert force, usually because it has no physical body (a banshee, for example) or because it doesn't move (a shrieker; see *Monster Manual*). The creature automatically fails Strength checks. If it can attack, it applies its Dexterity modifier to its base attack bonus instead of a Strength modifier.

Dexterity: Any creature that can move has at least 1 point of Dexterity.

A creature with no Dexterity score (a shrieker, for example; see *Monster Manual*) can't move. If it can act (such as by casting spells), it applies its Intelligence modifier to initiative checks instead of a Dexterity modifier. The creature fails all Reflex saves and Dexterity checks.

Constitution: Any living creature has at least 1 point of Constitution.

A creature with no Constitution score has no body (a banshee, for example) or no metabolism (a golem). It is immune to any effect that requires a Fortitude save unless the effect works on objects. For example, a runic guardian is unaffected by any type of poison but is susceptible to a *disintegrate* spell. The creature is also immune to ability damage, ability drain, and energy drain, and it always fails Constitution checks.

A creature with no Constitution score cannot heal damage on its own, though it can be healed by external means (a spell or an application of the Heal skill, for example). Negative energy (such as an *inflict* spell) can heal undead creatures. Constructs can be repaired in the same way an object can be (see the creature's description for details). The regeneration and fast healing special qualities work regardless of a creature's Constitution score (or lack of one).

Intelligence: Any creature that can think, learn, or remember has at least 1 point of Intelligence.

A creature with no Intelligence score operates on simple instincts or programmed instructions. It is immune to all mind-affecting effects (charms, compulsions, phantasms, patterns and morale effects) and automatically fails Intelligence checks.

Wisdom: Any creature that can perceive its environment in any fashion has at least 1 point of Wisdom.

Anything with no Wisdom score is an object, not a creature. Anything without a Wisdom score also has no Charisma score, and vice versa.

Charisma: Any creature capable of telling the difference between itself and things that are not itself has at least 1 point of Charisma.

Anything with no Charisma score is an object, not a creature. Anything without a Charisma score also has no Wisdom score, and vice versa.

CREATURE FEATS

Some of the creatures in this book possess feats that are not mentioned in the *Player's Handbook*. These "creature feats" are described below.

ABILITY FOCUS [General]

One of the creature's special attacks is more potent than normal.

Benefit: The Difficulty Class for all saving throws against the selected special attack increases by +2.

Special: This feat can be taken multiple times. Its effects do not stack. Each time it is taken, it applies to a different special attack.

FLYBY ATTACK [General]

The creature can attack on the wing.

Prerequisite: Fly speed.

Benefit: When flying, the creature can take a move action (including a dive) and another partial action at any point during the move. The creature cannot take a second move action during a round when it makes a flyby attack.

Normal: Without this feat, the creature takes a partial action either before or after its move.

HOVER [General]

The creature can halt its forward motion while flying, regardless of its maneuverability.

Prerequisite: Fly speed.

Benefit: While hovering, the creature can attack with all its natural weapons, except for wing attacks. Some creatures may be able to make additional attacks while hovering, as noted in the creature's descriptive text. If the creature has a breath weapon, it can use the breath weapon instead of making physical attacks.

If a creature hovers close to the ground in an area with lots of loose debris, the draft from its wings creates a hemispherical cloud with a radius specified in the creature's descriptive text. The winds so generated can snuff torches, small campfires, exposed lanterns, and other small, open flames of nonmagical origin. The cloud obscures vision, and creatures caught within it are blinded while inside and for 1 round after emerging. Each creature caught in the cloud must succeed at a Concentration check (DC 10 + 1/2 creature's HD) to cast a spell.

Normal: A creature without this feat cannot halt its forward motion without falling. A creature with average, poor, or clumsy maneuverability can slow its flying movement to only half of its fly speed. (See Tactical Aerial Movement in Chapter 3 of the *DUNGEON MASTER's Guide*.)

MULTIATTACK [General]

The creature is adept at using all its natural weapons at once.

Prerequisite: Three or more natural weapons.

Benefit: Each of the creature's secondary attacks with natural weapons takes only a –2 penalty.

Normal: Without this feat, each of the creature's secondary natural attacks takes a –5 penalty.

MULTIDEXTERITY [General]

The creature is adept at using all its hands in combat.

Prerequisite: Dex 15, three or more arms.

Benefit: The creature ignores all penalties for using an off hand.

Normal: Without this feat, a creature using an off hand takes a –4 penalty on attack rolls, ability checks, and skill checks. A creature has one primary hand, and all the others are off hands; for example, a four-armed creature has one primary hand and three off hands.

Special: This feat replaces the Ambidexterity feat for creatures with more than two arms.

MULTIWEAPON FIGHTING [General]

A creature with three or more hands can fight with a weapon in each hand. It can make one extra attack per round with each extra weapon.

Prerequisite: Three or more hands.

Benefit: Penalties for fighting with multiple weapons are reduced by 2.

Normal: A creature without this feat takes a –6 penalty on attacks made with its primary hand and a –10 penalty on attacks made with its off hands. (It has one primary hand, and all the others are off hands.) See Attacking with Two Weapons, page 124 in the *Player's Handbook*.

Special: This feat replaces the Two-Weapon Fighting feat for creatures with more than two arms.

QUICKEN SPELL-LIKE ABILITY [General]

The creature can use a spell-like ability with a moment's thought.

Benefit: Using a quickened spell-like ability is a free action that does not provoke an attack of opportunity. The creature can perform another action—including the use of another spell-like ability—in the same round that it uses a quickened spell-like ability. The creature may use only one quickened spell-like ability per round. A spell-like ability that duplicates a spell with a casting time greater than 1 full round cannot be quickened.

Each of a creature's spell-like abilities can be quickened only once per day, and the feat does not allow the creature to exceed its normal usage limit for any ability. Thus, if a demon chooses to quicken its *darkness* ability, it cannot use quickened *darkness* again the same day, though it could use its *darkness* ability again normally (since it can use *darkness* at will), or it could quicken another of its spell-like abilities, such as *desecrate*.

Normal: Normally the use of a spell-like ability requires a standard action and provokes an attack of opportunity unless noted otherwise.

Special: This feat can be taken multiple times. Each time it is taken, the creature can apply it to each of its spell-like abilities one additional time per day.

SNATCH [General]

The creature can grapple more easily with its claws or bite.

Prerequisite: Claws or bite as a natural weapon attack.

Benefit: A creature with this feat that hits with a claw or bite attack attempts to start a grapple as a free action without provoking an attack of opportunity. If it gets a hold with a claw on a creature four or more size categories smaller than itself, it squeezes each round for automatic claw damage. If it gets a hold with its bite on a creature three or more size categories smaller than itself, it automatically deals bite damage each round, or if it does not move and takes no other action in combat, it deals double bite damage. The snatched creature gets no saving throw against the creature's breath weapon (if any).

The creature can drop a foe it has snatched as a free action or use a standard action to fling it aside. The feet traveled and the damage taken by a flung foe are specified in the creature's descriptive text. If the foe is flung while the creature is flying, the foe takes the specified amount of damage or falling damage, whichever is greater.

Normal: Without this feat, the creature must conduct grapple attempts according to Chapter 8 of the *Player's Handbook*.

WINGOVER [General]

The creature can change direction quickly while flying.

Prerequisite: Fly speed.

Benefit: This feat allows a flying creature to turn up to 180 degrees once per round regardless of its maneuverability, in addition to any other turns it is normally allowed. A creature cannot gain altitude during the round when it executes a wingover, but it can dive.

Normal: A creature without this feat that has average, poor, or clumsy maneuverability is limited to a turn of 90 degrees or 45 degrees. (See Tactical Aerial Movement in Chapter 3 of the *DUNGEON MASTER's Guide*.)

SKILLS

This line gives the creature's skills along with each skill's modifier, which includes adjustments for ability scores, size, synergy bonuses, armor check penalties, magic items, feats, or racial traits unless otherwise noted in the descriptive text. All of a creature's skills were purchased as class skills unless the creature has a character class. Any skill not mentioned in the creature's entry is treated as a cross-class skill unless the creature has a character class, in which case it can purchase the skill as any other member of that class can. A creature's type and Intelligence score determine the number of skill points it has (see Type Descriptions, earlier in the introduction).

The Skills section of the creature's descriptive text recaps racial and other bonuses for the sake of clarity; these bonuses should not be added to the creature's skill modifiers unless otherwise noted. An asterisk (*) beside the relevant score and in the Skills section indicates a conditional adjustment.

FEATS

This line identifies the creature's feats. The creature's descriptive text may contain additional information if a feat works differently from the way it is described in this book or in Chapter 5 of the *Player's Handbook*. Some creatures also receive bonus feats, designated by (B) following the feat name in the statistics block. A creature need not meet the prerequisites for a bonus feat.

Most creatures use the same feats that are available to characters, but some have access to special feats. See the Creature Feats sidebar for descriptions of these feats.

SECONDARY STATISTICS BLOCK

This section includes information that the DM needs for campaign purposes but not (usually) during an encounter. In many cases when the main statistics block includes information for several related creatures and the secondary information for all those creatures is identical, the secondary statistics block appears only once.

CLIMATE/TERRAIN

This entry describes the locales where the creature is most often found.

Cold: Arctic and subarctic climes. Any area that has winter conditions for the greater portion of the year is cold.

Temperate: Any area that has alternating warm and cold seasons is temperate.

Warm: Tropical and subtropical climes. Any area that has summer conditions for the greater portion of the year is warm.

Aquatic: Fresh or salt water.

Desert: Any dry area with sparse vegetation.

Forest: Any area covered with trees.

Hill: Any area with rugged but not mountainous terrain.

Marsh: Low, flat, waterlogged areas; includes swamps.

Mountains: Rugged terrain, higher than hills.

Plains: Any fairly flat area that is not a desert, swamp, or forest.

Underground: A subterranean area.

ORGANIZATION

This line describes the kinds of groups the creature might form. A range of numbers in parentheses indicates how many combat-ready adults are in each type of group.

Many groups also have a number of noncombatants, expressed as a percentage of the fighting population. Noncombatants can include young, the infirm, slaves, or other individuals who are not inclined to fight. A creature's Society entry may include more details on noncombatants.

CHALLENGE RATING

This is the average level of a party of four adventurers for which a single creature would be an encounter of moderate difficulty. Assume a party of four fresh characters (full hit points, full spells, and equipment appropriate to their levels). Given reasonable luck, the party should be able to win the encounter with some damage but no casualties. For more information about Challenge Ratings, see Chapter 4 and Chapter 7 of the *Dungeon Master's Guide*.

TREASURE

This entry reflects how much wealth the creature owns and refers to Table 7–4: Treasure in the *Dungeon Master's Guide*. In most cases, a creature keeps valuables in its home or lair and has no treasure with it when it travels. Intelligent creatures that own useful, portable treasure (such as magic items) tend to carry and use these, leaving bulky items at home.

Note: The random dungeon generation tables in Chapter 4 of the *Dungeon Master's Guide* provide their own treasure information. Use that information instead of the monster's Treasure line whenever you refer to those tables.

Treasure can include coins, goods, and items. Creatures can have varying amounts of each, as follows.

Standard: Roll once under each type of treasure's column on the appropriate row for the creature's Challenge Rating (for groups of creatures, use the Encounter Level for the encounter instead).

Some creatures have double, triple, or even quadruple standard treasure; in these cases, roll under each treasure column two, three, or four times.

None: The creature collects no treasure of its own.

Nonstandard: Some creatures have quirks or habits that affect the types of treasure they collect. These creatures use the same treasure tables, but with special adjustments.

Fractional Coins: Roll on the Coins column, using the row for the creature's Challenge Rating, but divide the result as indicated.

% Goods or Items: The creature has goods or items only some of the time. Before checking for goods or items, roll

d%. On a result that indicates treasure, make a normal roll on the Goods column or the Items column (which may still result in no goods or items).

Double Goods or Items: Roll twice on the Goods or Items column.

Parenthetical Notes: Some entries for goods or items include notes that limit the types of treasure collected.

When a note includes the word "no," it means the creature does not collect or cannot keep that thing. If a random roll generates such a result, treat the result as "nothing" instead. For example, if a creature's "items" entry reads "no flammables," and a random roll generates a scroll, the creature instead has no item at all (the scroll burned up, or the creature left it behind).

When a note includes the word "only," the creature goes out of its way to collect treasure of the indicated type. If an entry for Goods or Items indicates "gems only," roll on the Goods or Items column and treat any "art" result as "gems" instead.

It sometimes will be necessary to reroll until the right sort of item appears. For example, if a creature's "items" entry reads "nonflammables only," roll normally on the Goods or Items column. If you get a flammable item, reroll on the same table until you get a nonflammable one. If the table you rolled on contains only flammable items, back up a step and reroll until you get to a table that can give you an appropriate item.

ALIGNMENT

This line gives the alignment that the creature is most likely to have. Every alignment line includes a qualifier that indicates how broadly that alignment applies to that kind of creature.

Always: The creature is born with the given alignment. The creature may have a hereditary predisposition to the alignment or come from a plane that predetermines it. It is possible for such individuals to change alignment, but such individuals are either unique or one-in-a-million exceptions.

Usually: The majority of these creatures have the given alignment. This may be due to strong cultural influences, or it may be a legacy of their origin. For example, most elves inherited their chaotic good alignment from their creator, the deity Corellon Larethian.

Often: The creature tends toward the listed alignment, by either nature or nurture, but not strongly. A plurality (40% to 50%) of individuals have the given alignment, but exceptions are common.

ADVANCEMENT

This book describes only the weakest and most common version of each creature. The Advancement line of a creature's entry shows how tough the creature can get, in terms of extra Hit Dice. (This is not an absolute limit, but exceptions are extremely rare.) In general, a creature should be able to gain up to three times its original Hit Dice (that is, a 3-HD creature should be able to advance up to 9 HD).

Size Increases

Creatures may become larger as they gain Hit Dice.

A size increase can affect a creature's physical ability scores, natural armor, Armor Class, attack bonus, and damage, as indicated on the following tables.

Old Size*	New Size	Str	Dex	Con	Natural Armor	AC/Attack
Fine	Diminutive	Same	–2	Same	Same	–4
Diminutive	Tiny	+2	–2	Same	Same	–2
Tiny	Small	+4	–2	Same	Same	–1
Small	Medium-size	+4	–2	+2	Same	–1
Medium-size	Large	+8	–2	+4	+2	–1
Large	Huge	+8	–2	+4	+3	–1
Huge	Gargantuan	+8	Same	+4	+4	–2
Gargantuan	Colossal	+8	Same	+4	+5	–4

*Repeat the adjustment if the creature moves up more than one size. For example, if a creature advances from Medium-size to Huge, it gains +16 Strength, –4 Dexterity, and –2 to attack bonus and Armor Class.

Old Damage (Each)*	New Damage
1d2	1d3
1d3	1d4
1d4	1d6
1d6	1d8
1d8 or 1d10	2d6
1d12	2d8

*Repeat the adjustment if the creature moves up more than one size category. For example, if a Medium-size creature with two claw attacks dealing 1d4 points of damage each advances from Medium-size to Huge, the damage dealt by each of its claw attacks increases to 1d8.

Skills and Feats

To determine the number of skill points and feats an advanced creature has, use the formulas given for its type in the Type Descriptions section of the introduction. The only difference is that if you need to calculate its extra Hit Dice for those formulas, use the minimum Hit Dice for its old size rather than its new size from the Typical Creature Statistics by Type table. (Doing this prevents the advanced creature from having fewer skill points and feats than it did when it was smaller.)

Other Improvements

As its Hit Dice increase, the creature's attack bonuses and saving throw modifiers might improve, and it could gain more feats and skills, depending on its type.

Saving throw bonuses are given in Table 3–1: Base Save and Base Attack Bonuses in the *Player's Handbook*. A "good" saving throw uses the higher of the given values.

Note that if the creature acquires a character class, it improves according to its class, not its type.

Creatures with Character Classes

If a creature acquires a character class, it follows the rules

for multiclassing given in Chapter 3 of the *Player's Handbook*. The creature's character level equals the number of class levels it has, plus the total Hit Dice for its kind, if greater than 1. For example, an ogre normally has 4 HD. If it picks up one level in the barbarian class, it becomes a 5th-level character: 1st-level barbarian/4th-level ogre (its "monster class") and adds 1d12 (for its barbarian Hit Die) to its hit point total. A creature with 1 or fewer HD trades out its creature Hit Die for its first level of a character class. Thus, it uses only its character level (see Monsters as Races in Chapter 2 of the *Dungeon Master's Guide* for details). In this case, the creature retains all its racial benefits and adjustments (such as racial bonuses to the use of skills) but gains no feats or skill points for its monster class. Additional Hit Dice from a character class never affect a creature's size.

A creature's monster class is always its favored class, and the creature never suffers XP penalties for having it.

Effective Character Level: Some of the creatures in this book are capable of having levels in a class, and when they do, they are significantly more powerful than the races described in the *Player's Handbook*. This difference in power is expressed as the creature's level adjustment (a positive number). This number and the creature's Hit Dice are added to the creature's class level to determine its effective character level, or ECL.

For instance, an avolakia PC has a level adjustment of +5 and 10 HD; thus, a 1st-level avolakia sorcerer has an ECL of 16, and it is the equivalent of a 16th-level character. The creature would be a good fit in a party whose other members were at or about 16th level, but it would be too powerful for a party of lower-level characters.

DESCRIPTIVE TEXT

The descriptive text opens with a short narrative about the monster: what it does, what it looks like, and what is most noteworthy about it. The following sections of the text describe how the creature fights and give details on special attacks, special qualities, skills, and feats.

EXAMPLE OF MONSTER ADVANCEMENT

The dune stalker is a Medium-size outsider with an advancement of 7–12 HD (Medium-size); 13–18 HD (Large). Creating a more powerful dune stalker with 13 Hit Dice requires the following adjustments.

	Old Statistics	New Statistics	Notes
Size/Type:	Medium-size outsider	Large outsider	New size due to 13 HD.
Hit Dice:	6d8+12 (39 hp)	13d8+52 (110 hp)	Constitution from 14 to 18 for becoming Large.
Initiative:	+4	+3	Dexterity from 10 to 8 due to size increase.
Speed:	40 ft., climb 20 ft.	40 ft., climb 20 ft.	No change.
AC:	17 (+7 natural), touch 10, flat-footed 17	17 (–1 size, –1 Dex, +9 natural), touch 8, flat-footed 17	Natural armor improves, but Dexterity and size penalties apply.
Attacks:	Slam +9 melee	Slam +20 melee	Base attack bonus for a 13-HD outsider is +13. Adjustments are +7 (for Strength 24), –1 (for Large size), and +1 (for Weapon Focus) for a primary attack bonus of +20.
Damage:	Slam 1d8+4	Slam 2d6+10	Each d8 becomes 2d6, Strength 24 provides bonus of +7 to damage.
Face/Reach:	5 ft. by 5 ft./5 ft.	5 ft. by 5 ft./10 ft.	Reach increases due to Large size.
Special Attacks:	Kiss of death, *shout*	Kiss of death, *shout*	The save DC against the creature's kiss of death attack rises from 15 to 20 (+3 for half of its additional Hit Dice rounded down, and +2 because its Constitution modifier rose from +2 to +4).
Special Qualities:	DR 10/+1, improved tracking, jump, outsider traits, SR 20	DR 10/+1, improved tracking, jump, outsider traits, SR 22	SR rises by 1 for each additional point of CR.
Saves:	Fort +7, Ref +5, Will +7	Fort +12, Ref +7, Will +10	At 13 HD, good saves have a base +8 bonus; all saves adjusted for ability scores.
Abilities:	Str 16, Dex 10, Con 14, Int 13, Wis 15, Cha 11	Str 24, Dex 8, Con 18, Int 13, Wis 15, Cha 11	Strength increases by 8, Constitution increases by 4, Dexterity decreases by 2.
Skills:	Balance +6, Climb +19, Hide +6, Intimidate +4, Jump +5, Knowledge (nature) +4, Listen +9, Move Silently +9, Search +7, Spot +8, Tumble +9	Balance +8, Climb +25, Hide +10, Intimidate +4, Jump +21, Knowledge (nature) +4, Listen +19, Move Silently +10, Search +16, Spot +19, Tumble +15	Adding 7 HD raises skill max ranks to 16 and adds 63 skill points.
Feats:	Alertness, Improved Initiative	Alertness, Improved Initiative, Power Attack, Weapon Focus (slam)	Advancing this creature to 13 HD adds two feats.
Challenge Rating:	9	11	Challenge Rating rises by 2, since the dune stalker's Hit Dice have been doubled (see Tougher Monsters in Chapter 4 of the *Dungeon Master's Guide*).

	Vassal Medium-Size Monstrous Humanoid	Soldier Large Monstrous Humanoid	Queen Medium-Size Monstrous Humanoid
Hit Dice:	1d8 (4 hp)	6d8+18 (45 hp)	14d8+42 (105 hp)
Initiative:	+1	+1	+5
Speed:	30 ft., fly 60 ft. (average)	40 ft., fly 90 ft. (good)	40 ft., fly 80 ft. (good)
AC:	11 (+1 Dex), touch 11, flat-footed 10	10 (−1 size, +1 Dex), touch 10, flat-footed 9	11 (+1 Dex), touch 11, flat-footed 10
Attacks:	2 claws +1 melee and sting −4 melee, or light flail +1 melee and sting −4 melee, or javelin +2 ranged	2 claws +11 melee and sting +6 melee, or Huge ranseur +11/+6 melee and sting +6 melee, or Huge masterwork mighty composite longbow (+6 Str bonus) +7/+2 ranged	2 claws +18 melee and sting +13 melee, or sickle +18/+13/+8 melee and sting +13 melee, or masterwork mighty composite longbow (+4 Str bonus) +16/+11/+6 ranged
Damage:	Claw 1d4, light flail 1d8, sting 1d6 plus poison, javelin 1d6	Claw 1d6+6, Huge ranseur 2d6+9/×3, sting 1d8+3 plus poison, Huge mighty composite longbow (+6 Str bonus) 2d6+6/×3	Claw 1d6+4, sickle 1d6+4, sting 2d4+2 plus poison, masterwork mighty composite longbow (+4 Str bonus) 1d8+4/×3
Face/Reach:	5 ft. by 5 ft./5 ft.	5 ft. by 5 ft./10 ft. (15 ft. with ranseur)	5 ft. by 5 ft./5 ft.
Special Attacks:	Drone, improved grab, poison	Drone, improved grab, poison, stormwing	Drone, improved grab, poison, spells
Special Qualities:	Darkvision 60 ft., hive mind	Darkvision 60 ft., DR 5/+1, hive mind, special enemy	Darkvision 60 ft., DR 10/+1, hive mind, SR 21
Saves:	Fort +0, Ref +3, Will +4	Fort +5, Ref +6, Will +6	Fort +9, Ref +10, Will +14
Abilities:	Str 11, Dex 13, Con 10, Int 10, Wis 14, Cha 9	Str 22, Dex 13, Con 16 Int 9, Wis 12, Cha 13	Str 18, Dex 13, Con 16 Int 15, Wis 21, Cha 18
Skills:	Craft (any one) +4, Intuit Direction +6, Knowledge (any one) +2, Listen +5, Search +4, Wilderness Lore +5	Intuit Direction +6, Knowledge (any one), +1, Listen +6, Sense Motive +4, Spot +6, Wilderness Lore +7	Concentration +13, Diplomacy +6, Intimidate +13, Knowledge (any two) +10, Listen +12, Sense Motive +10, Spot +6, Wilderness Lore +13
Feats:	Dodge	Dodge, Flyby Attack	Dodge, Flyby Attack, Great Fortitude, Improved Initiative, item creation feat (any one), metamagic feat (any one)
Climate/Terrain:	Temperate or warm hills, plains, or desert	Temperate or warm hills, plains, or desert	Temperate or warm hills, plains, or desert
Organization:	Solitary, pair, team (3–8), or crew (10–40)	Solitary, pair, team (3–8), or troop (10–20)	Solitary or hive (1 plus 20–100 vassals and 5–30 soldiers)
Challenge Rating:	2	6	12
Treasure:	Standard	Standard	Double standard
Alignment:	Usually lawful	Usually lawful	Usually lawful
Advancement:	By character class	By character class	By character class

Abeils are insectlike humanoids known for their industriousness and their complex social structure. They are commonly referred to as "bee people." Their society has an expansionist philosophy—a fact that troubles those whose lands they intrude upon. Rather than resorting to war, abeils prefer to overcome rivals through superior resourcefulness and industry.

An abeil looks like a cross between an elf and a bee. A vassal or queen stands more than 7 feet high and has slender but sinewy legs and arms. A soldier is at least 10 feet tall and considerably more muscular than either of the other two varieties. An abeil's hands and feet have four digits each. Its body is covered with bristly fur, colored in alternating bands of black and yellow. The creature's head and facial features resemble those of an elf, except that the abeil has black,

faceted eyes and long antennae. Like a bee, an abeil has translucent wings.

Abeils speak Common, Elven, and Sylvan.

COMBAT

All abeils prefer to fight from the sky, making ranged attacks and sonic assaults upon their foes below. If forced to fight on the ground, they coordinate their attacks to make the best use of their ranged weapons (and spells, for those capable of casting them). In melee, they prefer to swarm around particularly tough opponents and sting them with their enfeebling poison.

Abeils fight to the death because they believe that cowardice on the battlefield could doom the hive. They rarely wear armor because it impedes their ability to fly.

Drone (Su): As a full-round action, an abeil can beat its wings to create a droning buzz in a 60-foot spread. Each creature in the area must make a Will save (see below for DCs) or fall asleep as the *sleep* spell. There is no Hit Dice limit for this effect. Abeils are immune to their own drone attacks as well as those of other abeils.

Improved Grab (Ex): If an abeil hits a single target that is at least one size category smaller than itself with both claws, it deals normal damage and attempts to start a grapple as a free action without provoking an attack of opportunity (see below for grapple bonuses). If it gets a hold, it automatically hits with its sting. Thereafter, the abeil has the option to conduct the grapple normally, or simply use its claws to hold the opponent (–20 penalty on grapple check, but the abeil is not considered grappled). In either case, each successful grapple check it makes during successive rounds automatically deals damage from both claws and the sting.

Hive Mind (Ex): All abeils within 25 miles of their queen are in constant communication. If one is aware of a particular danger, they all are. If one in a particular group is not flat-footed, none of them are. No abeil in such a group is considered flanked unless they all are.

VASSAL

Vassals are the backbone of abeil society. It is they who provide the menial labor for the hive. They gather pollen, maintain the hive-city, and obey their queen's every command. Vassals produce the necessary goods for the abeil society, provide both mundane and specialized services, and advance the culture and techology of their hive city. A few even choose to leave behind their mundane tasks and pursue more individualistic paths, such as philosophy, art, religion, and politics. These abeils form an elite conclave called the vassal court that reports directly to the queen and serves as her council.

Combat

Unless ordered to attack, vassals flee combat to notify the hive of the threat. When armed for battle, they fight with light flails.

Drone (Su): Will save DC 9.

Improved Grab (Ex): A vassal's grapple bonus is +1.

Poison (Ex): A vassal delivers its poison (Fortitude save DC 10) with each successful sting attack. The initial and secondary damage is the same (1d4 points of Strength damage).

SOLDIER

These creatures account for fully a third of an abeil hive-city's population. The soldiers are the queen's army—the first and last line of defense for their hive. They are trained to respond swiftly to any danger. Soldiers consider most nearby civilizations to be threats and treat uninvited visitors with grave suspicion.

Combat

Abeil soldiers are often called stormwings because of the thunderous noise they make in battle. They prefer to meet a threat by using their stormwing attacks and bows first, then meleeing with ranseurs and stingers as needed.

Drone (Su): Will save DC 14.

Improved Grab (Ex): A soldier's grapple bonus is +16.

Poison (Ex): A soldier delivers its poison (Fortitude save DC 16) with each successful sting attack. The initial and secondary damage is the same (2d4 points of Strength damage).

Stormwing (Su): As a full-round action, a soldier in flight can hover and deliver a destructive sonic attack with its wings. The attack deals 6d6 points of damage to all (except other abeils) within a 40-foot burst (Reflex save DC 16 for half damage). Once the soldier uses this ability, it must wait 1d4 rounds before using it again.

MC

Special Enemy (Ex): An abeil soldier may select a type of creature as a special enemy. This ability is similar to the ranger's favored enemy ability, and the soldier may choose from the same list (see the Ranger entry in Chapter 3 of the *Player's Handbook*). Each soldier may select only one special enemy.

The soldier receives a +3 bonus on Bluff, Listen, Sense Motive, Spot, and Wilderness Lore checks when using these skills against its special enemy. Likewise, a soldier gets this same bonus on weapon damage rolls against creatures of the selected type.

QUEEN

At the pinnacle of any abeil society is the queen, who rules with absolute power. All the abeils in her realm live and die at her command. Though she was born to rule, the typical queen routinely seeks the advice of her court before committing to any major decisions.

The queen selects a mate from her vassal court and personally rears future queens. Each hive-city maintains 1–5 juvenile queens in addition to the reigning queen. Each such young queen has the same statistics as a vassal.

Combat

An abeil queen can cast powerful spells when threatened, and her poison is more virulent than that of any other abeil. However, she is rarely in combat because she depends primarily on her soldiers to protect her.

Drone (Su): Will save DC 21.

Improved Grab (Ex): A queen's grapple bonus is +18.

Poison (Ex): A queen delivers her poison (Fortitude save DC 20) with each successful sting attack. The initial and secondary damage is the same (1d2 points of Strength drain).

Spells: An abeil queen can cast divine spells as a 16th-level druid (spells/day 6/7/6/6/5/5/3/3/2; save DC 15 + spell level).

ABEIL SOCIETY

The hive-city is the central hub of the abeils' busy society. Vassals buzz here and there, ensuring that vital city services continue, while patrols of soldiers vigilantly keep the peace and protect the hive against outside threats.

Abeils are highly imperialistic, though they are not so much concerned with conquering other races as they are with setting up new hive-cities. Nevertheless, this goal puts them into conflict with nearly every other race they encounter, since soceieties in their path must fight for space and resources or be pushed out by the abeil civilization.

When a hive-city becomes too large, one of the young queens is given a substance called royal jelly, which converts her into a full-fledged queen. She then takes twenty vassals and five soldiers and leaves to set up a new hive-city at a previously scouted location.

ABEIL CHARACTERS

Although abeil society is extremely rigid, there is enough freedom within a hive to allow an individual abeil its own choice of profession. Even so, relatively few abeils desire to progress as characters. For those that do, the favored class is druid for queens or vassals and ranger for soldiers.

An abeil PC's effective character level (ECL) is its class level plus the appropriate modifier: vassal +3, soldier +11, queen +21. For example, a 1st-level vassal druid has an ECL of 4 and is the equivalent of a 4th-level character.

ASH RAT

Small Magical Beast (Fire)
Hit Dice: 1d10 (5 hp)
Initiative: +8
Speed: 40 ft., climb 20 ft.
AC: 16 (+1 size, +4 Dex, +1 natural), touch 15, flat-footed 12
Attacks: Bite +0 melee, or flame spit +6 ranged touch
Damage: Bite 1d4–2, flame spit 1d4 fire
Face/Reach: 5 ft. by 5 ft./5 ft.
Special Attacks: Flame spit, heat
Special Qualities: Darkvision 60 ft., fire heal, fire subtype, low-light vision, smoky hide
Saves: Fort +2, Ref +6, Will +1
Abilities: Str 6, Dex 18, Con 11, Int 2, Wis 13, Cha 3
Skills: Climb +14, Hide +9*, Move Silently +5
Feats: Improved Initiative

Climate/Terrain: Any warm land
Organization: Solitary, nest (10–40) or horde (41–60)
Challenge Rating: 1
Treasure: None
Alignment: Always chaotic neutral
Advancement: 2–3 HD (Small)

Spreading fires throughout towns, fields and forests, ash rats constitute a deadly menace to any civilized society. These little nomadic horrors are naturally drawn to large sources of flame; in fact, they get their nourishment from heat in a way that not even the sages understand. These creatures are so hot that they ignite any combustibles they touch.

An ash rat is a 2-foot-long rodent with orange eyes. It has the general shape of a rat, and its fur is black, gray, or brown. Its oversized front teeth are a dull yellow color. An ash rat's exact appearance is difficult for most onlookers to discern because it exudes a perpetual cloud of sooty smoke that hides it from view.

COMBAT

An ash rat normally flees from combat if possible. When cornered, it fights defensively, spitting fire at those who threaten it. Its heated body is painful to the touch, which prevents prudent foes from closing.

Flame Spit (Su): Once per round, an ash rat can spit flames at one target up to 10 feet away. This attack deals 1d4 points of fire damage.

Large Magical Beast (Cold)
Hit Dice: 4d10+8 (30 hp)
Initiative: +1
Speed: 60 ft., fly 30 ft. (good)
AC: 13 (−1 size, +1 Dex, +3 natural), touch 10, flat-footed 13
Attacks: 2 hooves +4 melee and bite −1 melee
Damage: Hoof 1d6+1, bite 1d6
Face/Reach: 5 ft. by 10 ft./5 ft.
Special Qualities: Cold subtype, darkvision 60 ft., dodge arrows, *feather fall*, low-light vision, ride the wind, telepathy, uncanny dodge, wind immunity
Saves: Fort +6, Ref +5, Will +2
Abilities: Str 13, Dex 12, Con 15, Int 13, Wis 12, Cha 10
Skills: Intimidate +7, Listen +10, Spot +10, Wilderness Lore +8
Feats: Alertness, Flyby Attack

Climate/Terrain: Any mountains
Organization: Solitary, pair, string (3–4), or herd (5–20)
Challenge Rating: 4
Treasure: None
Alignment: Always neutral good
Advancement: 5–6 HD (Medium-size)

Heat (Ex): An ash rat's body heat deals 1d2 points of fire damage to each creature (except another ash rat) that touches it. Any flammable item in contact with an ash rat must make a successful Reflex save (DC 10) or catch fire (see Catching on Fire in Chapter 3 of the DUNGEON MASTER'S *Guide*). When an ash rat dies, its body burns away completely in 1 round.

Fire Heal (Ex): Fire and heat heal an ash rat's wounds. For every round that the creature is exposed to flame or heat intense enough to deal at least 1 point of damage, the creature instead gains the benefit of a *cure minor wounds* spell (1 hit point healed). Two or more ash rats touching each other provide enough heat for fire healing.

Fire Subtype (Ex): An ash rat is immune to fire damage but takes double damage from cold unless a saving throw for half damage is allowed. In that case, the creature takes half damage on a success and double damage on a failure.

Smoky Hide (Ex): An ash rat continually sheds smoke from its body. This smoky haze is so thick that it grants the creature one-half concealment (20% miss chance) and makes hiding easier (see Skills, below). Though it is difficult to see the ash rat because of the smoke rising from its body, the smoke itself is visible, provided that the area has sufficient light by which to see it.

Skills: An ash rat uses its Dexterity modifier instead of its Strength modifier for Climb checks. *In smoky or foggy areas, an ash rat gains a +8 bonus on Hide checks.

At first glance, an asperi appears to be nothing more than an unusually beautiful horse. An individual asperi can be white, gray, or dun-colored, with a graceful, flowing mane of silver, white, or light gray. A secondary mane of the same shade as the first extends from the creature's front shoulders down along the backs of its front legs.

Unlike typical horses, asperis are intelligent magical beasts. They live in the permanent cold of remote mountain peaks, where they gallop across the glaciers and through the frigid skies. By catching prevailing winds and flying with them, asperis can move even faster through the skies than their normal flying speed permits. Their ability to "ride the wind" in this way has earned them the common name of wind steeds.

The typical asperi belongs to a herd with up to twenty members, but it spends much of its time roaming the skies alone or with just one or two chosen companions. Hippogriffs and griffons, the mortal enemies of the asperis, are almost never encountered in mountains where wind steeds live, since the far more intelligent asperis take pains to drive them off or kill them. Asperis also dislike rocs, but they get along well with pegasi. Lasting friendships between asperis and pegasi are rare, however, because the winged horses seldom venture into the cold mountain heights where the wind steeds live.

If captured when very young and raised with respect and consideration, an asperi can be trained as a steed. Any potential rider must realize that an asperi mount is not a mere animal; it is an intelligent, sentient being with opinions

and ideas of its own, and it demands to be treated as such. Under no circumstances will an asperi tolerate a rider who is chaotic or evil. A paladin might convince an adult wind steed to serve as a permanent mount, but full-grown asperis usually agree to bear riders only in the short term, since they value their independence.

Asperis with 5 or more HD are very rare. Such creatures have iridescent hides that glisten like snow and rainbow-hued manes and tails.

COMBAT

Asperis are inoffensive creatures by nature. Given their great speed, their usual response to danger is simply to fly away. Like most horses, however, they can fight ferociously when aroused. In combat, they usually kick and slash with their front hooves and bite with their powerful jaws.

Asperis prefer to fight from the air, which gives them a significant advantage against opponents on the ground, under the right conditions. Near their mountain homes, asperis always look for opportunities to attack intruders when the latter are at the edges of cliffs or maneuvering on narrow ledges. The wind steeds use combinations of charges, bull rushes, flyby attacks, and trip attacks (all while airborne) to force their enemies over precipices or into glacial crevasses. They usually prefer to use their speed and maneuverability to avoid combat until conditions are in their favor.

Cold Subtype (Ex): An asperi is immune to cold damage but takes double damage from fire unless a saving throw for half damage is allowed. In that case, the creature takes half damage on a success and double damage on a failure.

Dodge Arrows (Ex): A flying asperi gains a +2 dodge bonus to AC against any missile attack during any turn in which it takes a move action. If it has a rider, he or she also gains the bonus. The bonus lasts until the asperi's next turn.

Feather Fall **(Sp):** An asperi can use *feather fall* up to four times per day. Caster level 4th.

Ride the Wind (Su): This ability is similar to the effect of the *air walk* spell in most respects. When an asperi uses ride the wind, it gains bonus movement (+1 ft. to fly speed for each 1 mph of the prevailing wind) when moving with winds faster than 20 mph. Adverse winds do not slow the creature down, but they provide no bonus movement.

An asperi carrying a rider gallops through the air so smoothly that the rider can cast spells without making Concentration checks, provided that the asperi does not attack or perform any sudden aerial maneuvers.

Telepathy (Su): An asperi can communicate with any creature that has an Intelligence score of at least 1 through a form of telepathy. This communication has a range of 60 feet, and its complexity is limited by the Intelligence score of the other creature.

Uncanny Dodge (Ex): Because of its preternatural alertness, an asperi retains its Dexterity bonus to AC even when flat-footed, and it cannot be flanked.

Wind Immunity (Ex): Winds, either natural or magical, have no effect on an asperi unless it chooses to ride them for additional movement (see Ride the Wind, above). This benefit applies equally to mountain gales, magical windstorms, elemental whirlwinds, and other similar effects.

TRAINING AN ASPERI

Young asperis are worth 7,000 gp per head. They mature at the same rate as horses do. A professional trainer charges 2,000 gp to rear an asperi or to train it as a mount.

Training an asperi requires a successful Handle Animal check (DC 22 for a young asperi, DC 29 for an adult) and the willing cooperation of the creature. An asperi can fight while carrying a rider, but the rider cannot also attack unless he or she succeeds at a Ride check.

Carrying Capacity: A light load for an asperi is up to 150 pounds; a medium load, 151–300 pounds; and a heavy load, 301–450 pounds. Unlike most flying mounts, an asperi can fly with a medium or heavy load, thanks to its ride the wind ability.

	Pulverizer Medium-Size Construct	Hammerer Medium-Size Construct
Hit Dice:	3d10 (16 hp)	5d10 (27 hp)
Initiative:	+0	+0
Speed:	40 ft.	20 ft.
AC:	21 (+11 natural), touch 10, flat-footed 21	21 (+11 natural), touch 10, flat-footed 21
Attacks:	2 slams +7 melee	Slam +10 melee
Damage:	Slam 1d6+5	Slam 2d8+10
Face/Reach:	5 ft. by 5 ft./5 ft.	5 ft. by 5 ft./5 ft.
Special Attacks:	Sonic shriek	—
Special Qualities:	Blindsight 40 ft., construct traits, unreliable	Construct traits, unreliable
Saves:	Fort +1, Ref +1, Will +0	Fort +1, Ref +1, Will +0
Abilities:	Str 21, Dex 11, Con —, Int —, Wis 9, Cha 4	Str 25, Dex 11, Con —, Int —, Wis 9, Cha 4
Climate/Terrain:	Any land and underground	Any land and underground
Organization:	Solitary, pair, or team (3–5)	Solitary, pair, or team (3–5)
Challenge Rating:	3	3
Treasure:	None	None
Alignment:	Always neutral	Always neutral
Advancement:	4–8 HD (Medium-size); 9 HD (Large)	6–8 HD (Medium-size); 9–15 HD (Large)

An automaton is a creature built for labor or war. Although the construct is superficially similar to a golem, an automaton is actually quite different. It is built with clockwork parts and animated by means of powerful shadow magic. While the shadow consciousness of an automaton sometimes makes it difficult for the creature to interact with the physical world, it nevertheless can be a fearsome opponent.

COMBAT

Like golems, automatons are mindless but tenacious combatants. Since they are emotionless in combat, they are not easily provoked. Automatons don't use weapons, even if ordered to do so. Instead, they always strike with their limbs, which are formidable weapons in themselves.

An automaton follows the orders of its creator. The creature can be commanded directly by its creator if the latter is within 60 feet and both visible and audible to the automaton. If uncommanded, an automaton follows its last instruction to the best of its ability, though it returns any attacks directed at it. Typically, the creator gives an automaton a simple set of instructions (such as "Remain in this area and attack all creatures that enter," or "Attack all bipedal creatures you see," or "Ring a gong and attack," or the like) to govern its actions in his or her absence.

Construct Traits: An automaton is immune to mind-affecting effects, poison, *sleep*, paralysis, stunning, disease, death effects, necromantic effects, and any effect that requires a Fortitude save unless it also works on objects. The creature is not subject to critical hits, subdual damage, ability damage, ability drain, energy drain, or death from massive damage. It cannot heal itself but can be healed through repair. It cannot be raised or resurrected. An automaton has darkvision (60-foot range).

Unreliable (Ex): The shadow consciousness of an automaton is only quasi-real, like the consciousness of a

creation such as a simulacrum. The creature is thus some-times slow to react to the changing environment around it. At the beginning of each round in which an automaton attempts to act, roll 1d20. On a result of 11 or better, it acts normally; otherwise, it takes no action.

PULVERIZER

The pulverizer automaton was originally intended as a mining machine. Its sonic shriek was designed to weaken stone, and its wedges to finish the job of breaking it up. Thanks to its blindsight ability, this construct is particularly effective underground.

A pulverizer looks something like a four-legged, metal lobster with spiked wedges instead of claws. Instead of a head, it has a round opening at the top of its body from which it emits its sonic attacks.

Combat

When attacking, a lone pulverizer usually looses its sonic shriek, then moves in to use its slam attacks against any foes who are still moving. Teams of these creatures pose a formidable threat on the battlefield, since one or more can hang back and shriek every round while the others close with foes.

Sonic Shriek (Ex): Once per round as a standard action, a pulverizer can loose a cone of sonic energy 30 feet long. Everything within the cone takes 1d8 points of sonic damage. In addition, every creature within the cone that fails a Fortitude save (DC 13) is stunned for 1 round. (This value incorporates a +5 racial bonus to the save DC.)

Blindsight (Ex): A pulverizer is blind, but it maneuvers and fights as well as a sighted creature by using sonar, like that of a bat. This ability enables it to discern objects and creatures within 40 feet. The pulverizer usually does not need to make Spot or Listen checks to notice creatures within range of its blindsight. A *silence* spell negates this ability.

HAMMERER

The hammerer automaton is a roughly human-shaped, bipedal war machine adapted from another automaton that was designed for construction and heavy lifting. One of the creature's two arms ends in a massive claw or pincer, the other in an even more massive hammer.

Combat

Hammerers are not built for fancy tactical maneuvers, but they are still fearsome opponents. On the battlefield, com-manders simply point teams of these constructs at the enemy and let them go.

The powerful hammer-arm that gives the hammerer its name is a nasty piece of business—heavy, solid, and deadly. The pincer-arm is used mainly for lifting things. The con-struct can attack with only one arm at a time, and although it can slam with either arm, it favors the hammer-arm for all its attacks.

Large Aberration
Hit Dice: 10d8+30 (75 hp)
Initiative: +3
Speed: 20 ft.
AC: 18 (–1 size, +3 Dex, +6 deflection), touch 18, flat-footed 15
Attacks: Bite +10 melee and 8 claws +8 melee
Damage: Bite 2d6+4 plus poison, claw 1d4+2
Face/Reach: 5 ft. by 5 ft./10 ft.
Special Attacks: Poison, spell-like abilities, *suggestion*
Special Qualities: Darkvision 60 ft., *defensive aura*, fire resistance 10, immunities, regeneration 4, SR 21
Saves: Fort +6, Ref +6, Will +12
Abilities: Str 19, Dex 16, Con 17, Int 16, Wis 21, Cha 22
Skills: Bluff +14, Concentration +14, Diplomacy +18, Intimidate +8, Sense Motive +18, Spellcraft +11
Feats: Combat Casting, Combat Reflexes, Dodge, Multiattack, Quicken Spell-Like Ability

Climate/Terrain: Underground
Organization: Solitary, pair, band (3–8), or tribe (4–24 avo-lakias plus 3–30 zombies, 2–12 wights, and 1–6 mummies)
Challenge Rating: 10
Treasure: Standard coins, standard goods, double items
Alignment: Usually neutral evil
Advancement: By character class

The avolakia is a nauseating creature that combines the worst aspects of a worm, an octopus, and an insect. It has exceptional intelligence and is incredibly wise and glib. Avolakias are experts at infiltrating humanoid societies for a variety of nefarious purposes.

An avolakia stands 10 feet tall. Its wormlike body is pallid and gray, shimmering with a pale yellow slime. The creature supports itself and moves about on a set of six suckered tentacles, each of which is tipped with a multi-faceted yellow eye. Its "head" consists of a fleshy sheath that houses a set of three cruelly hooked mandibles. Eight long, spidery arms tipped with tiny insectoid claws that almost look like human hands protrude from a set of ridges about halfway up the creature's body. An avolakia reeks of mold and decay.

Although they can digest dead or living flesh, avolakias find both disgusting and resort to such sustenance only under dire circumstances. They prefer to eat undead flesh—"fresh" off a zombie's flank is best.

Avolakias speak their own language (a guttural, slobber-ing tongue). Many of them also understand Undercommon and other languages, though they do not have the vocal apparatus to speak them. With its *polymorph self* spell-like ability, however, an avolakia can assume a form that is capa-ble of speaking any language it desires. This ability also enhances its disguise capabilities and aids it in laying ambushes for unwary opponents.

COMBAT

An avolakia prefers to cast spells or use its spell-like abilities from a distance while its undead minions close to melee with the enemy. If forced into melee, an avolakia uses its poisonous bite and flails with its eight claws. Occasionally, the creature may choose to use poison against one or more foes, then assume humanoid form and use its *suggestion* ability to bend them to its will.

Poison (Ex): An avolakia delivers its poison (Fortitude save DC 18) with each successful bite attack. The initial damage is 1d6 points of Wisdom damage, and the secondary damage is 2d6 points of Wisdom damage.

Spell-Like Abilities: At will—*chill touch, cause fear, detect magic, disrupt undead, gentle repose, ghoul touch, halt undead, mage hand, polymorph self* (humanoid form only), *read magic, spectral hand*; 3/day—*animate dead, create undead, enervation, vampiric touch.* Caster level 14th; save DC 16 + spell level.

Suggestion **(Sp):** When in humanoid form, an avolakia has a melodious and hypnotic voice. By speaking soothingly to any one creature in range that understands its spoken words, the avolakia can create an effect identical to that of a quickened *suggestion* spell (caster level 10th; Will save DC 19). An opponent in eye contact with the creature while it makes its suggestion takes a –2 penalty on the saving throw. The avolakia can use this ability a number of times per day equal to its Charisma modifier (usually six times per day).

Defensive Aura **(Sp):** An avolakia has a +6 deflection bonus to Armor Class. This ability is always in effect.

Fire Resistance (Ex): The slime that an avolakia constantly exudes grants it fire resistance 10. It also helps the creature escape more easily (see Skills, below).

Immunities (Su): Because of its close association with undead, the avolakia has developed immunity to cold, disease, energy drain, and paralysis.

Regeneration (Ex): An avolakia takes normal damage from acid, fire, and electricity.

Skills: Because of the slime it constantly exudes, an avolakia gains a +10 competence bonus on Escape Artist checks.

AVOLAKIA SOCIETY

Avolakias band together in small tribes deep in the recesses of the earth. They delight in creating and modifying undead of all sorts, which they use for both food and defense. Avolakia clerics make good use of the *create greater undead* spell to create mummies, spectres, vampires, and ghosts. They often arm these greater undead with magic weapons, armor, and wondrous items to aid them in defending the avolakias' territory.

The majority of avolakias have taken to worshiping Kyuss, a little-known quasi-deity. Despite the fact that their deity's divine status does not enable him to grant spells, many avolakia clerics are quite powerful, drawing their spells from some unknown source. So eager are the avolakias to elevate Kyuss to full deity status that they actively recruit new worshipers for his cult. The creatures typically establish settlements beneath the communities of surface races, then use their *polymorph self* and *suggestion* abilities to infiltrate their target areas. Often a group of avolakias infiltrates a local religious institution and attempts to assume control of the funerary rites for the community. Should the avolakias succeed, they have access to plenty of corpses that they can use to create more undead. In addition, the disguised avolakias are in a perfect position to corrupt selected members of the community and slowly indoctrinate them into the cult of Kyuss.

Avolakias also interact with various Underdark races. Some, such as the drow, they infiltrate in much the same way as they do surface races. With others, such as mind flayers, they openly propose alliances for the two groups' mutual benefit. A typical agreement between mind flayers and avolakias stipulates that both groups hunt down and capture intelligent beings. The mind flayers consume the unfortunate victims' brains, then hand the bodies over to the avolakias, who use them to create undead. But such alliances tend to fall apart eventually, either when the mind flayers enslave captives for long periods before consuming their brains, or when the avolakias kill a few mind flayers to make more powerful undead creatures.

AVOLAKIA CHARACTERS

An avolakia's favored class is sorcerer, but avolakia clerics are also quite common, and tribal leaders are always clerics of Kyuss. Avolakia spellcasters of any sort tend to focus on necromantic magic. Though they may choose from any of Kyuss's domains (Death, Evil, Magic, or Trickery), the majority choose Death and Evil.

An avolakia PC's effective character level (ECL) is equal to its class level + 15; thus, a 1st-level avolakia sorcerer has an ECL of 16 and is the equivalent of a 16th-level character.

BANSHEE

Medium-Size Undead (Incorporeal)
Hit Dice: 26d12 (169 hp)
Initiative: +7
Speed: Fly 80 ft. (good)
AC: 16 (+3 Dex, +3 deflection), touch 16, flat-footed 13
Attacks: Incorporeal touch +16 melee
Damage: Incorporeal touch 1d8/19–20 plus 1d4 Charisma drain
Face/Reach: 5 ft. by 5 ft./5 ft.
Special Attacks: Charisma drain, horrific appearance, wail
Special Qualities: *Detect living*, incorporeal subtype, SR 28, stunt plants, undead traits
Saves: Fort +8, Ref +11, Will +19
Abilities: Str —, Dex 17, Con —, Int 16, Wis 15, Cha 17
Skills: Balance +5, Hide +13, Intuit Direction +7, Jump +2, Listen +24, Scry +13, Search +23, Spot +24, Tumble +16
Feats: Alertness, Blind-Fight, Combat Reflexes, Dodge, Expertise, Improved Critical (incorporeal touch), Improved Initiative, Iron Will, Mobility, Spring Attack

Climate/Terrain: Any land and underground
Organization: Solitary, pair, or brood (3–4)
Challenge Rating: 17
Treasure: Double standard
Alignment: Usually neutral evil
Advancement: 27–52 HD (Medium-size)

A banshee is the spirit of a strong-willed, selfish individual of a humanoid race. Because of its rage at the loss of its own life, it delights in bringing death to any living creature it encounters.

This creature appears as a translucent image of the form it held in life. With the passage of time, the banshee's image tends to become blurred and indistinct, though the creature remains recognizable as a humanoid.

The very presence of a banshee creates a pall over the landscape. Its ability to stunt the growth of plants combined with its deadly wail eventually reduces the surrounding territory to blasted heath and wasteland. Largely for this reason, many cultures consider a sudden blight upon the land to be an omen of death.

A banshee speaks the languages that it knew in life.

COMBAT

Banshees hate all living things with an unholy fury, and they readily attack anyone foolish enough to trespasses within their territories. A banshee typically uses its horrific appearance to drive off less powerful foes, then employs its howling wail one or more times to damage any who remain. Finally, it finishes off the intruders with its Charisma drain in melee. If overmatched, the creature flees into the earth, usually to a gravelike lair that it maintains beneath the surface.

Charisma Drain (Su): An individual struck by a banshee must make a Fortitude save (DC 26) or permanently lose 1d4 points of Charisma (or 2d4 points on a critical hit). The banshee heals 5 points of damage (10 on a critical hit) whenever it drains Charisma, gaining any excess as temporary hit points.

Horrific Appearance (Su): Any living creature within 60 feet that views a banshee must make a successful Fortitude save (DC 26) or permanently lose 1d4 points of Strength, 1d4 points of Dexterity, and 1d4 points of Constitution. A creature that successfully saves against this effect cannot be affected by the same banshee's horrific appearance for 24 hours.

Wail (Su): During the night, a banshee can loose a deadly wail. This attack can slay up to eighteen living creatures within a 30-foot spread centered on the banshee, or within a 60-foot cone extending from the banshee, at the creature's option. A successful Fortitude save (DC 26) negates the effect. Once a banshee wails, it must wait 1d4 rounds before it can do so again, and it can wail no more than three times per day.

Detect Living **(Sp):** This ability functions like the *commune with nature* spell, except that it detects only living creatures and the range is one-half mile. The banshee can use *detect living* up to three times per day.

Incorporeal Subtype: A banshee can be harmed only by other incorporeal creatures, +1 or better magic weapons, spells, spell-like abilities, and supernatural abilities. The creature has a 50% chance to ignore any damage from a corporeal source, except for force effects or attacks made with ghost touch weapons. A banshee can pass through solid objects, but not force effects, at will. Its attacks ignore natural armor, armor, and shields, but deflection bonuses and force effects work normally against them. A banshee always moves silently and cannot be heard with Listen checks if it doesn't wish to be.

Stunt Plants (Su): Once per day, a banshee can stunt all normal plants within a one-half mile radius. This ability otherwise functions like the stunt version of a *diminish plants* spell (caster level 18th).

Undead Traits: A banshee is immune to mind-affecting effects, poison, *sleep*, paralysis, stunning, disease, death effects, necromantic effects, and any effect that requires a Fortitude save unless it also works on objects. It is not subject

to critical hits, subdual damage, ability damage, ability drain, energy drain, or death from massive damage. A banshee cannot be raised, and resurrection works only if it is willing. The creature has darkvision (60-foot range).

BLADELING

Medium-Size Outsider (Lawful)

Hit Dice: 1d8 (4 hp)
Initiative: +5
Speed: 30 ft.
AC: 15 (+1 Dex, +4 natural), touch 11, flat-footed 14
Attacks: Claw +1 melee, or longsword +1 melee
Damage: Claw 1d6, longsword 1d8/19–20
Face/Reach: 5 ft. by 5 ft./5 ft.
Special Attacks: Razor storm
Special Qualities: Cold resistance 5, DR 5/+1 (slashing and piercing weapons only), fire resistance 5, immunities, outsider traits
Saves: Fort +2, Ref +3, Will +2
Abilities: Str 11, Dex 13, Con 11, Int 10, Wis 10, Cha 10
Skills: Craft (weaponsmithing) +4, Jump +4
Feats: Improved Initiative

Climate/Terrain: Any land
Organization: Solitary, pair, company (3–6), or squad (11–20)
Challenge Rating: 1
Treasure: None
Alignment: Always lawful (usually lawful neutral or lawful evil)
Advancement: By character class

Bladelings are xenophobic beings of humanoid shape. Though they hail from Acheron, most scholars believe that the race emigrated there from another plane, possibly the Nine Hells of Baator, the Bleak Eternity of Gehenna, or even some unknown metal-based plane.

A bladeling has skin of a dull metallic hue, spotted with patches of metallic spines. Its eyes gleam like shards of purple ice, and its blood is black and oily.

Bladelings speak Common, and those with high enough Intelligence scores to know an additional language usually speak Infernal as well.

COMBAT

Bladelings are quick to jump into battle, relying on their tough skins and natural agility to see them through any fight. They are also brave, so they usually focus their attacks on the most dangerous combatants they see.

Razor Storm (Ex): Once per day, a bladeling can expel shrapnellike bits of its skin in a 15-foot cone, dealing 2d6 points of piercing damage to any creature in the area. A Reflex save (DC 10) halves the damage. After this attack, the bladeling's natural armor bonus drops to +2 for 24 hours.

Immunities (Ex): A bladeling takes no d[...] and it is immune to rust attacks despite i[...]

Outsider Traits: A bladeling has dark[...] range). It cannot be raised or resurrected.

BLADELING SOCIETY

Most bladelings live in the city of Zoronor, on Ocanthus, the fourth layer of Acheron. Some, however, wander the other layers of Acheron or even the other planes.

Bladelings are superstitious and xenophobic creatures, so it's no surprise that they abhor intrusions into their home territory. (Of course, as residents of Ocanthus—a place of flying storms of blades—they rarely have visitors.) Their society is prone to internal strife, but they immediately band together against external dangers. Bladelings that travel the planes are reasonably amiable toward strangers, perhaps because they have picked up a degree of tolerance for other beings through constant contact. Even so, they tend not to trust anyone they do not know.

BLADELING CHARACTERS

A bladeling's favored class is fighter. Leaders are often cleric/fighters, and the race is known for its assassins as well. Bladeling clerics usually worship Hextor.

A bladeling PC's effective character level (ECL) is equal to its class level + 1; thus, a 1st-level bladeling fighter has an ECL of 2 and is the equivalent of a 2nd-level character.

BLOOD APE

Large Magical Beast

Hit Dice: 4d10+8 (30 hp)

Initiative: +2

Speed: 30 ft., climb 30 ft.

AC: 14 (–1 size, +2 Dex, +3 natural), touch 11, flat-footed 12

Attacks: 2 claws +8 melee and bite +3 melee

Damage: Claw 1d6+5, bite 1d8+2

Face/Reach: 5 ft. by 5 ft./10 ft.

Special Attacks: *Growth*, improved grab, rend 2d4+7

Special Qualities: Darkvision 60 ft., low-light vision, scent

Saves: Fort +6, Ref +6, Will +2

Abilities: Str 21, Dex 15, Con 14, Int 2, Wis 12, Cha 7

Skills: Climb +15, Listen +3, Spot +3

Feats: Power Attack

Climate/Terrain: Warm forest and mountains

Organization: Solitary, patrol (1 alpha male plus 1–4 males), or colony (1 alpha male plus 2–5 males and 7–21 noncombatants)

Challenge Rating: 6

Treasure: None

Alignment: Usually neutral

Advancement: 5–8 HD (Large); 9–12 HD (Huge)

Blood apes are peaceful diurnal foragers with a unique defense mechanism. The alpha male (or leader) of a troop or patrol has the magical ability to make himself and other members of the group larger. Their Huge forms (see *Growth*, below) allow them to deal more damage in combat, but the ability to return to Large size means that they require substantially less food than Huge creatures would. Sages and scholars suggest that this ability is a residual effect of exceptionally strong growth and form-altering magic practiced on the ancestors of the current blood apes millennia ago.

A blood ape resembles a red-furred mountain gorilla. Its body is compact but muscular, and its sinewy arms end in humanlike hands. The alpha male is typically the largest ape in a group. Unlike the rest of the group, he has silvery fur and a balding head.

Blood apes are exceptionally territorial, and they fight to the death to protect their young and their land from intruders. Patrols occasionally forage far from the colony's lair in search of new feeding grounds.

COMBAT

The alpha male in any group of blood apes begins using his *growth* ability on the other males at the first sign of intruders. After receiving the benefit of this power, all the males pair up to attack specific opponents. Blood apes give no warning and make no display before attacking. The alpha male uses his *growth* ability on himself last, then enters melee. If females and young are present, they beat a hasty retreat while the males fight.

Growth (Sp): The alpha male in every group of blood apes can use this power up to eight times per day. It functions like an *animal growth* spell (caster level 9th), except that it works only on adult male blood apes. The following changes apply to all subject blood apes as long as the effect of *growth* lasts: SZ Huge; HD 8d10+32 (76 hp); Init +1; AC 15 (–2 size, +1 Dex, +6 natural), touch 9, flat-footed 14; Atk +15 melee (2d4+9, 2 claws) and +10 melee (2d6+4, bite); SV Fort +10, Ref +7, Will +3; Face/Reach 10 ft. by 10 ft./10 ft.; Str 29, Dex 13, Con 18; Climb +19.

Improved Grab (Ex): If a blood ape hits an opponent that is at least one size category smaller than itself with a claw attack, it deals normal damage and attempts to start a grapple as a free action without provoking an attack of opportunity (grapple bonus +13, or +25 if under *growth* effect). If it hits with both claws, it can also rend in the same round. Once it has a hold, the blood ape has the option to conduct the grapple normally, or simply use its claw to hold the opponent (–20 penalty on grapple check, but the blood ape is not considered grappled). In either case, each successful grapple check it makes during successive rounds automatically deals claw damage.

Rend (Ex): If a blood ape hits with both claws, it latches onto the opponent's body and tears the flesh. This attack automatically deals an additional 2d4+7 points of damage (or 2d4+13 if under a *growth* effect; see above).

Scent (Ex): A blood ape can detect approaching enemies, sniff out hidden foes, and track by sense of smell.

BLOOD APE SOCIETY

One-third of the noncombatants in any colony are infants and youths, and the balance are adult females. The females have the same statistics as the males, but without the *growth*, improved grab, and rend abilities. The young have no combat ability.

The alpha male of a colony is the only one permitted to mate with the females of that group. As a colony grows larger, the younger males eventually break off and attempt to form their own colonies by stealing a few females. A male who succeeds immediately gains the *growth* ability, and over a period of six months he develops the characteristic silver fur and bald head of an alpha male.

BOGGLE

Small Monstrous Humanoid
Hit Dice: 4d8 (18 hp)
Initiative: +9
Speed: 40 ft., climb 30 ft.
AC: 18 (+1 size, +5 Dex, +2 natural), touch 16, flat-footed 13
Attacks: 2 claws +5 melee and bite +0 melee
Damage: Claw 1d4, bite 1d4
Face/Reach: 5 ft. by 5 ft./15 ft.
Special Attacks: Darkvision 60 ft., improved grab, rend 2d4
Special Qualities: *Dimension door*, DR 5/+1, fire resistance 5, grease, scent
Saves: Fort +1, Ref +9, Will +3
Abilities: Str 10, Dex 21, Con 11, Int 5, Wis 8, Cha 6
Skills: Climb +8, Escape Artist +17, Hide +11, Move Silently +10, Pick Pocket +12
Feats: Improved Initiative

Climate/Terrain: Any land and underground
Organization: Solitary, pair, or crew (3–5)
Challenge Rating: 3
Treasure: 50% coins, 50% goods, no items
Alignment: Usually chaotic neutral
Advancement: 5–8 HD (Small); 9–12 HD (Medium-size)

Boggles are clever, gibbering scavengers that behave much like some species of monkeys. They do not value treasure, but they do like to collect bright, shiny objects such as coins, precious gems, and jewelry, as well

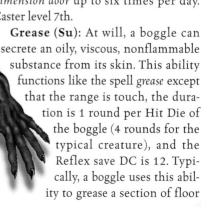

as bits of polished junk. In addition, they can often be tempted with food and sweets.

A boggle is a 3-foot-tall, hairless humanoid with a rubbery hide. It has a large, bulbous, bald head, huge ears, and disproportionate body parts, though the exact details vary from one individual to another. For example, a boggle's nose might be large and crooked, broad and flat, or nonexistent except for nostril slits. Arms, legs, hands, feet, torso, and abdomen vary from spindly to oversized but are almost always misshapen. Skin color may be any shade from dark gray to blackish-blue. A boggle can stretch and compress its body and limbs to a remarkable degree, which accounts for its impressive reach.

Boggles have their own rudimentary language of grunts and whistles.

COMBAT

Boggles are a cowardly lot. They taunt, bluster, and scold in their gibbering language, but always from a distance. If they know intruders are approaching, they often use their grease ability to make a section of floor slippery ahead of time, so that they can easily steal baubles from anyone who falls. When forced to fight, a boggle prefers to climb a wall and leap down on prey from above, so that it can bring its hind claws to bear for rending.

Improved Grab (Ex): If a boggle hits an opponent of up to one size category larger than itself with a claw attack, it deals normal damage and attempts to start a grapple as a free action without provoking an attack of opportunity (grapple bonus +5). If it hits with both claws, it can also rend in the same round. The boggle has the option to conduct the grapple normally, or simply use its claw to hold the opponent (−20 penalty on grapple check, but the boggle is not considered grappled). In either case, each successful grapple check it makes during successive rounds automatically deals claw damage.

Dimension Door (Sp): A boggle can use *dimension door* up to six times per day. Caster level 7th.

Grease (Su): At will, a boggle can secrete an oily, viscous, nonflammable substance from its skin. This ability functions like the spell *grease* except that the range is touch, the duration is 1 round per Hit Die of the boggle (4 rounds for the typical creature), and the Reflex save DC is 12. Typically, a boggle uses this ability to grease a section of floor

or wall, though it can use the ability in any of the ways that the spell can be used. This oily fluid also makes the boggle tougher to hold onto (see Skills, below). Boggles are immune to the effects of this substance.

Rend (Ex): If a boggle hits a single target with both claws, it latches onto the opponent's body and tears the flesh. This attack deals 2d4 points of damage.

Scent (Ex): A boggle can detect approaching enemies, sniff out hidden foes, and track by sense of smell.

Skills: Because of its perpetually oily skin, a boggle gains a +10 racial bonus on Escape Artist checks.

BOGUN

Tiny Construct
Hit Dice: 2d10 (11 hp)
Initiative: +3
Speed: 20 ft., fly 50 ft. (good)
AC: 15 (+2 size, +3 Dex), touch 15, flat-footed 12
Attacks: Nettles +1 melee
Damage: Nettles 1d4–2 plus poison
Face/Reach: 2 1/2 ft. by 2 1/2 ft./0 ft.
Special Attacks: Poison
Special Qualities: Construct traits
Saves: Fort +0, Ref +3, Will +1
Abilities: Str 7, Dex 16, Con —, Int 8, Wis 13, Cha 11

Climate/Terrain: Any land (typically forest)
Organization: Solitary
Challenge Rating: 1
Treasure: None
Alignment: Always neutral (same as the creator)
Advancement: 3–6 HD (Tiny)

A bogun is a small nature servant created by a druid. Like a homunculus, it is an extension of its creator. Thus, it has the same alignment and link to nature that its master has.

A bogun looks like a vaguely humanoid mound of compost. The creator determines its precise features, but the typical version stands about 18 inches tall and has a wingspan of about 2 feet. Its skin is covered with nettles and branches. Insect carapaces, feathers, scales, and other forest detritus may also be part of its form.

A bogun does not fight particularly well, but it can perform any simple action, such as attacking, carrying a message, or opening a door or window.

For the most part, the creature simply carries out its creator's instructions. Because it is self-aware and somewhat willful, however, its behavior is not entirely predictable. On rare occasions (5% of the time), a bogun may refuse to perform a particular task. In that case, the creator must make a Diplomacy check (DC 11) to convince the creature to cooperate. Success means the bogun performs the task as requested; failure indicates that it either does exactly the opposite or refuses to do anything at all for 24 hours (DM's option).

A bogun cannot speak, but the process of creating one links it telepathically with its creator. It knows what its creator knows and can convey to him or her everything it sees and hears, up to a range of 1,500 feet. A bogun never travels beyond this range willingly, though it can be removed forcibly. In such a case, it does everything in its power to regain contact with its creator.

Any attack that destroys a bogun deals its creator 2d10 points of damage. If the creator is slain, the bogun also dies, and its body collapses into a heap of rotting vegetation.

COMBAT

A bogun has very little offensive capability, since its primary purpose is to carry out small tasks. Nevertheless, it is capable of attacking, either on the command of its creator or in self-defense.

A bogun usually tries to flee from combat. If it is prevented from escaping, it attacks by raking opponents with its poisonous nettles.

Poison (Ex): A bogun's nettles deliver an irritating poison (Fortitude save DC 11) with each successful attack. The initial and secondary damage is the same (1d6 points of Dexterity damage). The creator of a bogun is immune to its poison.

Construct Traits: A bogun is immune to mind-affecting effects, poison, *sleep*, paralysis, stunning, disease, death effects, necromantic effects, and any effect that requires a Fortitude save unless it also works on objects. The creature is not subject to critical hits, subdual damage, ability damage, ability drain, energy drain, or death from massive damage. Although it is made of vegetable matter, a bogun is not a plant and is therefore not subject to spells that affect only plants or plant creatures. It cannot heal itself but can be healed through

repair. It cannot be raised or resurrected. A bogun has dark-vision (60-foot range).

CONSTRUCTION

Unlike a homunculus, a bogun is created from natural materials available in any forest. Thus, there is no gold piece cost for its creation. All materials used become permanent parts of the bogun.

The creator must be at least 7th level and possess the Craft Wondrous Item feat to make a bogun. Before casting any spells, the creator must weave a physical form out of living (or once-living) vegetable matter to hold the magical energy. A bit of the creator's own body, such as a few strands of hair or a drop of blood, must also be incorporated into this crude mannequin. The creator may assemble the body personally or hire someone else to do it. Creating the mannequin requires a Craft (basketweaving) or Craft (weaving) check (DC 12).

Once the body is finished, the creator must animate it through an extended magical ritual that requires a week to complete. He or she must labor for at least 8 hours each day in complete solitude in a forest grove; any interruption from another sentient creature undoes the magic. If the creator is personally weaving the creature's body, that process and the ritual can be performed together.

When not actively working on the ritual, the creator must rest and can perform no other activities except eating, sleeping, or talking. Missing even one day causes the process to fail. At that point, the ritual must be started anew, though the previously crafted body and the grove can be reused.

On the final day of the ritual, the creator must personally cast *control plants*, *wood shape*, and *beget bogun* (see below). These spells can come from outside sources, such as scrolls, rather than being prepared, if the creator prefers.

BEGET BOGUN

Conjuration (Creation)
Level: Drd 1
Components: V, S, M, XP
Casting Time: 1 action
Range: Touch
Effect: Tiny construct
Duration: Instantaneous
Saving Throw: None
Spell Resistance: No

Beget bogun allows you to infuse living magic into a small mannequin that you have created from vegetable matter. This is the final spell in the process of creating a bogun. See the bogun's description, above, for further details.

Material Component: The mannequin from which the bogun is created.

XP Cost: 25 XP.

BONE NAGA

Large Undead
Hit Dice: 15d12 (97 hp)
Initiative: +5
Speed: 40 ft.
AC: 16 (–1 size, +1 Dex, +6 natural), touch 10, flat-footed 15
Attacks: Sting +9 melee and bite +4 melee
Damage: Sting 2d4+3 plus poison, bite 1d4+1 plus poison
Face/Reach: 5 ft. by 5 ft. (coiled)/10 ft.
Special Attacks: Poison, spells
Special Qualities: Detect thoughts, guarded thoughts, immunities, SR 23, telepathy, undead traits
Saves: Fort +5, Ref +8, Will +11
Abilities: Str 16, Dex 13, Con —, Int 16, Wis 15, Cha 17
Skills: Bluff +12, Concentration +14, Diplomacy +7, Hide +11, Intimidate +12, Listen +12, Sense Motive +8, Spellcraft +14, Spot +12
Feats: Alertness, Combat Casting, Dodge, Improved Initiative, Lightning Reflexes, metamagic feat (any one), Spell Focus (any one school)

Climate/Terrain: Temperate and warm land and underground
Organization: Solitary
Challenge Rating: 11
Treasure: None
Alignment: Always lawful evil
Advancement: 16–21 HD (Large); 22–45 HD (Huge)

A bone naga was once a living dark naga. After its death, it was transformed into a skeletal undead creature by another dark naga through a horrific ritual.

A bone naga looks like a 12-foot-long, serpentine skeleton. Its skull bears an eerie resemblance to that of a human, except that the bone naga sports long fangs that can deliver a debilitating poison. A cold, cruel light burns in the creature's eye sockets, giving it an air of unspeakable hatred and malice. Its tail ends in a vicious bone stinger which, like its teeth, delivers poison with every hit.

Though it despises its servitude, a bone naga unswervingly obeys its creator, attacking even other nagas if so commanded. Should its master die, a bone naga becomes free-willed and can choose its own destiny.

COMBAT

Bone nagas under the control of masters are given explicit instructions on how to deal with enemies. Beyond that, these highly intelligent undead can make their own decisions about methods for defeating particular foes.

A bone naga typically uses its mind-reading abilities to determine its foes' strengths and weaknesses before joining combat. It often begins by trying to intimidate its enemies with telepathic taunts. Thereafter, it resorts to spellcasting to soften up the more powerful-looking

opponents before entering melee. A bone naga is likely to focus its melee attacks on living opponents rather than undead or constructs, since the living are susceptible to its poison.

Poison (Ex): A bone naga delivers its poison via successful bite or sting attacks. The poison from its bite (Fortitude save DC 17) has the same initial and secondary damage (1d4 points of Strength damage). The poison from its sting (Fortitude save DC 17) is more virulent; its initial damage is 1d4 points of Constitution drain, and the secondary damage is 1d4 points of Constitution damage.

Spells: A bone naga casts spells as a 14th-level sorcerer (spells known 9/5/5/4/4/3/2/1; spells/day 6/7/7/7/6/6/5/3; save DC 13 + spell level).

Detect Thoughts (Su): A bone naga can continuously detect the thoughts of those around it. This ability functions like a *detect thoughts* spell (caster level 9th; Will save DC 15), and it is always active.

Guarded Thoughts (Ex): Because of their ability to shield their thoughts, bone nagas are immune to any form of mind-reading.

Immunities (Ex): Bone nagas are immune to cold. Also, because they lack flesh or internal organs, they take only half damage from piercing weapons.

Telepathy (Su): A bone naga can communicate telepathically with any creature within 250 feet that has a language.

Undead Traits: A bone naga is immune to mind-affecting effects, poison, *sleep*, paralysis, stunning, disease, death effects, necromantic effects, and any effect that requires a Fortitude save unless it also works on objects. It is not subject to critical hits, subdual damage, ability damage, ability drain, energy drain, or death from massive damage. A bone naga cannot be raised, and resurrection works only if it is willing. The creature has darkvision (60-foot range).

BONE OOZE

Gargantuan Ooze
Hit Dice: 20d10+210 (320 hp)
Initiative: −5
Speed: 20 ft.
AC: 1 (−4 size, −5 Dex), touch 1, flat-footed 1
Attacks: 2 slams +26 melee
Damage: Slam 2d8+15 plus ability drain plus wounding
Face/Reach: 30 ft. by 30 ft./15 ft.
Special Attacks: Ability drain, bone meld, engulf, wounding
Special Qualities: Blindsight 60 ft., DR 30/+5, ooze traits, SR 32
Saves: Fort +15, Ref +1, Will +1
Abilities: Str 40, Dex 1, Con 28, Int —, Wis 1, Cha 1

Climate/Terrain: Any underground
Organization: Solitary
Challenge Rating: 21
Treasure: None
Alignment: Always neutral
Advancement: 21–30 HD (Gargantuan); 31–60 HD (Colossal)

Bone oozes slide along underground, scavenging for bones. These disgusting creatures are called rolling graveyards because of all the bones suspended in their bodies.

A bone ooze appears as an immense, undulating mass of goo the color of bleached bone. Jagged, bony protrusions jut from the monster's mass here and there, and more bones in various stages of digestion are suspended within its translucent body. A bone ooze normally maintains a roughly spherical shape, measuring more than 30 feet in diameter and weighing more than 40,000 pounds, though it can alter its shape to flow through a space as small as 5 feet by 5 feet. Because the bones it contains give its amorphous shape firmer support than the typical ooze has, it takes 1 round for a bone ooze to squeeze through an opening too small for its normal dimensions.

COMBAT

A bone ooze attacks by slamming opponents or by rolling over them. It tries to engulf opponents whenever possible, so that it can use its bone meld. A bone ooze's attacks also cause bleeding wounds.

Ability Drain (Ex): A successful slam attack from a bone ooze absorbs some of the victim's bone structure. Any melee hit deals 1d6 Strength drain, 1d6 Dexterity drain, and 1d6 Constitution drain. On a critical hit, it drains twice that amount from each affected score. A bone ooze heals 5 points of damage it has taken (10 on a critical hit) whenever it drains abilities. If the amount of healing is more than the damage the

creature has taken, it gains any excess as temporary hit points for 1 hour.

Bone Meld (Ex): Once per round, a bone ooze can attempt to absorb the skeleton of an engulfed creature into its own mass, pulling the bones out through the flesh. The victim must make a successful Fortitude save (DC 35) or die. After 1d3 rounds, the bone ooze leaves behind the fleshy parts of the victim and any treasure he or she carried.

Engulf (Ex): A bone ooze can simply bowl over Huge or smaller creatures as a standard action. This attack affects as many opponents as the creature's body can cover. Each target can make either an attack of opportunity against the bone ooze or a Reflex save (DC 35) to avoid being engulfed. A successful saving throw indicates that the target has been pushed back or aside (target's choice) as the ooze moves forward. A bone ooze cannot make a slam attack during a round in which it attempts to engulf, but each creature engulfed is considered grappled and trapped within the bone ooze's body. Such a creature takes automatic slam, ability drain, and wounding damage upon being engulfed and each succeeding round that it remains trapped. In the next round after engulfing, the bone ooze can attempt a bone meld attack.

Wounding (Ex): Because of the bone shards the creature's body contains, a bone ooze's slam or engulf attack causes a wound that bleeds for 5 points of damage per round thereafter, in addition to the attack's normal damage. Multiple wounds from the creature result in cumulative bleeding loss (two wounds for 10

points of damage per round, and so on). The bleeding can be stopped only by a successful Heal check (DC 15) or the application of a *cure* spell or some other healing spell (*heal*, *healing circle*, or the like).

Blindsight (Ex): A bone ooze is blind, but blindsight allows it to maneuver and fight as well as a sighted creature. Through this ability, it can discern objects and creatures within 60 feet. The bone ooze usually does not need to make Spot or Listen checks to notice creatures within range of its blindsight.

Ooze Traits: A bone ooze is immune to mind-affecting effects, poison, *sleep*, paralysis, stunning, and polymorphing. It is not subject to critical hits or flanking.

BRAXAT

Large Monstrous Humanoid
Hit Dice: 10d8+50 (95 hp)
Initiative: +1
Speed: 30 ft.
AC: 18 (–1 size, +1 Dex, +8 natural), touch 10, flat-footed 17
Attacks: Huge greatclub +16/+11 melee and gore +10 melee
Damage: Huge greatclub 2d6+9, gore 1d8+3
Face/Reach: 5 ft. by 5 ft./10 ft.
Special Attacks: Breath weapon, *mind blast*, psionics, spell-like abilities
Special Qualities: Darkvision 60 ft., DR 10/+1, telepathy
Saves: Fort +8, Ref +8, Will +10
Abilities: Str 23, Dex 12, Con 20, Int 15, Wis 12, Cha 11
Skills: Intimidate +9, Jump +11, Listen +12, Spot +13, Wilderness Lore +10
Feats: Expertise (B), Improved Bull Rush, Improved Disarm, Improved Trip, Iron Will, Power Attack (B), Weapon Focus (greatclub)

Climate/Terrain: Any desert or mountains
Organization: Solitary, pair, gang (3–6), warband (7–12), or tribe (20–80)
Challenge Rating: 9
Treasure: Standard
Alignment: Usually neutral evil
Advancement: By character class

Braxats are violent, nocturnal hunters that stalk mountainous and desert regions. These dangerous, evil humanoids prey exclusively on intelligent beings, whom they take great pleasure in torturing, killing, and eating. Their taste for humanoid flesh can take them deep into civilized lands, where prey is plentiful and easy to catch.

A braxat is a hulking, bipedal, lizard-like humanoid that towers over many giants at its full adult height of 15 feet. Its features are a

combination of those of a rhinoceros and a spiny beetle. The top of its head and its back are lined with thick, horn-covered plates, and a single, massive horn juts up from between its nostrils.

Braxats respect neither law nor authority, and they fear no one. Their awesome strength, psionic abilities, and damage reduction make them nearly unstoppable, and it is not uncommon for a single band of them to wipe out several humanoid settlements in the course of a year.

Occasionally a few survivors from braxat raids band together and try to hunt the creatures down, but rarely do they succeed in exacting vengeance. Experienced adventurers have been known to hunt braxats for sport, pitting their experience and cleverness against the creatures' raw cunning and psionic abilities. As such hunters have discovered to their dismay, braxats are quite proficient at protecting themselves with deadly traps and ambushes. Most such hunts end in victory for the braxats, but now and then one is successful, yielding a few braxat-horn trophies to the hunters. These horns have no value in themselves, but artists sometimes carve intricate sculptures on them and sell them as art objects.

Braxats speak Giant, and a few of the more civilized ones make the effort to learn Common as well.

COMBAT

Braxats relish the hunt. They delight in their victims' fear and like to prolong the agony of their prey by stalking it for long periods, using their telepathy to create false hopes, and then crushing those hopes with new ambushes. Alternatively, braxats may send their victims telepathic taunts, detailing the grisly fate that awaits them after capture.

In combat, braxats are cruel and cunning. They prefer to soften up opponents with *mind blasts* and psionic assaults before closing in for the kill. They usually save their breath weapons for particularly stubborn foes. Once the opponents are damaged, the braxats wade into combat with their greatclubs.

Breath Weapon (Su): A braxat can breathe a 30-foot-long cone of cold for 3d8 points of cold damage (Reflex save DC 20 half). Once it has used its breath weapon, the creature must wait 1d4 rounds before it can do so again.

Mind Blast (Sp): This mind-numbing blast extends from the braxat in a 30-foot-long cone. Anyone caught in the area must succeed at a Will save (DC 15) or be stunned for 3d4 rounds. (When using the *Psionics Handbook*, replace this ability with the *mind blast* attack mode, as noted below.)

Psionics (Sp): At will—*dimension door, mind blank*. Caster (or manifester) level 8th; save DC 10 + spell level.

Attack/Defense Modes: mind thrust, mind blast/thought shield, empty mind.

Spell-Like Abilities (Sp): At will—*blink*; 1/day—*confusion, feeblemind*. Caster level 8th; save DC 10 + spell level.

Telepathy (Su): A braxat can communicate telepathically with any creature within one mile that has a language.

BRAXAT SOCIETY

Braxats live in a tribal society in which males and females have equal social status and access to leadership positions. Each tribal leader must prove his or her worthiness annually in a ritual combat with a single challenger who has earned the right of contest through successful raiding over the past year.

Young braxats are trained to fight from the time they can stand. Deadly combat between young braxats over potential mates, lairs, or treasure is encouraged to ensure that only the strongest and cleverest survive to reproduce.

Once a young braxat is deemed worthy to join a warband, that group becomes his or her second family. Switching to a different warband occurs only rarely—usually when most of a band has been killed in battle. Aggression between bandmates is strictly forbidden, since cooperation is vital to a successful hunt. Killing a bandmate is punishable by the immediate execution of both the offender and his or her family.

BRAXAT CHARACTERS

Because of the braxat's affinity for hunting, its favored class is ranger, although some braxats prefer to take levels in barbarian or fighter. Evil druid braxats are rare, but not unknown.

A braxat PC's effective character level (ECL) is equal to its class level + 16. Thus, a 1st-level braxat ranger has an ECL of 17 and is the equivalent of a 17th-level character.

BREATHDRINKER

Medium-Size Elemental (Air, Evil)

Hit Dice: 8d8+24 (60 hp)

Initiative: +6

Speed: Fly 80 ft. (perfect)

AC: 16 (+2 Dex, +4 natural), touch 12, flat-footed 14

Attacks: Wind scythe +6 melee

Damage: Wind scythe 2d4

Face/Reach: 5 ft. by 5 ft./5 ft.

Special Attacks: Fear gaze, steal breath

Special Qualities: Air mastery, DR 10/+1, elemental traits, invisibility

Saves: Fort +5, Ref +8, Will +3

Abilities: Str 11, Dex 15, Con 16, Int 14, Wis 13, Cha 14

Skills: Hide +12, Move Silently +8, Search +12, Spot +7, Wilderness Lore +9

Feats: Flyby Attack, Improved Initiative, Track

Climate/Terrain: Temperate land or underground

Organization: Solitary

Challenge Rating: 7

Treasure: None

Alignment: Always chaotic evil

Advancement: 9–16 HD (Large); 17–24 (Huge)

The breathdrinker is a dreadful elemental that feeds on air extracted from the lungs of living creatures. How it actually derives sustenance from such a source is unknown, but the cruel monster seems to take great delight in stealing the breath of its helpless victims.

The breathdrinker is normally invisible, except when attacking. When it does become visible, it roughly mimics the form of its chosen victim, appearing as a misty, translucent duplicate. Its eyes resemble tiny, red spheres of light.

Most breathdrinkers reside on the Elemental Plane of Air. Occasionally, a breathdrinker summoned to the Material Plane by a spellcaster for a specific task (most often the slaying of a specific target) decides to stay on after completing the assignment. A creature that chooses this course nearly always does so because it enjoyed its task and wishes to continue bringing death and destruction.

Breathdrinkers speak Common and Auran.

COMBAT

A breathdrinker lurks invisibly most of the time, waiting for prey to wander near. It normally selects a single creature as a victim, then spends some time stalking and watching its quarry before deciding on the best method of approach. Often, it simply waits for its chosen prey to fall asleep before attempting to steal its breath. Alternatively, it may first attempt to render the creature helpless with its gaze attack, then follow up with its steal breath attack. The breathdrinker is single-minded to a fault—once it selects a victim, it does not rest until it has fully

fed from that creature's lungs. Unless the breathdrinker is killed, it persists with its breath-stealing attacks until its chosen victim dies, then flees to digest its meal (a process that usually takes several days) before setting out to hunt again.

If attacked by creatures other than the one it has selected, the breathdrinker usually defends itself with a wind scythe—a plane of pressurized air that it forms from its own body. The creature does not use this attack against its chosen victim, preferring to kill that creature entirely through breath-stealing.

Fear Gaze (Su): Anyone within 30 feet of a breathdrinker who meets the creature's glowing red eyes must succeed at a Will saving throw (DC 16) or be paralyzed with fear for 1d4 rounds.

Steal Breath (Su): As a full-round action, a breathdrinker can attempt to suck the air from the lungs of any helpless creature within reach. The target must make a successful Fortitude saving throw (DC 17) or take 1d6 points of Constitution damage. The target dies when his or her Constitution score reaches 0. The breathdrinker heals 5 points of damage for each point of Constitution the target loses, gaining any excess as temporary hit points. So long as the target remains helpless, the breathdrinker continues to use this attack against that creature every round until it dies.

Air Mastery (Ex): Any airborne creature takes a –1 penalty on attack and damage rolls made against a breathdrinker.

Elemental Traits (Ex): The breathdrinker is immune to poison, *sleep*, paralysis, and stunning. It is not subject to critical hits or flanking, and it cannot be raised or resurrected. The creature also has darkvision (60-foot range).

Invisibility (Su): A breathdrinker can make itself invisible at will as a free action. This ability functions like an *invisibility* spell (caster level 8th), except that it lasts until the breathdrinker ends the effect, either by choice or by attacking.

39

BRONZE SERPENT

Huge Construct
Hit Dice: 16d10 (88 hp)
Initiative: +9
Speed: 50 ft., burrow 30 ft., climb 20 ft.
AC: 26 (−2 size, +9 Dex, +9 natural), touch 17, flat-footed 17
Attacks: Bite +17 melee
Damage: Bite 1d6+10 plus electricity
Face/Reach: 10 ft. by 20 ft./10 ft.
Special Attacks: Constrict 2d8+10, improved grab, shocking bite
Special Qualities: Construct traits, DR 10/+1, electric healing, electricity resistance 10, SR 21
Saves: Fort +5, Ref +14, Will +6
Abilities: Str 25, Dex 28, Con —, Int —, Wis 13, Cha 3
Skills: Climb +15

Climate/Terrain: Any land and underground
Organization: Solitary, pair, or cluster (3–5)
Challenge Rating: 10
Treasure: None
Alignment: Always neutral
Advancement: 17–32 HD (Huge); 33–48 HD (Gargantuan)

First seen in tropical lands, bronze serpents are golemlike guardians that resemble the serpent gods whose temples they once protected. Over the course of centuries, the secret of the creatures' construction has spread far and wide, so now they may appear anywhere.

A bronze serpent is a 20-foot-long snake built of articulated bronze rings. Its eyes glow blue-white, and its powerful jaws are equipped with impressive fangs that drip fat electrical sparks instead of venom.

A bronze serpent cannot speak, but it can understand simple instructions in its creator's language.

COMBAT

A bronze serpent usually concentrates its initial attacks on the creatures that appear most vulnerable to its shocking bite. Once it hits with that attack, it wraps its body around the opponent, then continues biting while it constricts.

Constrict (Ex): With a successful grapple check, a bronze serpent can crush a grabbed opponent, dealing 2d8+10 points of bludgeoning damage.

Improved Grab (Ex): If a bronze serpent hits an opponent that is at least one size category smaller than itself with a bite attack, it deals normal damage and attempts to start a grapple as a free action without provoking an attack of opportunity (grapple bonus +27). If it gets a hold, it can also constrict in the same round. Thereafter, the creature has the option to conduct the grapple normally, or simply use its jaws to hold the opponent (−20 penalty on grapple check, but the bronze serpent is not considered grappled). In either case, each successful grapple check it makes during successive rounds automatically deals bite and constrict damage.

Shocking Bite (Su): A bronze serpent's bite deals 1d8+16 points of electricity damage in addition to the normal bite damage. The creature receives a +3 bonus on attack rolls against any opponent that is made out of metal, wearing metal armor, or carrying a a significant amount of metal.

Construct Traits: A bronze serpent is immune to mind-affecting effects, poison, *sleep*, paralysis, stunning, disease, death effects, necromantic effects, and any effect that requires a Fortitude save unless it also works on objects. The creature is not subject to critical hits, subdual damage, ability damage, ability drain, energy drain, or death from massive damage. It cannot heal itself but can be healed through repair or through its electric healing ability. It cannot be raised or resurrected. A bronze serpent has darkvision (60-foot range).

Electric Healing (Ex): Because of the bronze serpent's electrical affinity, any electricity attack directed at it cures 1 point of damage for each 3 points of damage it would otherwise deal. The creature gets no saving throw against electricity effects.

CONSTRUCTION

A bronze serpent's body is constructed from 1,000 pounds

of bronze. The creator must be at least 16th level and able to cast arcane spells. Completing the ritual drains 4,000 XP from the creator and requires the spells *geas/quest, limited wish, polymorph any object,* and *shocking grasp.*

The serpent costs 200,000 gp to create, including 1,500 gp for the body. Assembling the body requires a successful Craft (armorsmithing) or Craft (weaponsmithing) check (DC 25).

CATOBLEPAS

Huge Aberration
Hit Dice: 6d8+30 (57 hp)
Initiative: +1
Speed: 30 ft.
AC: 19 (–2 size, +1 Dex, +10 natural), touch 9, flat-footed 18
Attacks: Tail slam +10 melee, or death ray +3 ranged touch
Damage: Tail slam 1d6+12 plus stun
Face/Reach: 10 ft. by 20 ft./10 ft.
Special Attacks: Death ray, stun
Special Qualities: Darkvision 60 ft., scent
Saves: Fort +7, Ref +3, Will +6
Abilities: Str 26, Dex 13, Con 21, Int 2, Wis 13, Cha 8
Skills: Jump +10, Listen +3, Spot +3, Wilderness Lore +3

Climate/Terrain: Any marsh
Organization: Solitary, pair, or family (3)
Challenge Rating: 6
Treasure: 1/10 coins, 50% goods, 50% items
Alignment: Always neutral
Advancement: 7–12 HD (Huge); 13–18 HD (Gargantuan)

The catoblepas is a bizarre, loathsome creature that inhabits dismal swamps and marshes. It is thought to be the result of a magical experiment gone terribly wrong. Though it hunts for meat only occasionally, the creature's deadly nature is legendary.

The body of a catoblepas resembles that of a bloated buffalo, and its legs are stumpy, like those of a pygmy elephant or a hippopotamus. Its muscular tail, which it can move with blinding speed, ends in a chitinous knob. The head is perched upon a long, weak neck that can barely support its weight, so the creature tends to hold its head very low to the ground. The face looks like that of a warthog, but uglier.

Catoblepases mate for life, and when more than one is encountered, the group is either a mated pair or (10%

chance) a family consisting of a mated pair with a single offspring. The juvenile catoblepas in such a group has 3d8+15 HD (28 hp) and does not fight, nor does it have any of the adult creature's special attacks.

Catoblepases do not collect treasure. Any valuables in their vicinity are there because previous victims dropped them. The creature's lair is usually an area that offers both shelter and firm ground, hidden by by tall reeds or marsh grasses that the catolepas is canny enough not to consume. An adult catoblepas has little to fear from other marsh denizens, but its young are vulnerable to predators.

COMBAT

Normally, the catoblepas is a meandering grazer, wandering the marsh in search of the most succulent grasses and weeds. But once a month, usually under the light of a full moon, it hunts for meat to round out its diet of reeds and grasses. Usually it dines on easy prey such as fish, marsh birds, eels, rats, large amphibians, snakes, and other marsh animals during this period, but it is willing to hunt larger creatures if necessary.

The creature makes full use of its reach when attacking with its tail, and it never tries to engage more than one enemy at a time. It usually reserves its death ray attack for self-defense. A pair of catoblepases try to flank a single target and slay it before moving on to another.

Death Ray (Su): The catoblepas can project a thin, green ray up to 160 feet from its bloodshot eyes. Any living creature struck by this ray must make a Fortitude save (DC 18) or die instantly. Even on a success, the target takes 5d6 points of damage. After striking one target, the ray dissipates, and the attack cannot be used again for 1d4 rounds.

Stun (Ex): Any living creature struck by the catoblepas's tail must succeed at a Fortitude save (DC 18) or be stunned for 1 round. (A stunned character cannot act and loses any Dexterity bonus to Armor Class. An attacker gets a +2 bonus on attack rolls against a stunned opponent.) Success indicates that the target takes only the normal damage for the attack.

Scent (Ex): A catoblepas can detect approaching enemies, sniff out hidden foes, and track by sense of smell.

LGW

CELESTIAL

The Outer Planes that celestials call home foster a variety of good creatures. The goodness of celestials is of a quality and intensity that makes many a paladin feel diminished and inadequate.

Evil creatures in general and fiends in particular are anathema to celestials. They may not spend all their waking hours rooting out tanar'ri and baatezu from every corner of the multiverse, but when confronted by fiends of any sort, they seldom back down. Celestials are often involved in prolonged wars against fiends of various types, and armies of celestials occasionally take the battle to their enemies. Though celestials are generally peaceloving creatures, they are also terrible foes.

All celestials have comely looks, though their actual appearances vary widely. Guardinals, the type presented here, tend to have both humanoid and animal characteristics.

Celestials speak Celestial, Infernal, and Draconic.

COMBAT

Most celestials are armed with a variety of nonlethal attacks and special abilities, which they reserve primarily for those rare occasions when they must fight or subdue good beings. Against creatures of evil or beings who have somehow aroused their wrath, celestials are willing to unleash the full measure of their lethal, otherworldly powers. Most celestials have excellent skills in melee as well, and they do not hesitate to take on their foes hand-to-hand. For creatures that dislike killing, they are exceptionally good at it.

All celestials have the following characteristics.

Celestial Traits: A celestial can speak with any creature that has a language as though using a *tongues* spell (caster level 14th; always active). It is immune to electricity and petrification attacks, and it has acid resistance 20 and cold resistance 20. In addition, a celestial has low-light vision and a +4 racial bonus on Fortitude saves against poison.

Outsider Traits: A celestial has darkvision (60-foot range). It cannot be raised or resurrected.

GUARDINALS

The guardinals are the people of Elysium, just as demons (tanar'ri) are the people of the Abyss. Most guardinals resemble beautiful, muscular humans with noticeable animal-like traits.

Guardinals aren't numerous. In Elysium, they tend to live in small groups, watching their home plane for any sign of trouble while roaming its breathtaking landscape in nomadic bands. They live simply, taking only what they require from the land.

Guardinals have no tolerance for evil or injustice. Most of those that leave Elysium do so to seek out and address such wrongs. Thus, it is rare to find a guardinal roaming the planes for pleasure.

CERVIDAL

The most common of the guardinals of Elysium are the satyrlike cervidals. Their home, Amoria, is the uppermost layer of that plane. Cervidals take their guardianship of Amoria serioiusly and are rarely found elsewhere except in times of great need.

A cervidal's body is slim, muscular, and covered with short, dark red fur. Aside from its regal bearing, the creature's most striking feature is the pair of long, curved horns atop its head. A cervidal has hooves instead of feet, but its hands are like a human's, except that the backs are protected by hard plates of horn. This allows it to use its hands as punching weapons to deliver effective slam attacks.

Cervidals are peaceful and slow to anger, but in times of need they form the bulk of any guardinal army. One on one, a cervidal is a match for any comparable baatezu or tanar'ri, but cervidals seldom have the luxury of fighting an equal number of opponents.

	Cervidal Medium-Size Outsider (Good)	Lupinal Medium-Size Outsider (Good)
Hit Dice:	4d8+8 (26 hp)	8d8+8 (44 hp)
Initiative:	+3	+5
Speed:	50 ft.	50 ft.
AC:	19 (+3 Dex, +2 leather armor, +4 natural), touch 13, flat-footed 16	20 (+5 Dex, +3 natural, +2 leather armor), touch 15, flat-footed 15
Attacks:	2 slams +8 melee and butt +6 melee	2 claws +14 melee and bite +9 melee
Damage:	Slam 1d6+4, butt 1d3+2	Claw 1d4+6, bite 1d6+3
Face/Reach:	5 ft. by 5 ft./5 ft.	5 ft. by 5 ft./5 ft.
Special Attacks:	Charge, spell-like abilities	Fear aura, improved grab, spell-like abilities, trip
Special Qualities:	Celestial traits, horn powers, outsider traits	Celestial traits, dodge missiles, DR 20/+2, outsider traits, scent
Saves:	Fort +6, Ref +7, Will +7	Fort +7, Ref +11, Will +10
Abilities:	Str 18, Dex 17, Con 15, Int 12, Wis 17, Cha 16	Str 23, Dex 20, Con 13, Int 16, Wis 18, Cha 15
Skills:	Balance +9, Concentration +8, Heal +8, Intimidate +9, Jump +19, Spellcraft +7	Animal Empathy +13, Balance +16, Climb +17, Concentration +12, Hide +16, Listen +17, Move Silently +16, Spot +17
Feats:	Multiattack, Power Attack	Alertness, Power Attack, Track
Climate/Terrain:	Elysium or any forest	Elysium or any forest, plain, or hills
Organization:	Solitary, pair, or team (3–6)	Solitary, pair, or pack (3–8)
Challenge Rating:	3	5
Treasure:	None	None
Alignment:	Usually neutral good	Usually neutral good
Advancement:	5–12 HD (Medium-size)	9–24 HD (Medium-size)

Combat

A cervidal's horns are its favored weapon. It usually begins a fight by charging. Thereafter, it uses its slam and butt attacks to advantage in melee.

Charge (Ex): A cervidal can lower its head and charge an opponent, striking with its deadly horns. In addition to the normal benefits and hazards of a charge, this tactic allows the cervidal to make a single butt attack that deals 1d8+6 points of damage.

Spell-Like Abilities: At will—*bless, command, detect poison, light*; 1/day—*hold person, magic missile, suggestion.* Caster level 9th; save DC 13 + spell level.

Horn Powers (Su): A cervidal can deliver any of several effects by a touch of its horns. The horns can negate any poison or disease (as the spells *neutralize poison* and *remove disease*) in the creature touched, dispel an illusion (as a targeted *dispel magic* spell, except that it affects only spells of the Illusion school and is automatically successful), or dismiss (as a *dismissal* spell) a summoned, conjured, or extraplanar creature. Each of these horn powers can be used at will as a standard action. Except as noted, all these abilities function as the corresponding spells. Caster level 20th; save DC 13 + spell level.

Skills: Because of its powerful legs, a cervidal gains a +8 racial bonus on Jump checks.

LUPINAL

As the name implies, lupinals are half-human, half-wolf creatures. They are constantly on the prowl for evil intrusions into their territory, be it Elysium or a piece of the Material Plane that they have made their own. Lupinals are more likely than cervidals to make their homes outside Elysium and assist other beings in repelling evil incursions.

Perhaps because of their pack-based society, lupinals are more lawful than other natives of Elysium. In group activities, they operate in close cooperation and perfect harmony. Even solitary lupinals are rarely more than an hour away from allies (or even closer, via *ethereal jaunt*).

At first glance, a lupinal might be mistaken for a werewolf, with its long muzzle, fur, and backward-bending canine legs. But where lycanthropes are savage and animal-like, lupinals are intelligent, regal, and poised—though they are quick to anger and ferocious when aroused.

Combat

Lupinals are exceptionally skilled in combat. They use pack tactics (such as surrounding opponents, chasing down enemies, and the aid another action) with great skill. Their approach often involves ambush, deception, and misdirection as well.

Fear Aura (Ex): When a lupinal howls, every creature within 600 feet (except other celestials) who can hear it must make a Will saving throw (DC 16). On a failure, a creature with 7 or fewer Hit Dice becomes panicked for 4d6 rounds; one with 8 or more Hit Dice becomes shaken for 4d6

rounds. Success leaves the creature unaffected. Once a creature has either been affected by this ability or made a successful save, it cannot be affected by that lupinal's howl again for 24 hours.

Improved Grab (Ex): If a lupinal hits an opponent that is at least one size category smaller than itself with a bite attack, it deals normal damage and attempts to start a grapple as a free action without provoking an attack of opportunity (grapple bonus +14). The creature has the option to conduct the grapple normally, or simply use its jaws to hold the opponent (–20 penalty on grapple check, but the lupinal is not considered grappled). In either case, each successful grapple check it makes during successive rounds automatically deals bite damage.

Spell-Like Abilities: At will—*blink, blur, change self, darkness, ethereal jaunt;* 3/day—*cone of cold, cure light wounds, fly, magic missile.* Caster level 8th; save DC 12 + spell level.

Trip (Ex): A lupinal that hits with a bite attack can attempt to trip the opponent as a free action (see Trip in Chapter 8 of the *Player's Handbook*) without making a touch attack or provoking an attack of opportunity. If the attempt fails, the opponent cannot react to trip the lupinal.

Dodge Missiles (Ex): This ability operates like the Deflect Arrows feat, except that the lupinal can dodge any missile and it need not have its hands free. (The creature is dodging, not deflecting.) This ability is usable three times per round.

Scent (Ex): A lupinal can detect approaching enemies, sniff out hidden foes, and track by sense of smell.

CHAIN GOLEM

Medium-Size Construct
Hit Dice: 7d10 (38 hp)
Initiative: +3
Speed: 30 ft. (can't run)
AC: 21 (+3 Dex, +8 natural), touch 13, flat-footed 18
Attacks: 2 chain rakes +9 melee
Damage: Chain rake 1d8+4 plus wounding
Face/Reach: 5 ft. by 5 ft./10 ft.
Special Attacks: Chain barrier, wounding
Special Qualities: Construct traits, magic immunity, resistance to ranged attacks
Saves: Fort +2, Ref +5, Will +2
Abilities: Str 18, Dex 17, Con —, Int —, Wis 11, Cha 1
Feats: Dodge (B), Expertise (B), Improved Disarm (B), Improved Trip (B)

Climate/Terrain: Any land or underground
Organization: Solitary
Challenge Rating: 5
Treasure: None
Alignment: Always neutral
Advancement: 8–10 HD (Medium-size); 11–21 HD (Large)

Creations of the diabolical kytons (see the *Monster Manual*), chain golems serve as bodyguards for devils and as guardians of unholy places. Occasionally, one of these creatures is selected to carry out a special mission. When a chain golem appears on the Material Plane, it is usually delivering or retrieving a message or an item of particular interest to its kyton master.

The body of a chain golem is composed entirely of shifting chains that vary in size and shape, ranging from extremely thin and razor-sharp to thick and mounted with barbs, spikes, and blades. A chain golem clanks and screeches continually as its chains slide around its body. Because it has a mostly humanoid shape, it is often mistaken for a kyton.

A chain golem always obeys its master's commands to the letter, sacrificing itself in the execution of its duties if necessary. Should a chain golem's master die, the creature immediately becomes the servant of another kyton.

COMBAT

A chain golem typically uses its long reach to grab at foes and knock them to the ground. Then it activates its vicious chain barrier to shred the fallen creature's flesh.

Chain Barrier (Ex): As a full-round action, a chain golem can surround itself with a whirling, slicing shield of chains, similar in effect to a *blade barrier* spell. Anyone adjacent to a chain barrier must make a successful Reflex save (DC 17) or

take 7d6 points of damage. Any creature or object entering or passing through such a barrier automatically takes that amount of damage. The chain barrier moves with the golem and serves as one-half cover for it (+4 bonus to AC). Maintaining the barrier once it has been activated is a standard action.

Wounding (Ex): A wound resulting from a chain golem's chain rake attack bleeds for an additional 2 points of damage per round thereafter. Multiple wounds from such attacks result in cumulative bleeding loss (two wounds for 4 points of damage per round, and so on). The bleeding can be stopped only by a successful Heal check (DC 10) or the application of a *cure* spell or some other healing spell (*heal*, *healing circle*, or the like).

Construct Traits: A chain golem is immune to mind-affecting effects, poison, *sleep*, paralysis, stunning, disease, death effects, necromantic effects, and any effect that requires a Fortitude save unless it also works on objects. The creature is not subject to critical hits, subdual damage, ability damage, ability drain, energy drain, or death from massive damage. It cannot heal itself but can be healed through repair. It cannot be raised or resurrected. A chain golem has darkvision (60-foot range).

Magic Immunity (Ex): A chain golem is immune to all spells, spell-like abilities, and supernatural effects except as follows. An electricity effect slows it (as the *slow* spell) for 2 rounds (no saving throw). A fire effect breaks any *slow* effect on the chain golem and cures 1 point of damage for each 2 points of damage it would otherwise deal. A chain golem gets no saving throw against fire effects.

Resistance to Ranged Attacks (Su): A chain golem gains a +2 resistance bonus on saving throws against ranged spells or ranged magical attacks that specifically target it (except ranged touch attacks).

CONSTRUCTION

Kytons are the only beings known to be capable of creating chain golems, and they go to great lengths to keep the method of construction a secret from all other creatures—including other devils. Should another creature either develop or acquire the method of chain golem creation, the kytons would spare no effort to assassinate that individual before he or she could spread the knowledge further.

CHAOS ROC

Colossal Magical Beast
Hit Dice: 33d10+297 (478 hp)
Initiative: +2
Speed: 40 ft., fly 120 ft. (average)
AC: 25 (–8 size, +2 Dex, +21 natural), touch 4, flat-footed 23
Attacks: 2 claws +41 melee and bite +36 melee, or 2 wings +41 melee
Damage: Claw 2d8+16, bite 4d6+8, wing 2d6+16
Face/Reach: 80 ft. by 40 ft./15 ft.
Special Attacks: Prismatic spray, swallow whole
Special Qualities: DR 20/+3, SR 33
Saves: Fort +27, Ref +20, Will +12
Abilities: Str 42, Dex 15, Con 28, Int 2, Wis 13, Cha 13
Skills: Spot +4, Wilderness Lore +3
Feats: Flyby Attack, Snatch (B)

Climate/Terrain: Temperate and warm mountains
Organization: Solitary or pair
Challenge Rating: 22
Treasure: Standard
Alignment: Always chaotic neutral
Advancement: 34–99 HD (Colossal)

Almost too big to be believed, chaos rocs are immense birds of prey known for carrying off large animals (such as cattle, horses, or even elephants). These enormous birds lair in huge nests made from whole trees. They prefer to dwell high in the mountains, far from other large creatures such as rocs, dragons, and even other chaos rocs. This tactic ensures that the food supply in any one area is not compromised too severely. Each chaos roc usually hunts within a radius of about 10 miles around its own nest.

A chaos roc resembles a large eagle covered from head to tail with brilliant, shimmering plumage in rainbow hues. The creature measures 90 feet long from beak to tail, and its wingspan can be as wide as 240 feet.

COMBAT

Chaos rocs prefer to attack on the wing, using their prismatic spray ability to blind prey before attempting to snatch it up.

Any additional damage done by the spray effect simply makes the snatch attempt easier.

Prismatic Spray (Su): A chaos roc can emit a spray of colored light from its eyes at will. The effect is like that of the spell (caster level 20th; save DC 27), except that the range is 105 feet, and only the colors red, orange, yellow, green, blue, and indigo are present (roll 1d6 instead of 1d8 on the table given for *prismatic spray* in the *Player's Handbook*).

Swallow Whole (Ex): A chaos roc can swallow a snatched opponent that is Huge or smaller by making a successful grapple check (grapple bonus +65). Once inside the roc, the opponent takes 2d8+12 points of bludgeoning damage and 1d8 points of acid damage per round from the bird's gizzard. A successful grapple check allows the swallowed creature to climb out of the gizzard and return to the roc's beak, where another successful grapple check is needed to get free. Alternatively, a swallowed creature can try to cut its way out with either claws or a light piercing or slashing weapon. Dealing at least 25 points of damage to the gizzard (AC 20) in this way creates an opening large enough to permit escape. Once a single swallowed creature exits, muscular action closes the hole; thus, another swallowed opponent must cut its own way out. A chaos roc's gizzard can hold 2 Huge, 8 Large, 32 Medium-size, or 128 Small or smaller creatures.

Feats: A creature that is flung by a chaos roc after being snatched travels 100 feet and takes 10d6 points of damage. If the chaos roc is flying, the creature takes this damage or the appropriate falling damage, whichever is greater.

CLOAKED APE

Medium-Size Magical Beast
Hit Dice: 4d10+4 (26 hp)
Initiative: +2
Speed: 30 ft., climb 30 ft., fly 40 ft. (poor)
AC: 16 (+2 Dex, +4 natural), touch 12, flat-footed 14
Attacks: 2 claws +4 melee and bite −1 melee
Damage: Claw 1d6, bite 1d6
Special Attacks: Improved grab
Special Qualities: Darkvision 60 ft., DR 5/silver, fast healing 3, low-light vision, scent
Saves: Fort +5, Ref +6, Will +2
Abilities: Str 11, Dex 14, Con 12, Int 3, Wis 12, Cha 5
Skills: Climb +9, Listen +3, Spot +3, Tumble +4, Wilderness Lore +3
Feats: Flyby Attack

Climate/Terrain: Warm forest
Organization: Solitary, pair, or pack (5–20)
Challenge Rating: 2
Treasure: 50% coins and 50% goods (no items)
Alignment: Always neutral
Advancement: 5–8 HD (Medium-size); 9–12 HD (Large)

Cloaked apes inhabit the deep forests of tropical and subtropical lands, where they glide through the treetops in search of food. These diurnal foragers subsist primarily on a diet of fruit and nuts, though they do occasionally eat small animals that they manage to ambush from above.

The cloaked ape is named for the flaps of skin that stretch from its wrists to its ankles. When not extended for gliding through the treetops, these skin flaps resemble the folds of a cloak.

COMBAT

Cloaked apes are territorial, but they rarely attack unless they significantly outnumber the intruders. Otherwise they stay in the treetops, hooting and hurling loose branches and half-eaten fruit, berries, and nuts at their foes.

Improved Grab (Ex): If a cloaked ape hits an opponent that is its own size or smaller with both claw attacks, it deals normal damage and attempts to start a grapple as a free action without provoking an attack of opportunity (grapple bonus +4). The creature has the option to conduct the grapple normally, or simply use its claws to hold the opponent (−20 penalty on grapple check, but the cloaked ape is not considered grappled). In either case, each successful grapple check it makes during successive rounds automatically deals damage for two claw attacks.

Fast Healing (Ex): A cloaked ape regains lost hit points at the rate of 3 per round. Fast healing does not restore hit points lost from starvation, thirst, or suffocation, and it does not allow the cloaked ape to regrow or reattach lost body parts.

Scent (Ex): A cloaked ape can detect approaching enemies, sniff out hidden foes, and track by sense of smell.

	Electrum Horror Small Construct	Gold Horror Small Construct
Hit Dice:	4d10 (22 hp)	8d10 (44 hp)
Initiative:	+2	+2
Speed:	30 ft.	30 ft.
AC:	19 (+1 size, +1 Dex, +7 natural), touch 12, flat-footed 18	22 (+1 size, +2 Dex, +9 natural), touch 13, flat-footed 20
Attacks:	Razor saw +5 melee, or pressure dart +5 ranged	Razor saw +9 melee
Damage:	Razor saw 1d8+1, pressure dart 2d4+1	Razor saw 1d10+3
Face/Reach:	5 ft. by 5 ft./5 ft.	5 ft. by 5 ft./5 ft.
Special Attacks:	—	*Lightning bolt*
Special Qualities:	Construct traits, electricity immunity, linked mind, spell vulnerability, SR 17	Construct traits, electricity immunity, linked mind, spell vulnerability, SR 18
Saves:	Fort +1, Ref +2, Will +3	Fort +2, Ref +4, Will +5
Abilities:	Str 12, Dex 13, Con —, Int 5, Wis 14, Cha 5	Str 14, Dex 15, Con —, Int 9, Wis 16, Cha 11
Feats:	Point Blank Shot (B), Precise Shot (B)	Cleave (B), Power Attack (B), Sunder (B)
Climate/Terrain:	Any land and underground	Any land and underground
Organization:	Pair or component (3–8)	Module (1–2 plus 3–12 electrum horrors)
Challenge Rating:	4	5
Treasure:	50% coins, 50% goods (gems only)	50% coins, 50% goods (gems only)
Alignment:	Always lawful evil	Always lawful evil
Advancement:	—	—

	Platinum Horror Small Construct	Adamantine Horror Small Construct
Hit Dice:	12d10 (66 hp)	16d10 (88 hp)
Initiative:	+3	+8
Speed:	40 ft.	50 ft.
AC:	25 (+1 size, +3 Dex, +11 natural), touch 14, flat-footed 22	28 (+1 size, +4 Dex, +13 natural), touch 15, flat-footed 24
Attacks:	Razor saw +13 melee	Razor saw +18 melee
Damage:	Razor saw 1d12+4	Razor saw 2d10+7
Face/Reach:	5 ft. by 5 ft./5 ft.	5 ft. by 5 ft./5 ft.
Special Attacks:	*Lightning bolt*	Spell-like abilities
Special Qualities:	Construct traits, electricity immunity, linked mind, spell vulnerability, SR 20	Construct traits, electricity immunity, linked mind, spell vulnerability, SR 22
Saves:	Fort +4, Ref +7, Will +9	Fort +5, Ref +9, Will +12
Abilities:	Str 16, Dex 17, Con —, Int 13, Wis 20, Cha 15	Str 20, Dex 19, Con —, Int 17, Wis 24, Cha 21
Feats:	Cleave (B), Great Cleave (B), Power Attack (B), Sunder (B)	Cleave (B), Great Cleave (B), Improved Initiative (B), Power Attack (B), Sunder (B)
Climate/Terrain:	Any land and underground	Any land and underground
Organization:	Series (1 plus 1–2 gold horrors and 4–16 electrum horrors)	Assembly (1 plus 1–2 platinum horrors, 3–4 gold horrors, and 5–20 electrum horrors)
Challenge Rating:	7	9
Treasure:	50% coins, 50% goods (gems only)	50% coins, 50% goods (gems only)
Alignment:	Always lawful evil	Always lawful evil
Advancement:	—	—

Clockwork horrors are intelligent, arachnidlike constructs that live as a hierarchical collective. They exist solely to strip entire worlds of worked and raw metals, which they use to produce more horrors. These activities take clockwork horrors into areas where metal can be found, from underground mines to civilized areas where processed metal is often readily available. Clockwork horrors ignore nonmechanical creatures unless such beings

pose a threat or obviously possess metal. The horrors' searches are methodical and efficient, resulting in the destruction of nearly everything in their path. An army of horrors can devastate an entire nation in a matter of weeks.

A clockwork horror appears as a four-legged, mechanical arachnid with a body about 2 feet in diameter. It is made of a base metal (such as iron) overlaid with a thin patina of precious or semiprecious metal. A large gem is embedded in the creature's brow. A single razor saw is situated near the front of its head where a mouth would normally be located. The more powerful clockwork horrors are more fantastically designed and decorated than the lesser ones. Servant clockwork horrors with overlays of less precious metals are known to exist, but these serve the hierarchy primarily as laborers.

Clockwork horrors communicate in their own language of mechanical sounds. The linked mind that they share allows for instant communication among individual horrors within 10 miles of each other.

Logic indicates that since the horrors are mechanical beings, someone or something must have created them. What happened to that being is unknown. Some sages theorize that the adamantine horror rebelled against and slew its creator, then devised the other types of clockwork horrors to serve as its armies.

COMBAT

Clockwork horrors attack their foes with calculated, merciless precision. Lesser horrors unswervingly follow the orders of their superiors, fighting to the death if so commanded. In battle, clockwork horrors swarm around foes and whittle away at them while calling for reinforcements. A clockwork horror's weaponry is a part of its being, so it cannot be disarmed. When it dies, the gem in its brow disintegrates, and its body fuses into a mass of melted metal.

All clockwork horrors share the following qualities.

Construct Traits: A clockwork horror is immune to mind-affecting effects, poison, *sleep*, paralysis, stunning, disease, death effects, necromantic effects, and any effect that requires a Fortitude save unless it also works on objects. The creature is not subject to critical hits, subdual damage, ability damage, ability drain, energy drain, or death from massive damage. It cannot heal itself but can be healed through repair. It cannot be raised or resurrected. A clockwork horror has darkvision (60-foot range).

Linked Mind (Ex): All clockwork horrors within 10 miles of a gold, platinum, or adamantine horror are in constant communication. If one is aware of a particular danger, they all are. If one in a particular group is not flat-footed, none of them are. No clockwork horror in such a group is considered flanked unless they all are.

Spell Vulnerability (Ex): A clockwork horror is susceptible to the *shatter* spell, which blinds it for 1d4+1 rounds.

ELECTRUM HORROR

Electrum horrors are the shock troops of the clockwork horror collective. They are sent in to scout out areas, assess potential resistance, and overcome any opposition.

Combat

Electrum horrors advance into combat in precise battle lines, with the individual horrors spaced about 10 feet apart. They open fire with volleys of pressure darts. Upon closing with the enemy, some continue firing darts at perceived spellcasters or opponents using ranged weapons, while others slice away at nearby foes with their razor-sharp saws. After a battle, additional electrum horrors scavenge the area, retrieving fallen companions and any abandoned weapons for smelting down and making new horrors.

GOLD HORROR

Gold horrors are the commanders of the clockwork horror armies. They supervise the electrums and other lesser horrors, ensuring that the orders of their superiors are obeyed.

ombat

Gold horrors fight from behind a line of electrum guards, shooting *lightning bolts* at their foes. In melee, a gold horror strikes at an enemy's weapon to destroy it. Against magic weapons and items, a gold horror's razor saw functions as a +2 weapon.

Lightning Bolt (Sp): Once every 2 rounds, the monster can generate a *lightning bolt* 5 feet wide and 40 feet long that deals 6d6 points of damage. A successful Reflex save (DC 13) halves the damage.

LATINUM HORROR

Platinum horrors are the generals and governors of all the lesser clockwork horrors. It is they who identify targets, devise strategies, and decide how best to deploy other horrors to achieve their goals.

ombat

In combat, platinum horrors fire *lightning bolts* at opponents before closing with them. In melee, they use their razor saws to sunder the weapons and armor of their enemies. Against magic weapons and items, a platinum horror's razor saw functions as a +3 weapon.

Lightning Bolt (Sp): A platinum horror's *lightning bolt* ability produces more powerful *lightning bolts* than the gold horror can emit. Once every 2 rounds, the platinum horror can fire a *lightning bolt* 5 feet wide and 80 feet long, dealing 12d6 points of electricity damage. A successful Reflex save (DC 15) halves the damage.

DAMANTINE

An adamantine horror is the supreme leader of the entire clockwork horror collective. Only one is believed to exist.

The adamantine horror directs the harvesting of metal and the creation of new horrors. It alone decides which new horrors to make; thus it controls the composition of the collective. The adamantine horror holds the secret of animating a newly built horror body.

The adamantine horror's motives in its aggressive campaign to grow the collective are unknown. Some sages speculate that it strives to destroy rival cultures; others claim it has acquired a living thing's drive to reproduce. Whatever its motives, the creature is a master at destroying other civilizations.

ombat

An adamantine horror devastates foes with its spell-like abilities from afar. In melee, it slashes through its enemies with its razor saw. Against magic weapons and items, an adamantine horror's razor saw functions as a +5 weapon.

Spell-Like Abilities: At will—*disintegrate, implosion, Mordenkainen's disjunction.* Caster level 14th; save DC 15 + spell level.

Colossal Magical Beast
Hit Dice: 30d10+270 (435 hp)
Initiative: +1
Speed: Fly 40 ft. (poor)
AC: 8 (−8 size, +1 Dex, +5 natural), touch 3, flat-footed 7
Attacks: Bite +37 melee and tail slam +32 melee
Damage: Bite 3d10+15, tail slam 2d8+7
Face/Reach: 100 ft. by 60 ft./5 ft. (20 ft. with tail)
Special Attacks: Swallow whole
Special Qualities: Darkvision 60 ft., levitate, low-light vision, protection from arrows, telekinesis
Saves: Fort +26, Ref +18, Will +10
Abilities: Str 40, Dex 13, Con 28, Int 2, Wis 11, Cha 11
Skills: Hide +6*, Listen +5, Spot +5
Feats: Flyby Attack, Snatch (B)

Climate/Terrain: Temperate and warm desert, plains, marsh, and hills
Organization: Solitary or pair
Challenge Rating: 16
Treasure: None
Alignment: Always neutral
Advancement: 31–60 HD (Colossal)

Cloud rays are among the most majestic of all flying creatures. They do not truly fly; instead, they levitate while propelling themselves with their wing-flaps.

A cloud ray has an enormous, flattened, triangular body that resembles that of an aquatic ray, but on an immensely larger scale. Its vast body is mottled in shades of dark blue and gray, with similar, lighter colors underneath. Along each side of its body is a long, wing-shaped piece of muscular tissue, which it uses for maneuvering and propulsion. Its abdomen tapers into a long, agile tail, called a zip, which is covered with bony spines.

With the possible exception of dragons, cloud rays have no known predators. They typically prey on rocs, pegasi, manticores, hippogriffs, griffons, and other large flying creatures. Cloud rays do not deliberately seek out human prey, but they have been known to devour whole villages when the opportunities presented themselves.

COMBAT

Most often, a cloud ray attacks simply because it is hungry. It dives on its prey and tries to snatch it up in its 20-foot-wide mouth, then flies off to swallow it.

In melee, a cloud ray can use its Snatch feat, or it can slap a foe with its tail. When it does the latter, the tail moves so fast that it creates a thundrous sound, like the crack of a whip.

Swallow Whole (Ex): A cloud ray can swallow a snatched opponent that is Huge or smaller by making a successful grapple check (grapple bonus +61). The cloud ray, however, has no appreciable stomach. Instead it has a long throat, the whole length of which is equipped with teeth for grinding

JE

the effect cannot be dispelled and it does not discharge after absorbing a certain amount of damage.

Telekinesis (Su): Lacking any sort of hands or paws, the cloud ray instead uses telekinesis to manipulate objects. This ability works like the *telekinesis* spell (caster level 5th), so the creature can lift or throw 125 pounds.

Skills: Thanks to its coloration, a cloud ray has a +16 racial bonus on Hide checks. *When it tires of drifting through the sky, it settles to the ground for rest. Through a combination of telekinesis and moving its great wing-flaps, it covers itself with dust, dirt, rocks, logs, uprooted bushes, and whatever else is nearby. While it is thus camouflaged, its Hide modifier rises to +32. The ray may rest on the ground thus covered for a few hours or a few weeks.

Feats: A creature that is flung by a cloud ray after being snatched travels 100 feet and takes 10d6 points of damage. If the cloud ray is flying, the creature takes this damage or the appropriate falling damage, whichever is greater.

COROLLAX

Tiny Magical Beast
Hit Dice: 1d10 (5 hp)
Initiative: +3
Speed: 10 ft., fly 60 ft. (good)
AC: 17 (+2 size, +3 Dex, +2 natural), touch 15, flat-footed 14
Attacks: Claw +6 melee
Damage: Claw 1d3–5
Face/Reach: 2 1/2 ft. by 2 1/2 ft./0 ft.
Special Attacks: Color spray
Special Qualities: Darkvision 60 ft., DR 5/silver, low-light vision, SR 12
Saves: Fort +2, Ref +5, Will +2
Abilities: Str 1, Dex 17, Con 11, Int 2, Wis 14, Cha 16
Skills: Listen +4, Spot +4
Feats: Weapon Finesse (claws)

Climate/Terrain: Warm forest
Organization: Solitary, pair, or swarm (5–20)
Challenge Rating: 1/2
Treasure: None
Alignment: Usually neutral
Advancement: 2–6 HD (Tiny); 7–9 HD (Small)

Corollaxes are mischievous and curious insectivores that dwell in dense jungles in tropical and subtropical climates. They typically nest in large colonies that span several closely placed trees.

These colorful creatures are very curious and quite social. They can provide the unknowing traveler with a great deal of companionship and amusement—at least until startled. At that point, their natural defensive reaction erupts, and chaos usually ensues.

A corollax has a gray-black, curved beak and black eyes. Its plumage varies in color, but a typical male's feathers are

and tearing food. Its throat empties directly into its intestines, so the ray must chew its food thoroughly to ensure proper digestion. Once inside the ray's throat, the opponent takes 3d10+22 points of bludgeoning, slashing, and piercing damage per round from its teeth and muscular contractions. A successful grapple check allows the swallowed creature to climb out of the throat and return to the ray's mouth, where another successful grapple check is needed to get free. Alternatively, a swallowed creature can try to cut its way out with either claws or a light piercing or slashing weapon. Dealing at least 25 points of damage to the throat (AC 20) in this way creates an opening large enough to permit escape. Once a single swallowed creature exits, muscular action closes the hole; thus, another swallowed opponent must cut its own way out. A cloud ray's throat can hold 2 Huge, 8 Large, 32 Medium-size, or 128 Small or smaller creatures.

Levitate (Ex): The cloud ray controls its altitude by generating and manipulating lighter-than-air gases inside its body. This ability enables it to ascend 20 feet per round or, by neutralizing the levitating gases and letting gravity take its course, descend as much as 500 feet per round. In spite of its immense bulk, the ray can pull out of such a dive instantly simply by levitating again.

Protection from Arrows (Su): This ability allows a cloud ray to resist most ranged attacks. It works like a *protection from arrows* spell (DR 10/+2 against projectiles), except that

a mixture of bright red, orange, and yellow, and a female's are either brown or gray.

TRAINING A COROLLAX

A corollax can be trained with a successful Handle Animal check (DC 23) to accept a particular creature (not necessarily the one who made the check) as a member of its flock. Any bird so trained does not use its color spray attack against the designated individual.

These birds are also natural mimics. With a successful Handle Animal check (DC 23), a corollax can be trained to repeat a particular phrase. Each bird is capable of remembering up to nine different phrases, though each phrase requires a separate Handle Animal check. The birds don't seem to comprehend what they say, however, and many humanoids later come to regret teaching the precocious mimics to talk—particularly when they can't get the creatures to shut up.

COROLLAX COMPANIONS

Because it is a social creature, a corollax can sometimes be persuaded to accept humanoid companionship on a long-term basis. If a character offers food and makes a successful Handle Animal check (DC 25 if the character has not previously frightened or abused the bird, or DC 30 otherwise), the corollax considers the character a desirable companion and accompanies him or her willingly in all travels. A corollax adopted in this manner refuses to leave the character's side so long as food, grooming, and lots of attention are provided. A well-treated corollax makes every effort to rejoin its companion if forcibly separated, and the companion receives a +2 circumstance bonus on all subsequent Handle Animal checks involving the bird. If the corollax is mistreated, it leaves and attempts to find its own way home.

COMBAT

Corollaxes are not aggressive and do not attack unless someone attacks or harasses them first. If disturbed, a corollax screeches and flies about, unleashing its color spray attack. If forced into melee, the bird combines both claws into a single attack.

Color Spray (Su): Once per round, a corollax can unleash a vivid cone of clashing colors. This ability works like a *color spray* spell (caster level 1st; save DC 13). The creature is immune to its own color spray attack and to those of others of its kind.

Gargantuan Undead
Hit Dice: 30d12 (195 hp)
Initiative: +2
Speed: 40 ft., burrow 10 ft.
AC: 12 (–4 size, –2 Dex, +8 natural), touch 4, flat-footed 12
Attacks: Slam +23/+18/+13 melee
Damage: Slam 2d12+18/19–20
Face/Reach: 20 ft. by 20 ft./20 ft.
Special Attacks: Improved grab, ingest corpses, swallow whole
Special Qualities: Desanctifying aura, DR 10/+2, soul-binding, SR 30, undead traits, zombie-spawn
Saves: Fort +10, Ref +8, Will +17
Abilities: Str 34, Dex 7, Con —, Int 10, Wis 11, Cha 15
Skills: Climb +14, Jump +14, Listen +20, Search +16, Spot +18
Feats: Cleave, Improved Critical (slam), Improved Initiative, Power Attack

Climate/Terrain: Any land and underground
Organization: Solitary, pair, or cluster (3–5)
Challenge Rating: 19
Treasure: None
Alignment: Usually neutral
Advancement: 31–60 HD (Colossal)

A corpse gatherer is an animated graveyard empowered by a mean intelligence and a greed for more bodies. It exists only to increase its own size and power by devouring more dead bodies. It seeks corpses everywhere, from cemeteries to battlefields to scenes of natural disasters.

A corpse gatherer appears roughly humanoid, but its immense body is made up of corpses, tombstones, and grave earth. From a distance, the creature resembles a hulking giant made of earth and stones, but upon closer inspection, a viewer can detect the occasional dead hand, head, or other appendage protruding from its form.

These creatures are thought to spawn from the burial of a sentient undead creature (such as a vampire) in unconsecrated ground. The lingering taint of undeath somehow permeates the earth, causing the entire graveyard—corpses, tombstones, and all—to coalesce into a ravening undead monster.

Corpse gatherers feast upon dead flesh, but they are more than willing to create fresh corpses by slaying living creatures. A single corpse gatherer has been known to destroy several entire villages to sate its unceasing hunger.

Though corpse gatherers are not themselves evil, their undead taint extends to any living prey they devour. The soul of a creature consumed by a corpse gatherer is trapped within the latter's body along with its corpse. Thus, the soul cannot escape (so the creature cannot be raised or resurrected) until the corpse gatherer itself is destroyed.

COMBAT

A corpse gatherer fights by attempting to pound its opponents into mush. From time to time, it also grabs troublesome opponents and stuffs them into its porous body (see Swallow Whole, below). Those so absorbed are grasped and held fast by the hands of the corpses that make up the gatherer.

Improved Grab (Ex): If a corpse gatherer hits an opponent its own size or smaller with a slam attack, it deals normal damage and attempts to start a grapple as a free action without provoking an attack of opportunity (grapple bonus +39). If it gets a hold, it can try to swallow the opponent in the next round. Alternatively, the corpse gatherer has the option to conduct the grapple normally, or simply use its hand to hold the opponent (–20 penalty on grapple check, but the corpse gatherer is not considered grappled). In either case, its next successful grapple check deals automatic slam damage.

Ingest Corpses (Su): The corpse gatherer increases its hit points by adding bodies to its form. It gains 5 hit points for every corpse of a swallowed creature that it absorbs. The corpse gatherer can exceed its normal hit points in this manner, gaining any excess as temporary hit points. Opponents the creature has swallowed are not subject to ingestion until the round after they die.

Swallow Whole (Ex): A corpse gatherer can swallow a grabbed opponent that is at least one size category smaller than itself by making a successful grapple check (grapple bonus +39). The creature need not use its mouth to swallow; it can merely stuff the opponent into any convenient portion of its porous body. Once inside the gatherer, the opponent takes 1d12+12 points of bludgeoning damage per round from the roiling corpses, gravestones, and other objects inside the creature's body. A successful grapple check allows the swallowed creature to extract itself from the hands of the corpses inside the gatherer and return to the surface of the gatherer's body, where another successful grapple check

is needed to get free. Alternatively, a swallowed creature can try to cut its way out with either claws or a light piercing or slashing weapon. Dealing at least 25 points of damage to the corpse gatherer (AC 20) in this way creates an opening large enough to permit escape. Once a single swallowed creature exits, the other nearby corpses close the hole; thus, another swallowed opponent must cut its own way out. A Gargantuan corpse gatherer can hold 2 Huge, 8 Large, 32 Medium-size, or 128 Small or smaller creatures.

Desanctifying Aura (Su): A corpse gatherer projects a continual field of negative energy in a 100-foot-radius emanation. The area within this field is under the effect of a double-strength *desecrate* spell (caster level 15th), as if the corpse gatherer were a permanent feature dedicated to its own deity. Each turning attempt within this area has a –6 profane penalty. Further, each undead creature in the area (including the corpse gatherer) is entitled to a +2 profane bonus on its attack rolls, damage rolls and saving throws, as well as +2 hit points per HD. This aura lasts for 24 hours after the corpse gatherer has passed through.

Soul Binding (Su): Creatures slain and ingested by a corpse gatherer are affected as if by a *soul bind* spell, so they cannot be restored to life. Destroying the corpse gatherer negates this effect. Corpses that the creature devours without having slain them itself are not subject to soul binding.

Undead Traits: A corpse gatherer is immune to mind-affecting effects, poison, *sleep*, paralysis, stunning, disease, death effects, necromantic effects, and any effect that requires a Fortitude save unless it also works on objects. It is not subject to critical hits, subdual damage, ability damage, ability drain, energy drain, or death from massive damage. A corpse gatherer cannot be raised, and resurrection works only if it is willing. The creature has darkvision (60-foot range).

Zombie-Spawn (Su): Upon reaching 0 hit points, the corpse gatherer falls apart into its component corpses. The creature's animating force remains among the corpses that formerly composed its body, converting them into zombies. Upon its death, a corpse gatherer generates as many zombies as it has Hit Dice (that is, a 30-HD corpse-gatherer becomes thirty zombies). Unless circumstances dictate otherwise, these are all Medium-size zombies. They function normally as long as they remain in the desanctified area of the dead corpse gatherer, but outside its effect they revert to normal corpses.

CRIMSON DEATH

Medium-Size Undead (Incorporeal)
Hit Dice: 13d12 (84 hp)
Initiative: +9
Speed: Fly 30 ft. (perfect)
AC: 17 (Dex +5, deflection +2), touch 17, flat-footed 12
Attacks: 2 incorporeal touches +11 melee
Damage: Blood drain
Face/Reach: 5 ft. by 5 ft./5 ft.
Special Attacks: Blood drain, seize
Special Qualities: Incorporeal subtype, *lift*, undead traits
Saves: Fort +4, Ref +11, Will +10
Abilities: Str —, Dex 21, Con —, Int 17, Wis 15, Cha 14
Skills: Concentration +14, Hide +21*, Intuit Direction +7, Listen +20, Search +13, Spot +20
Feats: Alertness, Blind-Fight, Combat Reflexes, Dodge, Expertise, Improved Initiative, Lightning Reflexes (B), Mobility, Spring Attack (B)

Climate/Terrain: Any marsh
Organization: Solitary
Challenge Rating: 11
Treasure: Standard
Alignment: Always neutral evil
Advancement: 14–26 HD (Medium-size)

A crimson death is a vaporous creature that lives in marshes, on moors, or any place that is subject to frequent, thick fogs. To conceal its presence from the general populace, a crimson death usually carries the bodies of its victims back to its lair, which is a charnel-house piled with the corpses and treasure of its victims.

A crimson death resembles a knot of fog with a vaguely humanoid shape, including arms and a torso. Its lower body trails off into indistinct vapor. The creature's eyes glow white, but it has no other facial features. After it has fed, the blood of its victims stains its misty body red.

COMBAT

A crimson death's attack consists of extending a vaporous tendril and wrapping it around its opponent. The creature prefers to attack from ambush, and it avoids physically powerful targets that might easily break free of its grasp.

Blood Drain (Ex): A crimson death drains blood, dealing 1d4 points of Constitution damage immediately upon seizing an opponent with a tendril. Each round thereafter that the opponent remains seized, the creature automatically deals an additional 1d4 points of Constitution damage. The crimson death craves blood, so it usually presses its attack until it can deal at least 12 points of Constitution damage.

Seize (Ex): When a crimson death makes a successful incorporeal touch attack, one of its tendrils wraps around the opponent. The two creatures are not considered grappled, but the opponent can break free with a successful Escape Artist or grapple check (grapple bonus +11). Upon seizing an opponent, the crimson death begins draining blood (see above).

Incorporeal Subtype: A crimson death can be harmed only by other incorporeal creatures, +1 or better magic weapons, spells, spell-like abilities, and supernatural abilities. The creature has a 50% chance to ignore any damage from a corporeal source, except for force effects or attacks made with ghost touch weapons. A crimson death can pass through solid objects, but not force effects, at will. Its attacks ignore natural armor, armor, and shields, but deflection bonuses and force effects work normally against them. A crimson death always moves silently and cannot be heard with Listen checks if it doesn't wish to be.

Lift (Sp): As a free action, a crimson death can telekinetically lift another creature or an object weighing up to 300 pounds. This ability works like the *telekinesis* spell (sustained force version, caster level 12th), except that it works only on an opponent already seized by a tendril of the crimson death. Against a struggling opponent, use of this ability requires a successful grapple check (grapple bonus +11).

Undead Traits: A crimson death is immune to mind-affecting effects, poison, *sleep*, paralysis, stunning, disease, death effects, necromantic effects, and any effect that requires a Fortitude save unless it also works on objects. It is not subject to critical hits, subdual damage, ability damage, ability drain, energy drain, or death from massive damage. A crimson death cannot be raised, and resurrection works only if it is willing. The creature has darkvision (60-foot range).

Skills: *A crimson death's misty form makes it difficult to spot in fog. Before feeding, the creature receives a +8 bonus on Hide checks in smoky or foggy areas. After it has fed, the bonus drops to +4 because of its red coloration.

DARKTENTACLES

Large Aberration
Hit Dice: 9d8+27 (67 hp)
Initiative: +2
Speed: 5 ft., swim 20 ft.
AC: 18 (–1 size, +2 Dex, +7 natural), touch 11, flat-footed 16
Attacks: 12 slams +9 melee, or weapon +9/+4 melee and 11 light weapons +9 melee, or weapon +7/+2 melee and 11 weapons (at least one of which is not light) +7 melee
Damage: Slam 1d4+4, by weapon (damage bonus +4 for primary hand and +2 for each off hand)
Face/Reach: 10 ft. by 10 ft./15 ft.
Special Attacks: Constrict 2d6+6, improved grab, spell-like abilities
Special Qualities: Darkvision 60 ft., enhanced multiweapon fighting, tentacle regeneration, tremorsense, weapon use
Saves: Fort +6, Ref +5, Will +7
Abilities: Str 19, Dex 15, Con 17, Int 14, Wis 12, Cha 12
Skills: Concentration +11, Hide +14, Listen +6, Move Silently +14, Spot +6
Feats: Combat Reflexes, Multidexterity, Multiweapon Fighting

Climate/Terrain: Any marsh
Organization: Solitary
Challenge Rating: 7
Treasure: Standard
Alignment: Always chaotic evil
Advancement: 10–18 HD (Large); 19–27 HD (Huge)

The darktentacles is a justly feared swamp monster. Both intelligent and malicious, it often leaves treasure from previous victims scattered about to attract new prey. The creature can flatten its squishy body across the ground so as to be inconspicuous, and it usually hides in or near water.

A darktentacles resembles an octopus with thirty-six tentacles, each of which can be up to 20 feet long. Instead of suction cups, each of its tentacles is lined with eyes. The creature uses some tentacles for movement and others for combat, striking with whichever tentacles are convenient.

This creature is capable of wielding weapons in its tentacles, and it often does so. It has no innate sense for magic items, but it tends to select the most effective weapons at its disposal. Because it hides so well, many characters have no idea that a darktentacles is present

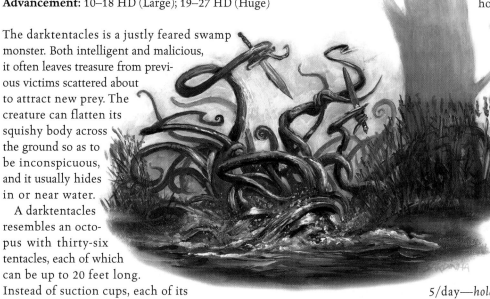

until abandoned weapons fly up from the ground and begin attacking them.

A darktentacles speaks Common and Aquan.

COMBAT

When creatures approach, a darktentacles typically uses its *charm monster* and *hold monster* powers first, concentrating these attacks on foes who seem to be physically powerful. Thereafter, it attacks anyone who comes within reach of its tentacles. If the darktentacles manages to grab someone, it uses its *wall of force* ability to keep any other opponents from lending the victim assistance.

A darktentacles can use only three tentacles at once against a Small or Medium-size opponent. Against a larger foe, it can use three additional tentacles for each extra 5 feet of face the opponent has, provided that it has the reach. Against a Tiny or smaller opponent, the creature can use only one tentacle. It can use a maximum of three tentacles against all foes in any single 5-foot by 5-foot area.

Constrict (Ex): With a successful grapple check, a darktentacles can crush a grabbed opponent, dealing 2d6+6 points of bludgeoning damage.

Improved Grab (Ex): If a darktentacles hits an opponent that is at least one size category smaller than itself with a slam attack, it deals normal damage and attempts to start a grapple as a free action without provoking an attack of opportunity (grapple bonus +30; includes a +16 racial bonus on grapple checks). If it gets a hold, it can also constrict in the same round. Thereafter, the darktentacles has the option to conduct the grapple normally, or simply use its tentacle to hold the opponent (–20 penalty on grapple check, but the darktentacles is not considered grappled). In either case, each successful grapple check it makes during successive rounds automatically deals slam and constrict damage.

Spell-Like Abilities: 5/day—*hold monster*; 3/day—*charm monster*; 1/day—*wall of force*. Caster level 10th; save DC 11 + spell level.

Enhanced Multiweapon Fighting (Ex): This ability lessens the penalty for off-hand weapon use by 2 for both primary and off hands. Combined with the Multidexterity and Multiweapon Fighting feats, this ability effectively negates all attack penalties for using one or more light off-hand weapons.

Tentacle Regeneration (Ex): Foes can attack the tentacles of a darktentacles, but only when those appendages are actually holding an opponent. A tentacle has an AC of 19 (touch 12) and can withstand 20 points of damage. The loss of a tentacle does not harm the creature (that is, the damage does not apply against its hit point total), and it regrows the limb within a day.

Tremorsense (Ex): A darktentacles can automatically sense the location of anything within 60 feet that is in contact with the ground.

Weapon Use (Ex): A darktentacles of Large size can wield a melee weapon of up to Huge size in each tentacle. It is proficient with all simple and martial melee weapons.

Skills: A darktentacles receives a +4 racial bonus on Hide checks.

DEATHBRINGER

Large Undead
Hit Dice: 30d12 (195 hp)
Initiative: +2
Speed: 40 ft.
AC: 32 (–1 size, +1 Dex, +16 natural, +6 banded mail), touch 10, flat-footed 31
Attacks: Heavy flail +16/+11/+6 melee and heavy flail +16 melee, or 2 slams +19 melee
Damage: Heavy flail 1d10+5/17–20, heavy flail 1d10+2/17–20, slam 1d8+5
Face/Reach: 5 ft. by 5 ft./10 ft.
Special Attacks: Greater dispelling, negative burst, trample 2d4+7
Special Qualities: Undead traits
Saves: Fort +10, Ref +12, Will +19
Abilities: Str 20, Dex 15, Con —, Int 13, Wis 14, Cha 7
Skills: Intimidate +22, Listen +26, Move Silently +20, Spot +25
Feats: Ambidexterity, Blind-Fight, Cleave, Great Cleave, Improved Bull Rush, Improved Critical (heavy flail), Power Attack, Two-Weapon Fighting, Weapon Focus (heavy flail)

Climate/Terrain: Any land and underground
Organization: Solitary, pair, or gang (3–5)
Challenge Rating: 17
Treasure: None
Alignment: Usually neutral evil
Advancement: 31–50 HD (Large); 51–70 HD (Huge); 71–90 HD (Gargantuan)

These powerful undead often lead undead armies assembled by necromancers, liches, demons, devils, or any other evil beings intent on inflicting pain and destruction on the living. Deathbringers care not whom they serve; they care only about inflicting widespread destruction.

A deathbringer is a hulking brute of humanoid shape. It has waxy gray skin and a bald head with no external ears. Its lips and eyelids appear to have been sewn shut with blue thread. The creature wears banded mail and wields two wickedly spiked heavy flails.

Deathbringers speak Common and either Abyssal or Infernal.

COMBAT

A deathbringer uses little subtlety in battle, but whenever it can make a full attack, it attempts to trip its opponent. If tripped during its own attempt, it drops its flail and attacks with its armored fists. When severely damaged, a deathbringer uses its negative burst power, centered on itself. This heals both the deathbringer and any undead compatriots it has in the area while also harming its opponents.

Greater Dispelling (Sp): A deathbringer can produce a *greater dispelling* effect at will. Caster level 20th.

Negative Burst (Su): A deathbringer can release a silent burst of negative energy at a range of up to 100 feet. The burst has a 20-foot radius and deals 1d8+10 points of negative energy damage to each living creature in the area (Will DC 23 half). Since undead are powered by negative energy, this effect heals the deathbringer and any other undead within the area of as much damage as it would otherwise deal. Once a deathbringer releases a negative burst, it must wait 1d4 rounds before it can do so again.

Trample (Ex): As a standard action during its turn each round, a deathbringer can trample opponents at least one size category smaller than itself. This attack deals 2d4+7 points of bludgeoning damage. A trampled opponent can attempt either an attack of opportunity at a –4 penalty or a Reflex save (DC 30) for half damage.

Undead Traits: A deathbringer is immune to mind-affecting effects, poison, *sleep*, paralysis, stunning, disease, death effects, necromantic effects, and any effect that requires a Fortitude save unless it also works on objects. It is not subject to critical hits, subdual damage,

ability damage, ability drain, energy drain, or death from massive damage. A deathbringer cannot be raised, and resurrection works only if it is willing. The creature has darkvision (60-foot range).

DEMON

In the countless, nearly infinite realms of the Abyss, demons grow numerous and varied. Though all embrace the path of evil, the tanar'ri stand as the supreme villains within the Abyssal hierarchy of iniquity. These creatures are constantly in conflict with every force of good in the universe, as well as with the lawful evil devils and baatezu of the Nine Hells.

The abyssal maw, abyssal skulker, and abyssal ravager are vicious but servile demons that can be found in the service of more powerful demons, or of evil mortals who treat with such beings. All three creatures speak Abyssal and Common, though abyssal maws and abyssal ravagers speak none too clearly, thanks to their low Intelligence scores and toothy maws.

The jovoc, palrethee, jarilith, and kelvezu appear wherever their demonic masters see fit to make use of them, be it the hidden reaches of their personal domains or out among mortals on the Material Plane. The zovvut, though not a tanar'ri itself, serves under and alongside those creatures. All five of these demons speak Abyssal, Celestial, and Draconic.

COMBAT

Demons are ferocity personified. They are willing to attack any creatures—even other demons—just for the sheer fun of it. Demons enjoy terrifying their victims before slaying them, and they often devour the slain. Many demons can create darkness, so they frequently blanket their enemies with it before joining battle.

All demons have the following abilities in common.

Outsider Traits: A demon has darkvision (60-foot range). It cannot be raised or resurrected.

In addition, all tanar'ri have the following abilities in common.

Tanar'ri Traits: Tanar'ri can communicate telepathically with any creature within 100 feet that has a language. Except as noted in the specific descriptions, a tanar'ri is immune to electricity and poison, and it has acid resistance 20, cold resistance 20, and fire resistance 20.

Summon Tanar'ri (**Sp**): All tanar'ri can summon other tanar'ri to their aid. This ability functions like a *summon monster* spell of the appropriate level, except that it has only a limited chance of success. Roll d% and compare the result with the creature's chance of success. On a failure, no tanar'ri answer the summons. Summoned tanar'ri automatically return whence they came after 1 hour. A tanar'ri that has just been summoned cannot use its own summon ability for 1 hour. Most tanar'ri do not use their summon ability lightly, since it leaves them beholden to the summoned creatures. In general, they use it only when necessary to save their own lives.

ABYSSAL MAW

An abyssal maw is a disgusting creature consisting mainly of teeth. Its appetite is legendary; one maw has been known to consume the better part of a centaur in less than a minute.

An abyssal maw looks like a huge, toothy mouth perched on a few stubby appendages. Its hide is a dull brown shade.

Combat

Abyssal maws serve as shock troops in evil armies. Since they lack ranged attacks, they usually rush into melee combat as soon as possible, where their gnashing teeth do the rest.

	Abyssal Maw Medium-Size Outsider (Chaotic, Evil)	Abyssal Skulker Small Outsider (Chaotic, Evil)	Abyssal Ravager Large Outsider (Chaotic, Evil)
Hit Dice:	2d8+2 (11 hp)	2d8+2 (11 hp)	3d8+9 (22 hp)
Initiative:	+0	+2	+4
Speed:	30 ft.	40 ft.	50 ft.
AC:	15 (+5 natural), touch 10, flat-footed 15	15 (+1 size, +2 Dex, +2 natural), touch 13, flat-footed 13	17 (−1 size, +4 Dex, +4 natural), touch 13, flat-footed 13
Attacks:	Bite +5 melee	2 claws +5 melee	Sting +6 melee
Damage:	Bite 2d8+4	Claw 1d2	Sting 1d4+4 plus poison
Face/Reach:	5 ft. by 5 ft./5 ft.	5 ft. by 5 ft./5 ft.	5 ft. by 10 ft./5 ft.
Special Attacks:	Rend fallen	—	Poison
Special Qualities:	Outsider traits	Outsider traits	Acid resistance 20, cold resistance 20, immunity to poison, outsider traits, scent
Saves:	Fort +4, Ref +3, Will +2	Fort +4, Ref +5, Will +5	Fort +6, Ref +7, Will +4
Abilities:	Str 17, Dex 10, Con 13, Int 6, Wis 9, Cha 8	Str 10, Dex 15, Con 12, Int 13, Wis 14, Cha 9	Str 17, Dex 19, Con 17, Int 6, Wis 12, Cha 8
Skills:	Climb +7, Jump +7, Listen +5, Spot +1	Hide +9, Listen +7, Move Silently +7, Spot +7	Jump +7, Listen +6, Move Silently +6, Sense Motive +4, Spot +4, Wilderness Lore +2
Feats:	Alertness	Weapon Finesse (claw)	Weapon Focus (sting)
Climate/Terrain:	Any land and underground	Any land and underground	Any land and underground
Organization:	Solitary, pair, or gang (3–5)	Solitary, pair, or gang (3–5)	Solitary, pair, or gang (3–5)
Challenge Rating:	2	2	5
Treasure:	None	None	None
Alignment:	Always chaotic evil	Always chaotic evil	Always chaotic evil
Advancement:	3–4 HD (Medium-size); 5–6 HD (Large)	3–4 HD (Small); 5–6 HD (Medium-size)	4–6 HD (Large); 7–9 HD (Huge)

Rend Fallen (Ex): An abyssal maw loves to tear into its downed foes. It automatically deals an additional 2d8+4 points of damage to any foe it drops with a melee attack.

ABYSSAL SKULKER

This demon is small but mean. Gangs of abyssal skulkers usually stalk ahead of evil armies and raiding parties to seek out and eliminate enemy scouts and pickets.

An abyssal skulker resembles a hairless ape with large hands and feet. Knobs of horn run along the crown of its head and down its spine. Although capable of walking upright, it habitually creeps about on all fours, keeping its body close to the ground.

Combat

Abyssal skulkers love to sneak up on their prey, then charge as a group. Their victims rarely have time to sound an alarm.

ABYSSAL RAVAGER

The abyssal ravager is a grotesque hybrid—part demon, part hyena, and all nasty. Although its exact origins are unclear, scholars agree that it is likely the result of demonic lust, which has no bounds and results in all manner of bizarre crossbreeds.

An abyssal ravager has baleful eyes and elongated jaws full of overlarge teeth. Patches of scaly hide show through its coarse, shaggy fur, and a row of curving spines juts from its backbone. Its long, warty tail is equipped with a vicious stinger. A full-grown specimen of either gender stands about 5 feet tall at the shoulder, measures nearly 10 feet from snout to base of tail, and weighs almost 2,000 pounds.

Combat

These demons are notoriously bad-tempered and aggressive. They tend to attack anything they see or smell, striking it repeatedly with their stingers.

Despite their formidable-looking teeth, abyssal ravagers do not use bite attacks. Their weak jaws are useful only for tearing apart prey that has already succumbed to their poisonous stings.

Poison (Ex): An abyssal ravager delivers its poison (Fortitude save DC 14) with each successful sting attack. The initial and secondary damage is the same (2d6 points of Strength damage).

Scent (Ex): An abyssal ravager can detect approaching enemies, sniff out hidden foes, and track by sense of smell.

	Jovoc (Tanar'ri) Small Outsider (Chaotic, Evil)	Palrethee (Tanar'ri) Medium-Size Outsider (Chaotic, Evil, Fire)	Zovvut Medium-Size Outsider (Chaotic, Evil)
Hit Dice:	4d8+18 (36 hp)	8d8+24 (60 hp)	10d8+20 (65 hp)
Initiative:	+2	+3	+1
Speed:	30 ft.	30 ft.	30 ft., fly 50 ft. (average)
AC:	16 (+1 size, +2 Dex, +3 natural), touch 13, flat-footed 14	23 (+3 Dex, +10 natural), touch 13, flat-footed 20	20 (+1 Dex, +9 natural), touch 11, flat-footed 19
Attacks:	2 claws +6 melee and bite +1 melee	+1 *flaming longsword* +14/+9, or 2 slams +12 melee	2 claws +13 melee
Damage:	Claw 1d3+1, bite 1d4	+1 *flaming longsword* 1d8+7/19–20 plus 1d6 fire, slam 1d8+4	Claw 1d12+3
Face/Reach:	5 ft. by 5 ft./5 ft.	5 ft. by 5 ft./5 ft.	5 ft. by 5 ft./5 ft.
Special Attacks:	—	Demonic burn, spell-like abilities	Draining gaze, spell-like abilities
Special Qualities:	Aura of retribution, DR 5/silver, fast healing 5, outsider traits, SR 13, *summon tanar'ri*, tanar'ri traits	DR 20/+2, *fiery shield*, fire subtype, outsider traits, SR 18, *summon tanar'ri*, tanar'ri traits	Create spawn, DR 20/+2, outsider traits, SR 20
Saves:	Fort +7, Ref +6, Will +4	Fort +9, Ref +9, Will +7	Fort +9, Ref +8, Will +10
Abilities:	Str 12, Dex 15, Con 16, Int 7, Wis 10, Cha 7	Str 19, Dex 16, Con 16, Int 13, Wis 12, Cha 11	Str 17, Dex 13, Con 15, Int 14, Wis 16, Cha 14
Skills:	Hide +8, Listen +7, Search +3, Sense Motive +3, Spot +7	Bluff +10, Diplomacy +10, Hide +9, Intimidate +2, Knowledge (any one) +12, Listen +6, Sense Motive +12, Search +12, Spellcraft +6, Spot +8	Bluff +10, Concentration +12, Diplomacy +6, Hide +11, Intimidate +4, Listen +13, Move Silently +11, Scry +11, +15, Sense Motive +16, Spellcraft +8, Spot +18
Feats:	Toughness (×2)	Dodge, Expertise, Weapon Focus (longsword)	Alertness, Dodge, Mobility
Climate/Terrain:	Any land and underground	Any land and underground	Any land and underground
Organization:	Solitary, pair, or gang (3–4)	Solitary	Solitary or squad (1 plus 2–4 wights)
Challenge Rating:	5	8	9
Treasure:	Standard	None	Standard
Alignment:	Always chaotic evil	Always chaotic evil	Always chaotic evil
Advancement:	5–8 HD (Small); 9–12 HD (Medium-size)	9–12 HD (Medium-size)	11–16 HD (Medium-size)

JOVOC

These vicious little black-hearted fiends were born to create strife. Their ability to inflict the damage they take on others makes them invaluable in the front lines of tanar'ri armies. A unit of jovocs can absorb repeated blows and spells from the enemy and still survive to exact a punishing revenge.

A jovoc is a 4-foot-tall, bloated, hairless creature of humanoid shape. It resembles the bruised and battered corpse of a gnome left too long to decay in the heat of summer, and the stench that emanates from its rough skin lends credence to this impression. Its skin is dark blue or black, and its eyes are vacant, black pools. Each of the creature's long arms ends in a three-fingered hand with long red fingernails, forever stained the color of blood.

Combat

Jovocs are not especially intelligent, but they are quick and experienced ambushers who know how to use their small size to best effect. Years of training and experience have taught them how to take advantage of their aura of retribution and fast healing abilities. They often adopt a hit-and-run strategy, jumping into a group of enemies to do as much damage as possible, then dashing off for a few rounds to heal.

Alternatively, jovocs fighting in pairs or trios can utilize their favorite tactic. Lurking just beyond the reach of their enemies (preferably concealed by darkness, a wall, or some other barrier), they begin to attack one another, automatically hitting with each swing. These attacks deal full damage not only on the jovocs, but also on anyone caught within their aura of retribution. After allowing a round or two for

their fast healing ability to close their wounds, the creatures begin to claw and bite one another again.

Aura of Retribution (Su): This effect is always active in a 30-foot spread centered on the jovoc. Whenever the creature takes damage from any source, every nontanar'ri within the area immediately takes an equal amount of damage. A successful Fortitude saving throw (DC 15) halves the damage. (For example, if an opponent deals 12 points of damage to a jovoc, that opponent and every other nontanar'ri within 30 feet also immediately take 12 points of damage each, or 6 points with a successful Fortitude save.) Regardless of the source of the damage to the jovoc, the damage dealt to nontanar'ri by this effect is not subject to negation or reduction because of resistance, immunity, damage reduction, spell resistance, or the like.

Fast Healing (Ex): A jovoc regains lost hit points at the rate of 5 per round. Fast healing does not restore hit points lost from starvation, thirst, or suffocation, and it does not allow the jovoc to regrow or reattach lost body parts.

Summon Tanar'ri (Sp): Once per day, a jovoc can attempt to summon another jovoc with a 25% chance of success.

PALRETHEE

According to legend, palrethees were once ambitious demons who yearned to rule the Abyss as balors. Despite their great malice and their sadism, these lost souls failed in some unknown trial by fire, and now they burn for all eternity. Many balors use palrethees as sergeants or messengers, taking great pleasure in reinforcing the ambitious demons' subservient positions. This connection between the two kinds of tanar'ri has lent credence to the bards' tales about the palrethees' origin.

A palrethee is a tall, emaciated creature of humanoid shape with blood-red or blue skin and bony, white, vestigial wings. The entire length of its body is sheathed in fire. The creature can alter the color and appearance of its flames at will, making them appear translucent and ghostly, or the red-orange shade of a fiery forge, or even blue-white and delicate. No matter how the flames look, their effects remain unchanged.

Combat

Palrethees have all the necessary combat abilities to enjoy the din of battle, but these arrogant fiends often believe themselves to be above the petty assignments they receive. Desperate to acquire magic, mortal souls, or some other currency with which they can gain power, they try to make bargains, use humans as tools, or trick unwary mortals into doing their bidding.

When forced into combat, a palrethee usually employs its *fear* spell-like ability first to scatter as many opponents as possible, then wades into melee with its flaming longsword.

Demonic Burn (Ex): Any creature hit by a palrethee's slam attack must succeed at a Reflex save (DC 17) or catch fire. The flame burns for 1d4 rounds (see Catching on Fire in Chapter 3 of the DUNGEON MASTER's Guide). A burning creature can take a move-equivalent action to put out the flame.

Spell-Like Abilities: At will—*detect good, detect magic, see invisibility;* 1/day—*fear* (30-foot radius). Caster level 8th; save DC 10 + spell level.

Fiery Shield (Sp): A palrethee is wreathed in scorching flames that cause damage to each creature that attacks it

	Jarilith (Tanar'ri) Large Outsider (Chaotic, Evil)	Kelvezu (Tanar'ri) Medium-Size Outsider (Chaotic, Evil)
Hit Dice:	10d8+80 (125 hp)	12d8+36 (90 hp)
Initiative:	+9	+14
Speed:	60 ft.	30 ft., fly 60 ft. (good)
AC:	32 (−1 size, +9 Dex, +14 natural), touch 18, flat-footed 23	35 (+10 Dex, +15 natural), touch 20, flat-footed 35
Attacks:	2 claws +22 melee and bite +19 melee	+1 *scimitar of greater wounding* +16/+11/+6 melee and +1 *dagger of wounding* +16/+11 melee
Damage:	Claw 2d6+12/18–20/×3, bite 2d8+6/18–20/×3	+1 *scimitar of greater wounding* 1d6+6/18–20 plus poison, +1 *dagger of wounding* 1d4+3/19–20 plus poison
Face/Reach:	10 ft. by 5 ft./5 ft.	5 ft. by 5 ft./5 ft.
Special Attacks:	Frightful presence, improved grab, pounce, rake 2d6+6/18–20, spell-like abilities	Poison, sneak attack +8d6, spell-like abilities
Special Qualities:	Augmented critical, DR 30/+3, outsider traits, scent, SR 25, *summon tanar'ri*, tanar'ri traits	DR 20/+2, enhanced detection, evasion, outsider traits, SR 26, *summon tanar'ri*, tanar'ri traits, uncanny dodge
Saves:	Fort +15, Ref +16, Will +8	Fort +11, Ref +18, Will +11
Abilities:	Str 35, Dex 29, Con 27, Int 8, Wis 12, Cha 14	Str 21, Dex 31, Con 16, Int 17, Wis 16, Cha 16
Skills:	Balance +14, Climb +14, Concentration +21, Hide +22*, Jump +14, Listen +12, Move Silently +25, Search +4, Spot +12	Bluff +15, Concentration +15, Diplomacy +7, Hide +33, Intimidate +5, Knowledge (any one) +13, Listen +18, Move Silently +33, Search +18, Sense Motive +16, Spellcraft +13, Spot +18
Feats:	Multiattack, Power Attack, Weapon Focus (claw)	Ambidexterity, Improved Initiative, Improved Two-Weapon Fighting, Two-Weapon Fighting
Climate/Terrain:	Any land and underground	Any land and underground
Organization:	Solitary, pair, or pride (6–10)	Solitary
Challenge Rating:	13	18
Treasure:	Standard	Standard coins; standard items, plus +1 *scimitar of greater wounding* and +1 *dagger of wounding*
Alignment:	Always chaotic evil	Always chaotic evil
Advancement:	11–23 HD (Large); 24–30 HD (Huge)	13–24 HD (Medium-size)

with a natural or hand-held melee weapon. Such an attack deals normal damage to the palrethee (assuming its damage reduction is overcome), but at the same time the attacker takes 1d6+8 points of fire damage (spell resistance applies; caster level 8th). Weapons with exceptional reach, such as longspears, do not endanger their users in this way.

Fire Subtype (Ex): A palrethee is immune to fire damage but takes double damage from cold unless a saving throw for half damage is allowed. In that case, the creature takes half damage on a success and double damage on a failure.

Summon Tanar'ri **(Sp):** Once per day, a palrethee can attempt to summon another palrethee with a 30% chance of success.

Tanar'ri Traits: Unlike most tanar'ri, palrethees have no resistance to cold attacks.

ZOVVUT

Zovvuts are the spawn of some terrible demon prince. The first of them were created during horrible blood rites centuries ago. Rumors link zovvuts to that master of demons and necromancy known as Orcus, though the secret of the creatures' creation has become widely known among the lords of the Abyss. Now zovvuts can be found in

many regions of the Abyss as well as on the Material Plane, doing the bidding of anyone powerful enough to intimidate them into obedience.

Zovvuts are often used by demonic agents in conjunction with more combative demons—the latter keep enemies at bay while the zovvuts' gaze attacks annihilate them. Zovvuts resent any creature with the power to command them and, like any demons, they constantly seek to undermine and betray authority.

A zovvut is a muscular, pale-skinned, hairless creature of humanoid shape. Its arms end in sharp, barbed claws that are well designed for rending flesh. Foul, feathered wings stretch upward from the zovvut's shoulders. A third eye is set into the center of its forehead.

Combat

Zovvuts are not afraid of combat. Though weaker than many other demons in terms of combat ability, they rely on their gaze attack to bring their foes to submission.

Draining Gaze (Su): Any living creature within 30 feet of a zovvut that meets its glowing red eyes must succeed at a Will saving throw (DC 17) or gain one negative level. For

each negative level bestowed, the zovvut heals 5 points of damage. If the amount of healing is more than the damage the creature has taken, it gains any excess as temporary hit points. If the negative level has not been removed (with a spell such as *restoration*) before 24 hours have passed, the afflicted opponent must succeed at a Fortitude save (DC 17) to remove it. Failure means the opponent's level (or HD) is reduced by one.

Spell-Like Abilities: At will—*clairaudience/clairvoyance, darkness, desecrate, detect good, detect thoughts, doom, suggestion, teleport without error* (self plus 50 pounds of objects only). Caster level 12th; save DC 12 + spell level.

Create Spawn (Su): Any humanoid slain by the zovvut's gaze attack (negative levels equal to current Hit Dice, or drained below 1st level) becomes a wight in 1d4 rounds. This creature is under the command of the zovvut that killed it, and it remains enslaved until either it or the zovvut dies. A spawn does not possess any of the abilities it had in life.

ARILITH

Jariliths, the elite hunting beasts of the Abyss, are terrifying feline creatures conjured up from the nightmares of a thousand generations of mortals. They prefer demonic flesh and are comfortable hunting their favorite prey in desert, jungle, waste, or forest. Jariliths are notoriously difficult to control, so even the most powerful balor must tread carefully around them. They sense weakness, and to them nearly any other creature seems weak.

A jarilith resembles a slightly larger than average male lion, complete with a glorious mane. Long teeth extend from its jaws, and its claws are longer still. The creature's blood-red coat reveals its origin, but it strikes so fast that the only clue most victims get to its presence is a slight reek of brimstone.

Jariliths do not speak, but they understand Abyssal. They communicate silently with one another through telepathy.

Combat

A jarilith is a direct, uncompromising foe in battle. Normally, it relies on its Power Attack feat and its augmented critical ability to deal horrendous amounts of damage to its foes. Though they often do not need the advantage, jariliths prefer to ambush their opponents.

Frightful Presence (Ex): When a jarilith charges or attacks, it inspires terror in all creatures within 30 feet that have fewer Hit Dice or levels than it has. Each potentially affected opponent must succeed at a Will save (DC 17) or become shaken—a condition that lasts until the opponent is out of range. A successful save leaves that opponent immune to that jarilith's frightful presence for 24 hours.

Improved Grab (Ex): If a jarilith hits an opponent that is at least one size category smaller than itself with a bite attack, it deals normal damage and attempts to start a grapple as a free action without provoking an attack of opportunity (grapple bonus +26). If it gets a hold, it can attempt to rake in the same round. Thereafter, the jarilith has the option to conduct the grapple normally, or simply use its jaws to hold the opponent (–20 penalty on grapple check, but the jarilith is not considered grappled). In either case, each successful grapple check it makes during successive rounds automatically deals bite damage and allows another rake attempt.

Pounce (Ex): If a jarilith charges, it can make a full attack (including a rake attempt, see below) even though it has moved.

Rake (Ex): On any round that a jarilith has a hold on an opponent (see Improved Grab, above), it can make two rake attacks (+21 melee) with its hind legs for 2d6+6 points of damage each. The jarilith can also attempt to rake when it pounces on an opponent.

Spell-Like Abilities: At will—*clairaudience/clairvoyance, darkness, detect good, detect thoughts, doom.* Caster level 12th; save DC 12 + spell level.

Augmented Critical (Ex): A jarilith threatens a critical hit on a natural attack roll of 18–20. On a successful critical hit with a bite, claw, or rake attack, it deals triple damage.

Scent (Ex): A jarilith can detect approaching enemies, sniff out hidden foes, and track by sense of smell.

Summon Tanar'ri (**Sp**): Once per day, a jarilith can attempt to summon another jarilith with a 35% chance of success.

Skills: A jarilith receives a +4 racial bonus on Balance, Hide, and Move Silently checks. *In areas of tall grass or heavy undergrowth, its Hide bonus improves to +12.

KELVEZU

Mariliths act as generals in tanar'ri armies, and balors are the mighty aristocrats of the Abyssal hierarchy. Both find the services of kelvezus—the infiltrators and assassins of the demonic realm—quite useful. Kelvezus rarely lead troops; instead, they surgically remove specific opponents (such as

devils, competing demons, or obstinate mortals) in accordance with the orders of more powerful demons.

The kelvezu is remarkable among the higher ranks of demonkind because of its size—it stands barely 5 feet tall. Because of its size and its humanoid shape, it can be mistaken for a human if it uses a touch of disguise to hide its rosy red skin.

Combat

Kelvezus strike from stealth, relying not only on their invisibility, but also on their gift for hiding and sneaking. Like their mortal counterparts, these assassins try to dispatch their targets quickly. If they cannot, they retreat and strike again when conditions are favorable. Every kelvezu carries a +1 *scimitar of greater wounding* (see below) that resembles a serpent's tail and a +1 *dagger of wounding* that resembles a serpent's tooth.

Poison (Ex): A kelvezu continually coats its weapons with an injury poison (Fortitude save DC 19) produced from its fingertips. The initial and secondary damage is the same (1d6 points of Constitution damage). Kelvezu poison is highly perishable, becoming inert 1 minute after the creature stops applying it.

Sneak Attack (Ex): Any time the kelvezu's target is denied a Dexterity bonus, or when it is flanked by the kelvezu, the latter deals an additional +8d6 points of damage on a successful melee attack.

Spell-Like Abilities: At will—*deeper darkness, desecrate, detect good, detect law, greater dispelling, improved invisibility* (self only), *read magic, suggestion, teleport without error* (self plus 50 pounds of objects only), *tongues* (self only), *unhallow.* Caster level 18th; save DC 13 + spell level.

Enhanced Detection (Su): In addition to its regular senses, a kelvezu perceives foes through *detect magic* and *see invisibility* effects (caster level 18th) that are always active.

Evasion (Ex): If exposed to any effect that normally allows a Reflex save for half damage, a kelvezu takes no damage on a successful saving throw.

Summon Tanar'ri **(Sp):** Once per day, a kelvezu can attempt to summon another kelvezu with a 25% chance of success.

Uncanny Dodge (Ex): A kelvezu retains its Dexterity bonus to AC even when flat-footed, and it cannot be flanked.

Skills: A kelvezu receives a +8 racial bonus on Hide and Move Silently checks.

New Melee Weapon Special Ability

Greater Wounding: A wound inflicted by a weapon of greater wounding bleeds for 2 points of damage per round thereafter, in addition to the normal damage the weapon deals. Multiple wounds from the weapon result in cumulative bleeding loss (two wounds deal 4 points of damage per round, and so on). The bleeding can be stopped only by a successful Heal check (DC 15) or the application of a *cure* spell or some other healing spell (*heal, healing circle,* and so on).

Caster Level: 15th; *Prerequisites:* Craft Magic Arms and Armor, *Mordenkainen's sword; Market Price:* +4 bonus.

DESMODU

Large Monstrous Humanoid

Hit Dice: 12d8+48 (102 hp)

Initiative: +3

Speed: 20 ft. (40 ft. when galloping), climb 30 ft.

AC: 20 (–1 size, +3 Dex, +5 natural, +3 masterwork studded leather), touch 12, flat-footed 17

Attacks: 2 claws +16 melee and bite +14 melee, or masterwork notbora +15/+10/+5 melee and masterwork notbora +15 melee and bite +14 melee, or Large heavy lance +16/+11/+6 melee, or masterwork mighty composite longbow (+4 Str bonus) with masterwork arrows +16/+11/+6 ranged

Damage: Claw 1d4+5, bite 1d6+2, or notbora 2d6+5/19–20 (primary), notbora 2d6+2 (off hand), Large heavy lance 2d6+7/×3, masterwork mighty composite longbow (+4 Str bonus) with masterwork arrows 1d8+4/×3

Face/Reach: 5 ft. by 5 ft./10 ft.

Special Attacks: Screech, sonic abilities, wounding

Special Qualities: Blindsight 120 ft., darkvision 60 ft., gallop, scent, speak with bats, +4 racial bonus on saves against sonic effects

Saves: Fort +10, Ref +11, Will +10

Abilities: Str 20, Dex 16, Con 18, Int 15, Wis 15, Cha 11

Skills: Animal Empathy +5, Balance +12, Climb +13, Handle Animal +5, Jump +14, Listen +11, Move Silently +8, Ride (bat) +10, Spot +11, Tumble +10, Use Rope +8

Feats: Ambidexterity (B), Combat Reflexes, Expertise, Great Fortitude, Multiattack, Quick Draw, Two-Weapon Fighting (B)

Climate/Terrain: Underground

Organization: Solitary, pair, company (4–7), troop (8–18 plus 1 leader of 2nd–5th level), colony (20–80 plus 5 3rd-level elders and 1 leader of 4th–6th level), or enclave (100–600 plus 10 3rd-level elders, 5 5th-level senior elders, and 1 leader of 5th–9th level)

Challenge Rating: 9

Treasure: No coins, 1/2 goods, standard items, plus equipment

Alignment: Usually neutral good

Advancement: By character class

Desmodus are massive, batlike humanoids who live in caverns deep underground. They are omnivorous and usually not dangerous unless attacked. Until recently, most sages thought them to be extinct, wiped out in an ancient war against the drow.

An adult desmodu stands 8 to 9 feet tall. Its body is covered with reddish-black or reddish-brown fur. The creature has long arms, short legs, and a head like that of a bat. A membrane of leathery, black skin stretches from each wrist to the corresponding ankle. A desmodu's hands and feet are long and narrow, with stubby, curving digits ending in retractable claws. The fingers and toes, along

with the heel and palms, are equipped with cilia that give the creature a very sure grip.

A desmodu is bipedal. Normally it walks upright with a rolling gait, but it can also can get down on all fours and gallop along at twice its base speed. The typical desmodu wears armor and a harness for carrying tools and weapons, but very little else.

Desmodus speak Undercommon and Terran in addition to a language of their own. This language, called Desmodu, includes both ultrasonic and subsonic utterances, so non-desmodus cannot speak it. Desmodus have deep, rich voices, though their speech includes the occasional sharp squeak or bass rumble when they are using a language other than their native tongue.

COMBAT

Desmodus use their sonic abilities to give themselves bonuses and their foes penalties. Their favorite melee weapon is the notbora, an exotic double weapon of their own invention.

These creatures often rush into melee on all fours, using smokesticks to blind foes. They follow up by using the Quick Draw feat to draw their notboras and attack as they stand up. Desmodus also are fond of dropping down on opponents from the ceiling of a cavern, and they make full use of their superior reach in melee. Once battle is joined, they jump and tumble to bypass the foes' front line and attack opposing spellcasters or set up flanking attacks.

Screech (Su): Once per day, a desmodu can produce a screech that can literally tear items apart. The creature can choose one of two effects.

Ray: A ray deals 5d6 points of sonic damage to any creature or object it strikes. This attack has a range of 30 feet.

Spread: A sonic concussion causes every creature (except other desmodus) within a 30-foot spread centered on the desmodu to be stunned for 1d4 rounds. A successful Fortitude save (DC 20) negates the effect.

Sonic Abilities (Su): At will, a desmodu can emit subsonic vibrations, choosing one of two effects. It takes a standard action to invoke an effect or to concentrate to maintain it.

Despair: Each foe in a 30-foot spread centered on the desmodu takes a –2 morale penalty on saving throws, attack rolls, ability checks, skill checks, and weapon damage rolls for as long as the desmodu concentrates and for 1d4 rounds thereafter. A successful Will save (DC 16) negates this sonic, mind-affecting effect.

Hope: Every ally in a 30-foot spread centered on the desmodu gains a +2 morale bonus on saving throws, attack rolls, ability checks, skill checks, and weapon damage rolls for as long as the desmodu concentrates and for 1d4 rounds thereafter.

Wounding (Ex): A desmodu's saliva contains an anticoagulant that causes bite wounds the creature inflicts to bleed freely. A wound resulting from a desmodu's bite attack bleeds for an additional 1 point of damage per round thereafter. Multiple wounds from such attacks result in cumulative bleeding loss (two wounds for 2 points of damage per round, and so on). The bleeding stops on its own after 1 minute. Alternatively, it can be stopped by a successful Heal check (DC 15) or the application of a *cure* spell or some other healing spell (*heal, healing circle,* or the like).

Blindsight (Ex): A desmodu emits high-frequency sounds, inaudible to most other creatures, that bounce off nearby objects and creatures. This ability enables it to discern objects and creatures within 120 feet. The desmodu usually does not need to make Spot or Listen checks to notice creatures within range of its blindsight. A *silence* spell negates this ability and forces the desmodu to rely on its vision (which is as good as a human's).

Gallop (Ex): A desmodu can get down on all fours and gallop along like an ape at a speed of 40 feet, provided that its hands are free.

Speak with Bats (Sp): This ability functions like a *speak with animals* spell (caster level 1st), except that it only works on bats and is usable at will.

Skills: A desmodu receives a +4 racial bonus on Spot and Listen checks, which is lost if its blindsight is negated. The creature also gets a +2 racial bonus on grapple checks. When wearing light armor or no armor, the creature gains a +2 bonus on Balance and Jump checks. All these racial bonuses are included in the statistics above. When a desmodu has its

hands free and deliberately jumps down from a height, subtract 10 feet from the distance fallen to determine damage. If it makes a successful Jump check (DC 15), reduce the effective distance fallen by another 10 feet.

DESMODU SOCIETY

Desmodus live in small, independent family groups that gather in loosely organized colonies or enclaves to pool resources and create a communal defense. They eschew complex social organizations, and individual families live as they please. Each family group includes several generations, with the eldest generation acting as the ruling body to settle all issues.

The oldest and most experienced desmodus in an enclave form a council to settle disputes between families and make recommendations about handling external affairs. Desmodus of the same age from different families frequently adopt each other as siblings. These adopted siblings are called age-mates, and they always refer to each other as though they were blood kin. The extended family ties that desmodus form in this manner can be both varied and complex, and they are usually not clear to anyone except other desmodus.

Desmodus live in large caverns festooned with stalactites and stalagmites. They tunnel into the ceilings to create living spaces, keeping the entrances concealed among the stalactites. They use the cavern floor to grow fungi, herd lizards, and conduct any other activities that might be difficult to perform on the ceiling. Desmodus breed a variety of bats to serve as steeds and guardians.

A desmodu settlement includes noncombatants (mostly children) equal to 20% of the fighting population. The society is egalitarian, so both males and females can be found filling almost every role.

Desmodus enjoy a simple lifestyle. They understand the value of weapons and tools, but they keep neither money nor valuables. They conduct trade through barter, and the only distinction they recognize as a status symbol is the number of bats and lizards a family owns.

Breeding, keeping, and training bats is a favorite activity among the desmodus. They consider it a mark of distinction to breed a new and useful type of bat, and thus countless varieties of bats exist within desmodu caverns. Three of the types that are of value in combat are detailed in the Desmodu Bats entry (see below), but there are many others as well.

Desmodu artisans produce a wide variety of ingenious and high-quality goods. Some of these devices that may be of interest to adventurers are described in the Desmodu Items section, below. These creatures also produce all manner of mundane items, including toys, household goods, and musical instruments. All desmodu appreciate good music and items that can produce or enhance sound. Their own music, however, is mostly inaudible to others because of its ultrasonic and subsonic components.

The chief desmodu deity is Vesperian, who is the creator and protector of the race. Typically there is a shrine dedicated to him in every enclave, and many dwellings also boast private altars to Vesperian.

DESMODU ITEMS

Desmodus have created a number of specialized items for their own use. Some of these items are detailed below.

Breathing Mask: This mask covers the user's face. It is fitted with goggles and a bag of an alchemical substance that allows the wearer to breathe for up to 4 hours. With the mask on, the wearer can ignore the effects of noxious fumes and inhaled toxins. The mask even enables the wearer to survive underwater or in an airless environment.

The item consists of a masterwork leather mask with goggles (cost 50 gp), and the alchemical air supply, which costs 950 gp and can be manufactured with a successful Alchemy check (DC 20). A partially used air supply cannot be combined with another partially used one to get a fresh supply, but it can be discarded and replaced with a new supply.

Cost: 1,000 gp; *Weight:* 5 lb.

Cable: This 100-foot-long metal cord is thinner, stronger, and lighter than even silk rope. It is too thin for most creatures to climb it easily (Climb DC 20), but desmodus using a cable can climb at their normal climb speed. The cable has a snap ring at each end so that it can be quickly attached to or detached from a piton, spike, grappling hook, or other item without a Use Rope check.

The cable has 10 hit points and hardness 5. It can be burst with a successful Strength check (DC 32). Its stiffness imposes a −2 circumstance penalty on Use Rope checks.

Cost: 50 gp; *Weight:* 4 lb.

Cablespool: This gadget carries 100 feet of cable in an enclosed reel. The reel is spring-wound and can pull in all 100 feet of cable in 1 round (pulling with an effective Strength score of 16). It can be set to reel or unreel the cable automatically as the user climbs, or to act as a brake, allowing the user to jump down 100 feet without harm.

Cost: 125 gp (175 with cable); *Weight:* 2 lb. (6 lb. with cable).

Harness: Desmodus cannot wear belts because of the flaps of skin attached to their flanks. Instead, they wear harnesses that loop over their shoulders and between their legs. Straps crisscross the front and back of the desmodu's body to keep the harness from slipping off.

Each desmodu harness is fitted with rings, hooks, and ties for carrying weapons and equipment. A reinforced hook hangs near the waist for carrying a cablespool.

Cost: 20 gp; *Weight:* 2 lb.

Frostfire: This sticky, adhesive substance drains away heat when exposed to air or moisture. A flask of frostfire can be thrown as a grenadelike weapon with a range increment of 10 feet, and a direct hit deals 1d6 points of cold damage. The target can then attempt to scrape off or wash away the frostfire, if desired. If this does not occur, the target takes an additional 1d6 points of cold damage on the round following the direct hit. Removing frostfire by scraping requires a successful Reflex saving throw (DC 15). Alternatively, the substance can be removed automatically by dousing it with at least 1 pint of an alcoholic or acidic solution (such as wine or vinegar). Either method requires a full-round action.

Cost: 40 gp; *Weight:* 1 lb.

Kinship Badge: This item resembles an exquisite cymbal or flattened bell, measuring 3 or 4 inches across. When struck, it emits a single musical note. It also resonates and produces a distinctive ultrasonic tone when a desmodu's echolocation sounds strike it. Desmodus usually exchange kinship badges with their age-mates and use them to identify each other in battle.

Cost: 5 gp; *Weight:* —.

Notbora: This Huge exotic double weapon looks like a big quarterstaff with a crook at one end. A notbora has a hinge in the middle so that it can be folded for storage. The wielder can unfold the weapon and lock the hinge by pressing a hidden catch (a free action when drawing the notbora). The notbora's straight end is actually a sheath that can be removed to reveal a blade. The hooked end can be used to make trip attacks. A wielder who is tripped during his or her own trip attempt can drop the notbora to avoid being tripped.

Each end of the notbora deals 2d6 points of damage. The hooked end is a blunt weapon that deals double damage on a critical hit and threatens a critical hit on an attack roll of 20. With the sheath in place, the straight end functions the same way. With the sheath removed, the straight end is a slashing weapon that deals double damage on a critical hit and threatens a critical hit on an attack roll of 19 or 20.

Cost: 20 gp; *Weight:* 2 lb.

DESMODU CHARACTERS

Desmodus sometimes become barbarians or rogues, but their favored class is fighter. A desmodu fighter usually leads a colony's council of elders, and fighters also lead most warbands, in those rare cases when the desmodu join to attack a common enemy. Wizards and clerics are unknown in the race. Some desmodu sorcerers and bards exist, but most desmodu spellcasters are adepts.

Because of its many special abilities, a desmodu PC's effective character level (ECL) is equal to its class level + 14. Thus, a 1st-level desmodu fighter has an ECL of 15 and is the equivalent of a 15th-level character.

DESMODU BAT

The desmodus love bats. They breed and maintain bats of all shapes and sizes as companions, guards, and draft animals. Three unique kinds of desmodu-bred bats are described here.

COMBAT

Like other bats, these creatures fight on the wing, swooping down to bite their foes.

Blindsight (Ex): A bat emits high-frequency sounds, inaudible to most other creatures, that bounce off nearby objects and creatures. This ability enables it to discern objects and creatures within 120 feet. The bat usually does not need to make Spot or Listen checks to notice creatures within range of its blindsight. A *silence* spell negates this ability and forces the bat to rely on its weak vision, which has a range of 10 feet.

Immunities: The bats the desmodu breed are immune to the despair and stunning screech abilities of desmodus.

HUNTING BAT

The desmodu breed these bats as hunting animals, in the same way that humans breed hunting dogs. When hunting for meat animals underground, a desmodu releases one or more hunting bats. When the bat discovers prey, it calls ultrasonically to its master, then begins chasing its quarry.

A hunting bat has a body like that of an ordinary bat and a head that resembles a wolf's. Its fur is usually black or gray.

Combat

When a hunting bat swoops down on its prey, it first attempts to trip its opponent. Whether or not this tactic succeeds, the bat follows up the attempt with bite attacks. The bat then picks up any prey that it has downed in its jaws and returns with it to its master.

Trip (Ex): A hunting bat that hits with a bite attack can attempt to trip the opponent as a free action without making a touch attack or provoking an attack of opportunity. If the attempt fails, the opponent cannot react to trip the bat.

RGM

	Hunting Bat Medium-Size Animal	Guard Bat Large Animal	War Bat Huge Animal
Hit Dice:	4d8+4 (22 hp)	4d8+12 (30 hp)	10d8+50 (95 hp)
Initiative:	+7	+6	+6
Speed:	20 ft., fly 60 ft. (good)	20 ft., fly 60 ft. (good)	20 ft., fly 40 ft. (good)
AC:	20 (+7 Dex, +3 natural), touch 17, flat-footed 13	20 (−1 size, +6 Dex, +5 natural), touch 15, flat-footed 14	23 (−2 size, +6 Dex, +9 natural), touch 14, flat-footed 17
Attacks:	Bite +10	Bite +5 melee	Bite +12 melee
Damage:	Bite 1d6+3	Bite 1d8+4 plus wounding	Bite 2d6+10
Face/Reach:	5 ft. by 5 ft./5 ft.	5 ft. by 5 ft./5 ft.	10 ft. by 10 ft./10 ft.
Special Attacks:	Trip	Wounding	—
Special Qualities:	Blindsight 120 ft., immunities, scent	Blindsight 120 ft., immunities	Blindsight 120 ft., immunities
Saves:	Fort +5, Ref +11, Will +4	Fort +7, Ref +10, Will +6	Fort +12, Ref +13, Will +9
Abilities:	Str 15, Dex 24, Con 13, Int 2, Wis 16, Cha 7	Str 17, Dex 22, Con 17, Int 2, Wis 14, Cha 7	Str 25, Dex 22, Con 21, Int 2, Wis 14, Cha 7
Skills:	Hide +16, Listen +14*, Move Silently +19, Spot +14*	Listen +15*, Move Silently +11, Spot +15*	Listen +11*, Move Silently +11, Spot +11*
Feats:	Weapon Finesse (bite) (B)	Dodge (B), Mobility (B), Spring Attack (B)	—
Climate/Terrain:	Underground	Underground	Underground
Organization:	Solitary or colony (5–8)	Solitary or colony (5–8)	Solitary or colony (5–8)
Challenge Rating:	3	3	5
Treasure:	None	None	None
Alignment:	Always neutral	Always neutral	Always neutral
Advancement:	5–12 HD (Large)	5–12 HD (Huge)	11–16 HD (Huge); 17–30 HD (Gargantuan)

Scent (Ex): A hunting bat can detect approaching enemies, sniff out hidden foes, and track by sense of smell.

Skills: A hunting bat receives a +4 racial bonus on Hide checks. It also receives a +8 racial bonus on Spot and Listen checks. *These latter two bonuses are lost if its blindsight is negated.

GUARD BAT

A guard bat is nearly identical to a dire bat, except that the former is more agile, has even keener senses, and has a particularly dangerous bite. The desmodus use these creatures primarily as sentries.

A guard bat looks like a very large flying fox, except that it has long teeth, like those of a vampire bat, and shaggy fur on its head and body.

Combat

In battle, a group of guard bats typically picks out a single target and swoops in to bite. Then each guard bat uses its Spring Attack feat to bite and fly out of reach before the foe can respond.

Wounding (Ex): A guard bat's saliva contains an anticoagulant that causes bite wounds the creature inflicts to bleed freely. A wound resulting from a guard bat's bite attack bleeds for an additional 1 point of damage per round thereafter. Multiple wounds from such attacks result in cumulative bleeding loss (two wounds for 2 points of damage per round, and so on). The bleeding can be stopped only by a successful Heal check (DC 15) or the application of a *cure* spell or some other healing spell (*heal, healing circle,* or the like).

Skills: A guard bat receives a +8 racial bonus on Spot and Listen checks. *These bonuses are lost if blindsight is negated.

WAR BAT

The desmodus breed these creatures as mounts and beasts of burden. Desmodus armed with huge heavy lances sometimes ride them into battle. A war bat has a wingspan of 16 to 18 feet. Except for its size, it looks like a normal bat.

RGM

Combat

War bats seldom fight on their own unless attacked first or ordered into battle by their masters.

Skills: A war bat receives a +4 racial bonus on Spot and Listen checks. *These bonuses are lost if blindsight is negated.

	Advespa (Baatezu) Large Outsider (Evil, Lawful)	Amnizu (Baatezu) Medium-Size Outsider (Evil, Lawful)	Malebranche (Baatezu) Huge Outsider (Evil, Lawful)
Hit Dice:	4d8+12 (30 hp)	9d8+9 (49 hp)	16d8+96 (168 hp)
Initiative:	+5	+4	−1
Speed:	30 ft., fly 40 ft. (good)	30 ft., fly 60 ft. (average)	40 ft., fly 120 ft. (average)
AC:	17 (−1 size, +1 Dex, +7 natural), touch 10, flat-footed 16	21 (+11 natural), touch 10, flat-footed 21	24 (−2 size, −1 Dex, +17 natural), touch 7, flat footed 24
Attacks:	4 claws +8 melee and sting +3 melee	Touch +10 melee	Huge masterwork trident +25/+20/+15/+10 melee and gore +22 melee, or Huge masterwork trident +25/+20/+15/+10 melee and bite +22 melee, or 2 claws +24 melee and gore +22 melee, or 2 claws +24 melee and bite +22 melee
Damage:	Claw 1d6+5, sting 1d4+2 plus poison	Touch 2d4 plus feeblemind	Huge masterwork trident 2d8+15, claw 2d4+10, gore 2d6+5, bite 2d6+5
Face/Reach:	5 ft. by 5 ft./10 ft.	5 ft. by 5 ft./5 ft.	10 ft. by 10 ft./15 ft.
Special Attacks:	Improved grab, poison, spell-like abilities	Feeblemind touch, spell-like abilities, *summon baatezu*	Charge, fear aura, improved grab
Special Qualities:	Baatezu traits, DR 5/+1, outsider traits, regeneration 2, SR 15	Baatezu traits, outsider traits, regeneration 4, secure intelligence, SR 18	Baatezu traits, DR 25/+2, outsider traits, regeneration 8, SR 20
Saves:	Fort +7, Ref +5, Will +4	Fort +7, Ref +6, Will +8	Fort +16, Ref +9, Will +9
Abilities:	Str 20, Dex 13, Con 17, Int 8, Wis 11, Cha 10	Str 12, Dex 11, Con 13, Int 16, Wis 15, Cha 10	Str 30, Dex 9, Con 23, Int 10, Wis 9, Cha 10
Skills:	Hide +4, Listen +5, Move Silently +5, Search +4, Spot +7	Balance +2, Concentration +13, Diplomacy +2, Hide +12, Jump +3, Knowledge (the planes) +9, Scry +6, Search +15, Sense Motive +14, Spellcraft +15, Spot +14, Swim +7, Tumble +12	Balance +1, Bluff +12, Climb +13, Diplomacy +2, Intimidate +13, Jump +25, Listen +17, Move Silently +17, Search +18, Spot +18, Tumble +17
Feats:	Flyby Attack, Improved Initiative	Combat Casting, Improved Initiative, Quicken Spell-Like Ability	Cleave, Flyby Attack, Great Cleave, Multiattack, Power Attack
Climate/Terrain:	Any land and underground	Any land and underground	Any land and underground
Organization:	Solitary, pair, team (3–4), squad (5–10), or swarm (11–20)	Solitary, pair, team (3–4), or troupe (1–3 amnizus plus 2–4 advespas)	Solitary, pair, team (3–4), or squad (5–10)
Challenge Rating:	3	7	9
Treasure:	None	Standard	Standard
Alignment:	Always lawful evil	Always lawful evil	Always lawful evil
Advancement:	5–8 HD (Large); 9–12 HD (Huge)	10–18 HD (Medium-size); 19–27 HD (Large)	17–32 HD (Huge); 33–48 HD (Gargantuan)

Devils are fiends from the plane of Baator, a lawful evil realm. The most numerous devils are the baatezu, who are infamous for their strength, evil temperament, and ruthlessly efficient organization. These creatures are constantly in conflict with every force of good in the universe, as well as with the chaotic evil demons and tanar'ri of the Abyss.

Baatezu have a rigid caste system, in which authority derives not only from power but also from station. These creatures occupy themselves with extending their influence throughout the planes, primarily by corrupting mortals. Baatezu who further this agenda are usually rewarded with improved stations.

Most baatezu have a Gothic gargoyle look. They are grotesque and unsightly by human standards, corrupted physically by the evil they embrace. A few have an infernal sort of beauty in their natural forms, but these are rare.

The advespa, amnizu, and malebranche are vicious devils usually found in the service of more powerful baatezu, or of evil mortals who treat with such beings. These baatezu appear wherever their infernal masters send them, though the amnizus in particular are rarely deployed on other planes.

Unless otherwise noted, devils speak Infernal, Celestial, and Draconic.

COMBAT

Devils enjoy bullying those weaker than themselves, and they often attack good creatures just to gain a trophy or three. Some devils are surrounded by fear auras, which they use to break up powerful groups so that they can defeat opponents piecemeal.

The baatezu tend to use their illusion abilities to delude and confuse foes as much as possible in combat. One of their favorite tricks is to create illusory reinforcements, so that enemies can never be entirely sure whether a threat is only a figment or a group of real devils that has been summoned to join the fray.

All devils share the following traits.

Outsider Traits: A devil has darkvision (60-foot range). It cannot be raised or resurrected.

In addition, all baatezu have the following abilities in common unless otherwise stated.

Summon Baatezu (**Sp**): Most baatezu can summon other baatezu to their aid. This ability functions like a *summon monster* spell of the appropriate level, except that it has only a limited chance of success. Roll d% and compare the result with the creature's listed chance of success. On a failure, no baatezu answer the summons. Summoned creatures automatically return whence they came after 1 hour. A baatezu that has just been summoned cannot use its own summon ability for 1 hour. Most baatezu do not use their summon ability lightly, since it leaves them beholden to the summoned creatures. In general, they use it only when necessary to gain victory or to save their own lives.

Baatezu Traits: Unless otherwise noted, a baatezu can communicate telepathically with any creature within 100 feet that has a language. In addition, it can see perfectly in darkness of any kind, even that created by a *deeper darkness* spell. A baatezu is immune to fire and poison, and it has acid resistance 20 and cold resistance 20.

ADVESPA

Advespas are female, wasplike devils that patrol the skies above the infernal planes. They are often found under the command of some more powerful baatezu.

An advespa appears as a huge, heavy-bodied wasp with a female face. It has small, antennalike horns, protruding humanoid features, dripping mandibles, a chitinous hide, and a pair of dark, resilient, insect wings. Its lower abdomen terminates in a barbed, poisonous stinger, which may be brought up over the creature's head in the manner of a scorpion's tail.

The most common advespa is entirely black; in fact, it looks as if it had been carved from obsidian or some other dark stone. The more powerful advespas (those with higher stations and slightly higher Charisma scores) have striations of yellow, red, and orange, and they tend to be smaller than the common advespas. These colorful advespas usually serve as the leaders of squads and swarms.

Combat

An advespa usually attacks from above, seeking to pounce upon and grapple an opponent. If it succeeds,

it stings with its poisonous tail until its foe succumbs, then flies off with its helpless prey.

Improved Grab (Ex): If an advespa hits an opponent that is at least one size category smaller than itself with both claws, it deals normal damage and attempts to start a grapple as a free action without provoking an attack of opportunity (grapple bonus +13). If it gets a hold, it automatically hits with its sting. Thereafter, the advespa has the option to conduct the grapple normally, or simply use its claws to hold the opponent (–20 penalty on grapple check, but the advespa is not considered grappled). In either case, each successful grapple check it makes during successive rounds automatically deals damage from both claws and the sting.

Poison (Ex): The advespa injects a dose of poison (Fortitude save DC 15) with each successful sting attack. The initial and secondary damage is the same (1d4 points of Strength damage).

Spell-Like Abilities: 3/day—*change self, command, produce flame, pyrotechnics.* Caster level 4th; save DC 10 + spell level.

Regeneration (Ex): An advespa takes normal damage from acid, and also from holy weapons and blessed weapons of at least +1 enhancement.

Summon Baatezu (Sp): Once per day, an advespa can attempt to summon 1d2 additional advespas with a 30% chance of success.

AMNIZU

Amnizus are short, stocky, winged devils that serve as guardians at the gates of the Nine Hells of Baator. The typical amnizu has one or more squads of advespas at its disposal at all times.

An amnizu has an oversized, elongated head, small pig-like eyes, a pug nose, and a large, fang-filled mouth. Its wings are large and batlike.

Amnizus speak Infernal and Common.

Combat

An amnizu's task is not so much to keep interlopers out of the infernal domains as it is to ensure that, once they enter, they never escape. To that end, the creature usually softens up opponents with quickened *fireballs* and the attacks of its advespa troops before attempting to use its feeblemind touch to capture and detain its foes.

Feeblemind Touch (Su): The touch of an amnizu duplicates the effect of a *feeblemind* spell (caster level 14th; Will save DC 14).

Spell-Like Abilities: At will—*major image*; 3/day—*fireball*; 1/day—*sequester.* Caster level 14th; save DC 10 + spell level.

Regeneration (Ex): An amnizu takes normal damage from acid, and also from holy weapons and blessed weapons of at least +1 enhancement.

Secure Intelligence (Ex): An amnizu is immune to any effect that would drain, damage, or otherwise reduce its Intelligence score.

Summon Baatezu (Sp): Once per day, an amnizu may summon 1d3 advespas or 1 amnizu with a 50% chance of success.

MALEBRANCHE

Malebranches are huge, hulking devils with wickedly curving horns. These creatures usually serve other, more intelligent members of the infernal hierarchy as warriors, enforcers, punishers, and occasionally as mounts. Within the Nine Hells of Baator, malebranches are usually armed with immense masterwork tridents wrought from cold iron. These aggressive baatezu tend to bully creatures smaller than themselves and grovel before those that are more powerful.

A malebranche is a massive, winged devil of humanoid shape with an underslung jaw and huge, slightly curved horns. Its feral eyes glow with flickering shades of red.

Malebranches speak only Infernal, but they understand Common—particularly orders and curses in that language.

Combat

Malebranches are heavy hitters—the brute force among the baatezu—and they utilize their great strength to the best of their ability. A malebranche usually charges into combat on silent wings, hoping to catch its opponents flat-footed with a gore attack. Then the creature wreaks havoc with its masterwork iron trident.

Charge (Ex): A malebranche typically begins a battle with a flying charge at an opponent on the ground. In addition to the normal benefits and hazards of a charge, this tactic allows the malebranche to make a single gore attack (+24 melee) that deals 6d6+15 points of damage. The creature can also charge while moving on the ground, if it wishes.

Improved Grab (Ex): If a malebranche hits an opponent that is at least one size category smaller than itself with a claw attack, it deals normal damage and attempts to start a grapple as a free action without provoking an attack of opportunity (grapple bonus +34). The creature has the option to conduct the grapple normally, or simply use its claw to hold the opponent (–20 penalty on grapple check, but the malebranche is not considered grappled). In either case, each successful grapple check it makes during successive rounds automatically deals claw damage.

Fear Aura (Su): As a free action, a malebranche can produce a fear effect. This ability functions like a *fear* spell (caster level 12th; save DC 18), except that it affects all creatures within a 15-foot radius around the malebranche. Any creature that makes a successful saving throw against the effect cannot be affected again by that malebranche's fear aura for 24 hours. All baatezu are immune to the malebranche's fear aura.

Regeneration (Ex): A malebranche takes normal damage from acid, and also from holy and blessed weapons of at least +3 enhancement.

DINOSAUR

Dinosaurs, or terrible lizards, are ancient reptilian beasts that may be related to dragons. Among the traits that the typical predatory dinosaur shares with many dragons are sharp teeth, a savage disposition, a well-developed sense of territory, and a ruthless drive to hunt. The herbivorous dinosaurs are not usually aggressive unless wounded or defending their young, but they may attack if startled or harassed.

Dinosaurs most often live in rugged or isolated areas that humanoids seldom visit: remote mountain valleys, inaccessible plateaus, tropical islands, and the densest jungles. They may also populate a campaign's "lost lands."

COMBAT

Dinosaurs take full advantage of their size and speed. The swift carnivores stalk prey, staying hidden in cover until they can get close enough to charge. The great herbivores frequently overrun and trample their opponents.

Scent (Ex): A dinosaur can detect approaching enemies, sniff out hidden foes, and track by sense of smell.

CRYPTOCLIDUS

Cryptoclidus is a plesiosaur, a 10-foot-long aquatic reptile much like elasmosaurus (see the *Monster Manual*). Its neck isn't as long, proportionately, as that of elasmosaurus, but the two creatures have similar ovoid bodies. Cryptoclidus propels itself through the water by "flapping" four paddle-like fins. Its tail is also finned.

Combat

Cryptoclidus normally hunts fish, darting its neck into traveling schools and snapping up prey with its sharp little teeth. However, it is capable of traveling on the surface of the water and occasionally seeks larger prey.

Improved Grab (Ex): If cryptoclidus hits an opponent that is at least one size category smaller than itself with a bite attack, it deals normal damage and attempts to start a grapple as a free action without provoking an attack of opportunity (grapple bonus +10). If it gets a hold, it can try to swallow the opponent. Alternatively, the cryptoclidus has the option to conduct the grapple normally, or simply use its jaws to hold the opponent (–20 penalty on grapple check, but cryptoclidus is not considered grappled). In either case, each successful grapple check it makes during successive rounds automatically deals bite damage.

Swallow Whole (Ex): Cryptoclidus can swallow a grabbed opponent that is at least two size categories smaller than itself by making a successful grapple check (grapple bonus +10). Once inside the gullet, the opponent takes 1d8+4 points of bludgeoning damage plus 1d6+2 points of acid damage per round from the dinosaur's digestive juices. A successful grapple check allows the swallowed creature to climb out of the gullet and return to the mouth, where another successful

	Cryptoclidus Large Beast (Aquatic)	Allosaurus Huge Beast	Ankylosaurus Huge Beast
Hit Dice:	3d10+9 (25 hp)	10d10+30 (85 hp)	9d10+72 (121 hp)
Initiative:	+3	+1	−2
Speed:	Swim 60 ft.	50 ft.	20 ft.
AC:	16 (−1 size, +3 Dex. +4 natural), touch 12, flat-footed 13	14 (−2 size, +1 Dex, +5 natural); touch 9, flat-footed 13	22 (−2 size, −2 Dex, +16 natural); touch 6, flat-footed 22
Attacks:	Bite +5 melee	Bite +12 melee and 2 claws +7 melee	Tail slap +13 melee
Damage:	Bite 1d8+6	Bite 2d8+7, claw 2d4+3	Tail slap 2d6+13
Face/Reach:	5 ft. by 10 ft./10 ft.	10 ft. by 10 ft./15 ft.	10 ft. by 30 ft./10 ft.
Special Attacks:	Improved grab, swallow whole	Improved grab, rake 2d8+3, swallow whole, trample 5d8+10	Trample 2d12+13
Special Qualities:	Darkvision 60 ft., low-light vision, scent	Darkvision 60 ft., low-light vision, scent	Darkvision 60 ft., low-light vision, scent
Saves:	Fort +6, Ref +6, Will +2	Fort +10, Ref +8, Will +5	Fort +14, Ref +4, Will +2
Abilities:	Str 18, Dex 16, Con 17, Int 2, Wis 13, Cha 9	Str 24, Dex 12, Con 17, Int 2, Wis 15, Cha 11	Str 29, Dex 7, Con 26, Int 1, Wis 9, Cha 8
Skills:	Hide +4, Listen +6, Spot +6	Listen +9, Spot +10	Listen +4, Spot +4
Climate/Terrain:	Warm aquatic	Warm forest, hills, plains, and marsh	Warm forest, hills, plains, and marsh
Organization:	Solitary or school (20–40)	Solitary or pair	Solitary, pair, or herd (20–40)
Challenge Rating:	3	7	7
Treasure:	None	None	None
Alignment:	Always neutral	Always neutral	Always neutral
Advancement:	4–6 HD (Large); 7–9 HD (Huge)	11–20 HD (Huge); 21–30 HD (Gargantuan)	10–18 HD (Huge); 19–27 HD (Gargantuan)

grapple check is needed to get free. Alternatively, a swallowed creature can try to cut its way out with either claws or a light piercing or slashing weapon. Dealing at least 25 points of damage to the digestive tract (AC 20) in this way creates an opening large enough to permit escape. Once a single swallowed creature exits, muscular action closes the hole; thus, another swallowed opponent must cut its own way out. A Large cryptoclidus's gullet can hold 1 Small, 4 Tiny, or 16 Diminutive or smaller opponents.

ALLOSAURUS

Allosaurus is a big flesh-eating dinosaur that inhabits warm areas. It eats both mammals and smaller dinosaurs.

Allosaurus is 36 feet long and weighs 1 1/2 tons. A long tail balances its big head, S-shaped "bulldog" neck, and bulky body. It has powerful hind limbs with clawed feet and short, strong, three-fingered forelimbs with digits ending in impressive claws. The top of its head has bony ridges and bumps, and its jaws hold serrated, bladelike teeth.

Combat

Allosaurus eats everything it can catch. If its prey is too big to swallow whole, the dinosaur latches on with its powerful jaws and begins raking until the creature is dead.

Improved Grab (Ex): If allosaurus hits an opponent that is at least one size category smaller than itself with a bite attack, it deals normal damage and attempts to start a grapple as a free action without provoking an attack of opportunity (grapple bonus +22). If it gets a hold, it can attempt to rake in the same round, and the next round it can try to swallow the opponent. Alternatively, allosaurus has the option to conduct the grapple normally, or simply use its jaws to hold the opponent (−20 penalty on grapple check, but allosaurus is not considered grappled). In either case, each successful grapple check it makes during successive rounds automatically deals bite damage and allows another rake attempt.

Rake (Ex): On any round that allosaurus has a hold on an opponent (see Improved Grab, above), it can make two rake attacks (+12 melee) with its hind legs for 2d8+3 points of damage each. Allosaurus can also attempt to rake when it pounces on an opponent.

Swallow Whole (Ex): Allosaurus can swallow a grabbed opponent that is at least two size categories smaller than itself by making a successful grapple check (grapple bonus +22). Once inside the gullet, the opponent takes 2d8+12

points of bludgeoning damage and 1d8 points of acid damage per round from the dinosaur's digestive juices. A successful grapple check allows the swallowed creature to climb out of the gullet and return to the mouth, where another successful grapple check is needed to get free. Alternatively, a swallowed creature can try to cut its way out with either claws or a light piercing or slashing weapon. Dealing at least 25 points of damage to the digestive tract (AC 20) in this way creates an opening large enough to permit escape. Once a single swallowed creature exits, muscular action closes the hole; thus, another swallowed opponent must cut its own way out. A Huge allosaurus's gullet can hold 1 Medium-size, 4 Small, 16 Tiny, or 64 Diminutive or smaller opponents.

Trample (Ex): As a standard action during its turn each round, allosaurus can trample opponents at least one size category smaller than itself. This attack deals 5d8+10 points of bludgeoning damage. A trampled opponent can attempt either an attack of opportunity at a −4 penalty or a Reflex save (DC 22) for half damage.

ANKYLOSAURUS

Ankylosaurus is a heavily armored, quadrupedal herbivore. It is a versatile plant-eater, equally at home among temperate forests, humid marshes, and dry grasslands. These creatues sometimes travel in herds for added protection from larger predators.

The typical ankylosaurus is 25 to 35 feet in length, 4 1/2 feet tall, and 7 to 8 feet wide. A bony, armored shell covered with spikes protects its back and sides, giving the dinosaur the appearance of some infernally armored siege machine. This carapace protects the dinosaur from most attacks—indeed, those who have wounded an ankylosaurus and lived to tell the tale swear that the only way to harm the beast is to strike it on its underbelly. Its wide, flat, armored head protects a tiny brain. Its four legs are quite muscular, and it can rear up on the hind pair to reach the tender leaves of some of its favorite plants. Its heavy tail is tipped with a massive club, which the ankylosaurus can swing with devastating force and accuracy. This can cause even the most determined predator to think twice before attempting to make a meal of ankylosaurus.

Combat

Ankylosaurus rarely attacks unless it or its herd is threatened. Though it is slow to action, once this dinosaur views

another creature as an enemy, it fights until either it or its attacker is dead. In battle, it stands put, swinging its tail at any creature that comes within reach. If it takes 80 or more points of damage or finds itself cornered, it attempts to flee, trampling any creatures in its path.

Trample (Ex): As a standard action during its turn each round, ankylosaurus can trample opponents at least one size category smaller than itself. This attack deals 2d12+13 points of bludgeoning damage. A trampled opponent can attempt either an attack of opportunity at a –4 penalty or a Reflex save (DC 23) for half damage.

QUETZALCOATLUS

Technically not a dinosaur, quetzalcoatlus is a massive flying reptile. This fearsome predator glides through the skies searching for meals. Although it is not averse to eating carrion, it prefers fresh meat or fish. Quetzalcoatlus has a long neck and head, and a relatively large brain. Its "wings" are flaps of skin extended and controlled by its forelimbs and specially evolved fingers.

Combat

When hunting over water, it flies low and scoops fish and aquatic reptiles from just below the water's surface. It also attacks small land creatures when it can find them. Vulnerable to other predators while it is on the ground, quetzalcoatlus prefers to swoop down, snatch its prey in its

	Quetzalcoatlus Huge Beast	Seismosaurus Colossal Beast	Spinosaurus Gargantuan Beast
Hit Dice:	10d10+50 (105 hp)	32d10+288 (464 hp)	20d10+120 (230 hp)
Initiative:	+1	–1	+1
Speed:	20 ft., fly 100 ft. (poor)	20 ft.	40 ft.
AC:	17 (–2 size, +1 Dex, +8 natural), touch 9, flat-footed 16	11 (–8 size, –1 Dex, +10 natural), touch 1, flat-footed 11	16 (–4 size, +1 Dex, +9 natural), touch 7, flat-footed 15
Attacks:	Bite +13 melee and 2 wings +8 melee	Tail slap +31 melee	Bite +24 melee and 2 claws +19 melee
Damage:	Bite 2d10+8, wing 2d6+4	Tail slap 4d10+22	Bite 2d8+13, claw 2d6+6
Face/Reach:	35 ft. by 10 ft./10 ft.	40 ft. by 120 ft./25 ft.	20 ft. by 20 ft./20 ft.
Special Attacks:	Swallow whole	Trample 10d10+22	Frightful presence, improved grab, swallow whole, trample 2d8+19
Special Qualities:	Darkvision 60 ft., low-light vision	Darkvision 60 ft., low-light vision, scent	Darkvision 60 ft., low-light vision, scent
Saves:	Fort +12, Ref +8, Will +6	Fort +27, Ref +17, Will +12	Fort +18, Ref +13, Will +8
Abilities:	Str 26, Dex 13, Con 20, Int 2, Wis 17, Cha 11	Str 40, Dex 9, Con 29, Int 1, Wis 14, Cha 14	Str 36, Dex 13, Con 23, Int 2, Wis 15, Cha 10
Skills:	Spot +16	Listen +7, Spot +7	Listen +11, Spot +11
Feats:	Flyby Attack (B), Snatch (B)	—	—
Climate/Terrain:	Warm forests, hills, mountains	Warm forests, plains, hills, and marsh	Warm forests, plains, hills, and marsh
Organization:	Solitary, pair, or covey (3–5)	Solitary, pair, or pod (5–20)	Solitary or pair
Challenge Rating:	8	12	13
Treasure:	None	None	None
Alignment:	Always neutral	Always neutral	Always neutral
Advancement:	11–20 HD (Huge); 21–30 HD (Gargantuan)	33–64 HD (Colossal)	21–40 HD (Gargantuan); 41–60 HD (Colossal)

jaws, and then struggle to regain altitude while swallowing its catch.

Swallow Whole (Ex): Quetzalcoatlus can swallow a snatched opponent that is at least two size categories smaller than itself by making a successful grapple check (grapple bonus +23). Once inside the dinosaur, the opponent takes 1d8+4 points of bludgeoning damage and 1d4 points of acid damage per round from its gizzard. A successful grapple check allows the swallowed creature to climb out of the gizzard and return to the beak, where another successful grapple check is needed to get free. Alternatively, a swallowed creature can try to cut its way out with either claws or a light piercing or slashing weapon. Dealing at least 15 points of damage to the gizzard (AC 15) in this way creates an opening large enough to permit escape. Once a single swallowed creature exits, muscular action closes the hole; thus, another swallowed opponent must cut its own way out. A Huge quetzalcoatlus's gizzard can hold 1 Medium-size, 4 Small, 16 Tiny, or 64 Diminutive or smaller opponents.

Feats: A creature that is flung by quetzalcoatlus after being snatched travels 100 feet and takes 10d6 points of damage. If quetzalcoatlus is flying, the creature takes this damage or the appropriate falling damage, whichever is greater.

SEISMOSAURUS

Seismosaurus is the largest known of the dinosaurs. It feeds on plants, often defoliating several square miles of terrain within the course of a few weeks.

Seismosaurus is an immense four-legged dinosaur with a small head, a bulky body, and a long neck and tail. Its nostrils are located high up on its head.

Combat

Seismosaurus is simply too big to have natural enemies—it dwarfs even the likes of allosaurus and tyrannosaurus (see the *Monster Manual*). Seismosaurus is more likely to inadvertently step on an opponent than to intentionally use its tail slap attack.

Trample (Ex): As a standard action during its turn each round, seismosaurus can trample opponents at least one size category smaller than itself. This attack deals 10d10+22 points of bludgeoning damage. A trampled opponent can attempt either an attack of opportunity at a −4 penalty or a Reflex save (DC 41) for half damage.

SPINOSAURUS

Spinosaurus is the largest bipedal predatory dinosaur, towering over even tyrannosaurus. It has longer arms than the latter, and it occasionally moves about on all fours. Spinosaurus also has a large, saillike, ribbed fin on its back. The purpose of this appendage is unclear, but spinosaurus has a relatively flexible spine, so when it arches its back, the sail spreads. Spinosaurus has a large head with sharp, straight, nonserrated teeth set into a powerful, crocodilelike lower jaw.

Combat

Though capable of running down prey, spinosaurus prefers to freeze opponents in their places with an unearthly, soul-searing bellow. When it must chase prey, it tramples smaller creatures and grabs larger ones with its powerful jaws while tearing with its claws.

Frightful Presence (Ex): When a spinosaurus bellows (a standard action), it inspires terror in all creatures within 30 feet that have fewer Hit Dice or levels than it has. Each potentially affected opponent must succeed at a Will save (DC 20) or become shaken for 5d6 rounds. A successful save leaves that opponent immune to that spinosaurus's frightful presence for 24 hours.

Improved Grab (Ex): If spinosaurus hits an opponent that is at least one size category smaller than itself with a bite attack, it deals normal damage and attempts to start a grapple as a free action without provoking an attack of opportunity (grapple bonus +40). If it gets a hold, it can try to swallow the opponent in the next round. Alternatively, spinosaurus has the option to conduct the grapple normally, or simply use its jaws to hold the opponent (−20 penalty on grapple check, but spinosaurus is not considered grappled). In either case, each successful grapple check it makes during successive rounds automatically deals bite damage.

Swallow Whole (Ex): Spinosaurus can swallow a grabbed opponent that is at least two size categories smaller than itself by making a successful grapple check (grapple bonus +40). Once inside the gullet, the opponent takes 2d8+10 points of bludgeoning damage plus 1d8+4 points of acid damage per round from the dinosaur's digestive juices. A successful grapple check allows the swallowed creature to climb out of the gullet and return to the mouth, where

another successful grapple check is needed to get free. Alternatively, a swallowed creature can try to cut its way out with either claws or a light piercing or slashing weapon. Dealing at least 25 points of damage to the digestive tract (AC 20) in this way creates an opening large enough to permit escape. Once a single swallowed creature exits, muscular action closes the hole; thus, another swallowed opponent must cut its own way out. A Gargantuan spinosaurus's gullet can hold 2 Large, 8 Medium-size, 32 Small, or 128 Tiny or smaller opponents.

Trample (Ex): As a standard action during its turn each round, spinosaurus can trample opponents at least one size category smaller than itself. This attack deals 2d8+19 points of bludgeoning damage. A trampled opponent can attempt either an attack of opportunity at a –4 penalty or a Reflex save (DC 33) for half damage.

Skills: Spinosaurus receives a +2 racial bonus on Listen and Spot checks.

DIRE ANIMAL

Dire animals are larger, tougher, and meaner versions of normal animals. They tend to have a feral, prehistoric look.

COMBAT

Dire animals are fierce fighters that prefer melee combat. They are territorial, attacking anything that enters their territory or threatens their lairs.

Saving Throws: A dire animal has all good saves.

DIRE TOAD

These amphibians are generally shy and nonagressive. They usually aren't dangerous to humanoids.

Combat

Though dire toads are not prone to fighting, they do bite if disturbed. A dire toad's tongue attack has a range of 10 feet with no range increment.

Poison (Ex): A dire toad delivers its poison (Fortitude save DC 14) with each successful bite attack. The initial and secondary damage is the same (1d6 points of Constitution damage).

Improved Grab (Ex): If a dire toad hits an opponent that is at least one size category smaller than itself with a bite attack or a tongue attack, it deals normal damage and attempts to start a grapple as a free action without provoking an attack of opportunity (grapple bonus +3). If it gets a hold, it can try to swallow the opponent. Alternatively, the dire toad has the option to conduct the grapple normally, or simply use its jaws to hold the opponent (–20 penalty on grapple check, but the dire toad is not considered grappled). In either case, each successful grapple check it makes during successive rounds automatically deals bite damage.

Swallow Whole (Ex): A dire toad can swallow a grabbed opponent that is at least one size category smaller than itself by making a successful grapple check (grapple bonus +3). Once inside the toad, the opponent takes 1d6 points of bludgeoning damage plus 1d4 points of acid damage per round from the dire toad's stomach. A successful grapple check allows the swallowed creature to climb out of the stomach and return to the toad's mouth, where another successful grapple check is needed to get free. Alternatively, a swallowed creature can try to cut its way out with either claws or a light piercing or slashing weapon. Dealing at least 10 points of damage to the gizzard (AC 13) in this way creates an opening large enough to permit escape. Once a single swallowed creature exits, muscular action closes the hole; thus, another swallowed opponent must cut its own way out. A Medium-size dire toad's stomach can hold 2 Small or 8 Tiny or smaller opponents.

Skills: A dire toad receives a +4 racial bonus on Hide, Listen, and Spot checks, and a +8 racial bonus on Jump checks.

DIRE HAWK

This bird of prey is capable of taking down pigs, sheep, and even the occasional small horse. The dire hawk prefers high, remote nesting spots.

A typical dire hawk is about 5 feet long and has a wingspan of about 11 feet. The upper part of its beak has a bony protrusion, and several long feathers trail gracefully from its lower body and tail.

Skills: *A dire hawk receives a +8 racial bonus on Spot checks in daylight.

DIRE SNAKE

The dire snake combines the strength and power of a constrictor with the venomous bite of a viper.

The dire snake looks like an enormous viper with dull green or brown scales and long fangs. Its head has two bony protrusions similar to horns placed just behind the eyes.

Combat

Constrict (Ex): With a successful grapple check, a dire snake can constrict a grabbed opponent, dealing 1d8+10 points of bludgeoning damage.

Poison (Ex): A dire snake delivers its poison (Fortitude save DC 16) with each successful bite attack. The initial and secondary damage is the same (1d6 points of Constitution damage).

Improved Grab (Ex): If a dire snake hits an opponent that is at least one size category smaller than itself with a bite attack, it deals normal damage and attempts to start a

	Dire Horse Large Animal	Dire Elk Huge Animal	Dire Elephant Gargantuan Animal
Hit Dice:	8d8+48 (84 hp)	12d8+60 (114 hp)	20d8+200 (290 hp)
Initiative:	+1	+0	+0
Speed:	60 ft.	50 ft.	30 ft., climb 10 ft.
AC:	16 (−1 size, +1 Dex, +6 natural), touch 10, flat-footed 15	15 (−2 size, +7 natural), touch 8, flat-footed 15	10 (−4 size, +4 natural), touch 6, flat-footed 10
Attacks:	2 hooves +11 melee and bite +6 melee	Slam +14 melee and 2 hooves +9 melee, or gore +14 melee	Slam +26 melee and 2 stamps +21 melee, or gore +26 melee
Damage:	Hoof 1d6+6, bite 1d4+3	Slam 2d6+7, hoof 2d4+3, gore 2d8+10	Slam 2d8+15, stamp 2d8+7, gore 4d6+22
Face/Reach:	5 ft. by 10 ft./5 ft.	10 ft. by 20 ft./10 ft.	20 ft. by 40 ft./10 ft.
Special Attacks:	—	Trample 2d8+10	Trample 4d6+22
Special Qualities:	Low-light vision, scent	Low-light vision, scent	Low-light vision, scent
Saves:	Fort +12, Ref +7, Will +8	Fort +13, Ref +8, Will +8	Fort +22, Ref +12, Will +14
Abilities:	Str 22, Dex 13, Con 22, Int 2, Wis 15, Cha 11	Str 24, Dex 11, Con 20, Int 2, Wis 11, Cha 7	Str 40, Dex 11, Con 30, Int 2, Wis 15, Cha 7
Skills:	Listen +8, Spot +8	Listen +6, Spot +6	Climb +23, Listen +8, Spot +8
Climate/Terrain:	Any land	Temperate and cold forest, hills, and mountains	Warm forest and plains
Organization:	Solitary or herd (6–30)	Solitary or herd (6–30)	Solitary or herd (6–30)
Challenge Rating:	4	7	10
Treasure:	None	None	None
Alignment:	Always neutral	Always neutral	Always neutral
Advancement:	9–16 HD (Large); 17–24 HD (Huge)	13–16 HD (Huge); 17–36 HD (Gargantuan)	21–30 HD (Gargantuan); 31–45 HD (Colossal)

grapple as a free action without provoking an attack of opportunity (grapple bonus +20). If it gets a hold, it can also constrict in the same round. Thereafter, the dire snake has the option to conduct the grapple normally, or simply use its jaws to hold the opponent (−20 penalty on grapple check, but the dire snake is not considered grappled). In either case, each successful grapple check it makes during successive rounds automatically deals bite and constrict damage.

Scent (Ex): A dire snake can detect approaching enemies, sniff out hidden foes, and track by sense of smell.

Skills: A dire snake receives a +4 racial bonus on Hide, Listen, and Spot checks, and a +8 racial bonus on Balance checks.

DIRE HORSE

These aggressive, wild equines roam the wilderness in herds. Dire horses resist domestication as much as any wild animal does.

A dire horse looks like a large version of a normal horse except for the bony plates on either side of its head. A dire horse's hooves often have jagged edges, and its mane tends to be shaggy.

Combat

A dire horse usually lashes out with its hooves and follows up with a bite attack. It can fight while carrying a rider, but the rider cannot also attack unless he or she succeeds at a Ride check (DC 10).

Carrying Capacity: A light load for a dire horse is up to 519 pounds; a medium load is 520–1,038 pounds; and a heavy load is 1,039–1,557 pounds. A dire horse can drag 7,785 pounds.

Scent (Ex): A dire horse can detect approaching enemies, sniff out hidden foes, and track by sense of smell.

DIRE ELK

A bull dire elk is an imposing and aggressive beast. Females are less aggressive

	Dire Toad Medium-Size Animal	Dire Hawk Medium-Size Animal	Dire Snake Huge Animal
Hit Dice:	4d8+8 (26 hp)	5d8+10 (32 hp)	7d8+21 (52 hp)
Initiative:	+2	+6	+5
Speed:	30 ft.	10 ft., fly 80 ft. (average)	30 ft., climb 20 ft., swim 20 ft.
AC:	15 (+2 Dex, +3 natural), touch 12, flat-footed 13	19 (+6 Dex, +3 natural), touch 16, flat-footed 13	18 (−2 size, +5 Dex, +5 natural), touch 13, flat-footed 13
Attacks:	Bite +5 melee, or tongue +5 ranged	2 claws +9 melee and bite +4 melee	Bite +10 melee
Damage:	Bite 1d4 plus poison, tongue —	Claw 1d4+1, bite 1d6	Bite 2d6 +10 plus poison
Face/Reach:	5 ft. by 5 ft./5 ft.	5 ft. by 5 ft./5 ft.	10 ft. by 10 ft. (coiled)/10 ft.
Special Attacks:	Poison	—	Constrict 1d6+10, improved grab, poison
Special Qualities:	Low-light vision	Low-light vision	Low-light vision, scent
Saves:	Fort +6, Ref +6, Will +6	Fort +6, Ref +10, Will +6	Fort +8, Ref +10, Will +6
Abilities:	Str 10, Dex 14, Con 15, Int 2, Wis 15, Cha 7	Str 12, Dex 22, Con 15, Int 2, Wis 15, Cha 11	Str 24, Dex 20, Con 16, Int 1, Wis 13, Cha 11
Skills:	Hide +12, Jump +11, Listen + 7, Spot +11	Listen +8, Move Silently +8, Spot +8*	Balance +14, Climb +15, Hide +7, Listen +9, Spot +9
Feats:	Weapon Finesse (bite) (B)	Weapon Finesse (bite) (B), Weapon Finesse (claw) (B)	—
Climate/Terrain:	Temperate and warm land, aquatic, and underground	Any forest, hill, plains, and mountains	Temperate and warm land, aquatic, and underground
Organization:	Solitary or swarm (10–100)	Solitary or pair	Solitary
Challenge Rating:	3	2	5
Treasure:	None	None	None
Alignment:	Always neutral	Always neutral	Always neutral
Advancement:	5–6 HD (Medium-size); 7–10 HD (Large)	5–8 HD (Medium-size); 9–12 HD (Large)	8–12 HD (Huge); 13–16 HD (Gargantuan)

than males, but a cow dire elk is still formidable when her calves are threatened.

A dire elk has dark-colored, shaggy hair covering its body. The bull's enormous antlers can span up to 12 feet, and he can weigh up to 3 tons. In the spring, he sheds his antlers, so his gore attack is not available until he regrows them the following autumn. A female is not antlered, so she never has access to a gore attack.

Combat

If a bull dire elk believes himself challenged, he tries to drive off the interloper by bellowing loudly and pawing the ground. If that doesn't work, he charges with his head lowered to deliver a vicious gore with his oversized antlers, then follows up with trample attacks.

Trample (Ex): As a standard action during its turn each round, a dire elk can trample opponents at least one size category smaller than itself. This attack deals 2d8+10 points of bludgeoning damage. A trampled opponent can attempt either an attack of opportunity at a −4 penalty or a Reflex save (DC 23) for half damage.

Scent (Ex): A dire elk can detect approaching enemies, sniff out hidden foes, and track by sense of smell.

Skills: A dire elk receives a +4 racial bonus on Hide checks.

DIRE ELEPHANT

These titanic herbivores are somewhat unpredictable and moody. Giants sometimes use dire elephants as mounts or beasts of burden.

A dire elephant is a much larger version of a normal elephant, with bony plates armoring its spine and huge, vicious tusks. Its eyes are small and mean.

Combat

A dire elephant attacks by slamming opponents with its massive trunk, then stamping them into the ground. When there are several opponents, it usually attempts to trample them.

Trample (Ex): As a standard action during its turn each round, a dire elephant can trample opponents at least one size category smaller than itself. This attack deals 4d6+22 points of bludgeoning damage. A trampled opponent can attempt either an attack of opportunity at a −4 penalty or a Reflex save (DC 35) for half damage.

Scent (Ex): A dire elephant can detect approaching enemies, sniff out hidden foes, and track by sense of smell.

DRAGON, GEM

Gem dragons are a subcategory of dragons that spend much of their time on the Inner Planes. All are psionically powerful, although to most observers their psychic talents are indistinguishable from sorcery. Gem dragons tend to be aloof, solitary, and self-centered.

All dragons become more powerful as they age. They range in length from several feet upon hatching to more than 100 feet after attaining the status of great wyrm.

DRAGON AGE CATEGORIES

	Category	Age (Years)
1	Wyrmling	0–5
2	Very young	6–15
3	Young	16–25
4	Juvenile	26–50
5	Young adult	51–100
6	Adult	101–200
7	Mature adult	201–400
8	Old	401–600
9	Very old	601–800
10	Ancient	801–1,000
11	Wyrm	1,001–1,200
12	Great wyrm	1,201+

Living primarily on the Inner Planes, gem dragons have developed unusual diets. While they enjoy variety in their meals, they can survive indefinitely by consuming elemental matter. The gem dragons are not native to the Inner Planes, and all kinds of gem dragons can be found on all the planes, but they do have favored environments.

Like all dragons, gem dragons are incredibly covetous. They hoard wealth, collecting mounds of coins and gathering as many gems, jewels, and magic items as possible. Those with large hoards become slightly paranoid, venturing out of their lairs only to patrol the immediate area or to get food. For dragons, there is never enough treasure: It's pleasing to look at, and they bask in its radiance. Dragons like to make beds of their hoards, shaping nooks and mounds to fit their bodies. By the time a dragon matures to the great wyrm stage, hundreds of gems and coins are embedded in its hide.

All dragons speak Draconic.

SIZE

A dragon's face and reach increase with its size according to the Dragon Face and Reach table, below.

DRAGON FACE AND REACH

Size	Face	Reach
Tiny	2 1/2 ft. by 2 1/2 ft.	5 ft.*
Small	5 ft. by 5 ft.	5 ft.
Medium-size	5 ft. by 5 ft.	5 ft.
Large	5 ft. by 10 ft.	10 ft.*
Huge	10 ft. by 20 ft.	10 ft.
Gargantuan	20 ft. by 40 ft.	15 ft.
Colossal	40 ft. by 80 ft.	15 ft.

*Greater than normal reach for a creature of this size.

COMBAT

At its younger ages, a dragon attacks with its powerful claws and bite. As it grows older and larger, it acquires other attack forms as well (see Dragon Attacks, below). In addition, it can use a breath weapon, and it may also have access to various special abilities specific to its kind (see individual descriptions).

A dragon usually prefers to fight on the wing, staying out of reach until it has worn down the enemy with ranged attacks. Older, more intelligent dragons are adept at sizing up the opposition and eliminating the most dangerous foes first—or avoiding them while it picks off weaker enemies.

The table below describes the physical attacks a dragon gains as it grows larger. The last two rows of the table give the attack modifiers and damage modifiers for each attack. The dragon gets its full attack bonus for its bite, which is always its primary attack. Claw, wing, and tail slap attacks are all secondary, so these are made at a –5 penalty. Crush and tail sweep are special attacks that do not require attack rolls (see below). To determine the damage bonus for each attack, multiply the value given in the last row by the dragon's Str bonus.

DRAGON ATTACKS

Size	Bite	Claw	Wing	Tail Slap	Crush	Tail Sweep
Tiny	1d4	1d3	—	—	—	—
Small	1d6	1d4	—	—	—	—
Medium-size	1d8	1d6	1d4	—	—	—
Large	2d6	1d8	1d6	1d8	—	—
Huge	2d8	2d6	1d8	2d6	2d8	—
Gargantuan	4d6	2d8	2d6	2d8	4d6	2d6
Colossal	4d8	4d6	2d8	4d6	4d8	2d8
Attack Bonus	full	–5	–5	–5	Reflex save	Reflex save
Damage Bonus	×1	×0.5	×0.5	×1.5	×1.5	×1.5

Bite: A dragon can also use its bite to snatch opponents (see the Snatch feat description in the introduction).

Claw: A dragon can also use its claws to snatch opponents (see the Snatch feat description in the introduction).

Wing: A dragon can slam opponents with its wings, even when flying.

Tail Slap: A dragon can slap one opponent each round with its tail.

Crush: A flying or jumping dragon of at least Huge size can land on opponents three or more size categories smaller than itself as a standard action, using its whole body to crush them. (Of course, it can still attempt normal overrun or grapple attacks against larger opponents.) A crush attack affects as many creatures as can fit under the dragon's body (see Dragon Face and Reach Table, above). Each creature in the affected area must succeed at a Reflex save (DC 10 + 1/2 dragon's HD + dragon's Constitution modifier) or be pinned, automatically taking the listed amount of bludgeoning damage. Thereafter, if the dragon chooses to maintain the

pin, treat it as a normal grapple attack. While pinned, the opponent takes crush damage each round.

Tail Sweep: A dragon of at least Gargantuan size can sweep with its tail as a standard action. The sweep affects creatures four or more size categories smaller than the dragon within a half-circle (diameter 30 feet for a Gargantuan dragon or 40 feet for a Colossal dragon), centered on the dragon's rear. Each affected creature that fails a Reflex save (DC 10 + 1/2 dragon's HD + dragon's Constitution modifier) takes the listed damage; a successful save halves the damage.

Grappling: Dragons do not favor grapple attacks, though their crush attacks and the Snatch feat (see the introduction) use normal grapple rules.

If grappled by a creature the same size category as itself or larger, a dragon can return the attack with its bite and all four legs (the rear legs deal claw damage). If snatched or crushed by a larger dragon, a dragon can respond only with grapple attacks to try winning free, or with bite or breath weapon attacks. If grappled by a creature smaller than itself, the dragon can respond with any of its physical attacks other than a tail sweep.

A dragon can always use its breath weapon while grappling, as well as its spell-like or supernatural abilities, provided it succeeds at a Concentration check.

Breath Weapon (Su): Using a breath weapon is a standard action. Once a dragon breathes, it must wait 1d4 rounds to do so again. A blast from a breath weapon always starts at the dragon's mouth and extends in a direction of its choice, with an area as noted below. If the breath weapon deals damage, each creature caught in the area can attempt a Reflex save (DC 10 + 1/2 dragon's HD + dragon's Charisma modifier; see individual entries for specific DCs) to take half damage. Saves against nondamaging breath weapons use the same DCs, but the types vary as noted in the variety descriptions.

Breath weapons come in two basic shapes: line and cone. The areas vary with the dragon's size, as shown on the table below.

DRAGON BREATH WEAPONS

Dragon Size	Line* (Length)	Cone** (Length)
Tiny	30 ft.	15 ft.
Small	40 ft.	20 ft.
Medium-size	60 ft.	30 ft.
Large	80 ft.	40 ft.
Huge	100 ft.	50 ft.
Gargantuan	120 ft.	60 ft.
Colossal	140 ft.	70 ft.

*A line is always 5 feet high and 5 feet wide.
**A cone is as high and wide as its length.

Frightful Presence (Ex): A young adult or older dragon can unsettle foes with its mere presence. The ability takes effect automatically whenever the dragon attacks, charges, or flies overhead. Creatures within a radius of 30 feet × the dragon's age category are subject to the effect if they have fewer HD than the dragon.

A potentially affected creature that succeeds at a Will save (DC 10 + 1/2 dragon's HD + dragon's Charisma modifier) remains immune to that dragon's frightful presence for 24 hours. On a failure, a creature with 4 or fewer Hit Dice becomes panicked for 4d6 rounds; one with 5 or more Hit Dice becomes shaken for 4d6 rounds. Dragons ignore the frightful presence of other dragons.

Special Abilities: A gem dragon's special abilities depend on its age and kind. It gains the abilities given for its age category plus all previous ones. The save DC is 10 + dragon's Charisma modifier + spell level.

Psionics (Sp): All gem dragons have psionic abilities, as given in their descriptive text. (When using the *Psionics Handbook*, treat a gem dragon's spell resistance as power resistance.)

Blindsight (Ex): A dragon can ascertain its surroundings by nonvisual means (mostly hearing and scent, but also by noticing vibration and other environmental clues). This ability enables it to discern objects and creatures within a range of 30 feet × the dragon's age category. The dragon usually does not need to make Spot or Listen checks to notice creatures within range of its blindsight.

Immunities (Ex): All dragons are immune to *sleep* and paralysis effects. Each kind of dragon is immune to one or two additional forms of attack no matter what its age, as given in its description.

Keen Senses (Ex): A dragon sees four times as well as a human in low-light conditions and twice as well in normal light. It also has darkvision with a range of 100 feet × the dragon's age category.

Skills: Every dragon starts with 6 skill points per Hit Die, plus bonus points equal to its Intelligence modifier × HD. The following skills are class skills for all dragons: Bluff, Concentration, Diplomacy, Escape Artist, Knowledge (any), Listen, Scry, Spot, and Search. Dragons cannot gain skills that are exclusive to a class.

Feats: Each dragon has one feat, plus an additional feat per 4 HD. Dragons favor Alertness, Cleave (claw or tail slap attacks only), Improved Initiative, Power Attack, Sunder, and Weapon Focus (claw or bite). They can also choose from the following feats, all of which are described in the Creature Feats sidebar in the introduction of this book: Ability Focus, Flyby Attack, Hover, Quicken Spell-Like Ability, Snatch, and Wingover.

Hover: If a dragon hovers close to the ground in an area with lots of loose debris, the draft from its wings creates a hemispherical cloud with a radius of 30 feet × the dragon's age category.

Snatch: A creature that is flung by a gem dragon after being snatched travels 10 feet and takes 1d6 points of damage per age category. If the dragon is flying, the creature takes this damage or the appropriate falling damage, whichever is greater.

Planar Travel (Su): Gem dragons have the innate ability to pass instantly between the Material Plane and the Inner Planes, where they often make their homes.

Resistances (Ex): Unless otherwise noted in an individual dragon's description, each gem dragon has fire resistance 30.

Movement: Each gem dragon has a swim speed and a burrow speed, in addition to being able to fly. Only the topaz dragon can breathe underwater, so the others are limited to surface areas—although older dragons can hold their breath for very long periods.

AMETHYST DRAGON

Dragon (Earth)

Climate/Terrain: Inner Planes, underground

Organization: Wyrmling, very young, young, juvenile, and young adult: solitary or clutch (2–5); adult, mature adult, old, very old, ancient, wyrm, or great wyrm: solitary, pair, or family (1–2 plus 2–5 offspring)

Challenge Ratings: Wyrmling 3; very young 4; young 6; juvenile 8; young adult 11; adult 14; mature adult 16; old 18; very old 19; ancient 21; wyrm 23; great wyrm 25

Treasure: Double standard

Alignment: Always neutral

Advancement: Wyrmling 7–8 HD (Small); very young 10–11 HD (Medium-size); young 13–14 HD (Medium-size); juvenile 16–17 HD (Large); young adult 19–20 HD (Large); adult 22–23 HD (Huge); mature adult 25–26 HD (Huge); old 28–29 HD (Huge); very old 31–32 HD (Huge); ancient 34–35 HD (Gargantuan); wyrm 37–38 HD (Gargantuan); great wyrm 40+ HD (Gargantuan)

Amethyst dragons are wise and regal. They sometimes serve as intermediaries between warring dragons, or even humanoid civilizations.

An amethyst dragon has lavender skin and scales that are shaped like naturally formed mineral crystals. When it first hatches, its scales are a light, translucent purple shade. As it grows older, they gradually darken and take on a crystalline quality.

Most amethyst dragons live in hollowed-out spaces on the Elemental Plane of Earth. These caverns can consist of many passages and chambers resplendent with crystals of all colors.

Combat

Younger amethyst dragons avoid combat by flying away if possible. Older ones use their special abilities, such as *invisibility*, to improve their chances of catching a target flat-footed. Even adults flee if it is obvious after the first few rounds of combat that they cannot overpower their opposition.

If an amethyst dragon is fighting to protect its lair or its young, however, it seldom flees a battle. A younger one uses its spell-like abilities, breath weapon, feats that are usable when flying, and any magic items it owns, while an older and larger one uses grapple, snatch, and crush attacks to even the odds.

AMETHYST DRAGONS BY AGE

Age	Size	Hit Dice (hp)	Str	Dex	Con	Int	Wis	Cha	Attack Bonus	Fort Save	Ref Save	Will Save	Breath Weapon (DC)	Frightful Presence DC	SR
Wyrmling	S	6d12+6 (45)	13	12	13	10	11	10	+8	+6	+5	+5	2d8 (14)	—	—
Very young	M	9d12+18 (76)	15	12	15	10	11	10	+11	+8	+6	+6	4d8 (16)	—	—
Young	M	12d12+24 (102)	17	12	15	12	13	12	+15	+10	+8	+9	6d8 (18)	—	—
Juvenile	L	15d12+45 (142)	19	12	17	14	15	14	+18	+12	+9	+11	8d8 (20)	—	—
Young adult	L	18d12+72 (189)	23	12	19	14	15	14	+23	+15	+11	+13	10d8 (23)	21	19
Adult	H	21d12+105 (241)	27	12	21	16	17	16	+27	+17	+12	+15	12d8 (25)	23	21
Mature adult	H	24d12+120 (276)	29	12	21	16	17	16	+31	+19	+14	+17	14d8 (27)	25	22
Old	H	27d12+162 (337)	31	12	23	18	19	18	+35	+21	+15	+19	16d8 (29)	27	24
Very old	H	30d12+180 (375)	33	12	23	18	19	18	+39	+23	+17	+21	18d8 (31)	29	25
Ancient	G	33d12+231 (445)	35	12	25	20	21	20	+41	+25	+18	+23	20d8 (33)	31	27
Wyrm	G	36d12+280 (507)	37	12	27	20	21	20	+44	+27	+20	+24	22d8 (35)	33	29
Great wyrm	G	39d12+312 (565)	39	12	27	22	23	22	+49	+29	+22	+27	24d8 (37)	35	31

AMETHYST DRAGON ABILITIES BY AGE

Age	Speed	Initiative	AC	Special Abilities	Caster Level
Wyrmling	40 ft., fly 100 ft. (average), burrow 20 ft., swim 10 ft.	+1	17 (+1 size, +5 natural, +1 Dex), touch 12, flat-footed 16	Force resistant, planar travel, poison immunity	—
Very young	40 ft., fly 150 ft. (poor), burrow 20 ft., swim 10 ft.	+1	19 (+8 natural, +1 Dex), touch 11, flat-footed 18		—
Young	40 ft., fly 150 ft. (poor), burrow 20 ft., swim 10 ft.	+1	22 (+11 natural, +1 Dex), touch 11, flat-footed 21		—
Juvenile	40 ft., fly 150 ft. (poor), burrow 20 ft., swim 10 ft.	+1	24 (−1 size, +14 natural, +1 Dex), touch 10, flat-footed 23	Stomp	1st
Young adult	40 ft., fly 150 ft. (poor), burrow 20 ft., swim 10 ft.	+1	27 (−1 size, +17 natural, +1 Dex), touch 10, flat-footed 26	DR 5/+1	3rd
Adult	40 ft., fly 150 ft. (poor), burrow 20 ft., swim 10 ft.	+1	29 (−2 size, +20 natural, +1 Dex), touch 9, flat-footed 28	*Explosive gem* (5d6), *invisibility*	5th
Mature adult	40 ft., fly 150 ft. (poor), burrow 20 ft., swim 10 ft.	+1	32 (−2 size, +23 natural, +1 Dex), touch 9, flat-footed 31	DR 10/+1	7th
Old	40 ft., fly 150 ft. (poor), burrow 20 ft., swim 10 ft.	+1	35 (−2 size, +26 natural, +1 Dex), touch 9, flat-footed 34	*Body equilibrium, explosive gem* (9d6)	9th
Very old	40 ft., fly 150 ft. (poor), burrow 20 ft., swim 10 ft.	+1	38 (−2 size, +29 natural, +1 Dex), touch 9, flat-footed 37	DR 15/+2	11th
Ancient	40 ft., fly 200 ft. (clumsy), burrow 20 ft., swim 10 ft.	+1	39 (−4 size, +32 natural, +1 Dex), touch 7, flat-footed 38	*Explosive gem* (13d6), *suggestion*	13th
Wyrm	40 ft., fly 200 ft. (clumsy), burrow 20 ft., swim 10 ft.	+1	42 (−4 size, +35 natural, +1 Dex), touch 7, flat-footed 41	DR 20/+3	15th
Great wyrm	40 ft., fly 200 ft. (clumsy), burrow 20 ft., swim 10 ft.	+1	45 (−4 size, +38 natural, +1 Dex), touch 7, flat-footed 44	*Amethyst telekinesis*	17th

Breath Weapon (Su): An amethyst dragon has one breath weapon, a line of concussive force. It can choose to deal subdual damage instead of normal damage.

Explosive Gem **(Sp):** Once per day, an amethyst dragon can spit a violet, crystalline lozenge up to 75 feet away with pinpoint accuracy. The gem explodes on impact, dealing bludgeoning damage to all creatures within a 20-foot radius. A target that succeeds at a Reflex saving throw (DC 17 + dragon's age category) takes half damage.

Amethyst Telekinesis **(Sp):** Once per day, an amethyst great wyrm can use a *telekinesis* effect. With this ability, it can lift up to 10 tons or hurl a Large or smaller creature against another object. The impact deals 20d6 points of damage to a Large creature, 15d6 to a Medium-size one, 10d6 to a Small one, 5d6 to a Tiny one, or 1d6 to a Diminutive or Fine creature.

Force Resistant (Ex): An amethyst dragon gains a +4 bonus on saving throws against force-based effects such as *magic missile*.

Stomp (Su): By stamping its foot, an amethyst dragon precipitates a shock wave that travels along the ground, toppling creatures and loose objects within 20 feet. The area is conelike and extends beneath the surface of the ground. (Any creatures above the surface are not affected.) Any creature standing in the area that fails its Reflex save (DC 10 + 1/2 dragon's Hit Dice + dragon's Strength modifier) is thrown to the ground and takes 1d4 points of subdual damage. This ability is usable three times per day. (When using the *Psionics Handbook*, replace this ability with the psionic power *stomp*.)

Body Equilibrium **(Sp):** Once per day, the dragon can adjust its body equilibrium to correspond with any solid or liquid. Thus, it can walk on water, quicksand, or even a spider's web without sinking or breaking through. (This does not confer any resistance to particularly sticky webs.) Movement is at normal speed, but running on a fragile, mushy, or liquid surface requires a Dexterity check (DC 10 or more, depending on the surface) to avoid breaking through. Falling damage is halved while this power is in effect. Body equilibrium lasts 1 minute per age category. (When using the *Psionics Handbook*, replace this ability with the psionic power *body equilibrium*.)

Psionics **(Sp):** 1/day— *invisibility, suggestion.* Caster (or manifester) level varies by age; save DC 10 + dragon's Charisma modifier + spell (or power) level.

Attack/Defense Modes: ego whip/mental barrier. An amethyst dragon manifests powers, and gains additional attack and defense modes, as if it were a psion with Psychokinesis as its primary discipline.

Age	Size	Hit Dice (hp)	Str	Dex	Con	Int	Wis	Cha	Attack Bonus	Fort Save	Ref Save	Will Save	Breath Weapon (DC)	Frightful Presence DC	SR
Wyrmling	S	5d12+5 (37)	13	10	13	10	11	11	+7	+5	+4	+4	2d6 (13)	—	—
Very young	M	8d12+16 (68)	15	10	15	10	11	11	+10	+8	+6	+6	4d6 (16)	—	—
Young	M	11d12+22 (93)	17	10	15	12	13	13	+14	+9	+7	+8	6d6 (17)	—	—
Juvenile	L	14d12+42 (133)	19	10	17	14	15	15	+17	+12	+9	+11	8d6 (20)	—	—
Young adult	L	17d12+68 (178)	23	10	19	14	15	15	+22	+14	+10	+12	10d6 (22)	20	19
Adult	H	20d12+100 (230)	27	10	21	16	17	17	+26	+17	+12	+15	12d6 (25)	23	21
Mature adult	H	23d12+115 (264)	29	10	21	16	17	17	+30	+18	+13	+16	14d6 (26)	24	22
Old	H	26d12+156 (325)	31	10	23	18	19	19	+34	+21	+15	+19	16d6 (29)	27	24
Very old	H	29d12+174 (362)	33	10	23	18	19	19	+38	+22	+16	+20	18d6 (30)	28	25
Ancient	G	32d12+224 (432)	35	10	25	20	21	21	+40	+25	+18	+23	20d6 (33)	31	27
Wyrm	G	35d12+280 (507)	37	10	27	20	21	21	+44	+27	+19	+24	22d6 (35)	32	28
Great wyrm	G	38d12+304 (551)	39	10	27	22	23	21	+48	+29	+21	+27	24d6 (37)	34	30

CRYSTAL DRAGON

Dragon (Air)

Climate/Terrain: Inner Planes, temperate and cold mountains

Organization: Wyrmling, very young, young, juvenile, and young adult: solitary or clutch (2–5); adult, mature adult, old, very old, ancient, wyrm, or great wyrm: solitary, pair, or family (1–2 plus 2–5 offspring)

Challenge Ratings: Wyrmling 2; very young 3; young 4; juvenile 7; young adult 10; adult 12; mature adult 15; old 17; very old 18; ancient 20; wyrm 21; great wyrm 23

Treasure: Double standard

Alignment: Always chaotic neutral

Advancement: Wyrmling 6–7 HD (Small); very young 9–10 HD (Medium-size); young 12–13 HD (Medium-size); juvenile 15–16 HD (Large); young adult 18–19 HD (Large); adult 21–22 HD (Huge); mature adult 24–25 HD (Huge); old 27–28 HD (Huge); very old 30–31 HD (Huge); ancient 33–34 HD (Gargantuan); wyrm 36–37 HD (Gargantuan); great wyrm 39+ HD (Gargantuan)

Crystal dragons are the friendliest of the gem dragons. They are always curious about the world, so they enthusiastically converse with willing visitors.

A wyrmling crystal dragon's scales are glossy white. As it ages, its scales become translucent. Moonlight and starlight cause them to luminesce, and full sunlight lends them a dazzling brilliance.

Crystal dragons prefer the Elemental Plane of Air, but they sometimes build incredible ice palaces atop high, cold mountain peaks on the Material Plane, where they can watch the stars and create sculptures out of ice and snow.

White dragons and crystal dragons sometimes come into conflict. Crystal dragons have been known to make off with white dragon eggs, possibly to foster the white wyrmlings and help them grow into friendlier dragons than they would otherwise become. Such white dragons are extremely

CRYSTAL DRAGON ABILITIES BY AGE

Age	Speed	Initiative	AC	Special Abilities	Caster Level
Wyrmling	40 ft., fly 100 ft. (average), burrow 5 ft., swim 40 ft.	+0	15 (+1 size, +4 natural), touch 11, flat-footed 15	Cold immunity, planar travel	—
Very young	40 ft., fly 150 ft. (poor), burrow 5 ft., swim 40 ft.	+0	17 (+7 natural), touch 10, flat-footed 17		—
Young	40 ft., fly 150 ft. (poor), burrow 5 ft., swim 40 ft.	+0	20 (+10 natural), touch 10, flat-footed 20		—
Juvenile	40 ft., fly 150 ft. (poor), burrow 5 ft., swim 40 ft.	+0	22 (–1 size, +13 natural), touch 9, flat-footed 22		—
Young adult	40 ft., fly 150 ft. (poor), burrow 5 ft., swim 40 ft.	+0	25 (–1 size, +16 natural), touch 9, flat-footed 25	DR 5/+1	—
Adult	40 ft., fly 150 ft. (poor), burrow 5 ft., swim 40 ft.	+0	27 (–2 size, +19 natural), touch 8, flat-footed 27	Charm person	5th
Mature adult	40 ft., fly 150 ft. (poor), burrow 5 ft., swim 40 ft.	+0	30 (–2 size, +22 natural), touch 8, flat-footed 30	DR 10/+1	7th
Old	40 ft., fly 150 ft. (poor), burrow 5 ft., swim 40 ft.	+0	33 (–2 size, +25 natural), touch 8, flat-footed 33	Color spray	9th
Very old	40 ft., fly 150 ft. (poor), burrow 5 ft., swim 40 ft.	+0	36 (–2 size, +28 natural), touch 8, flat-footed 36	DR 15/+2	11th
Ancient	40 ft., fly 200 ft. (clumsy), burrow 5 ft., swim 40 ft.	+0	37 (–4 size, +31 natural), touch 6, flat-footed 37	Domination	13th
Wyrm	40 ft., fly 200 ft. (clumsy), burrow 5 ft., swim 40 ft.	+0	40 (–4 size, +34 natural), touch 6, flat-footed 40	DR 20/+2	15th
Great wyrm	40 ft., fly 200 ft. (clumsy), burrow 5 ft., swim 40 ft.	+0	43 (–4 size, +37 natural), touch 6, flat-footed 43	Control winds	17th

rare, and the introduction of such creatures into a campaign is the purview of the DM. Crystal dragons tend to bear great enmity toward any local giants, since the latter occasionally join forces with white dragons to hunt for crystal dragon lairs or wyrmlings.

Combat

A crystal dragon rarely instigates a fight without cause. If a visitor is intriguing or seems friendly, the dragon attempts a conversation; otherwise it tries to avoid a meeting. If visitors dare to attack, however, a crystal dragon does not hesitate to respond in kind. It often uses its breath weapon first to weaken and blind foes, then takes to the air to make use of its psionic abilities and any other ranged attacks it has.

Breath Weapon (Su): A crystal dragon's breath weapon is a cone of brilliant light. A target who fails his or her Reflex saving throw takes the indicated damage and is blinded for 1d4 rounds.

Spell-Like Abilities: 3/day—*color spray*; 1/day—*control winds*. (When using the *Psionics Handbook*, replace *control winds* with the *control air* psionic power.) Caster level varies by age; save DC 10 + dragon's Charisma modifier + spell level.

Psionics (Sp): 3/day—*charm person*; 1/day—*domination*. Caster (or manifester) level varies by age; save DC 10 + dragon's Charisma modifier + spell (or power) level.

Attack/Defense Modes: *id insinuation/thought shield.* A crystal dragon manifests powers, and gains additional attack and defense modes, as if it were a psion with Telepathy as its primary discipline.

EMERALD DRAGON

Dragon (Air)
Climate/Terrain: Inner Planes, underground
Organization: Wyrmling, very young, young, juvenile, and young adult: solitary or clutch (2–5); adult, mature adult, old, very old, ancient, wyrm, or great wyrm: solitary, pair, or family (1–2 plus 2–5 offspring)
Challenge Ratings: Wyrmling 2; very young 4; young 6; juvenile 8; young adult 11; adult 14; mature adult 16; old 18; very old 19; ancient 21; wyrm 22; great wyrm 24
Treasure: Double standard
Alignment: Always lawful neutral

Advancement: Wyrmling 7–8 HD (Small); very young 10–11 HD (Medium-size); young 13–14 HD (Medium-size); juvenile 16–17 HD (Large); young adult 19–20 HD (Large); adult 22–23 HD (Huge); mature adult 25–26 HD (Huge); old 28–29 HD (Huge); very old 31–32 HD (Huge); ancient 34–35 HD (Gargantuan); wyrm 37–38 HD (Gargantuan); great wyrm 40+ HD (Gargantuan)

Emerald dragons are inquisitive, particularly about local history and customs. Often, their knowledge of particular areas surpasses that of the best sage. However, these dragons are also rather paranoid, so developing even a passing acquaintance with one can be quite difficult.

The scales of a wyrmling emerald dragon are translucent and sea-green. As it ages, its scales harden and take on every shade of green from deep emerald to mint, and they scintillate in even the dimmest light. An emerald dragon's pupils fade as it ages, so by the time it becomes a great wyrm, its eyes are featureless, glowing, green orbs.

The typical emerald dragon likes to settle near an area that is at least partly inhabited by civilized beings (of any type), but not so near that its presence becomes generally known. On the Material Plane, such dragons make their lairs in the cones of extinct (or seldom active) volcanoes. While on the Inner Planes, these dragons still watch their favored Material Plane spots.

Emerald dragons nurture their wyrmlings, so any given lair of a young adult or older dragon is likely to include at least one wyrmling.

Combat

Emerald dragons are quite distrustful of visitors, and their lairs bristle with hidden traps and both magic and mundane alarms. Should these measures fail to deter visitors, an emerald dragon first hides (with *improved invisibility*, if available), but reveals its presence if its treasure or its hatchlings are discovered.

When attacking, an emerald dragon prefers to blind its opponents with *fog cloud*, and then charge (or if it is flying, snatch up its opponents). These dragons are the least reluctant of all the gem dragons to engage foes in melee before thoroughly softening them up from a distance.

DRAGON

Age	Size	Hit Dice (hp)	Str	Dex	Con	Int	Wis	Cha	Attack Bonus	Fort Save	Ref Save	Will Save	Breath Weapon (DC)	Frightful Presence DC	SR
Wyrmling	S	6d12+6 (45)	13	10	13	14	15	14	+8	+6	+5	+7	2d6 (14)	—	—
Very young	M	9d12+18 (76)	15	10	15	14	15	14	+11	+8	+6	+8	4d6 (16)	—	—
Young	M	12d12+24 (102)	17	10	15	16	17	16	+15	+10	+8	+11	6d6 (18)	—	—
Juvenile	L	15d12+45 (142)	19	10	17	18	19	18	+18	+12	+9	+13	8d6 (20)	—	—
Young adult	L	18d12+72 (189)	23	10	19	18	19	18	+23	+15	+11	+15	10d6 (23)	23	20
Adult	H	21d12+105 (241)	27	10	21	20	21	20	+27	+17	+12	+17	12d6 (25)	25	22
Mature adult	H	24d12+120 (276)	29	10	21	20	21	20	+31	+19	+14	+19	14d6 (27)	27	23
Old	H	27d12+162 (337)	31	10	23	22	23	22	+35	+21	+15	+21	16d6 (29)	29	25
Very old	H	30d12+180 (375)	33	10	23	22	23	22	+39	+23	+17	+23	18d6 (31)	31	26
Ancient	G	33d12+231 (445)	35	10	25	24	25	24	+41	+25	+18	+25	20d6 (33)	33	28
Wyrm	G	36d12+288 (522)	37	10	27	26	27	26	+45	+28	+20	+28	22d6 (36)	36	29
Great wyrm	G	39d12+312 (565)	39	10	27	26	27	26	+49	+29	+21	+29	24d6 (37)	37	31

Against seafaring opponents, an emerald dragon usually either conjures up a storm or uses its tail to smash all the vessels it can reach (first the masts, then the hulls). If the creature is inclined toward leniency, it might merely becalm the ships, leave them fogbound, or snap some of their masts before allowing them to limp to safety. Alternatively, an emerald dragon might simply herd the nearly helpless ships to a location of its choice, thoroughly examine the crew and cargo, then either loot the vessel or hold the ship and its contents for ransom.

Breath Weapon (Su): An emerald dragon breathes a cone of keening sonic energy. In addition to making a Reflex saving throw against sonic damage, each creature within the cone must succeed at a Fortitude save (same DC) or be deafened for 1d4 rounds plus 1 round per age category of the dragon.

Spell-Like Abilities: At will—*legend lore*; 3/day—*fog cloud, improved invisibility, sculpt sound*. (When using the *Psionics Handbook*, replace *legend lore* with the *object reading* psionic power, replace *sculpt sound* with the *control sound* psionic power, and replace *improved invisibility* with the *augmented invisibility* psionic power.) Caster level varies with age; save DC 10 + dragon's Charisma modifier + spell level.

Psionics (Sp): 3/day—*nondetection, clairaudience/clairvoyance*. Caster (or manifester) level varies by age; save DC 10 + dragon's Charisma modifier + spell (or power) level.

Attack/Defense Modes: id insinuation, psychic crush/thought shield, tower of iron will. An emerald dragon manifests powers, and gains additional attack and defense modes, as if it were a psion with Clairsentience as its primary discipline.

Shield of Prudence (Sp): A great wyrm emerald dragon can extend its awareness a few fractions of a second into the future. This ability gives it a +6 insight bonus to AC for 6 hours. If it is caught flat-footed, it still gains a +4 insight bonus to AC. *Shield of prudence* is usable three times per day. (When using the *Psionics Handbook*, replace this with the *shield of prudence* psionic power.)

MERALD DRAGON ABILITIES BY AGE

Age	Speed	Initiative	AC	Special Abilities	Caster Level
Wyrmling	40 ft., fly 100 ft. (average) burrow 5 ft., swim 60 ft.	+0	16 (+1 size, +5 natural), touch 11, flat-footed 16	Object reading, planar travel, sonic immunity	—
Very young	40 ft., fly 150 ft. (poor), burrow 5 ft., swim 60 ft.	+0	18 (+8 natural), touch 10, flat-footed 18		—
Young	40 ft., fly 150 ft. (poor), burrow 5 ft., swim 60 ft.	+0	21 (+11 natural), touch 10, flat-footed 21	*Improved invisibility*	1st
Juvenile	40 ft., fly 150 ft. (poor), burrow 5 ft., swim 60 ft.	+0	23 (–1 size, +14 natural), touch 9, flat-footed 23	*Fog cloud*	3rd
Young adult	40 ft., fly 150 ft. (poor), burrow 5 ft., swim 60 ft.	+0	26 (–1 size, +17 natural), touch 9, flat-footed 26	DR 5/+1	5th
Adult	40 ft., fly 150 ft. (poor), burrow 5 ft., swim 60 ft.	+0	28 (–2 size, +20 natural), touch 8, flat-footed 28	*Legend lore*	7th
Mature adult	40 ft., fly 150 ft. (poor), burrow 5 ft., swim 60 ft.	+0	31 (–2 size, +23 natural), touch 8, flat-footed 31	DR 10/+1	9th
Old	40 ft., fly 150 ft. (poor), burrow 5 ft., swim 60 ft.	+0	34 (–2 size, +26 natural), touch 8, flat-footed 34	*Clairaudience/clairvoyance, nondetection*	11th
Very old	40 ft., fly 150 ft. (poor), burrow 5 ft., swim 60 ft.	+0	37 (–2 size, +29 natural), touch 8, flat-footed 37	DR 15/+2	13th
Ancient	40 ft., fly 200 ft. (clumsy), burrow 5 ft., swim 60 ft.	+0	38 (–4 size, +32 natural), touch 6, flat-footed 38	*Sculpt sound*	15th
Wyrm	40 ft., fly 200 ft. (clumsy), burrow 5 ft., swim 60 ft.	+0	41 (–4 size, +35 natural), touch 6, flat-footed 41	DR 20/+3	17th
Great wyrm	40 ft., fly 200 ft. (clumsy), burrow 5 ft., swim 60 ft.	+0	44 (–4 size, +38 natural), touch 6, flat-footed 44	*Shield of prudence*	19th

SAPPHIRE DRAGON

Dragon (Earth)
Climate/Terrain: Inner Planes, underground
Organization: Wyrmling, very young, young, juvenile, and young adult: solitary or clutch (2–5); adult, mature adult, old, very old, ancient, wyrm, or great wyrm: solitary, pair, or family (1–2 plus 2–5 offspring)
Challenge Ratings: Wyrmling 2; very young 4; young 6; juvenile 8; young adult 10; adult 13; mature adult 15; old 18; very old 19; ancient 21; wyrm 22; great wyrm 24
Treasure: Double standard
Alignment: Always lawful neutral
Advancement: Wyrmling 6–7 HD (Tiny); very young 9–10 HD (Small); young 12–13 HD (Medium-size); juvenile 15–16 HD (Medium-size); young adult 18–19 HD (Large); adult 21–22 HD (Large); mature adult 24–25 HD (Huge); old 27–28 HD (Huge); very old 30–31 HD (Huge); ancient 33–34 HD (Huge); wyrm 36–37 HD (Gargantuan); great wyrm 39+ HD (Gargantuan)

Sapphire dragons are quite territorial, particularly when it comes to other dragons that encroach on their territories, either on the Elemental Plane of Earth, or in the areas of the Material Plane that they call their own.

Sapphire dragons tend to be antisocial toward all beings, but they view the evil races of the Underdark as particular enemies and sometimes come into direct conflict with them over underground territory. These dragons don't go in for small talk unless the discussion revolves around military strategy, a subject on which they consider themselves experts, if not geniuses. In fact, a sapphire dragon may forgive visitors their presence if they offer it a game of strategy. Of course, it is never wise to let the dragon lose.

A sapphire dragon's scales range from light to dark blue in color, and they scintillate in any light, creating a cascade of ghostly glints on the walls of the caverns in which these creatures often lair. Unlike the scales of other gem dragons, those of a sapphire dragon do not change as the creature ages. Its pupils fade with time, however, so by the time it becomes a great wyrm, its eyes are featureless, glowing, sapphire orbs.

Sapphire dragons love the Elemental Plane of Earth, but they also like to lair in deep, dry, rocky caverns on the Material Plane. The typical sapphire dragon uses *move earth* and *stone shape* to hide the entrance to its lair. Inside, it spreads out its treasures through several chambers, arranging them in a somewhat decorative manner. Drow, illithid, and aboleth trophies are often prominently displayed to remind the dragon of its past victories over its enemies. A sapphire dragon often allows Large monstrous spiders to roam its lair, but only as a handy source of food. To keep such creatures close, the dragon also frequently allows their favorite prey species to inhabit portions of its lair.

Combat

A sapphire dragon uses its spider climb and *teleport* abilities to confuse its opponents and try to catch them flat-footed. It also uses its *skate* ability to enhance its own movement or push heavy objects down slopes at its enemies.

SAPPHIRE DRAGONS BY AGE

Age	Size	Hit Dice (hp)	Str	Dex	Con	Int	Wis	Cha	Attack Bonus	Fort Save	Ref Save	Will Save	Breath Weapon (DC)	Frightful Presence DC	SR
Wyrmling	T	5d12+5 (37)	11	12	13	12	13	12	+7	+5	+5	+5	2d4 (13)	—	—
Very young	S	8d12+8 (60)	13	12	13	12	13	12	+10	+7	+7	+7	4d4 (15)	—	—
Young	M	11d12+22 (93)	15	14	15	14	15	14	+13	+9	+9	+9	6d4 (17)	—	—
Juvenile	M	14d12+28 (119)	17	14	15	14	15	14	+17	+11	+11	+11	8d4 (19)	—	—
Young adult	L	17d12+51 (161)	19	16	17	16	17	16	+20	+13	+13	+13	10d4 (21)	21	19
Adult	L	20d12+60 (190)	23	16	19	16	17	16	+25	+16	+15	+15	12d4 (24)	23	21
Mature adult	H	23d12+115 (264)	27	18	21	18	19	18	+29	+18	+17	+17	14d4 (26)	25	23
Old	H	26d12+130 (299)	29	18	21	18	19	18	+33	+20	+19	+19	16d4 (28)	27	25
Very old	H	29d12+174 (362)	31	20	23	20	21	20	+37	+22	+21	+21	18d4 (30)	29	26
Ancient	H	32d12+192 (400)	33	20	23	20	21	20	+41	+24	+23	+23	20d4 (32)	31	28
Wyrm	G	35d12+245 (472)	35	22	25	22	23	22	+43	+26	+25	+25	22d4 (34)	33	29
Great wyrm	G	38d12+304 (551)	37	22	27	22	23	22	+47	+29	+27	+27	24d4 (37)	35	31

Sapphire Dragon Abilities by Age

Age	Speed	Initiative	AC	Special Abilities	Caster Level
Wyrmling	40 ft., fly 100 ft. (average), burrow 15 ft., swim 10 ft.	+1	16 (+2 size, +3 natural, +1 Dex), touch 13, flat-footed 15	Electricity immunity, spider climb	—
Very young	40 ft., fly 100 ft. (average), burrow 15 ft., swim 10 ft.	+1	18 (+1 size, +6 natural, +1 Dex), touch 12, flat-footed 17		—
Young	40 ft., fly 150 ft. (poor), burrow 10 ft., swim 10 ft.	+2	21 (+9 natural, +2 Dex), touch 12, flat-footed 19		1st
Juvenile	40 ft., fly 150 ft. (poor), burrow 10 ft., swim 10 ft.	+2	24 (+12 natural, +2 Dex), touch 12, flat-footed 22	Sense psychoportation	3rd
Young adult	40 ft., fly 150 ft. (poor), burrow 5 ft., swim 10 ft.	+3	27 (–1 size, +15 natural, +3 Dex), touch 12, flat-footed 24	DR 5/+1	5th
Adult	40 ft., fly 150 ft. (poor), burrow 5 ft., swim 10 ft.	+3	30 (–1 size, +18 natural, +3 Dex), touch 12, flat-footed 27	*Skate, stone shape*	7th
Mature adult	40 ft., fly 150 ft. (poor), burrow 5 ft., swim 10 ft.	+4	32 (–2 size, +20 natural, +4 Dex), touch 12, flat-footed 28	DR 10/+1	9th
Old	40 ft., fly 150 ft. (poor), burrow 5 ft., swim 10 ft.	+4	35 (–2 size, +23 natural, +4 Dex), touch 12, flat-footed 31	*Teleport*	11th
Very old	40 ft., fly 150 ft. (poor), burrow 5 ft., swim 10 ft.	+5	39 (–2 size, +26 natural, +5 Dex), touch 13, flat-footed 34	DR 15/+2	13th
Ancient	40 ft., fly 150 ft. (poor), burrow 5 ft., swim 10 ft.	+5	42 (–2 size, +29 natural, +5 Dex), touch 13, flat-footed 37	*Wall of stone*	15th
Wyrm	40 ft., fly 200 ft. (clumsy), burrow 5 ft., swim 10 ft.	+6	44 (–4 size, +32 natural, +6 Dex), touch 12, flat-footed 38	DR 20/+3	17th
Great wyrm	40 ft., fly 200 ft. (clumsy), burrow 5 ft., swim 10 ft.	+6	47 (–4 size, +35 natural, +6 Dex), touch 12, flat-footed 41	*Move earth*	19th

It enjoys panicking creatures with its breath weapon, then using its *skate* ability to facilitate their departure.

Breath Weapon (Su): A sapphire dragon breathes a cone of nearly inaudible sonic energy. In addition to making a Reflex saving throw against sonic damage, each creature within the cone must succeed at a Will save (same DC) or become panicked for 1d4 rounds.

Spider Climb (Ex): A sapphire dragon can climb on stone surfaces as though using the *spider climb* spell. This ability is always active.

Sense Psychoportation (Su): The dragon can sense the use of any power or spell that enhances movement or allows instant transit from one place to another. This ability is always active, and it functions at a range of 100 feet + 10 feet per caster level of the detected power or spell. The dragon does not need a line of sight; it is instantly aware of the distance and direction to the detected power. (When using the *Psionics Handbook*, replace this ability with the *sense psychoportation* psionic power.)

Skate (Sp): This ability allows the sapphire dragon, another willing creature, or an unattended object to slide along any solid surface with no friction. An intelligent creature can control its movement by thought alone, skating, turning, or stopping as desired. The subject's base speed is its normal speed + 15 feet. The subject can move up or down inclines that he or she could otherwise walk on, but skating upward reduces speed to normal, while skating downward adds 30 feet (instead of 15) to the skater's speed. An object under the influence of the *skate* effect can be dragged across the ground as if it weighed only one-tenth its normal weight. This ability is usable three times per day. (When using the *Psionics Handbook*, replace this ability with the *skate* psionic power.)

Spell-Like Abilities: 2/day—*stone shape*; 1/day—*move earth, wall of stone*. Caster level varies by age; save DC 10 + dragon's Charisma modifier + spell level.

Psionics (Sp): 1/day—*teleport*. Caster (or manifester) level varies by age; save DC 10 + dragon's Charisma modifier + spell (or power) level.

Attack/Defense Modes: id insinuation, ego whip/thought shield, empty mind. A sapphire dragon manifests powers, and gains additional attack and defense modes, as if it were a psion with Psychoportation as its primary discipline.

Skills: A sapphire dragon has the Climb skill for free at 1 rank per Hit Die.

TOPAZ DRAGON

Dragon (Water)

Climate/Terrain: Inner Planes, any aquatic

Organization: Wyrmling, very young, young, juvenile, and young adult: solitary or clutch (2–5); adult, mature adult, old, very old, ancient, wyrm, or great wyrm: solitary, pair, or family (1–2 plus 2–5 offspring)

Challenge Ratings: Wyrmling 3; very young 4; young 6; juvenile 9; young adult 12; adult 14; mature adult 17; old 19; very old 20; ancient 22; wyrm 23; great wyrm 25

Treasure: Double standard

Alignment: Always chaotic neutral

Advancement: Wyrmling 8–9 HD (Small); very young 11–12 HD (Medium-size); young 14–15 HD (Medium-size); juvenile 17–18 HD (Large); young adult 20–21 HD (Large); adult 23–24 HD (Huge); mature adult 26–27 HD (Huge); old 29–30 HD (Huge); very old 32–33 HD (Huge); ancient 35–36 HD (Gargantuan); wyrm 38–39 HD (Gargantuan); great wyrm 41+ HD (Colossal)

Topaz dragons tend to be unfriendly and selfish. Though they are not malevolent, their erratic behavior makes any dealings with them unpleasant and dangerous.

A topaz wyrmling's scales are dull yellow with orange highlights. As it ages, its color slowly brightens until its individual scales become scarcely visible. From a distance, the creature looks as if it had been sculpted from pure topaz. A topaz dragon's pupils fade as it

ages, so by the time it becomes a great wyrm, its eyes resemble glowing orbs of fire.

Topaz dragons spend most of their time on the Elemental Plane of Water. During their brief forays onto the Material Plane, they lair on secluded beaches or caves below the waterline. Even on the Elemental Plane of Water, however, topaz dragons keep their lairs completely dry.

These dragons love to lounge on outcroppings that are lashed by waves and wind-blasted

TOPAZ DRAGONS BY AGE

Age	Size	Hit Dice (hp)	Str	Dex	Con	Int	Wis	Cha	Attack Bonus	Fort Save	Ref Save	Will Save	Breath Weapon (DC)	Frightful Presence DC	SR
Wyrmling	S	7d12+7 (52)	13	10	13	14	15	14	+9	+6	+5	+7	2d8 (14)	—	—
Very young	M	10d12+20 (85)	15	10	15	14	15	14	+12	+9	+7	+9	4d8 (17)	—	—
Young	M	13d12+26 (110)	17	10	15	16	17	16	+16	+10	+8	+11	6d8 (18)	—	—
Juvenile	L	16d12+ 48 (152)	19	10	17	18	19	18	+19	+13	+10	+14	8d8 (21)	—	—
Young adult	L	19d12+76 (199)	23	10	19	18	19	18	+24	+15	+11	+15	10d8 (23)	23	20
Adult	H	22d12+110 (253)	27	10	21	20	21	20	+28	+18	+13	+18	12d8 (26)	26	22
Mature adult	H	25d12+125 (287)	29	10	21	20	21	20	+32	+19	+14	+19	14d8 (27)	27	24
Old	H	28d12+168 (350)	31	10	23	22	23	22	+36	+22	+16	+22	16d8 (30)	30	26
Very old	H	31d12+186 (387)	33	10	23	24	25	24	+40	+23	+17	+24	18d8 (31)	32	27
Ancient	G	34d12+238 (459)	35	10	25	26	27	26	+42	+26	+19	+27	20d8 (34)	35	29
Wyrm	G	37d12+333 (573)	39	10	29	28	29	28	+47	+29	+20	+29	22d8 (37)	37	30
Great wyrm	C	40d12+400 (660)	43	10	31	30	31	30	+48	+32	+22	+32	24d8 (40)	40	32

TOPAZ DRAGON ABILITIES BY AGE

Age	Speed	Initiative	AC	Special Abilities	Caster Level
Wyrmling	40 ft., fly 100 ft. (average), burrow 5 ft., swim 60 ft.	+0	17 (+1 size, +6 natural), touch 11, flat-footed 17	Cold immunity, water breathing	—
Very young	40 ft., fly 150 ft. (poor), burrow 5 ft., swim 60 ft.	+0	19 (+9 natural), touch 10, flat-footed 19		—
Young	40 ft., fly 150 ft. (poor), burrow 5 ft., swim 60 ft.	+0	22 (+12 natural), touch 10, flat-footed 22		—
Juvenile	40 ft., fly 150 ft. (poor), burrow 5 ft., swim 60 ft.	+0	24 (−1 size, +15 natural), touch 9, flat-footed 24	Feather fall	3rd
Young adult	40 ft., fly 150 ft. (poor), burrow 5 ft., swim 60 ft.	+0	27 (−1 size, +18 natural), touch 9, flat-footed 27	DR 5/+1	5th
Adult	40 ft., fly 150 ft. (poor), burrow 5 ft., swim 60 ft.	+0	29 (−2 size, +21 natural), touch 8, flat-footed 29	Fog cloud	7th
Mature adult	40 ft., fly 150 ft. (poor), burrow 5 ft., swim 60 ft.	+0	32 (−2 size, +24 natural), touch 8, flat-footed 32	DR 10/+1	9th
Old	40 ft., fly 150 ft. (poor), burrow 5 ft., swim 60 ft.	+0	35 (−2 size, +27 natural), touch 8, flat-footed 35	Control winds	11th
Very old	40 ft., fly 150 ft. (poor), burrow 5 ft., swim 60 ft.	+0	38 (−2 size, +30 natural), touch 8, flat-footed 38	DR 15/+2	13th
Ancient	40 ft., fly 200 ft. (clumsy), burrow 5 ft., swim 60 ft.	+0	39 (−4 size, +33 natural), touch 6, flat-footed 39	Control weather	15th
Wyrm	40 ft., fly 200 ft. (clumsy), burrow 5 ft., swim 60 ft.	+0	42 (−4 size, +36 natural), touch 6, flat-footed 42	DR 20/+3	17th
Great wyrm	40 ft., fly 200 ft. (clumsy), burrow 5 ft., swim 60 ft.	+0	41 (−8 size, +39 natural), touch 2, flat-footed 41	Shapechange	19th

sea spray. Of course, such vantages also allow them to spot passing prey, such as sharks and large squids.

Because they inhabit similar territories, topaz dragons and bronze dragons often come into conflict. Duels between the two are always furious and deadly.

Combat

Topaz dragons generally dislike intruders, but they prefer to begin any potential confrontation with conversation. They quickly attack intruders who prove either hostile or boring.

When outdoors, a topaz dragon prefers to express its displeasure first through its wind and weather control abilities, then with physical attacks. Indoors, it usually leads off with its breath weapon.

Breath Weapon (Su): A topaz dragon breathes a cone of dehydration that looks like a watery blast. When directed against an aqueous liquid (water or a liquid composed mainly of water), this effect evaporates one cubic foot of water per hit point of damage dealt. Each creature within the cone takes the indicated damage, or half that amount with a successful Reflex save.

Water Breathing (Ex): Topaz dragons breathe water as readily as air.

Spell-Like Abilities: 3/day—*control winds, fog cloud*; 1/day—*control weather*. Caster level varies by age; save DC 10 + dragon's Charisma modifier + spell level. (When using the *Psionics Handbook*, replace *control winds* with the *control air* psionic power.)

Psionics (Sp): 3/day—*shapechange*; 2/day—*feather fall*. Caster (or manifester) level varies by age; save DC 10 + dragon's Charisma modifier + spell (or power) level.

Attack/Defense Modes: mind thrust, ego whip/thought shield, mental barrier. A topaz dragon manifests powers, and gains additional attack and defense modes, as if it were a psion with Psychometabolism as its primary discipline.

Skills: A topaz dragon has the Swim skill for free at 1 rank per Hit Die.

DREAD GUARD

Medium-Size Construct
Hit Dice: 5d10 (27 hp)
Initiative: +0
Speed: 20 ft. (can't run)
AC: 17 (+6 masterwork banded mail, +1 masterwork small steel shield), touch 10, flat-footed 17
Attacks: Longsword +6 melee
Damage: Longsword 1d8+3/19–20
Special Qualities: Cold resistance 10, construct traits, fire resistance 10
Saves: Fort +1, Ref +1, Will +2
Abilities: Str 17, Dex 11, Con —, Int 6, Wis 13, Cha 2

Climate/Terrain: Any land and underground
Organization: Solitary, pair, or company (3–5)

Challenge Rating: 2
Treasure: None
Alignment: Always neutral
Advancement: 6–10 HD (Medium-size); 11–15 HD (Large)

A dread guard appears to be an armored undead, still bearing the weapons and shield it carried in life. In fact, it is an animated suit of armor, little different from a golem. Those who create dread guards usually do so to obtain guardians for their strongholds—guardians that can never be bribed and rarely fooled.

A dread guard obeys simple commands from its creator, but these are limited to one or two rudimentary concepts. Typical orders include "Stay in this room and attack anyone but me who enters," and "Kill each person who opens this chest until I tell you otherwise."

A dread guard never speaks, but it understands commands in its creator's language.

COMBAT

Dread guards attack mindlessly with their weapons. They are unsubtle and straightforward in combat.

Construct Traits: A dread guard is immune to mind-affecting effects, poison, *sleep*, paralysis, stunning, disease, death effects, necromantic effects, and any effect that requires a Fortitude save unless it also works on objects. The creature is not subject to critical hits, subdual damage, ability damage, ability drain, energy drain, or death from massive damage. It cannot heal itself but can be healed through repair. It cannot be raised or resurrected. A dread guard has darkvision (60-foot range).

CONSTRUCTION

A dread guard may be constructed from any suit of master-work heavy armor, and a Medium-size one may wield any Medium-size or Large martial weapon. A Large dread guard may wield any Large or Huge martial weapon.

The cost of creating a dread guard is 40,000 gp. This amount includes the cost of a masterwork suit of heavy armor and, if desired, a masterwork shield. Construction requires a martial weapon, but it need not be a masterwork weapon. Assembling the body requires a success-ful Craft (armorsmithing) check (DC 25).

The creator must be at least 15th level and able to cast arcane spells. Completing the ritual drains 800 XP from the creator and requires the *fabricate*, *geas/quest*, and *polymorph any object* spells.

DUNE STALKER

Medium-Size Outsider (Earth, Evil)
Hit Dice: 6d8+12 (39 hp)
Initiative: +4
Speed: 40 ft., climb 20 ft.
AC: 17 (+7 natural), touch 10, flat-footed 17
Attacks: Slam +9 melee
Damage: Slam 1d8+4
Face/Reach: 5 ft. by 5 ft./5 ft.
Special Attacks: Kiss of death, *shout*
Special Qualities: DR 10/+1, improved tracking, jump, outsider traits, SR 20
Saves: Fort +7, Ref +5, Will +7
Abilities: Str 16, Dex 10, Con 14, Int 13, Wis 15, Cha 11
Skills: Balance +6, Climb +19, Hide +6, Intimidate +4, Jump +5, Knowledge (nature) +4, Listen +9, Move Silently +9, Search +7, Spot +8, Tumble +9
Feats: Alertness, Improved Initiative

Climate/Terrain: Any desert and underground
Organization: Solitary
Challenge Rating: 9
Treasure: None
Alignment: Always neutral evil
Advancement: 7–12 HD (Medium-size); 13–18 HD (Large)

Dune stalkers are creatures native to the Elemental Plane of Earth, though they are also frequently found on the Gray Waste of Hades. These monsters revel in evil and take their only joy from spreading its blight. They despise the Material Plane and avoid it as much as possible. Even so, they are sometimes summoned there by evil characters to kill targets or carry out other quests.

A dune stalker appears humanoid. It stands approximately 7 feet tall, but it would be taller if stretched out or forced to stand erect. Its head is triangular, and the neck attaches near the top of the head, causing its leering, toothy face and pointed chin to hang below its shoulders. The dune stalker's gangly body is hairless, and its red, dusty, abrasive skin has no pores. The combination of short legs, long arms, and stooped posture causes its hands to drag on the ground. Its fingers and toes (four on each limb) are long and bony. The creature has massive shoulders and an enormous chest, which tapers to a narrow waist and hips.

A dune stalker that has been assigned a mission by its summoner pursues the literal fulfillment of its instructions to the exclusion of all else. It resents its time on the Material Plane and wants to make its stay there as short as possible. Occasionally, a summoner's instructions are phrased in such a way that the dune stalker cannot actually carry them out. In this case, it is trapped on the Material Plane, where it takes out its frustration by killing all creatures it finds.

Despite their sonic abilities, dune stalkers do not speak, though they understand Common and Terran.

COMBAT

A dune stalker's preferred tactic is to hide in a rocky area and attack from ambush. When possible, it tries to gain higher ground on its opponents by climbing up on a rock or a structure to conceal itself.

It often begins an assault by using its *shout* ability to dis-orient a group of opponents, then leaping into combat to deliver its kiss of death. Against foes within its reach, a dune stalker usually prefers to deliver a kiss of death against just one target rather than a *shout* against the whole group. The

preferred target is the one it seeks to slay, or the one that presents the greatest danger, or the one that appears to have the strongest good alignment. (Given the dune stalker's demented psychology, this last could be just about anyone, but paladins usually stand out.)

Kiss of Death (Su): The kiss of death is a sonic and death effect delivered with the dune stalker's face pressed directly against the victim's. If the dune stalker makes a successful melee touch attack (+9 melee), the opponent must attempt a Fortitude saving throw (DC 15). Success leaves the opponent stunned for 1 round; failure sets up lethal vibrations in the opponent's body that result in instant death. This ability is usable at will.

Shout **(Sp):** Three times per day, the dune stalker can create an effect identical to that of a *shout* spell (caster level 6th; Fort save DC 14), except that the actual sound produced resembles a loud, rasping cough.

Improved Tracking (Ex): A consummate tracker, the dune stalker tracks as well as an invisible stalker does. Like that creature, it uses Spot checks rather than Wilderness Lore checks to follow its quarry's trail.

Jump (Ex): A dune stalker can produce a *jump* effect (caster level 6th) at will.

Outsider Traits: A dune stalker has darkvision (60-foot range). It cannot be raised or resurrected.

Skills: A dune stalker gains a +4 racial bonus on Intimidate checks.

EFFIGY

Medium-Size Undead (Fire, Incorporeal)

Hit Dice: 27d12 (175 hp)
Initiative: +6
Speed: Fly 60 ft. (perfect)
AC: 20 (+2 Dex, +3 deflection, +5 natural), touch 15, flat-footed 18
Attacks: 2 incorporeal touches +16 melee touch
Damage: Incorporeal touch 1d6/19–20 plus 2d6 fire plus energy drain plus infuse
Face/Reach: 5 ft. by 5 ft./ 5 ft.
Special Attacks: Energy drain, infuse
Special Qualities: Fire subtytpe, incorporeal subtype, SR 28, undead traits
Saves: Fort +11 Ref +13, Will +20
Abilities: Str —, Dex 15, Con —, Int 16, Wis 17, Cha 17
Skills: Balance +4, Escape Artist +17, Hide +17, Jump +2, Listen +20, Search +23, Spot +25, Tumble +17
Feats: Alertness, Blind-Fight, Expertise, Great Fortitude, Improved Critical (incorporeal touch), Improved Initiative, Iron Will, Lightning Reflexes, Run, Weapon Focus (incorporeal touch)

Climate/Terrain: Any land and underground
Organization: Solitary, pair, or brood (3–5)
Challenge Rating: 17

Treasure: None
Alignment: Always chaotic evil
Advancement: 28–54 HD (Medium-size)

An effigy is an envious undead that hates living creatures and lusts after the life energy they possess. It seeks to possess a living creature and take over its life, but it cannot maintain its usurped body for long. Eventually the fires of its own raw hatred literally immolate the body it has possessed.

An effigy appears as a translucent humanoid shape composed of multicolored flame. Its eyes glow white within the flickering fires of its insubstantial body, but it has no other discernible facial features.

COMBAT

An effigy seeks to join its undead force with the body of a living host, which it then burns out from within. It need not be joined with a body to attack, but it often keeps its most recent body's ashes animated within its fiery heart.

Energy Drain (Su): Any living creature struck by an effigy's incorporeal touch attack must succeed at a Fortitude saving throw (DC 26) or gain two negative levels. For each negative level bestowed, the effigy heals 5 points of damage. If the amount of healing is more than the damage the creature has taken, it gains any excess as temporary hit points. If the negative level has not been removed (with a spell such as *restoration*) before 24 hours have passed, the afflicted opponent must succeed at a Fortitude save (DC 26) to remove it.

Failure means the opponent's level (or Hit Dice) is reduced by one.

Infuse (Su): When an effigy hits a humanoid or monstrous humanoid that is no more than two size categories larger than itself with its incorporeal touch attack, the opponent must make a successful Will save (DC 26) or become infused with the effigy's spirit. The effects of infusion on the opponent are similar to those of a *magic jar* spell, except as noted here. Upon infusion, the effigy gains control of the infused creature. While infused, it uses the body's physical ability scores but its own mental ability scores. It also uses whatever attack forms the subject has available. Such attacks still do 2d6 points of additional fire damage, but they do not bestow negative levels.

An infused effigy automatically deals fire damage and inflicts energy drain on its host body each round. The subject dies upon reaching –10 hit points or dropping below 1st level. At that point, the body becomes a flaming corpse.

Each round after infusion occurs, the subject must make an opposed Wisdom check against the effigy. Success casts the effigy out, forcing it to retreat 30 feet. Thereafter, it may not attempt to infuse the same target again for 1 round per point of difference between the check results. A failed save leaves the effigy in control of the body. If an effigy is turned while infused in a host, it abandons the body to flee.

Fire Subtype (Ex): An effigy is immune to fire damage but takes double damage from cold unless a saving throw for half damage is allowed. In that case, it takes half damage on a success and double damage on a failure.

Incorporeal Subtype: An effigy can be harmed only by other incorporeal creatures, +1 or better magic weapons, spells, spell-like abilities, and supernatural abilities. The creature has a 50% chance to ignore any damage from a corporeal source, except for force effects or attacks made with ghost touch weapons. An effigy can pass through solid objects, but not force effects, at will. Its attacks ignore natural armor, armor, and shields, but deflection bonuses and force effects work normally against them. An effigy always moves silently and cannot be heard with Listen checks if it doesn't wish to be.

Undead Traits: An effigy is immune to mind-affecting effects, poison, *sleep*, paralysis, stunning, disease, death effects, necromantic effects, and any effect that requires a Fortitude save unless it also works on objects. It is not subject to critical hits, subdual damage, ability damage, ability drain, energy drain, or death from massive damage. An effigy cannot be raised, and resurrection works only if it is willing. The creature has darkvision (60-foot range).

Weirds are cryptic beings of elemental force who are powerful in the art of divination. They are oracles, soothsayers, and seers of knowledge past, present, and future. Each weird is composed of material from one of the four elements (air, earth, fire, or water) and has special knowledge of the particular aspect of fate with which its element is associated (see below). These creatures dwell in remote or hidden locations on the Material Plane—a fact that makes travel difficult for those seeking their counsel.

The upper body of a weird always resembles that of a beautiful female humanoid. The lower half may be either humanoid or a serpentine column. A weird rises from a pool of the appropriate element, which it can never leave.

A weird can divine information that could change the very course of history. It has its finger on the pulse of fate and knows exactly where possible courses of action might lead. Like most seers, an elemental weird never provides a clear, concise prophecy. Some of the message may seem forthright, but some is always confusing or just difficult to decipher because the listener does not have enough information to understand the weird's meaning. Though its messages can be misinterpreted, a weird's warnings and advice are never wrong. Its counsel is seldom free, however, so anyone beseeching a weird had best bring offerings or be prepared to undertake a quest of vital importance to the creature.

A weird can communicate with any creature that has a language.

COMBAT

Elemental weirds do not fight if they can avoid it. If they must fight, they begin by summoning elementals to defend them. If any other elementals are present (regardless of type), the weird attempts to gain control of them and turn them against its foes. Meanwhile, the weird remains in the center of its pool, using divination magic to foresee possible consequences of the battle and acting accordingly.

If forced into melee, a weird uses its reach to lash out at nearby foes. If seriously threatened, a weird retreats back to its plane of origin.

Elemental Command (Su): A weird can attempt to gain control over any elemental within 100 feet regardless of the latter's elemental type. The elemental must make a successful Will save (DC 23) or succumb to the weird's control. An elemental that saves against this attack is immune to that weird's elemental command ability for 24 hours. There is no limit to the number of elementals that a weird can control.

Once under the weird's control, an elemental serves the weird until either it or the weird dies, until the weird dismisses it, or until the duration for its summoning expires. It obeys the weird explicitly, even if ordered to attack the being who originally summoned it. The weird does not need to concentrate to maintain control over any elemental it commands.

	Air Weird	**Earth Weird**
	Large Elemental (Air)	Large Elemental (Earth)
Hit Dice:	15d8+45 (112 hp)	15d8+45 (112 hp)
Initiative:	+6	+6
Speed:	30 ft., fly 60 ft. (perfect)	30 ft., burrow 30 ft.
AC:	15 (−1 size, +2 Dex, +4 natural), touch 11, flat-footed 13	15 (−1 size, +2 Dex, +4 natural), touch 11, flat-footed 13
Attacks:	Slam +15/+10/+5 melee	Slam +15/+10/+5 melee
Damage:	Slam 2d6+7	Slam 2d6+7
Face/Reach:	5 ft. by 5 ft./10 ft.	5 ft. by 5 ft./10 ft.
Special Attacks:	Elemental command, spells	Elemental command, spells
Special Qualities:	Air mastery, air pool, breathsense, DR 20/+2, elemental traits, prescience, regeneration 10, SR 25	DR 20/+2, earth mastery, earth pool, elemental traits, prescience, regeneration 10, SR 25, tremorsense
Saves:	Fort +10, Ref +13, Will +11	Fort +14, Ref +9, Will +11
Abilities:	Str 21, Dex 14, Con 17, Int 20, Wis 23, Cha 22	Str 21, Dex 14, Con 17, Int 20, Wis 23, Cha 22
Skills:	Concentration +10, Diplomacy +17, Intimidate +15, Knowledge (any three) +12, Listen +8, Scry +14, Sense Motive +13, Spot +8	Concentration +10, Diplomacy +17, Intimidate +15, Knowledge (any three) +12, Listen +8, Scry +14, Sense Motive +13, Spot +8
Feats:	Alertness, Dodge, Empower Spell, Flyby Attack (B), Great Fortitude, Improved Initiative, Lightning Reflexes, Maximize Spell	Alertness, Dodge, Empower Spell, Great Fortitude, Improved Initiative, Lightning Reflexes, Maximize Spell

	Fire Weird	**Water Weird**
	Large Elemental (Fire)	Large Elemental (Water)
Hit Dice:	15d8+45 (112 hp)	15d8+45 (112 hp)
Initiative:	+6	+6
Speed:	30 ft., fly 60 ft. (perfect)	30 ft., swim 30 ft.
AC:	15 (−1 size, +2 Dex, +4 natural), touch 11, flat-footed 13	15 (−1 size, +2 Dex, +4 natural), touch 11, flat-footed 13
Attacks:	Slam +15/+10/+5 melee	Slam +15/+10/+5 melee
Damage:	Slam 2d6+7 plus 2d6 fire	Slam 2d6+7
Face/Reach:	5 ft. by 5 ft./10 ft.	5 ft. by 5 ft./10 ft.
Special Attacks:	Burn, elemental command, spells	Drench, elemental command, spells
Special Qualities:	DR 20/+2, elemental traits, fire pool, fire subtype, prescience, regeneration 10, SR 25	DR 20/+2, elemental traits, prescience, regeneration 10, SR 25, water mastery, water pool
Saves:	Fort +10, Ref +13, Will +11	Fort +14, Ref +9, Will +11
Abilities:	Str 21, Dex 14, Con 17, Int 20, Wis 23, Cha 22	Str 21, Dex 14, Con 17, Int 20, Wis 23, Cha 22
Skills:	Concentration +10, Diplomacy +17, Intimidate +15, Knowledge (any three) +12, Listen +8, Scry +14, Sense Motive +13, Spot +8	Concentration +10, Diplomacy +17, Intimidate +15, Knowledge (any three) +12, Listen +8, Scry +14, Sense Motive +13, Spot +8, Swim +13
Feats:	Alertness, Dodge, Empower Spell, Great Fortitude, Improved Initiative, Lightning Reflexes, Maximize Spell	Alertness, Dodge, Empower Spell, Great Fortitude, Improved Initiative, Lightning Reflexes, Maximize Spell

Climate/Terrain: Any land or underground, or appropriate element
Organization: Solitary, pair, or charm (3–4)
Challenge Rating: 12
Treasure: Double standard
Alignment: Usually neutral
Advancement: 16–30 HD (Large); 31–45 HD (Huge)

Elemental Pool (Su): Each weird dwells within a large pool (at least 20 feet across and 40 feet deep) filled with the purest form of its element. The pool is always secured to a flat surface (floor, wall, or ceiling; see individual entries for possible orientations) such that its depth forms a hollow within that surface. The surface must have sufficient depth

to accommodate the pool. An elemental pool can also exist as a separate area inside a larger volume of the same element; for example, a water weird's pool might be situated at the bottom of an ocean or lake.

The base of the pool contains a *portal* to the weird's native plane. Three times per day, the weird can summon forth 2d4 huge elementals, 1d2 greater elementals, or 1 elder elemental through this portal. Any nonelemental creature entering a pool without the weird's permission must succeed at a Fortitude save (DC 20) each round or be irrevocably transformed into the elemental material of the pool. Creatures granted access to the pool by the weird are not subject to transformation. However, creatures allowed to enter a pool must still provide their own protection from the elemental material, as well as the means to breathe and move within that enviroment. Otherwise, they suffer the effects given in the individual entry.

A weird is physically tied to its pool and cannot leave except to return to its native plane through the *portal*. A weird may rise up to a height of 10 feet above the surface of its pool, but the lower part of its body must always remain in contact with the elemental material. Once a weird exits the pool for its native plane, the *portal* closes, and the pool loses its special effects.

Elemental Traits (Ex): An elemental weird is immune to poison, *sleep*, paralysis, and stunning. It is not subject to critical hits or flanking, and it cannot be raised or resurrected. The creature also has darkvision (60-foot range).

Prescience (Su): At will and as a free action, a weird can duplicate the effect of any of the following divination spells: *analyze dweomer, clairaudience/clairvoyance, contact other plane, detect thoughts, discern location, find the path, foresight, greater scrying, legend lore, locate creature, locate object, tongues, true seeing, vision.* Caster level 18th; save DC 16 + spell level.

AIR WEIRD

Air weirds are elemental spirits that offer direction and guidance to those traveling into unknown areas. They can point out paths not considered, reveal unknown doors into new worlds, and describe what may be needed to survive such journeys. An air weird's pool is often found outside, in an open-air place such as a windy plain or on a mountaintop.

An air weird appears as a ghostly, translucent woman composed of flowing vapors. Its eyes are deep blue, and its hair appears windblown. The lower half of the creature's body is a tendril of mist that trails back into its pool.

Spells: An air weird can cast arcane spells and divine spells from the Air and Travel domains as an 18th-level sorcerer (spells known 9/5/5/4/4/4/3/3/2/1; spells/day 6/8/8/7/7/7/7/6/5/3; save DC 16 + spell level).

Air Mastery (Ex): An air weird gains a +1 bonus on attack and damage rolls if its foe is airborne.

Air Pool: An air weird's pool is filled with billowing, gusting vapors of breathable air and mist. Creatures without the ability to fly cannot move through it, except by falling. An air weird's pool may be affixed to any vertical or horizontal surface, and it may be right side up or upside down (if affixed to a ceiling, for example).

Breathsense (Ex): An air weird can automatically sense the location of any breathing creature within 60 feet.

EARTH WEIRD

Earth weirds are foretellers of death and doom. They can pronounce an individual's impending fate or warn of a coming apocalypse. They are also prognosticators of wealth and fortune, foreseeing who shall succeed or fail in the pursuit of material possessions. An earth weird's pool is often situated at the base of a mountain or deep underground.

An earth weird's upper body resembles that of a beautiful human woman. The creature has sparkling gemstones for eyes and hair the brown color of earth, streaked with veins of gold and silver. The lower body is a shifting column of stone and dirt that connects to the earth pool.

Spells: An earth weird can cast arcane spells and divine spells from the Earth and Destruction domains as an 18th-level sorcerer (spells known 9/5/5/4/4/4/3/3/2/1; spells/day 6/8/8/7/7/7/7/6/5/3; save DC 16 + spell level).

Earth Mastery (Ex): An earth weird gains a +1 bonus on attack and damage rolls if its foe is touching the ground.

Earth Pool: This pool is filled with churning mud, rocks, and earth. Every creature within it (except the earth weird) takes 4d8 points of damage per round from the ever-grinding earth. In addition, creatures entering the pool suffocate if they do not have a way to breathe and are entombed (unable to move) if they cannot burrow. An earth weird's pool may be affixed only to a horizontal surface, and it may appear only in a right side up position (such as in the floor of a cavern).

Tremorsense (Ex): An earth weird can automatically sense the location of anything within 60 feet that is in contact with the ground.

FIRE WEIRD

Fire weirds are the diviners of hope. They shed light when all is dark and illuminate lore that has been long lost and nearly forgotten. They guide the long-suffering and ignorant to new peace and prosperity.

The beautiful, feminine half of a fire weird is a humanoid form composed of flickering flames and wreathed with smoke. The lower half of the body snakes away in a fiery trail into the hazy, flame-filled pool.

Burn (Ex): Any creature that is hit by the fire weird's slam attack (or that hits the fire weird with a natural weapon or an unarmed attack) must succeed at a Reflex save (DC 20) or catch fire (see Catching on Fire in Chapter 3 of the *Dungeon Master's Guide*). The fire burns for 1d4 rounds.

Spells: A fire weird can cast arcane spells and divine spells from the Fire and Sun domains as an 18th-level sorcerer (spells known 9/5/5/4/4/4/3/3/2/1; spells/day 6/8/8/7/7/7/7/6/5/3; save DC 16 + spell level).

Fire Pool: This pool contains a torrent of dancing flames that burn and smoke continually. Unprotected flammable materials within a fire pool catch on fire immediately, and any creature within the pool takes 3d10 points of fire damage per round. Creatures without the ability to fly

cannot move through this pool, except by falling. A fire weird's pool may be affixed to any vertical or horizontal surface, and it may appear only in a right side up position (such as on the floor of a cavern).

Fire Subtype (Ex): A fire weird is immune to fire damage but takes double damage from cold unless a saving throw for half damage is allowed. In that case, the creature takes half damage on a success and double damage on a failure.

WATER WEIRD

Water weirds are soothsayers that bring words of healing to the wounded. They offer curative knowledge for suffering lands and new options for people who seek a

better way. When there is little hope for life, water weirds offer a way to snatch victory from the jaws of defeat against all odds.

A water weird appears as a translucent, blue humanoid woman composed entirely of water. Its feet remain below the surface of its pool at all times.

Drench (Ex): A water weird's touch puts out torches, campfires, and other open flames of its own size category or smaller, as long as they are nonmagical.

Spells: A water weird can cast arcane spells and divine spells from the Water and Healing domains as an 18th-level sorcerer (spells known 9/5/5/4/4/4/3/3/2/1; spells/day 6/8/8/7/7/7/7/6/5/3; save DC 16 + spell level).

Water Mastery (Ex): A water weird gains a +1 bonus on attack and damage rolls if its opponent is touching water.

Water Pool: This pool is filled with bubbling, swirling water. Any creature within it that cannot breathe water immediately begins to drown (see The Drowning Rule in Chapter 3 of the *Dungeon Master's Guide*). Any creature without the ability to swim cannot move through a water pool, except by falling. A water weird's pool may be affixed only to a horizontal surface, and it may appear only in a right side up position (such as on the floor of a cavern).

WEIRD SOCIETY

All weirds, regardless of their elemental subtypes, are connected to each other in fundamental ways. They share a unique, secret bond that is evidenced in their level of cooperation. A weird that cannot provide the desired knowledge to a supplicant usually guides him or her to another weird for better counsel. Weirds of different elements often place their pools close to one another to broaden the range of divination services available to supplicants in an area.

Weirds are strongly linked to the Material Plane. They have all chosen to leave their native planes and serve as diviners for the humanoid races. Though they are bound to their pools, weirds can interact with other races though mortal agents that specialize in divination magic.

ETHER SCARAB

Tiny Outsider
Hit Dice: 1d8 (4 hp)
Initiative: +6
Speed: 10 ft.
AC: 14 (+2 size, +2 Dex), touch 14, flat-footed 12
Attacks: Bite +2 melee
Damage: Bite 1d3–1
Face/Reach: 2 1/2 ft. by 2 1/2 ft./0 ft.
Special Attacks: Wounding
Special Qualities: Death burst, outsider traits, planar rip
Saves: Fort+2, Ref +4, Will +1
Abilities: Str 8, Dex 15, Con 10, Int 1, Wis 9, Cha 4
Skills: Hide +11, Listen +0, Spot +0
Feats: Improved Initiative

Climate/Terrain: Any land or underground
Organization: Solitary, pair, cluster (3–5), or swarm (6–11)
Challenge Rating: 1
Treasure: None
Alignment: Always neutral
Advancement: 2–3 HD (Small)

These panicky, harmless-looking beetles are native to the Ethereal Plane. A wide variety of ethereal predators eat ether scarabs, so the latter have developed the ability to flee across planar boundaries. They often appear on the Material Plane next to buildings or other large objects near which they have made their lairs on the Ethereal Plane.

An ether scarab has six tentaclelike legs and a hard, amethyst-veined, chitinous shell marked by swirling, colorful pat-terns. It sports two pairs of

vicious-looking mandibles, which it uses to tear through planar boundaries.

COMBAT

The timid ether scarab almost always runs from trouble. If forced into battle, it bites with its mandibles. Ether scarabs do not enjoy the gravity of the Material Plane, so they return to their home plane as soon as it is safe to do so.

Wounding (Ex): A wound resulting from an ether scarab's bite attack bleeds for an additional 1 point of damage per round thereafter. Multiple wounds from such attacks result in cumulative bleeding loss (two wounds for 2 points of damage per round, and so on). The bleeding can be stopped only by a successful Heal check (DC 10) or the application of a *cure* spell or some other healing spell (*heal, healing circle*, or the like).

Death Burst (Ex): An ether scarab that dies on the Material Plane explodes harmlessly, causing a planar rip (see above) between the Material Plane and the Ethereal Plane. This hole in the planar fabric lasts 1d4+1 rounds.

Outsider Traits: An ether scarab has darkvision (60-foot range). It cannot be raised or resurrected.

Planar Rip (Su): By ripping at the planar fabric with its mandibles, an ether scarab can create a two-way *portal* between its own plane and another (usually the Material). This hole between the planes appears tiny, but it can accommodate any Large or smaller creature traveling in either direction. A planar rip closes in 1d4+1 rounds.

ETHEREAL DOPPELGANGER

Medium-Size Shapechanger
Hit Dice: 20d8 (90 hp)
Initiative: +5
Speed: 30 ft.
AC: 14 (+1 Dex, +3 natural), touch 11, flat-footed 13
Attacks: 2 claws +16 melee
Damage: Claw 1d4–1
Special Attacks: Assume identity, brain lock, mind wipe
Special Qualities: Darkvision 60 ft., DR 25/+3, fast healing 8, *plane shift*, SR 20
Saves: Fort +12, Ref +13, Will +13
Abilities: Str 8, Dex 13, Con 10, Int 14, Wis 13, Cha 15
Skills: Bluff +12, Diplomacy +6, Disguise +25, Intimidate +4, Listen +3, Sense Motive +11, Spot +7
Feats: Alertness, Blind-Fight, Dodge, Expertise, Improved Initiative, Mobility, Weapon Finesse (claw)

Climate/Terrain: Any land and underground
Organization: Solitary or squad (1 plus 4–16 jann)
Challenge Rating: 15
Treasure: Standard
Alignment: Usually lawful evil
Advancement: By character class

Ethereal doppelgangers live on the Ethereal Plane, in buildings that serve as combination showrooms, vaults, prisons, and shops. Ethereal doppelgangers are fond of magic items, and they frequently visit the Material Plane to acquire new ones for their collections. During their stays there, they usually disguise themselves as members of some other race. An ethereal doppelganger often interacts with or joins an adventuring party that it believes can lead it to, or near, a magic item it desires.

In its natural form, an ethereal doppelganger appears as a gangly humanoid with slick skin and white eyes that have no pupils. While traveling on the Material Plane, it usually takes the form of an attractive member of the same race as the group it has joined.

An ethereal doppelganger speaks Common, Infernal, and at least one elemental language (Auran, Aquan, Ignan, or Terran).

COMBAT

When it plans an extended stay on the Material Plane, an ethereal doppelganger uses its brain lock ability to render a chosen subject helpless, then takes that creature back to its floating home on the Ethereal Plane. In its sanctum, the doppelganger makes the subject comfortable and offers a deal. If the subject allows the doppelganger to assume his or her identity and acquire the desired item, the doppelganger will ensure the subject's comfort in the interim and return him or her unharmed to any desired location on the Material Plane afterward. If the subject refuses, the doppelganger wipes any memory of itself from the subject's mind, returns the creature to the Material Plane, and tries again with a new subject. Should the subject agree to the deal and then attempt to escape, the doppelganger sells him or her into extraplanar slavery. But if the subject accepts the agreement and complies with its terms, the doppelganger is as good as its word.

Assume Identity (Su): An ethereal doppelganger can absorb another creature's mind, memories, and personality. This process requires 1 hour of unbroken physical contact per level or Hit Die of the subject. The target may attempt a Will save (DC 22); if that is successful, the process is negated and the ethereal doppelganger must begin again. A willing creature can choose to waive the saving throw.

After consuming the target creature's identity, the ethereal doppelganger can assume its form with 100% accuracy.

The doppelganger possesses the other creature's memories, plus its alignment and all of its abilities, except for cleric spells of 2nd level or higher, a paladin's special abilities, and other powers granted by deities. (This does not deprive the subject of those memories or abilities; it only duplicates them in the ethereal doppelganger.) The doppelganger retains its own damage resistance, darkvision, fast healing, and spell resistance in its new form.

If an ethereal doppelganger commits an act that runs counter to its new identity's alignment, it is immediately forced back into its natural form for 1d10 rounds. It still retains the basic memories of the assumed identity, though not the deeper memories. If the subject dies before the contract is complete, the ethereal doppelganger immediately reverts to its natural form and loses all of that subject's memories and abilities.

Brain Lock (Su): As a standard action, an ethereal doppelganger can lock away the higher mind of an opponent up to 300 feet away, provided both are on the same plane and the doppelganger has line of sight to its subject. A successful Will save (DC 22) negates the attempt; failure leaves the subject mentally paralyzed. A brain-locked creature is not stunned, so attackers get no special advantage against it. Furthermore, it can still defend itself against attacks (its Dexterity bonus to AC, if any, still applies), but it cannot move or initiate any actions. A brain lock can negate various forms of special movement and cause harm to the creature thereby. For example, a brain-locked flying creature falls because it cannot flap its wings, and a brain-locked swimming creature may drown because it can no longer move its limbs. The effect lasts 20 rounds, but it can be dismissed earlier.

Mind Wipe (Su): With any successful melee touch attack, an ethereal doppelganger can wipe all memory of its existence from an opponent's mind (no saving throw).

Fast Healing (Ex): An ethereal doppelganger regains lost hit points at the rate of 3 per round. Fast healing does not restore hit points lost from starvation, thirst, or suffocation, and it does not allow the ethereal doppelganger to regrow or reattach lost body parts.

Plane Shift **(Sp):** An ethereal doppelganger can use *plane shift* (caster level 20th; Will save DC 17) at will.

ETHEREAL SLAYER

Medium-Size Outsider (Chaotic, Evil)
Hit Dice: 16d8+32 (104 hp)
Initiative: +8
Speed: 50 ft.
AC: 24 (+4 Dex, +10 natural), touch 14, flat-footed 20
Attacks: 2 claws +18 melee and bite +15 melee
Damage: Claw 1d8+1, bite 1d6
Face/Reach: 5 ft. by 5 ft./10 ft.
Special Qualities: Detect magic, dimensional anchor, DR 20/+2, outsider traits, plane shift, SR 23
Saves: Fort +12, Ref +14, Will +13
Abilities: Str 12, Dex 19, Con 14, Int 5, Wis 16, Cha 9
Skills: Hide +20, Jump +17, Listen +21, Move Silently +20, Spot +21
Feats: Alertness, Dodge, Improved Initiative, Weapon Finesse (bite), Weapon Focus (claw)

Climate/Terrain: Any
Organization: Solitary
Challenge Rating: 12
Treasure: None
Alignment: Always chaotic evil
Advancement: 17–24 HD (Medium-size); 25–32 HD (Large); 33–40 HD (Huge); 41–48 HD (Gargantuan)

Ethereal slayers are carnivorous predators that lie in ambush on the Ethereal Plane, waiting for unwitting creatures to enter. They typically wait in spots

that have significant cross-planar traffic, such as beside Material Plane buildings that are rich in magical auras. If several attempts have already been made to access a particular Material Plane location via ethereal travel, there is a good chance that a slayer has taken notice and gravitated to that spot.

A spiny, chitinous shell armors an ethereal slayer's body, and four mandibles surround its drooling mouth. It has two thick, birdlike legs and two arms that end in wicked, four-foot claws, like those of a praying mantis.

COMBAT

Ethereal slayers are ambush predators. They use their detect magic ability to locate strong magical auras, then wait near them for creatures to travel past on the Ethereal Plane. When a creature appears nearby, the slayer uses its dimensional anchor ability to fix its prey on the Ethereal Plane, then attacks with its claws. Should its opponent manage to flee to the Material Plane, the slayer uses its plane shift ability to pursue.

Detect Magic (Su): An ethereal slayer can produce a *detect magic* effect (caster level 9th) at will.

Dimensional Anchor (Su): An ethereal slayer can produce a *dimensional anchor* effect (caster level 9th) at will.

Outsider Traits: An ethereal slayer has darkvision (60-foot range). It cannot be raised or resurrected.

Plane Shift (Su): Twice per day, an ethereal slayer can produce a *plane shift* effect (caster level 9th; self only; save DC 14).

FAMINE SPIRIT

Medium-Size Undead
Hit Dice: 32d12 (208 hp)
Initiative: +4
Speed: 60 ft.
AC: 18 (+8 natural), touch 10, flat-footed 18
Attacks: Bite +19 melee and 2 claws +17 melee
Damage: Bite 1d8+3/19–20/vorpal bite, claw 1d6+1
Face/Reach: 5 ft. by 5 ft./5 ft.
Special Attacks: Aura of pain, vorpal bite
Special Qualities: Create spawn, ethereal jaunt, fast healing 10, scent, see invisibility, undead traits
Saves: Fort +10, Ref +10, Will +20
Abilities: Str 16, Dex 11, Con —, Int 14, Wis 15, Cha 15
Skills: Listen +37, Search +36, Spot +37
Feats: Cleave, Expertise, Great Cleave, Improved Bull Rush, Improved Critical (bite), Improved Initiative, Improved Trip, Multiattack, Power Attack, Sunder

Climate/Terrain: Any land and underground
Organization: Solitary, pair, brood (3–5), or band (2–5 plus 2–8 ghasts and 4–16 ghouls)
Challenge Rating: 19
Treasure: None

Alignment: Always neutral evil
Advancement: 33–64 HD (Medium-size)

The famine spirit, also called a ravenous ghoul, is a corporeal undead motivated entirely by hunger. It seeks to consume in death all that it was denied in life. It eats everything and anything that a living being could, but its hunger is never sated. A famine spirit can consume the comestibles of a *Mordenkainen's magnificent mansion* (caster level 14th) in a mere 5 hours and still be hungry for more. In a day, it can consume as many as one hundred humans.

A famine spirit appears as an obscenely obese humanoid or monstrous humanoid with a mouth full of razor-sharp teeth. Should the need present itself, a famine spirit can unhinge its jaw to swallow objects too large for it to consume normally.

Undead are among the few creatures that a famine spirit does not eat, so it may attract groups of ghouls and ghasts that serve it and feast in its wake.

COMBAT

Famine spirits ignore most other living things, turning on them only if they get in the way of its feasting, or if there is nothing else to consume. It fights primarily with its jaws, attempting to bite off the heads of any opponents.

Aura of Pain (Su): The famine spirit radiates a continual *symbol of pain* effect (save DC 28) as a 60-foot-radius emanation. A creature that fails its save is affected while within the area and for 10 minutes after leaving it. A successful save makes a creature immune to that famine spirit's aura of pain for 24 hours.

Vorpal Bite (Ex): The bite of a famine spirit severs the head of a Large or smaller opponent on a critical hit.

Create Spawn (Su): A famine spirit rarely leaves corpses in its wake, but sometimes it is forced to flee and leave slain opponents behind. Each of these corpses rises in 1d3 days as a famine spirit, unless a *protection from evil* spell is cast upon it before that time.

Ethereal Jaunt (Su): Three times per day, a famine spirit can produce an *ethereal jaunt* effect (caster level 20th). It uses this ability primarily to enter storehouses or to deal with ethereal interlopers.

See Invisibility (Su): A famine spirit can see invisible objects and beings as if under the effect of a *see invisibility* spell. This ability is always active.

Undead Traits: A famine spirit is immune to mind-affecting effects, poison, *sleep*, paralysis, stunning, disease, death effects, necromantic effects, and any effect that requires a Fortitude save unless it also works on objects. It is not subject to critical hits, subdual damage, ability damage, ability drain, energy drain, or death from massive damage. A famine spirit cannot be raised, and resurrection works only if it is willing. The creature has darkvision (60-foot range).

FELLDRAKE

The small, wingless dragons known as felldrakes trace their origin to Bahamut the Platinum Dragon. After helping a group of powerful elf wizards turn back a demonic invasion, Bahamut created the felldrakes to guard the elves against future incursions. All felldrakes have the blood of Bahamut in their veins and are fierce, loyal, and good at heart.

Felldrakes speak Draconic and Sylvan.

COMBAT

Felldrakes are impulsive attackers. Aggressive and eager to fight, they seek to close with opponents immediately.

Dragon Traits: Felldrakes are immune to *sleep* and paralysis effects. They have darkvision (60-foot range) and low-light vision.

CRESTED FELLDRAKE

Elves often employ crested felldrakes as guards for settlements and in border patrols.

A crested felldrake looks like a small, wingless dragon with powerful hind legs and a bright crest on its head.

Combat

When crested felldrakes fight in a group, some charge into battle and try to pin down the enemy, while their comrades move to encircle the foe.

	Crested Felldrake Small Dragon	Spitting Felldrake Medium-Size Dragon	Horned Felldrake Medium-Size Dragon
Hit Dice:	2d12+4 (17 hp)	3d12+3 (22 hp)	4d12+8 (34 hp)
Initiative:	+0	+2	+0
Speed:	40 ft.	30 ft.	30 ft.
AC:	15 (+1 size, +4 natural), touch 11, flat-footed 15	16 (+2 Dex, +4 natural), touch 12, flat-footed 14	17 (+7 natural), touch 10, flat-footed 17
Attacks:	Bite +3 melee	Bite +6 melee, or spit +5 ranged touch	Horn +8 melee
Damage:	Bite 1d8	Bite 1d6+3, spit 2d4 acid	Horn 2d6+4
Face/Reach:	5 ft. by 5 ft./5 ft.	5 ft. by 5 ft./ 5 ft.	5 ft. by 5 ft./5 ft.
Special Attacks:	—	—	Charge 4d6+6
Special Qualities:	Dragon traits, scent	Dragon traits	Dragon traits
Saves:	Fort +5, Ref +3, Will +4	Fort +4, Ref +5, Will +3	Fort +6, Ref +4, Will +5
Abilities:	Str 11, Dex 10, Con 15, Int 6, Wis 12, Cha 9	Str 14, Dex 15, Con 13, Int 8, Wis 10, Cha 9	Str 17, Dex 10, Con 15, Int 5, Wis 12, Cha 8
Skills:	Hide +6, Jump +2, Listen +5, Spot +5	Hide +7, Jump +4, Listen +4, Spot +4	Hide +3, Jump +6, Listen +6, Spot +6
Feats:	Alertness	Weapon Focus (bite)	Alertness, Weapon Focus (horn)
Climate/Terrain:	Any land and underground	Temperate plains, forest, hills and underground	Any land and underground
Organization:	Solitary, pair, gang (3–5), or pack (4–16)	Solitary, pair, or gang (3–5)	Solitary, pair, gang (3–5), or pack (4–16)
Challenge Rating:	1	2	3
Treasure:	None	None	None
Alignment:	Always neutral good	Always neutral good	Always neutral good
Advancement:	3–4 HD (Small); 5–6 HD (Medium-size)	4–9 HD (Medium-size)	5–8 HD (Medium-size); 9–12 HD (Large)

SPITTING FELLDRAKE

Because of its snaky body, a spitting felldrake can squeeze through small spaces. Thus, it is ideal for the underground expeditions so contrary to elven nature.

The spitting felldrake is slightly larger than its crested cousin. Its body is long and sinuous, like that of a snake.

Combat

A spitting felldrake usually pauses to spit acid before closing to melee. It can spit acid up to 30 feet as a ranged touch attack with no range increment.

HORNED FELLDRAKE

Horned felldrakes are often used to protect important individuals or cities.

This creature is larger than the other felldrakes. Its head sports several horns, which it uses to impale foes.

Combat

Horned felldrakes usually charge foes first, then use their horns in melee.

Charge (Ex): A horned felldrake typically begins a battle by charging at its opponent. In addition to the normal benefits and hazards of a charge, this allows the horned felldrake to make a single horn attack (+8 melee) that deals 4d6+6 points of damage.

FIENDWURM

Gargantuan Magical Beast
Hit Dice: 24d10+216 (348 hp)
Initiative: +5
Speed: 60 ft., burrow 60 ft.
AC: 27 (−4 size, +1 Dex, +20 natural), touch 7, flat-footed 26
Attacks: Bite +33 melee
Damage: Bite 2d8+19
Face/Reach: 10 ft. by 40 ft./10 ft.
Special Attacks:
   Death rift,
   demonic belch,
   improved grab,
   swallow whole
Special Qualities:
   Acidic hide, acid
   immunity, darkvision
   60 ft., DR 15/−, low-light
   vision, portal, tremorsense
Saves: Fort +23, Ref +15,
   Will +10
Abilities: Str 36,
   Dex 13, Con 29,
   Int 7, Wis 14, Cha 8
Skills: Intuit Direction
   +9, Listen +11, Spot +12
Feats: Alertness, Dodge,
   Improved Initiative

Climate/Terrain: Any desert, plains, and underground
Organization: Solitary or troupe (1 plus 2–8 dretches, quasits, or vrocks)
Challenge Rating: 28
Treasure: None
Alignment: Always chaotic evil
Advancement: 25–72 HD (Colossal)

A fiendwurm is the result of demonic magic applied to an ordinary earthworm. This tormented monster is constantly wracked with unbearable pain from the planar portal embedded in its belly. Eating relieves the creature's pain for a short while, so it attempts to swallow any creature it encounters. Its tortured existence keeps it constantly on the hunt.

A fiendwurm is a 40-foot-long, serpentine creature with a mottled gray and pink hide. Its huge maw is filled with long, snakelike fangs. The creature is never at rest; its intense pain causes it to writhe and squirm constantly.

Fiendwurms are in such terrible agony that they are unable to communicate at all.

COMBAT

A fiendwurm immediately lunges to bite and swallow any living creature it chances upon. If it seems to be overmatched, it uses its demonic belch ability to summon aid. A fiendwurm does not stop attacking until it is slain.

Death Rift (Su): Upon its death, a fiendwurm's portal implodes. Every creature within 5 feet of the fiendwurm that fails a Reflex save (DC 31) is drawn into the collapsing portal and transported to the Abyss. The implosion destroys the fiendwurm's body along with the portal. Thus, any creatures transported to the Abyss via a death rift must find another means of returning to their original planes.

Demonic Belch (Su): Three times per day, a fiendwurm can use its connection with the Abyss to bring 1d4 demons to its aid. It expels these creatures from its mouth with a great belching sound. The demons arrive unharmed, but the fiendwurm's pain may cause it to attack them thereafter, if they seem to be easier prey than the opponents, or if there are no other creatures left to eat. Roll d% to determine the kind of demons that arrive: 01–50 jovocs, 51–75 quasits, 76–100 vrocks. These demons cannot use their summoning abilities for one hour after being snatched out of the Abyss. Once a fiendwurm uses this ability, it must wait 1d4 rounds before using it again.

Improved Grab (Ex): If a fiendwurm hits an opponent that is at least one size category smaller than itself with a bite attack, it deals normal damage and attempts to start a grapple as a free action without provoking an attack of opportunity (grapple bonus +49). If it gets a hold, it can try to swallow the opponent in the next round. Alternatively, the fiendwurm has the option to conduct the grapple normally, or simply use its jaws to hold the opponent (−20 penalty on grapple check, but the fiendwurm is not considered grappled). In either case, each successful grapple check it makes during successive rounds automatically deals bite damage.

Swallow Whole (Ex): A fiendwurm can swallow a grabbed opponent that is at least two size categories smaller than itself by making a successful grapple check (grapple bonus +49). Once inside the fiendwurm, the opponent takes 2d8+13 points of bludgeoning damage and 1d8 points of acid damage per round from the creature's gizzard. A successful

grapple check allows the swallowed creature to climb out of the gizzard and return to the fiendwurm's mouth, where another successful grapple check is needed to get free. Alternatively, a swallowed creature can try to cut its way out with either claws or a light piercing or slashing weapon. Dealing at least 25 points of damage to the gizzard (AC 20) in this way creates an opening large enough to permit escape. Once a single swallowed creature exits, muscular action closes the hole; thus, another swallowed opponent must cut its own way out. A Gargantuan fiendwurm's gizzard can hold 2 Huge, 8 Large, 32 Medium-size, or 128 Small or smaller creatures.

Acidic Hide (Ex): A fiendwurm produces a highly caustic mucus that coats its entire body. Touching its hide deals 3d6 points of acid damage to an organic creature or object, 5d8 points of acid damage to a metallic creature or object, or 1d10 points of acid damage to a stony creature (such as an earth elemental) or object. A gallon or more of water is needed to wash off the mucus.

Portal (Su): Lining the lowest part of the fiendwurm's gizzard is a portal to the Abyss that is activated by the presence of a living creature. A swallowed creature must make a Reflex save (DC 31) each round to avoid falling into or being squeezed through the portal. The Abyssal side of the portal is stationary, but the other side moves with the fiendwurm. If this portal is permanently closed, the fiendwurm instantly dies but does not implode.

Tremorsense (Ex): A fiendwurm can automatically sense the location of anything within 120 feet that is in contact with the ground.

FIHYR

Fihyrs are the collected fears of humanity made corporeal. These creatures were once thought to be related to beholders, but in fact there is no connection between the two kinds of monsters aside from a superficial resemblance.

As the remnants of hundreds of people's nightmares swirl through the ether, they somehow combine with leftover magical power and coalesce into these physical monsters. A few random dream images aren't enough; it takes the strong emotional energy of a mass of people under duress to spawn a fihyr. The right combination of conditions is most often found in cities that are under siege, or being terrorized by monsters, or suffering from famine, civil war, or some other mass trauma.

Great fihyrs are larger, more intelligent, and much more dangerous than the smaller variety. A great fihyr forms when a number of small fihyrs combine.

All fihyrs have the same general appearance; the two kinds differ mainly in size. A fihyr is a roughly spherical blob of soft tissue and pulsating gray matter, much like a gigantic brain with a partial layer of skin stretched over it. The body of a fihyr is about 2 feet in diameter; that of a great fihyr is closer to 7 feet. Two large tentacles hang below the body and serve as the creature's legs. A mass of much smaller, constantly writhing and twining tentacles projects from its body; these help it maintain its balance. Numerous mouths and eyes are placed at random along the "front" side of the creature's body. The eyes are a startling gold color with horizontal black pupils, and the mouths are lined with needle-sharp teeth. The mottled skin of a fihyr runs the full spectrum of colors, but

	Fihyr Small Aberration	Great Fihyr Medium-Size Aberration
Hit Dice:	4d8 (18 hp)	16d8 +16 (88 hp)
Initiative:	+3	+6
Speed:	30 ft.	30 ft., fly 50 ft. (good)
AC:	18 (+1 size, +3 Dex, +4 natural), touch 14, flat-footed 15	18 (+2 Dex, +6 natural), touch 12, flat-footed 16
Attacks:	Bite +2 melee	4 bites +12 melee
Damage:	Bite 1d4–2	Bite 2d6
Face/Reach:	5 ft. by 5 ft./5 ft.	10 ft. by 10 ft./5 ft.
Special Attacks:	Frightful presence	*Emotion control*, frightful presence
Special Qualities:	Darkvision 60 ft., SR 10, vulnerable to sunlight	Darkvision 60 ft., invisibility, SR 18
Saves:	Fort +1, Ref +4, Will +5	Fort +8, Ref +9, Will +14
Abilities:	Str 7, Dex 16, Con 10, Int 5, Wis 12, Cha 7	Str 11, Dex 14, Con 12, Int 14, Wis 15, Cha 15
Skills:	Hide +10, Move Silently +9, Spot +8	Hide +16, Move Silently +21, Open Lock +17, Spot +12
Feats:	—	Dodge, Great Fortitude, Improved Initiative, Iron Will, Lightning Reflexes
Climate/Terrain:	Any city, town, or village	Any
Organization:	Solitary, pair, or brood (3–4)	Solitary
Challenge Rating:	3	15
Treasure:	None	None
Alignment:	Always chaotic evil	Always chaotic evil
Advancement:	5–8 HD (Small); 9–12 HD (Medium-size)	17–24 HD (Medium-size); 25–48 HD (Large)

GREAT FIHYR

Great fihyrs begin any conflict by using their *emotion control* ability to generate negative emotions on which they can feed. Once they decide to become visible, they immediately attack so as to use their frightful presence ability.

Great fihyrs are unaffected by sunlight, but they despise it. Thus, they prefer to lay low during the day in dark, secluded spots, such as caves, dungeons, abandoned buildings, and the like.

Frightful Presence (Ex): Any creature that witnesses a great fihyr attacking becomes panicked if it fails a Will save (DC 20).

Emotion Control (Sp): At will, the great fihyr can produce an effect like that of an *emotion* spell (*despair, fear,* or *hate* only; caster level 16th; Will save DC 16), except that its range is 260 feet, its radius is 15 feet, and it lasts as long as the creature concentrates on it. The great fihyr can use this ability and remain invisible.

Invisibility (Ex): A great fihyr can become invisible at will. This effect is like that of the *invisibility* spell, except that the creature can remain invisible as long as it wishes, even while using its *emotion control* ability. Normally, a great fihyr is visible only immediately after delivering a melee attack.

FIRBOLG

Large Giant

Hit Dice: 13d8+78 (136 hp)

Initiative: +1

Speed: 40 ft.

AC: 25 (–1 size, +1 Dex, +3 masterwork studded leather, +12 natural), touch 10, flat-footed 24

Attacks: Huge greatsword +21/+16 melee, or rock +10 ranged

Damage: Huge greatsword 2d8+19/19–20, rock 2d6+13

Face/Reach: 5 ft. by 5 ft./10 ft.

Special Attacks: Rock throwing, spell-like abilities, trample 2d8+19

Special Qualities: Darkvision 60 ft., fast healing 3, rock catching

Saves: Fort +14, Ref +5, Will +6

Abilities: Str 36, Dex 13, Con 23, Int 14, Wis 15, Cha 14

Skills: Knowledge (nature) +5, Move Silently +5, Spot +8, Wilderness Lore +8

Feats: Deflect Arrows, Dodge, Improved Unarmed Strike

Climate/Terrain: Temperate hills and forest

Organization: Solitary, pair, gang (3–8), squad (9–16), or troop (20–40)

Challenge Rating: 12

Treasure: Standard

Alignment: Usually neutral

Advancement: By character class

always in dull, sickly shades. An oily sheen covers the surface of the creature's body.

Fihyrs rarely survive beyond the night of their formation, and they never leave the troubled area that spawned them. Great fihyrs, on the other hand, survive until slain. They have been known to wander for hundreds of miles, from one tormented spot to another, feeding on the fear and despair of the inhabitants.

COMBAT

Both kinds of fihyrs attack by biting. The real purpose of a fihyr's bite is not to deal damage, but to spread fear in others.

FIHYR

Fihyrs never hesitate to attack, but they prefer to do so in front of as many witnesses as possible, to make use of their frightful presence ability.

Frightful Presence (Ex): Any creature that witnesses a fihyr attacking becomes panicked if it fails a Will save (DC 10).

Vulnerable to Sunlight (Ex): Fihyrs die instantly when exposed to sunlight, hissing and bubbling away into acrid smoke. They have no fear of sunlight, however, and they don't seek shelter to wait out the day. Magical sunlight can destroy a fihyr if it penetrates the creature's spell resistance, though if the fihyr succeeds at any allowed saving throw, it avoids the instant death effect.

Firbolgs are reclusive giants who tend to avoid contact with humanoid races and even other kinds of giants. Unlike some of the more brutish giantkin, firbolgs do not depend heavily on raiding for subsistence, nor do they rely solely on force to resolve problems.

A firbolg looks like a 10-foot-tall human and weighs more than 800 pounds. Its skin is a fleshy pink color, and it can have hair of almost any shade, although blond and red are the most common. A firbolg of either gender wears its hair long, and the typical male sports a great, thick beard.

Firbolgs speak Giant and Common.

COMBAT

Firbolgs are both cautious and crafty. They have learned to distrust and fear the "civilized" races, such as humans and elves. If possible, they avoid encounters with humanoids altogether, either by hiding or by deception.

If forced to fight, firbolgs employ effective combat strategy, using the terrain and situation to best effect. They always operate as a team, not as a collection of individuals.

Rock Throwing (Ex): An adult firbolg receives a +1 racial bonus on attack rolls when throwing rocks. It can throw rocks weighing 40 to 50 pounds each (Small objects) up to five range increments (range increment 130 feet).

Spell-Like Abilities: 1/day—*alter self, detect magic, feeblemind, know direction.* Caster level 13th; save DC 12 + spell level.

Trample (Ex): As a standard action during its turn each round, a firbolg can trample opponents at least one size category smaller than itself. This attack deals 2d8+19 points of bludgeoning damage. A trampled opponent can attempt either an attack of opportunity at a –4 penalty or a Reflex save (DC 29) for half damage.

Fast Healing (Ex): A firbolg regains lost hit points at the rate of 3 per round. Fast healing does not restore hit points lost from starvation, thirst, or suffocation, and it does not allow the firbolg to regrow or reattach lost body parts.

Rock Catching (Ex): A firbolg can catch Small, Medium-size, or Large rocks (or projectiles of similar shape). Once per round, a firbolg that would normally be hit by a rock can make a Reflex save to catch it as a free action. The DC is 15 for a Small rock, 20 for a Medium-size one, and 25 for a

Large one. (If the projectile has a bonus on attack rolls because of magic, the DC increases by that amount.) The firbolg must be ready for and aware of the attack.

FIRBOLG SOCIETY

Firbolgs usually live in well-fortified colonies, either in the depths of the forest or in cavern complexes dug into hillsides. All firbolg settlements are protected by guard towers. These creatures live primarily by hunting and gathering, but each colony also practices simple agriculture.

FIRBOLG CHARACTERS

A troop of firbolgs usually has a druid as its leader. Any other ranked members have levels in the barbarian class. A firbolg's favored class is druid.

A firbolg PC's effective character level (ECL) is equal to its class level + 18. Thus, a 1st-level firbolg druid has an ECL of 19 and is the equivalent of a 19th-level character.

FIRE BAT

Small Elemental (Fire)
Hit Dice: 6d8–6 (21 hp)
Initiative: +3
Speed: 10 ft., fly 50 ft. (good)
AC: 16 (+1 size, +3 Dex, +2 natural), touch 14, flat-footed 13
Attacks: Bite +8 melee
Damage: Bite 1d6–1 plus 1d6 fire
Face/Reach: 5 ft. by 5 ft./5 ft.
Special Attacks: Attach, burn, devour
Special Qualities: Blindsight 120 ft., elemental traits, fire subtype, regeneration 5
Saves: Fort +1, Ref +8, Will +0
Abilities: Str 8, Dex 17, Con 8, Int 6, Wis 7, Cha 5
Skills: Hide +15, Listen +9, Spot +9
Feats: Flyby Attack, Weapon Finesse (bite) (B)

Climate/Terrain: Elemental Plane of Fire or volcanoes
Organization: Solitary or swarm (11–20)
Challenge Rating: 3
Treasure: None
Alignment: Always neutral evil
Advancement: 7–12 HD (Small); 13–18 HD (Medium-size)

Fire bats are native to the Elemental Plane of Fire, but unlike fire elementals, they are not composed solely of elemental material. They can fly through the flames and magma of the Elemental Plane of Fire as easily as normal bats fly through

the air. They propel themselves by expelling heated gases from tubes within their bodies, flapping their wings only to steer during flight.

A fire bat cannot enter water or any other nonflammable liquid. A body of water is an impassible barrier unless the fire bat can step, jump or fly over it.

Fire bats feed on living creatures, attaching to targets and devouring flesh until they are sated. A sated fire bat has a 25% chance of splitting into two hungry fire bats during the next 24 hours.

A fire bat's body is about 2 feet long, and its wingspan is about 4 feet. The creature burns continuously with an unbearably hot, red flame, which makes it look larger than it really is. Until it is slain and its body cools, it's impossible to tell that it is not just swirling fire in the shape of a large bat.

Fire elementals get along well with fire bats, but salamanders, efreet, and most other creatures of fire prey on them. Such a check on their population is vital, since they not only regenerate but also multiply very quickly where food is plentiful. Without natural predators, they could overrun the entire Elemental Plane of Fire within weeks.

COMBAT

In combat, fire bats display a level of cunning that belies their limited intelligence, dividing their attacks evenly among all the possible targets. Once a fire bat is sated (see devour, below), it breaks off and leaves the fight. When one-fourth of the swarm is sated or slain, all the remaining fire bats break off and flee, only to shadow their prey and attack again when the time is right. They repeat this pattern until the whole swarm has fed.

Attach (Ex): If a fire bat hits with its bite attack, it latches onto the opponent's body. An attached fire bat is effectively grappling its prey. The fire bat loses its Dexterity bonus to AC (giving it an AC of 13) but holds on with great tenacity, dealing 1d6 points of fire damage each round it remains attached. An attached fire bat can be struck with a weapon or grappled itself. To remove an attached fire bat through grappling, the opponent must achieve a pin (see Grapple in Chapter 8 of the *Player's Handbook*) against the fire bat. Each grapple attempt subjects the opponent to the fire bat's burn attack.

Burn (Ex): Any creature that is hit by a fire bat's bite attack (or that hits the fire bat with a natural weapon or an unarmed attack) must succeed at a Reflex save (DC 12) or catch fire (see Catching on Fire in Chapter 3 of the *DUNGEON MASTER'S Guide*). The fire burns for 1d4 rounds. Immersing a fire bat in at least 10 gallons of water extinguishes its flames and prevents it from flying but does not otherwise harm the creature. The fire bat's flames reignite after 10 rounds.

Devour (Ex): Once it is attached, a fire bat devours the opponent's flesh, automatically dealing 1d6–1 points of bite damage and 1d6 points of fire damage each round it remains attached. After dealing 6 points of damage, the fire bat is sated; on the next round it detaches and flies away to digest the meal.

Blindsight (Ex): A fire bat emits high-frequency sounds, inaudible to most other creatures, that bounce off nearby objects and creatures. This ability enables it to discern objects and creatures within 120 feet. The fire bat usually does not need to make Spot or Listen checks to notice creatures within range of its blindsight. A *silence* spell negates this ability and forces the fire bat to rely on its weak vision (which has a maximum range of 10 feet).

Elemental Traits (Ex): A fire bat is immune to poison, *sleep*, paralysis, and stunning. It is not subject to critical hits or flanking, and it cannot be raised or resurrected. The creature also has darkvision (60-foot range).

Fire Subtype (Ex): A fire bat is immune to fire damage but takes double damage from cold unless a saving throw for half damage is allowed. In that case, the creature takes half damage on a success and double damage on a failure.

Regeneration (Ex): Cold attacks deal normal damage to a fire bat.

Skills: A fire bat receives a +4 racial bonus on Spot and Listen checks. *These bonuses are lost if its blindsight is negated.

FIRE BAT FAMILIARS

If your campaign uses the Improved Familiar feat from *Tome and Blood: A Guide Book to Wizards and Sorcerers*, a fire bat is an appropriate improved familiar for a 15th-level or higher arcane spellcaster of the fire subtype. Like other improved familiars, a fire bat familiar provides no special benefits to its master beyond the standard familiar benefits (see Familiars in Chapter 3 of the *Player's Handbook*).

FLESH JELLY

Gargantuan Ooze
Hit Dice: 18d10+108 (237 hp)
Initiative: –2
Speed: 20 ft.
AC: 4 (–4 size, –2 Dex), touch 4, flat-footed 4
Attacks: 4 slams +20 melee
Damage: Slam 2d8+11
Face/Reach: 30 ft. by 30 ft./15 ft.
Special Attacks: Absorb, disease, engulf
Special Qualities: Blindsight, horrid stench, ooze traits
Saves: Fort +12, Ref +4, Will +1
Abilities: Str 32, Dex 6, Con 23, Int —, Wis 1, Cha 1

Climate/Terrain: Warm forest, plains or marsh
Organization: Solitary
Challenge Rating: 19
Treasure: None
Alignment: Always neutral
Advancement: 19–36 HD (Colossal)

A flesh jelly is a nauseating mound of stinking flesh that gorges itself on any creatures unfortunate enough to cross its path. These ravenous oozes are usually found in tropical regions.

A flesh jelly is a blob of soft, fleshy tissue surrounded by a filthy membrane composed of skin, hair, and fur. When it moves, a few of the loose bones inside it press against the outer membrane, causing its disgusting body to bulge out here and there. The creature has no eyes, ears, or mouth.

COMBAT

Driven by its raging hunger, a flesh jelly simply rolls over its foes, absorbing them into its body mass. When facing a group, it usually concentrates on engulfing one target, then defends itself by lashing out at other opponents with its fleshy pseudopods while attempting to absorb its meal.

Absorb (Ex): A flesh jelly feeds by absorbing other creatures into its bulk. Any creature engulfed by the monster must succeed at a Fortitude save (DC 25) or be absorbed into its mass and die. A successful save prevents absorption that round. Each absorbed creature heals a flesh jelly of 2d6 points of damage. A flesh jelly expels the absorbed creature's personal belongings from its body 1d3

rounds after absorption. Nothing short of a *wish* or similar magic can restore a creature that has been absorbed.

Disease (Ex): Any creature engulfed by a flesh jelly or hit by its slam attack must succeed at a Fortitude save (DC 25) or contract filth fever. The incubation period is 1d3 days, and the disease deals 1d3 points of Dexterity damage and 1d3 points of Constitution damage (see Disease in Chapter 3 of the *Dungeon Master's Guide*).

Engulf (Ex): A flesh jelly can simply bowl over creatures up to one size category smaller than itself as a standard action. This attack affects as many opponents as the flesh jelly's body can cover. Each target can make either an attack of opportunity against the flesh jelly or a Reflex save (DC 30) to avoid being engulfed. A successful saving throw indicates that the target has been pushed back or aside (target's choice) as the ooze moves forward. An engulfed creature is considered grappled and trapped within the flesh jelly's body. A flesh jelly cannot make a slam attack during a round in which it attempts to engulf, but each engulfed creature takes automatic slam damage and must save against disease (see above) on that round and every round thereafter that it remains trapped. On any round after engulfing a creature, the flesh jelly can attempt to absorb it.

Blindsight (Ex): A flesh jelly is blind, but its entire body is a primitive sensory organ that can ascertain prey by scent and vibration. This ability enables it to discern objects and creatures within 60 feet. The flesh jelly usually does not need to make Spot or Listen checks to notice creatures within range of its blindsight.

Horrid Stench (Ex): Any corporeal creature with 10 or fewer Hit Dice that comes within 50 feet of a flesh jelly must make a Fortitude saving throw (DC 25) or be nauseated for the next 2d6 rounds. Another save is required at the end of that time if the creature is still within range. A single successful save against this effect renders the creature immune to that flesh jelly's horrid stench for 24 hours. A nauseated creature cannot attack, cast spells, concentrate on spells, or do anything else requiring attention. The only action permitted is a single move or move-equivalent action.

Ooze Traits: A flesh jelly is immune to mind-affecting effects, poison, *sleep*, paralysis, stunning, and polymorphing. It is not subject to critical hits or flanking.

FOMORIAN

Huge Giant

Hit Dice: 15d8+90 (157 hp)

Initiative: +1

Speed: 40 ft.

AC: 21 (–2 size, +1 Dex, +9 natural, +3 hide armor), touch 9, flat-footed 20

Attacks: Gargantuan heavy flail +21/+16/+11 melee, or 2 slams +21 melee

Damage: Gargantuan heavy flail 2d8+18/19–20, slam 1d8+12

Face/Reach: 10 ft. by 5 ft./15 ft.

Special Attacks: Trample 2d10+18

Special Qualities: DR 5/–, fast healing 5, scent

Saves: Fort +15, Ref +6, Will +6

Abilities: Str 34, Dex 12, Con 22, Int 11, Wis 13, Cha 9

Skills: Listen +3, Move Silently +16, Spot +12

Feats: Alertness, Cleave, Power Attack

Climate/Terrain: Any mountains and underground

Organization: Solitary, pair, or gang (3–5)

Challenge Rating: 11

Treasure: Standard

Alignment: Usually neutral evil

Advancement: By character class

Fomorians are grossly deformed behemoths that live in mountain caves, abandoned mines, or other subterranean areas. They rarely modify their homes for comfort or convenience; they simply adapt to their surroundings. Their territories are commonly marked by the partially consumed bodies of their victims.

Each fomorian has a different set of physical deformities. These can include a misplaced or misshapen limb, a misplaced facial feature, a hunchback, a bulging body part, drooping flesh, flapping ears, a huge snout, large feet on short legs, and many others. Patches of hair as tough as wire are scattered over its pale white skin, and large warts and other growths dot its thick hide.

Unlike other giants, fomorians can survive on relatively little food, considering the size of their bodies. They eat almost any organic matter they come across, from molds and lichens to humanoid prey, which is their favorite.

A fomorian speaks Giant and one other language (usually Common).

COMBAT

Fomorians usually try to sneak up on opponents and hit as hard as they can. If they bother to keep captured opponents alive after combat, it is only for the entertainment they gain from crude torture before eating their fallen foes. Fomorians do not throw or catch rocks as other giants do.

Trample (Ex): As a standard action during its turn each round, a fomorian can trample opponents at least one size category smaller than itself. This attack deals 2d10+18 points of bludgeoning damage. A trampled opponent can attempt either an attack of opportunity at a –4 penalty or a Reflex save (DC 29) for half damage.

Fast Healing (Ex): A fomorian regains lost hit points at the rate of 5 per round. Fast healing does not restore hit points lost from starvation, thirst, or suffocation, and it does not allow the fomorian to regrow or reattach lost body parts.

Scent (Ex): A fomorian can detect approaching enemies, sniff out hidden foes, and track by sense of smell.

Skills: A fomorian has a +10 racial bonus on Move Silently checks.

FOMORIAN SOCIETY

Depravity and wickedness rule fomorian society. The strongest and cruelest rules over all the others within reach, and women and children are treated as slaves in every household. Acts of violence, sometimes resulting in permanent injury or death, are common among fomorians. Anyone who can completely dominate a fomorian can use the creature as an ally, but such an alliance lasts only as long as the fomorian fears the dominant being.

FOMORIAN CHARACTERS

A fomorian's favored class is barbarian. Gang leaders are either druids or barbarian/druids.

A fomorian PC's effective character level (ECL) is equal to its class level + 17. Thus, a 1st-level fomorian barbarian has an ECL of 18 and is the equivalent of a 18th-level character.

FOREST SLOTH

Large Beast
Hit Dice: 14d10+70 (147 hp)
Initiative: +5
Speed: 40 ft., brachiation 40 ft., climb 60 ft.
AC: 21 (−1 size, +5 Dex, +7 natural), touch 14, flat-footed 16
Attacks: 2 claws +16 melee and bite +11 melee
Damage: Claw 2d4+7, bite 2d8+3
Face/Reach: 5 ft. by 10 ft./10 ft.
Special Attacks: Improved grab, swallow whole
Special Qualities: Darkvision 60 ft., low-light vision, poison immunity, scent
Saves: Fort +14, Ref +14, Will +5
Abilities: Str 25, Dex 20, Con 21, Int 2, Wis 12, Cha 9
Skills: Climb +15*, Listen +7, Move Silently, +8*, Spot +6*

Climate/Terrain: Warm forests
Organization: Solitary, pair, or family (3–5)
Challenge Rating: 11
Treasure: None
Alignment: Always neutral
Advancement: 15–21 HD (Large); 22–42 HD (Huge)

The territorial forest sloth is a nocturnal hunter that roams tropical forests and jungles. This creature is not the slow-moving beast its name implies; in fact, it possesses lightning-fast reflexes and can travel as quickly over land as it does through trees. It is particularly fond of halfling flesh.

Standing 8 feet tall, a forest sloth is a sinewy beast with a large, toothy mouth. Its tremendous jaws support a row of oversized, needle-sharp front teeth. Each of a forest sloth's limbs ends in three toes tipped with huge, curved claws. Its fur color ranges from olive to brown.

Forest sloths communicate with each other using screeches and grunts.

COMBAT

The forest sloth typically attacks by leaping on prey with a frenzy of bite and claw attacks. Families of forest sloths often hunt together, using one as a scout to lure prey into the trees where the rest of the group waits in ambush.

Improved Grab (Ex): If a forest sloth hits an opponent that is at least one size category smaller than itself with both claw attacks, it deals normal damage and attempts to start a grapple as a free action without provoking an attack of opportunity (grapple bonus +21). If it gets a hold, it transfers the opponent to its mouth as a free action and automatically hits with its bite attack in the same round. It can then try to swallow its prey in the next round. Alternatively, the forest sloth has the option to conduct the grapple normally, or simply use its jaws to hold the opponent (−20 penalty on grapple check, but the forest sloth is not considered grappled). In either case, each successful grapple check it makes during successive rounds automatically deals bite damage.

Swallow Whole (Ex): A forest sloth can swallow a creature that is at least two size categories smaller than itself by making a successful grapple check (grapple bonus +21), provided that the opponent is already in its mouth at the start of its turn. Once inside the sloth, the opponent takes 2d4+7 points of bludgeoning damage plus 1d8 points of acid damage per round from the sloth's gullet. A successful grapple check allows the swallowed creature to climb out of the gullet and return to the sloth's mouth, where another successful grapple check is needed to get free. Alternatively, a swallowed creature can try to cut its way out with either claws or a light piercing or slashing weapon. Dealing at least 25 points of damage to the gullet (AC 20) in this way creates an opening large enough to permit escape. Once a single swallowed creature exits, muscular action closes the hole; thus, another swallowed opponent must cut its own way out. A Large forest sloth's gullet can hold 2 Small, 8 Tiny, or 32 Diminutive or smaller creatures.

Scent (Ex): A forest sloth can detect approaching enemies, sniff out hidden foes, and track by sense of smell.

Skills: *A forest sloth receives a +4 racial bonus on Climb, Move Silently, and Spot checks when in forested areas.

FROST SALAMANDER

Medium-Size Magical Beast (Cold)
Hit Dice: 12d10+12 (78 hp)
Initiative: +2
Speed: 30 ft., climb 30 ft.
AC: 17 (+2 Dex, +5 natural), touch 12, flat-footed 15
Attacks: 4 claws +12 melee and bite +10 melee
Damage: Claw 1d6/19–20, bite 1d6
Face/Reach: 5 ft. by 10 ft./5 ft.
Special Attacks: Cold aura
Special Qualities: Cold subtype, darkvision 60 ft., DR 15/+1, low-light vision
Saves: Fort +9, Ref +10, Will +5
Abilities: Str 11, Dex 15, Con 12, Int 6, Wis 12, Cha 7
Skills: Climb +8, Hide +14, Listen +3, Move Silently +13, Spot +3
Feats: Alertness, Improved Critical (claw), Multiattack

Climate/Terrain: Any cold and underground
Organization: Solitary or pair
Challenge Rating: 7
Treasure: Standard
Alignment: Always chaotic evil
Advancement: 13–18 HD (Large); 19–24 HD (Huge); 25–36 HD (Gargantuan)

Frost salamanders can be found in many extremely cold places on the Material Plane. Ice caves, glaciers, frozen lakes, and other places where the temperature seldom rises above freezing are their favorite haunts.

A frost salamander's ice-blue, serpentine body has six legs, a long tail, and a reptilian head. Its claws are equipped with talons that resemble icicles. These claws not only make vicious weapons, they allow the creature to climb any ice-covered surface—even a vertical wall.

Frost salamanders are omnivorous, but they prefer their food frozen. If prey is plentiful, they may keep particularly delectable items, such as yetis and adventurers, frozen in their lair for years until the right craving strikes them.

COMBAT

In combat, a frost salamander rears up on its two hind legs and slashes with all four front legs while biting with its vicious teeth. It might also try bull rushing an enemy backward into a pool of freezing water.

Cold Aura (Ex): A frost salamander emanates such intense cold that each creature within 20 feet takes 1d8 points of cold damage per round (no saving throw). Magical effects that shield against cold work against this aura, but normal measures (such as heavy furs or insulation) do not.

Cold Subtype (Ex): A frost salamander is immune to cold damage but takes double damage from fire unless a saving throw for half damage is allowed. In that case, the creature takes half damage on a success and double damage on a failure.

GALEB DUHR

Medium-Size Elemental (Earth)
Hit Dice: 8d8+40 (76 hp)
Initiative: –3
Speed: 10 ft., burrow 10 ft.
AC: 22 (–3 Dex, +15 natural), touch 7, flat-footed 22
Attacks: 2 slams +7 melee
Damage: Slam 1d6+1
Face/Reach: 5 ft. by 5 ft./5 ft.
Special Attacks: Spell-like abilities
Special Qualities: DR 15/+1, elemental traits, freeze, SR 21, tremorsense
Saves: Fort +11, Ref –1, Will +7
Abilities: Str 13, Dex 5, Con 20, Int 11, Wis 16, Cha 12
Skills: Concentration +12, Diplomacy +3, Knowledge (geography) +7, Perform +10 (ballad, chant, sing, storytelling, and five others), Sense Motive +14
Feats: Iron Will

Climate/Terrain: Any mountain
Organization: Solitary, pair, or tumble (3–5)
Challenge Rating: 9
Treasure: No coins; standard goods (gems only); standard items (potions only)
Alignment: Always neutral
Advancement: 9–15 HD (Medium-size); 16–24 HD (Large)

Galeb duhrs are among the oddest creatures that an adventurer can encounter, but they are seldom dangerous. They live only in the mountains and seldom, if ever, venture onto other terrain. It is not known whether galeb duhrs can reproduce on the

Material Plane, or whether the ones found there have all come from the Elemental Plane of Earth.

To all appearances a galeb duhr is a living boulder with two dark, brooding eyes, a mouth, and rough-hewn appendages that serve as hands and feet. The typical galeb duhr stands about 4 feet tall, though advanced versions can reach heights of up to 16 feet.

When sitting perfectly still (an activity that occupies much of its time), a galeb duhr is nearly indistinguishable from the surrounding stone—so much so that many travelers walk right past one without realizing it. Galeb duhrs do love to sing, however, and occasionally their deep, resonant, slow, and often palpably sad songs reveal their presence. The frequency of much of their singing falls below the range of human hearing, but the subsonic tones can be felt through the ground for many miles and tend to make horses nervous.

As one might imagine, galeb duhrs are slow-moving, slow to anger, slow to action, and always take the long view. They have no known enemies except time. Now and then reckless monsters or adventurers attack them, hoping to acquire either gems or information about where to find rich veins of gold or other precious ore. Such attempts are generally doomed before they even begin. Galeb duhrs do know all there is to know about their mountain homes, both aboveground and below, but forcing them to give up those details is difficult in the extreme.

To further complicate matters, galeb duhrs are quite territorial, even to the point of feeling protective about rocks and boulders, in much the same way that a treant feels responsible for the forest in which it lives. Anyone damaging,

destroying, or even mining the mountains near a galeb duhr's home often discovers some very staunch opposition.

COMBAT

Galeb duhrs are usually solitary creatures, though they occasionally live with a few of their own kind. When approached, a galeb duhr can easily make it itself unnoticed. When irritated into combat, however, it attacks with its slams.

Spell-Like Abilities: At will—*animate objects* (stone only), *stone shape*; 1/day—*move earth*, *passwall*, *transmute rock to mud*, *wall of stone*. Caster level 20th; save DC 11 + spell level.

Elemental Traits (Ex): A galeb duhr is immune to poison, *sleep*, paralysis, and stunning. It is not subject to critical hits or flanking, and it cannot be raised or resurrected. The creature also has darkvision (60-foot range).

Freeze (Ex): A galeb duhr can hold itself so still that it appears to be a boulder. An observer must succeed at a Spot check (DC 30) to notice that it is really alive.

Tremorsense (Ex): A galeb duhr can automatically sense the location of anything within 300 feet that is in contact with the ground.

GAMBOL

Large Magical Beast
Hit Dice: 8d10+16 (60 hp)
Initiative: +4
Speed: 30 ft., climb 15 ft.
AC: 18 (–1 size, +4 Dex, +5 natural), touch 13, flat-footed 14
Attacks: Bite +13 melee and 2 claws +11 melee
Damage: Bite 2d8+6, claw 1d4+3
Face/Reach: 5 ft. by 10 ft./10 ft.
Special Attacks: Fear aura, great leap
Special Qualities: Darkvision 60 ft., evasion, haste, low-light vision, masterful dodge
Saves: Fort +8, Ref +12, Will +3
Abilities: Str 23, Dex 18, Con 15, Int 2, Wis 12, Cha 9
Skills: Balance +6, Climb +14, Jump +33, Tumble +14
Feats: Lightning Reflexes, Multiattack

Climate/Terrain: Warm forest
Organization: Solitary, pack (5–20) or troop (21–40)
Challenge Rating: 5
Treasure: None
Alignment: Usually chaotic neutral
Advancement: 9–12 HD (Large); 13–24 HD (Huge)

These carnivorous cousins of the ape are fiercely territorial marauders. They obsessively prowl the jungle, attacking anything that enters the area they claim.

A gambol is a baboonlike primate that stands 9 feet tall and weighs more than 1,000 pounds. Its purple skin is covered with dense, silky, blue hair. A gambol has elongated jaws and a hairless, doglike muzzle.

COMBAT

Gambols tumble into combat, clawing and biting their foes. They take advantage of their reach to grapple and trip advancing foes. Their constant maneuvering makes them difficult targets for foes attacking from a distance.

Fear Aura (Su): When a gambol howls, every creature within a 100-foot radius must succeed at a Will save (DC 13) or become panicked for 1d6+1 rounds. Whether or not the save is successful, the creature is then immune to that gambol's howl for 24 hours. The howl is a sonic, mind-affecting fear effect.

Great Leap (Ex): A gambol gains a +25 bonus on Jump checks. Maximum distance restrictions do not apply to its jumps.

Evasion (Ex): A gambol that makes a successful Reflex saving throw against an effect that would normally deal half damage instead avoids damage altogether.

Haste (Su): A gambol can take an extra partial action each round. This ability is always active.

Masterful Dodge (Ex): As a free action once per round, a gambol can dodge one ranged weapon attack, one reach melee weapon attack, or one spell that requires an attack roll by making a successful Reflex save (DC 20). An attack using a weapon with an enhancement bonus increases the save DC by the amount of the bonus, and a spell adds its spell level to the save DC. To use this ability, the gambol must be aware of the attack and not be flat-footed.

GIANT

Giants are humanoid-shaped beings of great size with even greater strength. They accomplish much through sheer determination and brute force, and in fact most rely on their might to solve problems. Giants can inflict tremendous damage on those who anger or oppose them, but they can also put their strength to good use in aiding their allies.

Many giants subsist by hunting or taking what they want from smaller, weaker beings. A few are not so cruel, raising what crops and livestock they need to survive.

All giants speak Giant. A giant with an Intelligence score of at least 10 also speaks Common.

COMBAT

Giants relish melee combat. They favor massive weapons, especially two-handed ones, and wield them with impressive skill. They possess enough cunning to soften up a foe with ranged attacks before closing, if they can. A giant's favorite ranged weapon is a big rock.

Rock Throwing (Ex): An adult giant is an accomplished rock thrower, so he or she receives a +1 racial bonus on attack rolls when throwing rocks. A giant of at least Huge size can hurl rocks weighing 60 to 80 pounds each (Medium-size objects) up to five range increments. The size of the range increment varies with the giant's kind (see individual entries). A Colossal giant can hurl rocks weighing 160 to 200 pounds (Huge objects).

Rock Catching (Ex): A giant of at least Huge size can catch Small, Medium-size, Large, or Huge rocks (or projectiles of similar shape). A Colossal giant can catch rocks of up to Colossal size. Once per round, a giant that would normally be hit by a rock can make a Reflex save to catch it as a free action. The DC to catch a rock is based on the rock's size (see table below). If the projectile has a bonus on attack rolls because of magic, the DC increases by that amount. The giant must be ready for and aware of the attack.

Rock Size	DC
Small	15
Medium-size	20
Large	25
Huge	30
Gargantuan	35
Colossal	40

GIANT SOCIETY

Solitary giants are usually young adults striking out on their own. Gangs are usually made up of young adults who hunt or raid (or both) together. Giant bands typically consist of young adults and their mates, servants, or guards. About a third of the giants in a band or tribe are children.

	Forest Giant Huge Giant	Sun Giant Huge Giant (Fire)
Hit Dice:	13d8+78 (136 hp)	13d8+91 (149 hp)
Initiative:	+5	+2
Speed:	40 ft.	40 ft.
AC:	20 (−2 size, +1 Dex, +11 natural), touch 9, flat-footed 19	20 (−2 size, +2 Dex, +10 natural), touch 10, flat-footed 18
Attacks:	Gargantuan greatclub +18/+13 melee, or Gargantuan mighty composite longbow (+4 Str bonus) +8/+3 ranged, or rock +9 ranged	Gargantuan longspear +20/+15 melee, or rock +10 ranged
Damage:	Gargantuan greatclub 2d8+16, Gargantuan mighty composite longbow (+4 Str bonus) 2d8+4/×3, rock 2d8+11	Gargantuan longspear 2d8+19/×3, rock 2d8+13
Face/Reach:	10 ft. by 10 ft./15 ft.	10 ft. by 10 ft./15 ft.
Special Attacks:	Poisoned arrows, rock throwing	Rock throwing, spell-like abilities
Special Qualities:	Darkvision 60 ft., rock catching	Darkvision 60 ft., fire subtype, rock catching
Saves:	Fort +14, Ref +5, Will +7	Fort +15, Ref +6, Will +8
Abilities:	Str 33, Dex 12, Con 22, Int 14, Wis 16, Cha 21	Str 37, Dex 14, Con 25, Int 15, Wis 18, Cha 14
Skills:	Hide +5*, Listen +5, Sense Motive +6, Spot +7	Handle Animal +6, Hide +8*, Listen +8, Spot +7
Feats:	Improved Initiative, Point Blank Shot, Precise Shot	Alertness, Point Blank Shot, Precise Shot
Climate/Terrain:	Any forest	Warm and temperate deserts
Organization:	Solitary, pair, gang (3–5), band (6–9 plus 35% noncombatants plus 1 1st–2nd level druid), or hunting/raiding party (6–9 plus 35% noncombatants plus 1 3rd–5th level druid)	Solitary, pair, gang (3–5), or family (3–8 plus 1–4 noncombatants plus 1 4th–6th level adept, cleric, or sorcerer)
Challenge Rating:	11	12
Treasure:	Standard coins; double goods; standard items	Standard
Alignment:	Usually neutral	Usually neutral
Advancement:	By character class	By character class

Giant children can be formidable opponents in their own right. When a group of giants includes children, roll d% for each child to determine his or her maturity level: 01–25 infant (no combat ability); 26–50 juvenile (two size categories smaller than an adult, 8 fewer Hit Dice, −8 to Strength and Constitution scores, and 1 rank in each skill that an adult has); 51–100 adolescent (one size category smaller than an adult, 4 fewer Hit Dice, −4 to Strength and Constitution scores, and 2, 3, or 4 ranks in each skill that an adult has). Giant children can throw rocks if they meet the minimum size requirement. Except as noted, giant children are identical with adults of the same kind.

FOREST GIANT

Forest giants are among the tallest specimens of giantkind, and they can live to be up to 200 years old. They are powerful hunters that pose a threat to all animals that dwell in the woods.

An adult forest giant stands 18 feet tall but weighs only 3,000 pounds. The lanky, muscular body resembles that of a wood elf but appears much sturdier. The creature has deep, earth-yellow skin and pale green hair that is usually wild and unkempt. The typical clothing for either gender is made of fur or leather, and each forest giant also wears some bone jewelry, particularly necklaces and earrings.

A forest giant's bag contains everything needed to survive in the wilderness, including tools to make and repair weapons, 2d4 rocks, 1d4+4 mundane items, and the giant's personal wealth. These items tend to be parts of things it killed for food, such as scraps of fur and hide, dried insects, and bones.

Combat

Forest giants target opponents from afar with their poisoned arrows. Though they are not averse to attacking with their clubs, their poison-tipped, ranged weapons often end a battle quickly with few casualties for the giants. Forest giants use their natural camouflage abilities to hide among the trees and wait in ambush for the next creature that crosses their path. Their thrown rocks have a range increment of 120 feet.

Poison (Ex): Forest giants coat their arrows with poison (Fortitude save DC 22). The initial and secondary damage is the same (unconsciousness for 4d4 rounds).

Skills: A forest giant has a +4 racial bonus on Hide checks. * In wooded areas, this bonus rises to +8.

Forest Giant Society

Forest giants live solely in wooded areas regardless of the climate. These ravenous meat-eaters hunt nearly any kind

of animal or beast for its flesh. Forest giants maintain friendly relations with fey, and they cooperate with other primitive woodland beings who enjoy the same hunting lifestyle as they do.

Forest Giant Characters

A forest giant's favored class is ranger. Many groups of forest giants include both druids and rangers.

A forest giant PC's effective character level (ECL) is equal to its class level + 16. Thus, a 1st-level forest giant ranger has an ECL of 17 and is the equivalent of a 17th-level character.

SUN GIANT

Sun giants are cruel nomads who eke out a living raising livestock under the bleakest of conditions. Most are grim and brutal, caring little for the trappings of civilization. Despite their harsh existence, they are long-lived beings, often reaching 400 years or more in age.

A sun giant's skin is parched and wrinkled from years of living in harsh, desertlike conditions. Hair that is soft and black in childhood becomes dry, ashen, and brittle with the passing of time. Only the creature's eyes seem unaffected by the desert—they sparkle a bright blue color. The typical sun giant stands 16 feet tall and weighs 7,000 pounds. The usual garb for either gender is a loose, light-colored robe that covers the legs, body, and arms, plus a cloth burnoose looped around the head and face to protect the skin from the burning sun. A sun giant never wears shoes, either for walking or riding.

A sun giant's bag contains 1d2 rocks, 1d6+4 mundane items, and the giant's personal wealth. Personal possessions usually include simple things such as sand sculptures, coins, and prized gifts from esteemed sun giant leaders.

Combat

Sun giants use their natural camouflage ability to hide amid the sand dunes, where they lie in wait for enemies with spears at the ready. They rarely throw rocks, but when they do, the range increment is 120 feet. In melee, sun giants prefer to pound opponents with their fists. During times of war, they fight mounted, seated upon Gargantuan steeds that they raise and train themselves. When weaponless, a sun giant uses its spell-like abilities to keep foes at bay.

Spell-Like Abilities: At will—*spike stones, stone shape, wall of stone.* Caster level 13th; save DC 12 + spell level.

Fire Subtype (Ex): A sun giant is immune to fire damage but takes double damage from cold unless a saving throw for half damage is allowed. In that case, the giant takes half damage on a success and double damage on a failure.

Skills: A sun giant has a +4 racial bonus on Hide checks. *In desert areas, this bonus rises to +8.

Sun Giant Society

Sun giants dwell in the desert, but they never set up permanent homes there because they enjoy the freedom that comes with living in tents. They almost always ride rather than traveling on foot. They prefer living mounts such as rocs and giant lizards, but when such creatures are scarce, they are quite willing to have their clerics animate dead mounts.

As herders, sun giants see all land as theirs for the taking, so they graze their animals anywhere food is available. This destructive practice often strips fields bare and turns the land barren, earning sun giants few friends in the desert.

Sun Giant Characters

Most groups of sun giants include clerics with access to any two of the following domains: Destruction, Fire, Sun, Travel, and War. A sun giant's favored class is ranger.

A sun giant PC's effective character level (ECL) is equal to its class level + 16. Thus, a 1st-level sun giant ranger has an ECL of 17 and is the equivalent of a 17th-level character.

OCEAN GIANT

The noble ocean giants are deep-sea dwellers who delight in the tossing waves and the rich life of the underwater world. These usually peaceful creatures are nevertheless quick to anger when anyone finds fault with their ways. Ocean giants frequently live to be 600 years old.

The barrel-chested body of an ocean giant is powerfully built, and the face has an almost leonine quality. Coppery skin is complemented by flowing white hair that streams out in waves as the giant swims. In natural form, an ocean giant has a fishlike tail like that of a merfolk,

	Ocean Giant **Huge Giant (Cold, Aquatic)**	**Mountain Giant** **Colossal Giant (Earth)**
Hit Dice:	18d8+162 (243 hp)	30d8+390 (525 hp)
Initiative:	+6	+0
Speed:	40 ft., swim 80 ft.	80 ft.
AC:	26 (−2 size, +2 Dex, +16 natural), touch 10, flat-footed 24	31 (−8 size, +29 natural), touch 2, flat-footed 31
Attacks:	Gargantuan trident +25/+20/+15 melee and tail slap +20 melee, or 2 slams +25 melee and tail slap +20 melee, or rock +14 ranged	Mountain giant club +30/+25/+20/+15 melee, or 2 slams +30 melee, or rock +15 ranged
Damage:	Gargantuan trident 4d6+21, slam 1d6+14, tail slap 1d10+7, rock 2d8+14	Mountain giant club 4d8+24/19–20, slam 2d6+16, rock 4d8+16
Face/Reach:	10 ft. by 10 ft./15 ft.	40 ft. by 40 ft./25 ft.
Special Attacks:	Rock throwing	Crush 2d6+24, fling, grapple, rock throwing, trample 4d6+24
Special Qualities:	Amphibious, blunt weapon immunity, cold subtype, darkvision 60 ft., landform, rock catching	Darkvision 60 ft., rock catching, scent, *summon giants*
Saves:	Fort +20, Ref +8, Will +8	Fort +30, Ref +10, Will +10
Abilities:	Str 39, Dex 15, Con 28, Int 11, Wis 14, Cha 18	Str 43, Dex 10, Con 37, Int 6, Wis 10, Cha 7
Skills:	Diplomacy +6, Listen+8, Sense Motive +8, Spot +10, Swim +22	Jump +18, Listen +16, Spot +16
Feats:	Combat Reflexes, Far Shot, Improved Initiative, Point Blank Shot	Alertness, Cleave, Combat Reflexes, Great Cleave, Improved Critical (mountain giant club), Power Attack, Sunder
Climate/Terrain:	Any aquatic	Any mountains
Organization:	Solitary, pair, or family (3–8 plus 1–4 noncombatants plus 1 7th–10th level cleric or sorcerer and 2–8 sea lions)	Solitary or family (2 plus 1–3 noncombatants)
Challenge Rating:	19	26
Treasure:	Double standard	Standard
Alignment:	Usually good	Usually chaotic
Advancement:	By character class	By character class

though the landform ability (see below) provides an alternate form in which the tail is replaced by legs. An ocean giant of either gender measures 16 feet in length and weighs more than 4,000 pounds. On land, the typical ocean giant wears light clothing that is unlikely to impede swimming should that become necessary. Underwater, clothing is spurned except for a belt pouch to carry personal effects.

An ocean giant's bag contains 1d2 rocks, 1d6+4 mundane items, and the giant's personal wealth. These items tend to be sea-related items such as navigation instruments, sea shells, pearls, and treasure found on sunken ships.

Combat

Whether fighting on the surface or underwater, an ocean giant usually wields a massive trident. On land, ocean giants prefer to keep their foes at a distance. They hurl rocks (range increment 120 feet) at closing enemies and even ships that are not welcome in their territory. In close combat on land, or when unarmed, they hammer opponents with their fists and slap with their tails.

Amphibious (Ex): Although ocean giants have gills for breathing underwater, they can also breathe air and can survive indefinitely on land.

Blunt Weapon Immunity (Ex): An ocean giant takes no damage from bludgeoning weapons.

Cold Subtype (Ex): An ocean giant is immune to cold damage but takes double damage from fire unless a saving throw for half damage is allowed. In that case, the giant takes half damage on a success and double damage on a failure.

Landform (Su): This ability allows an ocean giant to assume the form of a Huge humanoid-shaped giant or return to its natural form at will. An ocean giant in landform is able to walk on land, but it has no tail attack. A change wrought by landform cannot be dispelled, nor does the ocean giant revert to its natural form when killed. A *true seeing* spell, however, reveals the ocean giant's natural shape if it is in landform.

Ocean Giant Society

Ocean giants live in magnificent, underwater mansions situated near barrier reefs. They live off the sea, hunting large sea creatures and harvesting aquatic plants and shellfish. Elderly ocean giants often raise domestic animals on deserted islands

to supplement their clans' diet. Many young ocean giants desire to travel the seas aboard sailing ships, so they sign up to become sailors. Of course, their incredible size limits them to only the largest vessels. Merfolk and aquatic storm giants view ocean giants as plunderers of the sea's wealth, so relations between them are strained at best.

Ocean Giant Characters

An ocean giant's favored class is sorcerer, but many also choose to become clerics. An ocean giant cleric can choose two of the following domains: Luck, Protection, and Water.

An ocean giant PC's effective character level (ECL) is equal to its class level + 23; thus, a 1st-level ocean giant sorcerer has an ECL of 24 and is the equivalent of a 24th-level character.

MOUNTAIN GIANT

Among the largest giants in existence, mountain giants are primitive creatures given to cruelty and capriciousness. They take great pleasure in flinging boulders down upon passing smaller creatures, trying to hit them as they flee. Mountain giants often live to be 100 years old.

A mountain giant resembles a titanic hill giant, standing more than 40 feet tall and weighing nearly 50,000 pounds. Greasy, jet-black hair frames a face with bulbous features and a skin tone that can be any shade from tan to reddish brown. The typical mountain giant wears only minimal clothing—usually a breechcloth and a shirt made of rough animal hide that barely covers a large pot belly.

A mountain giant's bag contains 3d4 rocks, 1d4+2 mundane items, and the giant's personal wealth. These items tend to be humanoid artifacts that the mountain giant considers playthings, such as broken wagons, small huts, and furniture, including tables and beds.

Combat

Mountain giants attack in a straightforward manner, stepping forth to overrun opponents whenever possible. They also enjoy picking up foes and hurling them against a mountainside. Many an armed foe has foiled a mountain giant's initial grab attempt only to be scooped up by the monster's other hand.

In melee, mountain giants use their height to smash their clubs down on the heads of their foes. A mountain giant that feels seriously threatened often uses its *summon giants* ability to engage its foes

with other opponents, then steps back to hurl boulders. Against groups of smaller foes, mountain giants prefer their trample or crush attacks.

Crush (Ex): A mountain giant that jumps at least 20 feet into the air (or jumps down from a height of at least 20 feet) can land on opponents two or more size categories smaller than itself as a standard action, using its whole body to crush them. A crush attack affects as many creatures as can fit under the giant's body. (This is normally a 40-foot square, but the giant can instead opt to come down on its seat and cover a 40-foot by 60-foot area.) Each creature in the affected area must succeed at a Reflex save (DC 38) or be pinned, automatically taking 2d6+24 points of bludgeoning damage. Thereafter, if the giant chooses to maintain the pin, treat it as a normal grapple attack. While pinned, the opponent takes crush damage each round.

Fling (Ex): A mountain giant that sucessfully grapples a foe two or more size categories smaller than itself can hurl the creature as a standard action. A flung creature travels up to 120 feet and takes 12d6 points of damage. A creature that is flung off a mountain takes this amount of damage or the appropriate falling damage, whichever is greater. The giant also can throw the flung creature as though it were a boulder. In this case, the flung creature takes 12d6+16 points of damage, and any opponent it strikes takes 4d8+16 points of damage.

Grapple (Ex): If a mountain giant hits an opponent that is at least one size category smaller than itself with a slam (used as a melee touch attack), it deals normal damage and attempts to start a grapple (grapple bonus +54). If it gets a hold, it can fling the opponent in the next round. Alternatively, the mountain giant has the option to conduct the grapple normally, or simply use one hand to hold the opponent (–20 penalty on grapple check, but the mountain giant is not considered grappled). In either case, each successful grapple check it makes during successive rounds automatically deals slam damage.

Trample (Ex): As a standard action during its turn each round, a mountain giant can trample opponents at least one size category smaller than itself. This attack

deals 4d6+24 points of bludgeoning damage. A trampled opponent can attempt either an attack of opportunity at a –4 penalty or a Reflex save (DC 41) for half damage.

Scent (Ex): A mountain giant can detect approaching enemies, sniff out hidden foes, and track by sense of smell.

Summon Giants **(Sp):** Once per day, a mountain giant can attempt to summon 1d8+1 ogres, 1d6+1 trolls, or 1d4+1 hill giants with a 25% chance of success.

Skills and Feats: A mountain giant has EHD as though it were a Huge creature.

Mountain Giant Society

Mountain giants live largely solitary lives in desolate mountain ranges and volcanic peaks. Though most of them resent intruders, some like to keep a few dwarves and humans as pets. When more than one mountain giant is encountered, it is usually a mated pair with children.

Mountain Giant Characters

A mountain giant's favored class is barbarian, though the cleric class is also popular among the race. Mountain giant clerics can choose any two of the following domains: Earth, Strength, and Trickery.

A mountain giant PC's effective character level (ECL) is equal to its class level + 25. Thus, a 1st-level mountain giant barbarian has an ECL of 26 and is the equivalent of a 26th-level character.

GLIMMERSKIN

Medium-Size Outsider (Incorporeal)
Hit Dice: 12d8+24 (78 hp)
Initiative: +1
Speed: Fly 50 ft. (perfect)
AC: 14 (+1 Dex, +3 deflection), touch 14, flat-footed 13
Attacks: Energy touch +13
Damage: Energy touch
Face/Reach: 5 ft. by 5 ft./5 ft.
Special Attacks: Energy touch
Special Qualities: DR 5/+1, heroic bond, incorporeal subtype, outsider traits, *plane shift*, SR 15, telepathy
Saves: Fort +10, Ref +9, Will +10
Abilities: Str —, Dex 13, Con 14, Int 11, Wis 15, Cha 16
Skills: Bluff +17, Diplomacy +16, Intimidate +5, Knowledge (arcana) +14, Knowledge (the planes) +14, Search +15, Sense Motive +17, Spot +17
Feats: Cleave, Great Cleave, Power Attack, Sunder

Climate/Terrain: Any land and underground
Organization: Solitary
Challenge Rating: 8
Treasure: None
Alignment: Usually neutral
Advancement: By character class

Glimmerskins are thrill-seeking parasites from the Positive Energy Plane. These creatures travel to the Material Plane solely to engage in mortal combat.

Since a glimmerskin lacks a material form, it cannot engage an opponent in physical melee unaided. To circumvent this difficulty, it solicits a willing host to harbor it. In exchange for this service, the glimmerskin temporarily grants the host augmented fighting skills and abilities.

A glimmerskin appears as a vaguely humanoid-shaped being made of pulsing white light. Despite its alien appearance, it possesses a recognizably intelligent, elflike face. When bonded with a host, a glimmerskin cosmetically alters its shape to one more appropriate for battle, usually appearing as a full suit of radiant armor or a glowing, hooded robe. A glimmerskin envelops only its host's body; it cannot cover the latter's shield or drawn weapons.

When on the Material Plane, glimmerskins usually seek out large-scale battles, since these offer a greater variety of potential hosts. The creature is not concerned with alignment, nor is it interested in its host's intentions, nor does it care whether its host lives or dies—it desires only combat.

A glimmerskin can remain away from the Positive Energy Plane for a number of hours equal to half its Constitution score. Each round that it exceeds this limit, it must make a Fortitude save (DC 20) or die from energy dispersion. This danger keeps most glimmerskins from making frequent trips to the Material Plane.

Some enterprising adventurers who are familiar with the planes and aware of the glimmerskins' limited time frames arrange one-time "bondings" between glimmerskins and willing hosts. This often occurs during times of war and similar unrest, but bondings also occur between glimmerskins and adventurers seeking some extra power for an upcoming confrontation. Whoever arranges such a bonding first determines what physical challenges the host expects to meet, then apprises the glimmerskin of the offer and selects a time and place for the bonding. The host usually pays the arranger a stipend (or "finder's fee") ahead of time for this service.

Combat

Glimmerskins revel in combat, but they cannot actually control their hosts. Instead, they communicate their wishes telepathically, acting as combat advisors. A host who ignores a glimmerskin's requests risks termination of the bond, since the monster is quite willing to abandon a host in favor of a more accommodating or interesting one. Before abandoning a host, a glimmerskin usually contacts its next prospect via telepathy to arrange a transfer. If badly wounded, a

glimmerskin escapes to the Positive Energy Plane rather than continuing to fight.

Energy Touch (Su): The positively energized touch of a glimmerskin heals a target of 5 points of damage per round or grants 5 additional temporary hit points per round to a creature already at full hit points. These temporary hit points fade 1d6 rounds after the creature ceases physical contact with the glimmerskin. However, this benefit has an unfortunate side effect. For each round that its hit points (including temporary ones) exceed its normal hit point total, the target creature must make a successful Fortitude save (DC 19) or explode in a 20-foot burst of radiant energy. Each creature caught in the blast (including the target) takes damage equal to 2d6 points + the number of excess hit points the target had at the time. A Reflex save (DC 19) reduces the damage by half. A glimmerskin's host automatically benefits from the additional hit points but is allowed no saving throw to reduce the damage from the blast. Glimmerskins rarely inform their hosts of this side effect.

Heroic Bond (Su): A glimmerskin bonds by enveloping its host. A bonded host gains a +4 bonus on melee attack rolls, a +2 armor bonus to AC, access to the glimmerskin's feats (with the prerequisite Strength score of at least 13), and any class features the glimmerskin may have. Additionally, a host who can turn undead gains a +5 bonus on the roll to determine Hit Dice affected. In exchange, the host shares half of any earned experience points with the glimmerskin. Spells that protect against Positive Energy Plane effects prevent a glimmerskin from bonding to a host.

Incorporeal Subtype: A glimmerskin can be harmed only by other incorporeal creatures, +1 or better magic weapons, spells, spell-like abilities, and supernatural abilities. The creature has a 50% chance to ignore any damage from a corporeal source, except for force effects or attacks made with ghost touch weapons. A glimmerskin can pass through solid objects, but not force effects, at will. Its attacks ignore natural armor, armor, and shields, but deflection bonuses and force effects work normally against them. A glimmerskin always moves silently and cannot be heard with Listen checks if it doesn't wish to be.

Outsider Traits: A glimmerskin has darkvision (60-foot range). It cannot be raised or resurrected.

Plane Shift **(Sp):** A glimmerskin can use *plane shift* at will (caster level 12th; Will save DC 18).

Telepathy (Su): A glimmerskin can communicate telepathically with any creature within 100 feet that has a language.

Feats: A glimmerskin's feats become usable only when the creature is bonded with a host who has a Strength score of at least 13.

GLIMMERSKIN CHARACTERS

A glimmerskin's favored class is fighter.

A glimmerskin PC's effective character level (ECL) is equal to its class level + 15. Thus, a 1st-level glimmerskin fighter has an ECL of 16 and is the equivalent of a 16th-level character.

Golems are magically created constructs of great power. Constructing one involves the use of mighty magic and elemental forces. The animating force for a golem is a spirit from the Elemental Plane of Earth. The process of creation binds the unwilling spirit to the artificial body and subjects it to the will of the golem's creator.

Golems have no language of their own, but they can understand simple instructions from their creators.

COMBAT

Golems are tenacious in combat. Since they are mindless, they can do nothing in the absence of orders from their creators. They always follow instructions explicitly and are incapable of any strategy or tactics. They are emotionless in combat and cannot be provoked.

If a golem's creator is within 60 feet of it and both visible and audible to it, he or she can command the creature directly. An uncommanded golem usually follows its last instruction to the best of its ability, though it returns any attacks made against it. The creator can give the golem a simple program (such as "Remain in an area and attack all creatures [or creatures of a specific type] that enter," or "Ring a gong and attack," or the like) to govern its actions in his or her absence.

Since golems do not need to breathe and are immune to most forms of energy, they can press an attack against an opponent almost anywhere, from the bottom of the sea to the frigid top of the tallest mountain.

Construct Traits: A golem is immune to mind-affecting effects, poison, *sleep*, paralysis, stunning, disease, death effects, necromantic effects, and any effect that requires a Fortitude save unless it also works on objects. The creature is not subject to critical hits, subdual damage, ability damage, ability drain, energy drain, or death from massive damage. It cannot heal itself but can be healed through repair. It cannot be raised or resurrected. A golem has darkvision (60-foot range).

Magic Immunity (Ex): Golems completely resist most magical and supernatural effects, except as noted below.

CONSTRUCTION

The cost given for each golem includes the price of the physical body, plus all the materials and spell components that are consumed during the process or become a permanent part of the golem.

The first task is carving or assembling the golem's physical body. The creator can do this personally or hire someone else to do the job. The builder must have the requisite skill, which varies with the golem. The real work of creation involves extended magical rituals requiring two months to complete. Understanding the rituals requires a character of the appropriate level with the Craft Magic Arms and Armor and Craft Wondrous Item feats. The creator must labor for at least 8 hours each day in a specially prepared laboratory or workroom. This chamber is similar to an alchemist's laboratory and costs 500 gp to establish.

	Stained Glass Golem Medium-Size Construct	Brass Golem Large Construct	Dragonflesh Golem Large Construct
Hit Dice:	12d10 (66 hp)	16d10 (88 hp)	30d10 (165 hp)
Initiative:	+0	+0	+0
Speed:	30 ft. (can't run)	30 ft. (can't run)	40 ft. (can't run), fly 120 ft. (poor)
AC:	15 (+5 natural), touch 10, flat-footed 15	31 (−1 size, +22 natural), touch 9, flat-footed 31	23 (−1 size, +14 natural), touch 9, flat-footed 23
Attacks:	2 rakes +10 melee	Huge +3 *wounding greataxe* +19/+14/+9 melee, or butt +16 melee	Bite +27 melee and 2 claws +22 melee and 2 wings +22 melee and tail slap +22 melee
Damage:	Rake 1d8+1/19–20	Huge +3 *wounding greataxe* 2d8+10/×3, butt 1d8+7	Bite 2d6+6, claw 1d8+3, wing 1d6+3, tail slap 1d8+9
Face/Reach:	5 ft. by 5 ft./5 ft.	5 ft. by 5 ft./10 ft.	5 ft. by 10 ft./10 ft.
Special Attacks:	—	Maze	Frightful presence
Special Qualities:	Construct traits, DR 10/+2, fast healing 5, keen, magic immunity	Construct traits, DR 15/+3, magic immunity, scent	Blindsight 150 ft., construct traits, DR 15/+3, magic immunity
Saves:	Fort +4, Ref +4, Will +5	Fort +5, Ref +5, Will +7	Fort +10, Ref +10, Will +13
Abilities:	Str 13, Dex 10, Con —, Int 4, Wis 13, Cha 7	Str 20, Dex 11, Con —, Int 3, Wis 14, Cha 7	Str 22, Dex 11, Con —, Int 4, Wis 17, Cha 17
Skills:	Hide +0*	Wilderness Lore +2*	—
Climate/Terrain:	Any land and underground	Any land and underground	Any land and underground
Organization:	Solitary, pair, or crew (3–5)	Solitary	Solitary
Challenge Rating:	5	10	13
Treasure:	None	None	None
Alignment:	Always neutral	Always neutral	Always neutral
Advancement:	13–24 HD (Medium-size); 25–36 HD (Large)	17–32 HD (Large); 33–48 HD (Huge)	31–60 HD (Large); 61–90 HD (Huge)

When not working on the rituals, the creator must rest and can perform no other activities except eating, sleeping, or talking. If personally constructing the golem's body, the creator can perform the building and the rituals together. Missing a day of rituals means the process fails and must be started again. Any money spent is lost, but XP are not. The golem's body can be reused, as can the laboratory.

Completing the ritual drains the appropriate XP from the creator and requires casting any spells on the final day. The creator must cast the spells personally, but they can come from outside sources, such as scrolls.

STAINED GLASS GOLEM

Beautiful stained glass windows not only indicate the wealth of a temple or stronghold, they may also be the site's guardians. These beautiful constructs are built to harmonize with a structure's decor so that their presence is not obvious to any except intruders.

Stained glass golems are flat, two-dimensional replicas of living beings. When they move, they produce a tinkling sound like that made by delicate crystal wind chimes. When moving through a lighted area, they flash and flicker as the light striking them breaks down into its component hues. Stained glass golems never communicate in any way.

Combat

Stained glass golems attack by slashing with their "arms," which are as sharp as broken glass.

Keen (Su): A stained glass golem's rake attack threatens a critical hit on a natural attack roll of 19–20.

Magic Immunity (Ex): A stained glass golem is immune to all spells, spell-like abilities, and supernatural effects, except as follows. A *shatter* spell affects it normally. A *mending* spell heals 2d6 points of damage the golem has taken. Sonic attacks affect it normally.

Skills: *A stained glass golem receives a +20 competence bonus on Hide checks when standing motionless in a window frame.

Construction

A stained glass golem's body is constructed from 50 pounds of glass shards and costs 10,000 gp to create. Assembling the body requires a successful Craft (glass-making) check (DC 25).

The creator must be 16th level and able to cast arcane spells. Completing the ritual drains 200 XP from the creator and requires the *geas/quest*, *limited wish*, and *polymorph any object* spells.

RASS GOLEM

A brass golem exists to fulfill one goal, set at the time of its creation. It waits with absolute patience until activated, then it becomes a terrible instrument of destruction. If its goal becomes unattainable—for example, if it was created to guard a temple that no longer exists—the brass golem loses its enchantment entirely and becomes nothing more than a statue.

A brass golem is most often forged to resemble a minotaur. Until activated, it appears as a large, brass statue armed with a gleaming greataxe.

Combat

A brass golem fights primarily with its greataxe.

Maze (Sp): Once per day, a brass golem can target a *maze* effect (caster level 16th) against a single quarry. The golem is immune to the effects of its own *maze* ability and that of others of its kind, and it can freely enter its own *maze* to track a target.

Magic Immunity (Ex): A brass golem is immune to all spells, spell-like abilities, and supernatural effects, except as follows. An electricity effect slows it (as the *slow* spell) for 3 rounds, with no saving throw. A fire effect breaks any *slow* effect on the golem and cures 1 point of damage for each 3 points of damage it would otherwise deal. (For example, a brass golem hit by a *fireball* cast by a 5th-level wizard gains back 6 hit points if the damage total is 18.) The golem does not get a saving throw against fire effects.

Skills: *A brass golem is a relentless tracker. It gains a +20 competence bonus on Wilderness Lore checks for the purpose of tracking a foe designated by its creator, or in connection with any other goal set by its creator. When tracking a foe through its own *maze*, the creature gains a +20 insight bonus on Wilderness Lore checks.

Construction

A brass golem's body is constructed from 1,000 pounds of brass and costs 200,000 gp to create. (This amount includes 1,500 gp for the body and 32,320 gp for the +3 *wounding greataxe*.) Assembling the body requires one successful Craft (armorsmithing) check (DC 25) and one successful Craft (weaponsmithing) check (DC 25).

The creator must be 16th level and able to cast arcane spells. Completing the ritual drains 4,000 XP from the creator and requires the *geas/ quest, limited wish, maze, Mordenkainen's sword,* and *polymorph any object* spells.

DRAGONFLESH GOLEM

Dragonflesh golems, sometimes called drolems, are built from parts of dragons. These creatures can remember more complex commands than most golems can, but because they cannot think, they obey commands to the letter rather than evaluating the intent. Drolems have been known to kill their creators because a complex or incautiously worded command allowed such an option for fulfillment.

True dragons hate dragonflesh golems and attack them on sight. Once a dragon has slain a drolem, it hunts down the creator as well, to exact retribution for the atrocities committed against dragonkind in creating such a creature.

The dragonflesh golem is a hideous patchwork of rotting, mismatched dragon parts rudely stitched together. Despite its appearance, a dragonflesh golem is a construct, not an undead.

Combat

A drolem lacks the breath weapons and the spellcasting abilities of true dragons. It usually prefers to land in the midst of a group of opponents and lash out in all directions with its teeth, claws, wings, and tail.

Frightful Presence (Ex): When a drolem charges, attacks, or flies overhead, it inspires terror in all creatures within 30 feet that have fewer Hit Dice or levels than it has. Each potentially affected opponent must succeed at a Will save (DC 28) or become shaken for 5d6 rounds. A successful save leaves that opponent immune to that drolem's frightful presence for 24 hours.

Blindsight (Ex): A drolem can ascertain its surroundings by nonvisual means (mostly hearing and scent, but also by noticing vibrations and other environmental clues). This ability enables it to discern objects and creatures within 150 feet.

The drolem usually does not need to make Spot or Listen checks to notice creatures within range of its blindsight.

Magic Immunity (Ex): A drolem is immune to all spells, spell-like abilities, and supernatural effects, except as follows. Fire- and cold-based effects slow the monster (as the *slow* spell) for 2d6 rounds, with no saving throw. An electricity effect breaks any *slow* effect on the drolem and cures 1 point of damage for each 3 points of damage it would otherwise deal. For example, a drolem hit by a *lightning bolt* cast by a 5th-level wizard gains back 6 hit points if the damage total is 18. The drolem does not get a saving throw against electricity effects.

Construction

A drolem's body is constructed from either an entire dragon corpse, or enough parts of dragon corpses to assemble a whole dragon.

The drolem costs 200,000 gp to create. Assembling the body requires one successful Knowledge (nature) check and one successful Heal check (both DC 25).

The creator must be 16th level and able to cast arcane spells. Completing the ritual drains 4,000 XP from the creator and requires the *geas/quest*, *limited wish*, and *polymorph any object* spells.

GRAVECRAWLER

Small Undead (Earth)
Hit Dice: 25d12 (162 hp)
Initiative: +2
Speed: 20 ft., burrow 20 ft.
AC: 17 (+1 size, +2 Dex, +4 natural), touch 13, flat-footed 15
Attacks: Bite +13
Damage: Bite 1d4/19–20 plus 1d4 Constitution drain
Face/Reach: 5 ft. by 5 ft./5 ft.
Special Attacks: Calcifying aura, Constitution drain
Special Qualities: Burrow, speak with dead, SR 30, tremorsense, turn resistance +6, undead traits
Saves: Fort +8, Ref +10, Will +16
Abilities: Str 10, Dex 15, Con —, Int 16, Wis 11, Cha 11
Skills: Balance +4, Bluff +5, Diplomacy +12, Escape Artist +10, Hide +21, Intimidate +2, Jump +2, Knowledge (history) +20, Knowledge (local) +20, Knowledge (undead) +20, Listen +7, Sense Motive +5, Spot +2, Tumble +7
Feats: Alertness, Blind-Fight, Combat Reflexes, Dodge, Improved Critical (bite), Iron Will, Mobility, Skill Focus (Knowledge [history]), Skill Focus (Knowledge [local]), Skill Focus (Knowledge [undead])

Climate/Terrain: Any land and underground
Organization: Solitary, pair, or gang (3–4)

Challenge Rating: 16
Treasure: Standard
Alignment: Always neutral
Advancement: 26–52 HD (Medium-size)

The gravecrawler, sometimes called the ancestor worm, is an intelligent, sluglike undead with the power to turn flesh (dead or living) to stone. Gravecrawlers can be found in wilderness areas, but they are most often found in cemeteries, boneyards, and necropoli. There they slowly turn the surrounding dead bodies to a brittle stone that cannot be animated even by the *animate dead* spell.

A gravecralwer resembles a bloated, pale, segmented worm about 3 feet in length. Its face looks like that of a human or humanoid, except that it has no eyes—not even vestigial ones.

Gravecrawlers can communicate with the spirits of the dead they consume, and as such they often become repositories of local lore, history, and gossip. Because of this fact, some societies view gravecrawlers as beneficial creatures. Even those who consider them benefactors, however, tend to give their lairs a wide berth, since the presence of these creatures has a grievous effects on the living. Gravecrawlers are frequently sought out by those who seek hidden knowledge and lost bits of history, but they are hated both by necromancers and by corpse-devouring creatures such as the ghoul and the corpse gatherer.

COMBAT

Gravecrawlers would rather be venerated than fought. If seriously threatened, they usually try to flee below ground. Occasionally, a gravecrawler may try to ambush

its opponents, erupting from the ground to expose a whole group of intruders to its calcifying aura, then following up with its debilitating bite. Gravecrawlers tend to be more forgiving if propitiated with fresh bodies and uncalcified bones.

Calcifying Aura (Su): The presence of a gravecrawler is enough to cause flesh (living or dead) to harden and calcify, turning slowly into stone. This effect is a 30-foot-radius emanation centered on the gravecrawler, and it is always active. Every creature within the area must make a Fortitude save (DC 22) each round or take 1d2 points of Constitution damage. (Unlike the drain from its bite, the loss from the gravecrawler's calcifying aura is restored at the rate of 1 point per day.) A character brought to a Constitution score of 0 in this manner turns completely to stone. A gravecrawler is immune to its own calcifying aura and to those of others of its kind.

Constitution Drain (Su): Any creature bitten by a gravecrawler must make a Fortitude save (DC 22) or permanently lose 1d4 points of Constitution (or twice that amount on a critical hit). The gravecrawler heals 5 points of damage (10 on a critical hit) whenever it drains Constitution, gaining any excess as temporary hit points. A creature affected by this Constitution drain finds parts of its flesh turned to hard, brittle stone. At 0 Constitution, the target becomes a stone statue. A gravecrawler is immune to its own Constitution drain and to those of others of its kind.

Burrow (Ex): Gravecrawlers can move through stone, dirt, and earth, leaving no indication of their passage. A *move earth* spell cast on an area containing a burrowing gravecrawler flings the creature back 30 feet and stuns it for 1 round, unless it succeeds at a Fortitude save (DC 22).

Speak with Dead (Su): At will, a gravecrawler can produce an effect like that of a *speak with dead* spell (caster level 20th), except that it can be used to communicate with only one corpse per week. This ability does not allow communication with calcified remains.

Tremorsense (Ex): A gravecrawler can automatically sense the location of anything within 60 feet that is in contact with the ground.

Turn Resistance (Ex): A gravecrawler is treated as an undead with 31 Hit Dice for the purpose of turn, rebuke, command, and bolster attempts.

Undead Traits: A gravecrawler is immune to mind-affecting effects, poison, *sleep*, paralysis, stunning, disease, death effects, necromantic effects, and any effect that requires a Fortitude save unless it also works on objects. It is not subject to critical hits, subdual damage, ability damage, ability drain, energy drain, or death from massive damage. A gravecrawler cannot be raised, and resurrection works only if it is willing. The creature has darkvision (60-foot range).

Large Magical Beast
Hit Dice: 10d10+30 (85 hp)
Initiative: +3
Speed: 20 ft., climb 20 ft.
AC: 13 (–1 size, –1 Dex, +5 natural), touch 8, flat-footed 13
Attacks: 2 claws +13 melee and bite +8 melee
Damage: Claw 1d6+4, bite 1d8+2
Face/Reach: 5 ft. by 10 ft./5 ft.
Special Attacks: *Reverse gravity*
Special Qualities: Darkvision 60 ft., DR 5/+1, low-light vision, SR 19
Saves: Fort +10, Ref +6, Will +4
Abilities: Str 19, Dex 8, Con 17, Int 2, Wis 13, Cha 8
Skills: Climb +16, Hide +9*, Listen +5, Spot +5
Feats: Ability Focus (*reverse gravity*), Alertness, Improved Initiative

Climate/Terrain: Any underground
Organization: Solitary
Challenge Rating: 8
Treasure: Standard
Alignment: Always neutral
Advancement: 11–15 HD (Large); 16–20 HD (Huge); 21–25 HD (Gargantuan); 26–30 HD (Colossal)

A gravorg is a carnivorous predator that lairs underground. These monsters are only rarely encountered in the wilderness; they tend to move from cave to cave or dungeon to dungeon in search of prey. The sound of armor and flesh repeatedly striking stone often means that a gravorg has found another victim. The beast is so voracious that the remnants of such an encounter may be nothing more than piles of bones and equipment strewn haphazardly over a dungeon floor.

RGM

A gravorg is a 10-foot-long, four-legged animal that vaguely resembles a sloth. Its fur is a mixture of white, gray, and black hairs. This coloration makes it look like a lump of stone when motionless.

COMBAT

A gravorg uses *reverse gravity* to bounce its prey off ceilings or other overhangs, then dismisses the effect to drop the opponents back to the floor. Only when its victims appear unconscious or dead does a gravorg come out of hiding and begin to feed.

A gravorg caught outdoors uses its *reverse gravity* ability to throw predators in the air repeatedly until the latter either flee or become disabled. The monster uses its claws and teeth almost entirely for tearing open its prey rather than for self-defense.

Reverse Gravity (Sp): At will, a gravorg can produce an effect like that of a *reverse gravity* spell (caster level 10th; Reflex save DC 18), except that the range is 200 feet and it affects an area of up to five 10-foot cubes. The monster simply stacks the cubes to reach a ceiling or other overhang, then uses any remaining area to disrupt the prey's companions.

Skills: *A gravorg receives a +10 bonus on Hide checks in subterranean areas.

GREENVISE

Huge Plant
Hit Dice: 12d8+48 (102 hp)
Initiative: +0
Speed: 10 ft.
AC: 16 (−2 size, +8 natural), touch 8, flat-footed 16
Attacks: 4 slams +16 melee and bite +11 melee
Damage: Slam 2d4+9, bite 1d6+4
Face/Reach: 10 ft. by 10 ft./15 ft.
Special Attacks: Death fog, improved grab, swallow whole
Special Qualities: Acid immunity, plant traits, woodsense
Saves: Fort +12, Ref +4, Will +4
Abilities: Str 29, Dex 10, Con 18, Int 3, Wis 11, Cha 6

Climate/Terrain: Temperate or warm hills, plains or marsh
Organization: Solitary, pair, or patch (3–8)
Challenge Rating: 10
Treasure: None
Alignment: Always neutral
Advancement: 13–18 HD (Huge); 19–36 HD (Gargantuan)

Greenvises are ambulatory vegetable horrors that stalk the fringes of some humanoid settlements. These carnivorous plants are not bold—they prefer to ambush lone prey that happens to come too near. Greenvises rest at night and actively hunt during daylight hours, repositioning themselves throughout the day if prey in a particular hunting area proves scarce.

A greenvise is a larger, sturdier version of the venus flytrap, with a thick, green, trunklike stem and four sturdy tendrils that hang down like vines. When the creature opens its mouth, a mottled pink maw lined with toothlike thorns is revealed; when closed, the mouth structure resembles an ordinary leafy bush. A greenvise has small, tendrillike roots that it uses to move.

COMBAT

After setting itself up in an appropriate location, a greenvise lies in wait for prey to pass. It lunges at the first living creature it senses, using all its tendrils to grab the prey and transfer it to its maw. An extremely hungry or seriously hurt greenvise releases a death fog to weaken its opponents and obscure their vision. Although multiple greenvises are sometimes found together, they do not share their prey and thus do not assist each other in combat unless many potential victims are present.

Death Fog (Su): Twice per day, a greenvise can emit an acidic fog that functions like an *acid fog* spell, except as follows. The death fog's area is a 40-foot-high spread with a 60-foot radius. Within this area, all sight, including darkvision, is limited to 5 feet. A creature within 5 feet has one-half concealment (attacks against it have a 20% miss chance). Creatures farther away have total concealment (50% miss chance, and the attacker can't use sight to locate the target). Any creature attempting to move through the death fog progresses at one-tenth normal speed, and each of its melee attack and melee damage rolls incurs a −2 circumstance penalty. A death fog prevents effective ranged weapon attacks, except for magic rays and the like.

RGM

In addition to obscuring sight, a death fog is highly acidic. Each round, the fog deals 3d8 points of acid damage to every creature and object within it (no saving throw). A severe wind (31+ mph) disperses these vapors in 1d2 rounds; otherwise, the effect lasts for 3d6+1 rounds. The greenvise is not impeded by its own death fog, so it can move and fight within the fog freely.

Improved Grab (Ex): If a greenvise hits an opponent that is at least one size category smaller than itself with a slam attack, it deals normal damage and attempts to start a grapple as a free action without provoking an attack of opportunity (grapple bonus +26). If it gets a hold, it can transfer the opponent to its maw with another successful grapple check, dealing automatic bite damage, then try to swallow in the next round. Alternatively, the greenvise has the option to conduct the grapple normally, or simply use its tendrils or maw to hold the opponent (–20 penalty on grapple check, but the greenvise is not considered grappled). In either case, each successful grapple check it makes during successive rounds automatically deals slam or bite damage, as appropriate.

Swallow Whole (Ex): A greenvise can swallow a single creature that is at least one size category smaller than itself by making a successful grapple check (grapple bonus +26), provided it already has that opponent in its maw (see Improved Grab, above). Once inside the greenvise, the opponent takes 2d6+9 points of bludgeoning damage and 2d4 points of acid damage per round from the plant's stomach. A successful grapple check allows the swallowed creature to climb out of the stomach and return to the greenvise's maw, where another successful grapple check is needed to get free. Alternatively, a swallowed creature can try to cut its way out with either claws or a light piercing or slashing weapon. Dealing at least 20 points of damage to the stomach (AC 18) in this way creates an opening large enough to permit escape. Once a single swallowed creature exits, muscular action closes the hole; thus, another swallowed opponent must cut its own way out. A greenvise's stomach can hold 1 Large, 4 Medium-size, 16 Small, or 64 Tiny or smaller opponents.

Plant Traits (Ex): A greenvise is immune to poison, *sleep*, paralysis, stunning, and polymorphing. It is not subject to critical hits or mind-affecting effects. The creature also has low-light vision.

Woodsense (Ex): A greenvise can automatically sense the location of anything within 60 feet that is in contact with vegetation, even objects or creatures that are not in contact with the same vegetation as it is.

Medium-Size Aberration
Hit Dice: 5d8+10 (32 hp)
Initiative: +2
Speed: 5 ft., fly 30 ft. (perfect)
AC: 16 (+2 Dex, +4 natural), touch 12, flat-footed 14
Attacks: 10 tentacles +4 melee and bite –1 melee
Damage: Tentacle 1d4+1 plus paralyzation, bite 2d4
Face/Reach: 5 ft. by 5 ft./5 ft. (10 ft. with tentacle)
Special Attacks: Improved grab, paralysis
Special Qualities: Blindsight 60 ft., flight, immunities, tentacle regeneration
Saves: Fort +3, Ref +3, Will +4
Abilities: Str 12, Dex 15, Con 14, Int 10, Wis 11, Cha 9
Skills: Hide +12, Listen +4, Move Silently +12, Spot +8
Feats: Flyby Attack

Climate/Terrain: Any land or underground
Organization: Solitary, pair, or pack (3–7)
Challenge Rating: 3
Treasure: None
Alignment: Usually neutral evil
Advancement: 6–10 HD (Medium-size); 11–15 HD (Large)

These horrible, misshapen creatures resemble giant, floating brains with tentacles. They inhabit dungeons, underground passages, remote caves, and other places where light never reaches. Humanoids of all kinds are their favorite prey.

This vicious predator has a large, bulbous body composed of wrinkled, light gray flesh that seems to float in the air of its own volition. Ten long, spiny tentacles hang from the bottom of its body, twisting in the air like ropes. A grell has a sharp beak that it uses for tearing the flesh of its prey, but no other visible facial features.

COMBAT

A grell prefers to wait in ambush for potential prey. When a suitable target passes, the monster attempts to paralyze it with its tentacles, then escape to its lair with its helpless prey. Grells are cunning enough to avoid direct confrontations with large groups, since they are aware of the dangers that foes capable of teamwork can present.

A grell occasionally shadows a group that is too large to attack directly, following along inconspicuously and using its Hide skill to stay out of sight. When a member of the target group lags behind, or

LGW

the group is distracted by some other hazard, the grell attacks a straggler and tries to drag away its meal unnoticed. Grells also sometimes lurk near dangerous areas, such as pit traps, quicksand, or the lairs of other monsters, hoping to prey upon trapped, helpless, or wounded creatures.

In melee combat, a grell can attack as many foes as it can reach, using as many of its tentacles as it wishes against any single opponent. It uses its bite only against paralyzed prey or as a last resort.

Improved Grab (Ex): If a grell hits an opponent that is at least one size category smaller than itself with a tentacle attack, it deals normal damage and attempts to start a grapple as a free action without provoking an attack of opportunity (grapple bonus +20, including a +16 racial bonus on grapple checks). If it gets a hold, it has the option to conduct the grapple normally, or simply use a single tentacle to hold the opponent (–20 penalty on grapple check, but the grell is not considered grappled). In either case, each successful grapple check it makes during successive rounds automatically deals tentacle damage.

Paralysis (Ex): A grell's tentacles are lined with small spiny barbs, much like a squid's. (This is clearly a classic case of convergent evolution, since the two creatures are completely unrelated.) Any creature hit by a grell's tentacle must make a Fortitude save (DC 14) or be paralyzed for 4 rounds.

Blindsight (Ex): A grell is blind, but it maneuvers and fights as well as a sighted creature by using scent and vibration to ascertain its surroundings. This ability enables it to discern objects and creatures within 60 feet. The grell usually does not need to make Spot or Listen checks to notice creatures within range of its blindsight.

Flight (Ex): A grell's body is unusually buoyant. The creature continuously produces an effect like that of the *fly* spell, which it can use to move at a speed of 30 feet (perfect maneuverability). This buoyancy also grants the grell a permanent *feather fall* effect with personal range.

Immunities (Ex): A grell is immune to electricity and paralysis effects.

Tentacle Regeneration (Ex): Foes can attack a grell's tentacles, but only when those appendages are actually holding an opponent. A tentacle has an AC of 19 (touch 12) and can withstand 10 points of damage. The loss of a tentacle does not harm the creature (that is, the damage does not apply against its hit point total), and it regrows the limb within a day.

Skills: A grell gains a +2 racial bonus on Hide and Move Silently checks.

GRIMALKIN

Medium-Size Shapechanger
Hit Dice: 4d8 (18 hp)
Initiative: +5
Speed: 40 ft.
AC: 12 (+1 Dex, +1 natural), touch 11, flat-footed 11
Attacks: 2 claws +2 melee and bite –3 melee
Damage: Claw 1d4–1, bite 1d6–1
Face/Reach: 5 ft. by 5 ft./5 ft.
Special Qualities: Darkvision 60 ft., empathy, polymorph
Saves: Fort +4, Ref +5, Will +5
Abilities: Str 9, Dex 12, Con 11, Int 8, Wis 13, Cha 12
Skills: Climb +6, Hide +3, Jump +6, Listen +3, Move Silently +8, Spot +3
Feats: Improved Initiative

Climate/Terrain: Temperate plains
Organization: Solitary
Challenge Rating: 2
Treasure: None
Alignment: Usually neutral
Advancement: 5–8 HD (Medium-size); 9–12 HD (Large)

Prized pets and dedicated guard animals, the shapeshifting grimalkins are found among many civilized societies. Most of these unusual creatures are domesticated, so it is rare to see one in the wild.

The mutable nature of the grimalkin allows it to take on a wide variety of animal forms, though its preferred form is its natural one—that of an oversized, blue-gray housecat. When it is feeling playful, a grimalkin performs for its master by changing into amusing or beguiling forms. It adopts a more threatening form when defending itself from an attack.

A grimalkin bonds with one master and remains his or her loyal companion for life. Its personality is extremely malleable, and over time the grimalkin takes on a disposition similar to that of its owner.

Grimalkins speak Common. They are chatty creatures that never know when to keep quiet.

COMBAT

A grimalkin changes its shape each round during a battle to confuse its foes. This makes it very difficult to adopt any sort of strategy for fighting it. A grimalkin fights to the death when defending its master, though it is quite willing to flee a battle that is going badly for it while it is alone.

Empathy (Ex): A grimalkin can detect the surface emotions of any creature within 50 feet that it can see. It can sense basic needs, drives, and emotions, but not thoughts. A successful Will save (DC 13) allows a target to avoid being sensed in this way by that grimalkin for 24 hours thereafter.

Polymorph (Su): As a free action, a grimalkin can produce an effect like that of a *polymorph self* spell, except as follows. The creature may take the form of any Medium-size or smaller animal, beast, or vermin, but it does not regain hit points when changing forms.

Skills: A grimalkin has a +4 racial bonus on Move Silently checks and a +2 racial bonus on Climb and Jump checks.

GRIZZLY MASTODON

Huge Beast
Hit Dice: 15d10+90 (172 hp)
Initiative: +0
Speed: 40 ft.
AC: 16 (–2 size, +8 natural), touch 8, flat-footed 16
Attacks: Slam +21 melee and 2 stamps +16 melee, or gore +21 melee
Damage: Slam 2d6+12, stamp 2d6+6, gore 4d8+12
Face/Reach: 10 ft. by 20 ft./10 ft.
Special Attacks: Trample 4d8+18
Special Qualities: Darkvision 60 ft., low-light vision, scent
Saves: Fort +15, Ref +9, Will +7
Abilities: Str 35, Dex 10, Con 23, Int 2, Wis 15, Cha 7
Skills: Listen +10, Spot +9

Climate/Terrain: Cold and temperate hills and forests
Organization: Solitary or herd (6–30)
Challenge Rating: 13
Treasure: None
Alignment: Always neutral
Advancement: 16–21 HD (Huge); 22–45 HD (Gargantuan)

These larger, more temperamental cousins of the elephant roam subarctic and arctic lands. The great strength and endurance of these tremendous herbivores make them highly desirable to giants, who capture and tame them for use as mounts and beasts of burden.

Suspicious and unfriendly by nature, grizzly mastodons are highly protective of their young and their feeding grounds. They never hesitate to drive away intruders, stomping underfoot any who are unwise enough to persist. Grizzly mastodons are among the most aggressive creatures alive when it comes to defending their territories from other groups of mastodons or large herbivores and protecting their mates and offspring from predators of all kinds. More than one hungry creature that thought to make a meal of a young grizzly mastodon has learned a harsh lesson at the sharp tusks and stomping feet of several furious adults.

A grizzly mastodon is a shaggy, elephantine creature covered in gray, brown, or black fur. It is called grizzly because of the sprinkling of gray hairs throughout its coat, like that of a grizzly bear. Unlike an elephant, a grizzly mastodon has two pairs of ivory tusks. The typical adult specimen is 20 feet tall and weighs 22,000 pounds.

COMBAT

In combat, grizzly mastodons gore with their four tusks, then trample opponents underfoot. They prefer to attack in groups, but they show no fear even when overmatched if the safety of their young is at stake.

Trample (Ex): As a standard action, a grizzly mastodon can trample opponents at least one size category smaller than itself. This attack deals 4d8+18 points of bludgeoning damage. A trampled opponent can attempt either an attack of opportunity at a –4 penalty or a Reflex save (DC 29) for half damage.

Scent (Ex): A grizzly mastodon can detect approaching enemies, sniff out hidden foes, and track by sense of smell.

HALF-FIEND, DURZAGON

Medium-Size Outsider (Evil, Lawful)
Hit Dice: 5d8+10 (32 hp)
Initiative: +6
Speed: 30 ft.
AC: 13 (+2 Dex, +1 natural), touch 12, flat-footed 11
Attacks: 2 claws +7 melee and bite +2 melee and beard +2 melee
Damage: Claw 1d6+2, bite 1d6+1, beard 1d3+1 plus poison
Face/Reach: 5 ft. by 5 ft./5 ft.
Special Attacks: Beard, poison, spell-like abilities
Special Qualities: Acid resistance 20, cold resistance 20, darkvision 120 ft., DR 10/+1, duergar traits, electricity resistance 20, fire resistance 20, immunities, light sensitivity, outsider traits, SR 15
Saves: Fort +6, Ref +6, Will +4
Abilities: Str 15, Dex 14, Con 15, Int 14, Wis 11, Cha 8
Skills: Appraise +10, Diplomacy +3, Listen +11, Move Silently +14, Search +10, Sense Motive +8, Spot +11
Feats: Alertness (B), Improved Initiative, Power Attack

Climate/Terrain: Any underground
Organization: Solitary, team (1 plus 2–4 duergar), squad (1 plus 11–20 duergar), or clan (1 plus 30–100 duergar)
Challenge Rating: 4
Treasure: Double standard
Alignment: Usually lawful evil
Advancement: By character class

A durzagon is the result of secret crossbreeding between a devil and an unsuspecting duergar. From time to time, powerful devils disguised as gray dwarves infiltrate duergar society, seeking out the best mates to bear durzagon children. Most duergar are unaware that they have attracted the attention of diabolical forces. The birth of a half-fiend durzagon is cause for much celebration in the infernal realms.

A durzagon is slightly taller and leaner than a gray dwarf, usually reaching a height of about 5 feet. The half-fiend is bald but sports a wiry, gray beard tinged with red streaks. Its rust-colored skin radiates a palpable heat, and its fingers end in wickedly sharp claws.

Durzagons speak Dwarf and Undercommon. Those who learn of their diabolic ancestry also speak Infernal.

COMBAT

Though durzagons relish physical combat, they usually prefer to use spell-like abilities from behind the protection of duergar guards. In melee, durzagons show no fear; they would rather fight to the death than submit to an enemy.

Beard (Ex): If a durzagon hits a single opponent with both claw attacks, it automatically hits with its beard as well.

Poison (Ex): A durzagon's poison (Fortitude save DC 14) is a sulfuric fluid delivered with each successful beard attack. The initial damage is 1d4 points of Strength damage, and the secondary damage is 1d2 points of Strength drain.

Spell-Like Abilities: 3/day—*darkness*, 1/day—*desecrate, enlarge* (self only), *invisibility, unholy blight.* Caster level 10th; save DC 9 + spell level.

Duergar Traits: A durzagon gains a +1 bonus on attack rolls against orcs and goblinoids, a +2 bonus on Will saves against spells and spell-like abilities, and a +4 dodge bonus against giants. It also has stonecunning (+2 racial bonus on checks to notice unusual stonework; intuit depth).

Immunities (Ex): A durzagon is immune to paralysis, phantasms, and poisons.

Light Sensitivity: Exposure to bright light (such as sunlight or a *daylight* spell) imposes a –2 circumstance penalty on a durzagon's attack rolls.

Outsider Traits: A durzagon cannot be raised or resurrected.

Skills: A durzagon gains a +4 racial bonus on Move Silently checks and a +1 racial bonus on Listen and Spot checks.

DURZAGON SOCIETY

Durzagons almost always hold leadership positions in duergar society, and a large duergar city may have several durzagon residents. The gray dwarves revere these creatures as powerful leaders. Durzagons go to great lengths to keep the knowledge of their powers a secret from their enemies and their allies.

DURZAGON CHARACTERS

A durzagon's favored class is cleric. Like duergar, most durzagons worship the cruel dwarven deity, Laduguer. Durzagon clerics can choose two of the following domains: Evil, Law, Magic, and Protection.

A durzagon PC's effective character level (ECL) is equal to its class level + 7; thus, a 1st-level durzagon cleric has an ECL of 8 and is the equivalent of a 8th-level character.

HELLFIRE WYRM

Huge Dragon (Fire)
Hit Dice: 23d12+184 (333 hp)
Initiative: +4
Speed: 60 ft., burrow 30 ft., fly 250 ft. (clumsy)
AC: 36 (–2 size, + 28 natural), touch 8, flat-footed 36
Attacks: Bite +30 melee and 2 claws +25 melee
Damage: Bite 2d8+9, claw 2d6+4
Face/Reach: 10 ft. by 40 ft./10 ft.
Special Attacks: Breath weapon, crush 2d8+13, frightful presence, spell-like abilities
Special Qualities: DR 20/+5, fiendish form, fire subtype, immunities, infernal aura, keen senses, SR 37, *summon baatezu*
Saves: Fort +21, Ref +13, Will +21
Abilities: Str 29, Dex 10, Con 27, Int 23, Wis 26, Cha 28
Skills: Bluff +26, Diplomacy +32, Intimidate +35, Jump +28, Knowledge (any four) +31, Listen +34, Scry +29, Search +26, Spot +34
Feats: Flyby Attack, Hover, Improved Initiative, Power Attack, Quicken Spell-Like Ability, Snatch

Climate/Terrain: Any land and underground
Organization: Solitary, pair, or clutch (3–5)
Challenge Rating: 26
Treasure: Double standard
Alignment: Always lawful evil
Advancement: 24–46 HD (Gargantuan)

Hellfire wyrms are draconic agents of the Nine Hells of Baator that live among humanoid races on the Material Plane. They are masterful power brokers, manipulating people and events in subtle ways. Hellfire wyrms can steer rulers to fight in unjust wars, or support unholy alliances, or even commit despotic acts against their people.

A hellfire wyrm is a diabolic-looking, winged dragon with vicious bone spikes jutting from its head and shoulders. Smoke rises continually from its scales, and its eyes burn an intense yellow. The monster's scales shift in color to give the appearance of flowing molten lava, and they stink of brimstone.

Hellfire wyrms entrench themselves in regional politics by using their knowledge, wealth, and persuasive abilities to force through their foul agendas. The typical wyrm does not limit its actions to any one kingdom, and it often has a different identity for each realm it visits. It takes great pains to hide its draconic form, usually assuming the shape of a charismatic tiefling when dealing with humanoids and assassinating anyone who learns its true identity. Hellfire wyrms retreat to secret lairs when not actively scheming.

A hellfire wyrm speaks Draconic, Infernal, and Common, as well as the languages of any nearby humanoid races.

COMBAT

Utterly fearless and almost unstoppable in battle, hellfire wyrms are expert tacticians. They keep to the air, slinging mind-affecting spells and withering breath attacks at their enemies.

Breath Weapon (Su): A hellfire wyrm can breathe a 50-foot cone of infernal flame that deals 14d10 points of damage. Each creature caught in the area can attempt a Reflex save (DC 29) to take half damage. One-half of the damage from this attack derives from infernal power and is therefore not subject to reduction by protective elemental magic. Once the wyrm breathes, it must wait 1d4 rounds before using its breath weapon again.

Crush (Ex): A flying hellfire wyrm can land on opponents three or more size categories smaller than itself as a standard action, using its whole body to crush them. A crush attack affects as many creatures as can fit under the wyrm's body. Each creature in the affected area must succeed at a Reflex save (DC 29) or be pinned, automatically taking 2d8+13 points of bludgeoning damage. Thereafter, if the wyrm chooses to maintain the pin, treat it as a normal grapple attack (grapple bonus +40). While pinned, the opponent takes crush damage each round.

Frightful Presence (Ex): When a hellfire wyrm charges, attacks, or flies overhead, it inspires terror in all creatures within 240 feet that have fewer Hit Dice or levels than it has. Each potentially affected opponent must attempt a Will save (DC 30). On a failure, a creature with 4 or fewer Hit Dice becomes panicked for 4d6 rounds, and one with 5 or more Hit Dice becomes shaken for 4d6 rounds. A successful save leaves that opponent immune to that hellfire wyrm's frightful presence for 24 hours. Dragons ignore the frightful presence effect of a hellfire wyrm.

Spell-Like Abilities: At will—*blasphemy, charm person, demand, desecrate, dictum, fire storm, greater dispelling, hold person, improved invisibility, misdirection, pyrotechnics, sending, suggestion, teleport*

without error, true seeing (divine version), *unholy aura, unhallow, wall of fire.* Caster level 20th; save DC 19 + spell level.

Fiendish Form (Su): At will, a hellfire wyrm can produce an effect like that of a *shapechange* spell, except that only the normal form of any tiefling or devil may be assumed.

Fire Subtype (Ex): A hellfire wyrm is immune to fire damage but takes double damage from cold unless a saving throw for half damage is allowed. In that case, it takes half damage on a success and double damage on a failure.

Immunities: A hellfire wyrm is immune to sleep and paralysis effects.

Infernal Aura (Su): Any creature within 5 feet of a hellfire wyrm automatically takes 5d4 points of fire damage per round. It can suppress this aura as a free action.

Keen Senses (Ex): A hellfire wyrm sees four times as well as a human in low-light conditions and twice as well in normal light. It also has darkvision with a range of 120 feet.

Summon Baatezu **(Sp):** Once per day, a hellfire wyrm may summon a single barbazu, cornugon, or gelugon with a 100% chance of success. This ability functions like a *summon monster* spell of the appropriate level. A summoned devil automatically returns whence it came after 1 hour. A baatezu that has just been summoned cannot use its own summon ability for 1 hour.

Feats: A creature that is flung by a hellfire wyrm after being snatched travels 100 feet and takes 10d6 points of damage. If the hellfire wyrm is flying, the creature takes this damage or the appropriate falling damage, whichever is greater.

HOOK HORROR

Large Aberration

Hit Dice: 10d8+20 (65 hp)

Initiative: +3

Speed: 20 ft., climb 20 ft.

AC: 22 (–1 size, +3 Dex, +10 natural), touch 12, flat-footed 19

Attacks: 2 claws +13 melee and bite +8 melee

Damage: Claw 1d6+7, bite 2d6+3

Face/Reach: 5 ft. by 5 ft./10 ft.

Special Attacks: Improved grab, power sunder, rending bite

Special Qualities: Blindsight 60 ft., light sensitivity

Saves: Fort +5, Ref +6, Will +8

Abilities: Str 24, Dex 17, Con 14, Int 7, Wis 12, Cha 9

Skills: Climb +16, Hide +8*, Jump +15, Listen +13

Feats: Cleave, Improved Trip (B), Power Attack

Climate/Terrain: Any underground

Organization: Solitary, pack (5–20), or clan (21–40)

Challenge Rating: 6

Treasure: Standard

Alignment: Usually neutral

Advancement: 11–15 HD (Large); 16–30 (Huge)

Sly hunters of cavernous subterranean areas, hook horrors are territorial monsters that distrust intruders and fiercely protect their hunting grounds. Underground areas where hook horrors dwell echo with the constant clacking and scraping sounds of their hooks against stone, as they wend their way across cliffsides and cavern walls.

A hook horror stands about 9 feet tall and weighs approximately 400 pounds. Its long, powerfully built arms and legs end in wickedly curved hooks. Its head resembles a vulture's, with a monstrous beak. Its torso is shaped like a beetle's body and covered with a rough, stonelike exoskeleton, studded with sharp, bony protuberances.

Hook horrors normally live in extended family groups or clans, each of which is ruled by the eldest female. The eldest male usually leads the clan's hunters and warriors. The clan stores its eggs communally, in a central, well-defended area of its home system of caverns or warrens.

Hook horrors are omnivores, consuming lichens, fungi, plants, and any animals they can catch. Meat is their preferred food, and drow is rumored to be one of their favorite meals.

Hook horrors speak Undercommon.

COMBAT

Hook horrors attack in groups, using their climbing skills to ambush foes from above. They fight cooperatively and work together against the largest and best armed opponents. Hook horrors use their arm hooks to trip foes. If a battle goes poorly, they retreat by scaling walls.

Improved Grab (Ex): If a hook horror hits an opponent that is at least one size category smaller than itself with both claw attacks, it deals normal damage and attempts to start a grapple as a free action without provoking an attack of opportunity (grapple bonus +18). If it gets a hold, it automatically hits with its rending bite attack on the same round. (This replaces its normal bite attack for that round.) Thereafter, the hook horror has the

option to conduct the grapple normally, or simply use its claws to hold the opponent (–20 penalty on grapple check, but the hook horror is not considered grappled). In either case, each successful grapple check it makes during successive rounds automatically deals damage for both claw attacks and a rending bite.

Power Sunder (Ex): A hook horror attempting to strike a foe's weapon or shield does not incur an attack of opportunity. On a successful power sunder attack, a hook horror deals double damage.

Rending Bite (Ex): A hook horror can automatically bite a grabbed foe for 3d6+10 points of damage.

Blindsight (Ex): A hook horror emits high-frequency sounds, inaudible to most other creatures, that bounce off nearby objects and creatures. This ability enables it to discern objects and creatures within 60 feet. The hook horror usually does not need to make Spot or Listen checks to notice creatures within range of its blindsight. A *silence* spell negates this ability and forces the hook horror to rely on its weak vision, which has a range of 10 feet.

Light Sensitivity (Ex): Exposure to bright light (such as sunlight or a *daylight* spell) imposes a –2 penalty on a hook horror's attack rolls.

Skills: *A hook horror receives a +8 racial bonus on Hide checks when in subterranean areas.

IMMOTH

Large Elemental (Air, Cold, Water)
Hit Dice: 10d8+40 (85 hp)
Initiative: +3
Speed: 30 ft., fly 30 ft. (perfect), swim 30 ft.
AC: 18 (–1 size, +3 Dex, +6 natural), touch 12, flat-footed 15
Attacks: 2 claws +10 melee and tail slap +5 melee
Damage: Claw 1d4+4 plus 1d6 cold, tail slap 1d6+2 plus 1d6 cold plus poison
Face/Reach: 5 ft. by 5 ft./10 ft.
Special Attacks: *Ice runes*, poison, spells
Special Qualities: Cold subtype, DR 5/+1, elemental traits, icewalking, immunities, SR 23
Saves: Fort +11, Ref +10, Will +4
Abilities: Str 18, Dex 16, Con 19, Int 14, Wis 13, Cha 21
Skills: Climb +12, Hide +11, Jump +13, Spot +12, Swim +12
Feats: Cleave, Combat Reflexes, Power Attack

Climate/Terrain: Any cold
Organization: Solitary
Challenge Rating: 9
Treasure: Standard
Alignment: Usually neutral
Advancement: By character class

Immoths originate from the coldest regions of the Elemental Planes of Air and Water, although their thirst for knowledge takes them to many other planes of existence. They tend to dwell in forbidding, freezing regions. Though they are solitary creatures, immoths maintain contact with others of their kind, sharing secrets and coming to each other's aid when necessary. An immoth appears as a gleaming, 8-foot-tall giant carved from dense, translucent ice. It resembles a bearded, hulking dwarf with icy talons and a large, crystalline tail. The creature covers itself with gemlike nuggets of enchanted ice called *ice runes*.

Immoths seem to be highly curious about all forms of humanoid life, as well as arcane and divine magic, but they generally take a great interest in all things. They barter with intelligent beings for information but show no compunction about taking what they want by force if more peaceful methods fail. These relentless gatherers of knowledge and secrets hide their information in icy libraries.

One legend that planar travelers tell speaks of why the immoths seek out information. The tale goes that long ago, a powerful, mad sorcerer tried to recruit elementals to serve him. When they refused, he punished them with a vile curse: They must seek out and collect the words of his curse and return them to their planar home—a place referred to in the tale as the Mountain of Ultimate Winter. According to the story, this place was so cold that spoken words froze in the air and fell to the ground. The cursed elementals who lived there took on new forms and became the creatures now known as immoths. They then began traveling the planes to find the sorcerer's words.

This tale bolsters the widely held theory that immoths believe words themselves to have power. (Certainly, the verbal components of spells lend some credence to the idea.) Though the true reasons for their diligent search for knowledge are unknown, it is clear that the monsters prize words for their own sake, not merely the knowledge those words convey.

Immoths eat any sort of living creatures, feeding on the life essence rather than the actual flesh—though they

nonetheless consume the latter. It is not known how, or even whether, immoths reproduce.

Immoths speak Aquan, Auran, and Common.

COMBAT

Before wading into battle, an immoth casts spells designed to bolster its physical and defensive capabilities. In melee, it immobilizes as many foes as possible with its tail poison and uses rune magic to overcome any serious threats. Most immoths prefer runes that inflict pain or can debilitate opponents. When seriously threatened, these monsters flee by walking up the nearest icy cliff. Then, from on high, they cast damaging spells to deter foes from following.

Ice Runes (Sp): Any spell an immoth has prepared can be inscribed on an ice nugget. The creature can trigger the spell contained in such an *ice rune* as a free action. An *ice rune* remains magical until triggered by the immoth. Each immoth has at least 3d4+2 *ice runes* embedded on its body. Some wonder whether this ability lends credence to the story about frozen words in the Mountain of Ultimate Winter.

Poison (Ex): An immoth delivers its freezing venom (Fortitude save DC 19) with each successful tail attack. The initial damage is paralysis (1d6+2 rounds), and the secondary damage is 1 point of Intelligence drain per round of paralysis.

Spells: An immoth can cast arcane spells as a 12th-level sorcerer (spells/day 6/8/7/7/7/6/3; spells known 9/5/5/4/3/2/1; save DC 15 + spell level). It cannot cast spells with the fire descriptor.

Cold Subtype (Ex): An immoth is immune to cold damage but takes double damage from fire unless a saving throw for half damage is allowed. In that case, the creature takes half damage on a success and double damage on a failure.

Elemental Traits (Ex): An immoth is immune to poison, *sleep*, paralysis, and stunning. It is not subject to critical hits or flanking, and it cannot be raised or resurrected. The creature also has darkvision (60-foot range).

Icewalking (Ex): This ability works like the *spider climb* spell, except that it applies to all icy surfaces and it is always active.

Immunities (Ex): Because of its dense crystalline body, an immoth takes only half damage from piercing and slashing weapons.

IXITXACHITL

An ixitxachitl is an aquatic creature very similar to a ray—indeed, many adventurers have mistaken one for the other. The greatest difference between rays and ixitxachitls is that the former are simple, inoffensive creatures and the latter are intelligent, organized, and evil.

Ixitxachitls create lairs by hollowing out coral reefs to form bewildering mazes. From these strongholds, they wage war on sahuagins, locathahs, merfolk, coastal humans, and any other intelligent creatures that encroach on their territory. They tend to treat their homes as badly as they do their enemies, however, stripping them clean of all plant and animal life before moving on to new, unspoiled reefs.

Ixitxachitls are universally despised by all undersea races for their rapacious lifestyle, their aggression, and their habit of enslaving captives. A large ixitxachitl settlement often contains twice as many slaves as it does ixitxachitls. Anything that can survive underwater can be found captive in an ixitxachitl maze, including nixies, gargoyles, and even humans or elves who are wearing magic items that allow underwater breathing.

LGW

AVERAGE IXITXACHITL

Like a manta ray, an average ixitxachitl has a plain brown or black topside with a lighter-colored underside and a long tail. But this is where the resemblance ends. An ixitxachitl's large mouth is filled with triangular, razor-sharp teeth, and its eyes are intelligent and cruel.

Combat

Individually, ixitxachitls are quite weak. They seldom attack unless they have overwhelming numbers or the opportunity to spring an ambush. They have been known to conceal

	Average Ixitxachitl Small Aberration (Aquatic)	Vampiric Ixitxachitl Small Aberration (Aquatic)
Hit Dice:	1d8+1 (5 hp)	2d8+2 (11 hp)
Initiative:	+3	+3
Speed:	Swim 30 ft.	Swim 30 ft.
AC:	16 (+1 size, +3 Dex, +2 natural), touch 14, flat-footed 13	16 (+1 size, +3 Dex, +2 natural), touch 14, flat-footed 13
Attacks:	Bite +2 melee	Bite +3 melee
Damage:	Bite 1d6+1	Bite 1d6+1 plus energy drain
Face/Reach:	5 ft. by 5 ft./5 ft.	5 ft. by 5 ft./5 ft.
Special Attacks:	—	Energy drain
Special Qualities:	Darkvision 60 ft.	Darkvision 60 ft., fast healing 5
Saves:	Fort +1, Ref +3, Will +3	Fort +1, Ref +3, Will +4
Abilities:	Str 12, Dex 16, Con 13, Int 12, Wis 13, Cha 7	Str 12, Dex 16, Con 13, Int 12, Wis 13, Cha 7
Skills:	Hide +11, Intuit Direction +5, Knowledge (nature) +5, Listen +5, Spot +5, Swim +9, Tumble +7	Hide +11, Intuit Direction +5, Knowledge (nature) +5, Listen +6, Spot +6, Swim +9, Tumble +7
Feats:	Dodge	Dodge
Climate/Terrain:	Warm aquatic	Warm aquatic
Organization:	Solitary, pair, pod (5–12 plus 1 2nd-level cleric), or shoal (10–100 plus 5 2nd-level clerics, 2 5th-level clerics, and 20–200 slaves)	Solitary, pair, pod (1–2 plus 5–12 average ixitxachitls and 1 2nd-level cleric), or shoal (1–2 plus 10–100 average ixitxachitl, 5 2nd-level clerics, 2 5th-level clerics, and 20–200 slaves)
Challenge Rating:	1	3
Treasure:	No coins, no goods, double items (wearable items only)	No coins, no goods, double items (no weapons, potions, or scrolls)
Alignment:	Always chaotic evil	Always chaotic evil
Advancement:	By character class	3–4 HD (Small); 5–6 HD (Medium-size); 7–8 HD (Large); or by character class

themselves in the sand and muck of the sea bottom, waiting for enemies to pass by so they can rush in among them.

VAMPIRIC IXITXACHITL

Vampiric ixitxachitls are not undead, though they do share several traits with vampires, such as long canine teeth and the ability to drain energy. Vampiric ixitxachitls are immune to turning attempts and do not possess the standard undead traits. One of these monsters usually leads any group of average ixitxachitls.

Combat

Vampiric ixitxachitls prefer to hang back, hidden, and allow their underlings to enter combat while they size up the opposition. If the fight is going well, they join in, looking for easy targets. If the outcome seems doubtful, they try to support their underlings in strikes against the most dangerous-looking foe.

Energy Drain (Su): Any living creature hit by a vampiric ixitxachitl's bite attack gains one negative level. For each negative level bestowed, the vampiric ixitxachitl heals 5 points of damage. If the amount of healing is more than the damage the creature has taken, it gains any excess as temporary hit points.

If the negative level has not been removed (with a spell such as *restoration*) before 24 hours have passed, the afflicted opponent must succeed at a Fortitude save (DC 12) to remove it. (The vampiric ixitxachitl uses its Constitution modifier instead of its Charisma modifier to determine the save DC.) Failure means the opponent's level (or Hit Dice) is reduced by one.

Fast Healing (Ex): A vampiric ixitxachitl regains lost hit points at the rate of 5 per round. Fast healing does not restore hit points lost from starvation, thirst, or suffocation, and it does not allow the vampiric ixitxachitl to regrow or reattach lost body parts.

IXITXACHITL SOCIETY

Though they are occasionally encountered in rivers that empty into the sea, most ixitxachitls live in shallow ocean depths or coral reefs. Once they have selected a site for their lair, they have their slaves carve out a lair for them. Any group of ixitxachitls is led by a single powerful individual (usually a cleric or a vampiric ixitxachitl) that rules by intimidation.

IXITXACHITL CHARACTERS

Some ixitxachitls are accomplished clerics, generally serving any chaotic evil deity (and having access to the Chaos

and Evil domains), but occasionally following Erythnul specifically. An ixitxachitl's favored class is cleric.

An average ixitxachitl PC's effective character level (ECL) is equal to its class level + 2. Thus, a 1st-level ixitxachitl cleric has an ECL of 3 and is the equivalent of a 3rd-level character. A vampiric ixitxachitl PC's effective character level (ECL) is equal to its class level + 5. Thus, a 1st-level vampiric ixitxachitl cleric has an ECL of 6 and is the equivalent of a 6th-level character.

JAHI

Tiny Undead (Incorporeal)
Hit Dice: 25d12 (162 hp)
Initiative: +4
Speed: Fly 60 ft. (perfect)
AC: 16 (+2 size, +4 deflection), touch 16, flat-footed 16
Attacks: Incorporeal touch +14 melee
Damage: Incorporeal touch 1d3 plus 1d4 Charisma damage
Face/Reach: 2 1/2 ft. by 2 1/2 ft./0 ft.
Special Attacks: Charisma damage, Charisma drain, *dominate person*
Special Qualities: Incorporeal subtype, invest Charisma, SR 27, undead traits
Saves: Fort +8, Ref +10, Will +18
Abilities: Str —, Dex 11, Con —, Int 15, Wis 15, Cha 18
Skills: Balance +2, Bluff +9, Diplomacy +16, Escape Artist +15, Hide +18, Intimidate +6, Jump +2, Listen +14, Search +12, Sense Motive +12, Spot +14, Tumble +15
Feats: Ability Focus (*dominate person*), Alertness, Blind-Fight, Expertise, Flyby Attack, Improved Initiative, Iron Will, Lightning Reflexes, Quicken Spell-Like Ability

Climate/Terrain: Any land and underground
Organization: Solitary or harim (1 plus 1 14th-level chosen one and 4–20 7th-level followers)
Challenge Rating: 16
Treasure: Double standard
Alignment: Usually lawful evil
Advancement: 26–50 HD (Tiny)

The jahi is an incorporeal undead made of unfulfilled desires. It attacks by magically dominating its prey.

The jahi appears as a ghostly image of a serpentine, scaled worm with three elongated faces. Normally, it is found wrapped around the throat or chest of a creature it has selected to be its "chosen one."

A jahi prefers to work behind the mask of its chosen one, letting the blame for any excesses fall upon the latter. Once it has a chosen one, the monster begins to accumulate a group of dominated followers, who form the nucleus of a debauched cult dedicated to the jahi's worship. The creature feeds off the Charisma of these followers, all the while encouraging them to greater heights of hedonistic excess.

COMBAT

Jahis are sometimes encountered alone, but more often they have numerous enslaved individuals nearby. If encountered alone, the monster selects the individual with the most pleasing appearance as its chosen one. If it can successfully dominate that opponent, it drains his or her Charisma and replaces it with its own.

Charisma Damage (Su): Any creature hit by a jahi's incorporeal touch attack takes 1d4 points of Charisma damage (or twice that amount on a critical hit). The jahi heals 5 points of damage (or 10 on a critical hit) whenever it deals Charisma damage.

Charisma Drain (Su): Each day, a jahi's chosen one (if any) must make a Fortitude save (DC 26) or permanently lose 1d3 points of Charisma. The jahi heals 5 points of damage whenever it drains Charisma, gaining any excess as temporary hit points.

Dominate Person (Sp): Up to four times per day, a jahi can use *dominate person* (caster level 20th; save DC 20).

Incorporeal Subtype: A jahi can be harmed only by other incorporeal creatures, +1 or better magic weapons, spells, spell-like abilities, and supernatural abilities. The creature has a 50% chance to ignore any damage from a corporeal source, except for force effects or attacks made with ghost touch weapons. A jahi can pass through solid objects, but not force effects, at will. Its attacks ignore natural armor, armor, and shields, but deflection bonuses and force effects work normally against them. A jahi always moves silently and cannot be heard with Listen checks if it doesn't wish to be.

Invest Charisma (Ex): After draining all the Charisma from its chosen one, a jahi can automatically adhere to that creature (usually by wrapping around its throat or chest) and replace the lost Charisma with its own. While so invested, the creature uses the jahi's Charisma for all

Charisma-based checks. This investment lasts as long as the jahi and the chosen one are in physical contact. If seriously threatened, or if it decides to select another chosen one, the jahi detaches, removing the investment of its Charisma. At that point, the chosen one's Charisma score falls to 0 and he or she becomes unconscious until at least 1 point of Charisma has been regained.

Undead Traits: A jahi is immune to mind-affecting effects, poison, *sleep*, paralysis, stunning, disease, death effects, necromantic effects, and any effect that requires a Fortitude save unless it also works on objects. It is not subject to critical hits, subdual damage, ability damage, ability drain, energy drain, or death from massive damage. A jahi cannot be raised, and resurrection works only if it is willing. The creature has darkvision (60-foot range).

JERMLAINE

Tiny Fey

Hit Dice: 1/2 d6–1 (1 hp)

Initiative: +3

Speed: 40 ft.

AC: 15 (+2 size, +3 Dex), touch 15, flat-footed 12

Attacks: Diminutive dart +5 ranged, or Tiny shortspear –2 melee

Damage: Diminutive dart 1d3–4, Tiny shortspear 1d3–4/×3

Face/Reach: 2 1/2 ft. by 2 1/2 ft./0 ft.

Special Qualities: Low-light vision, *speak with rats*

Saves: Fort –1, Ref +5, Will +5

Abilities: Str 3, Dex 17, Con 8, Int 8, Wis 16, Cha 5

Skills: Animal Empathy +1, Craft (trapmaking) +3, Hide +15, Listen +9, Move Silently +7, Spot +9

Feats: Alertness

Climate/Terrain: Underground

Organization: Solitary, pair, gang (3–5), raiding party (4–16 plus 2–8 rats or 1–4 giant rats), or plague (10–60 plus 4–16 rats or 2–8 giant rats)

Challenge Rating: 1/2

Treasure: Standard

Alignment: Usually neutral evil

Advancement: 1–2 HD (Tiny)

Jermlaines, sometimes called jinxkin or banemidges, are tiny humanoid-shaped beings with foul dispositions and evil designs. They are remarkably adept at hiding and sneaking, so they are the enemies of all who venture underground.

A jermlaine appears to be a shaggy humanoid about 1 foot tall. Its eyes are tiny and beady, and its hair is sparse and filthy. It either dresses in dirty rags and scraps of hide or simply goes naked. Its skin is baggy, wrinkled, and always crusted with filth.

Jermlaines' speech amounts to high-pitched chitters and squeaks that are easily mistaken for the noises produced by rats or bats. (Indeed, rats are among the few living creatures that will have anything to do with them.) A few jermlaines can speak Common, Dwarf, Gnome, Goblin, or Orc, but seldom can any individual speak more than one of those languages.

COMBAT

Jermlaines attack only from ambush. If an ambush is impossible, they hide and wait until it is feasible. They always try to single out injured, ill, or sleeping foes as their first targets. Jermlaines enjoy sneaking into camps and vandalizing or stealing equipment, so long as they stand a good chance of getting away without combat.

Rather than confront an enemy, jermlaines prefer to dig pits or build net-dropping traps and other devices that can capture prey without a fight. Once an enemy is caught in a pit or a net, jermlaines swarm over him, pummeling to cause subdual damage until the target is knocked out. They have also been known to pour acid or flaming oil over trapped foes that appeared too dangerous to approach directly, even while trapped.

Speak with Rats **(Sp):** At will, a jermlaine can produce an effect like that of a *speak with animals* spell (caster level 3rd), except that it enables communication only with rats and dire rats.

JUGGERNAUT

Huge Construct
Hit Dice: 18d10 (99 hp)
Initiative: –4
Speed: 10 ft.
AC: 29 (–2 size, –4 Dex, +25 natural), touch 4, flat-footed 29
Attacks: 6 slams +21 melee
Damage: Slam 2d6+10
Face/Reach: 10 ft. by 10 ft./15 ft.
Special Attacks: Improved grab, spell-like abilities, squash 10d10+20
Special Qualities: All-around vision, DR 20/+2, construct traits, fast healing 10, immunities, SR 36
Saves: Fort +6, Ref +2, Will +8
Abilities: Str 31, Dex 3, Con —, Int —, Wis 15, Cha 16

Climate/Terrain: Any
Organization: Solitary
Challenge Rating: 11
Treasure: None
Alignment: Always neutral
Advancement: 19–32 HD (Huge); 33–54 HD (Gargantuan)

A juggernaut is a stony behemoth that serves as a weapon of war. Whether deployed to soften up the enemy prior to an invasion or used for defensive purposes, a juggernaut combines sheer size and magical abilities into a potent, nearly unstoppable force.

A juggernaut appears as a squat, square or round stone building situated atop wide stone rollers. Six sturdy stone arms jut from its sides, three on the right and three on the left. A juggernaut is often decorated with frightening stone carvings and horrific painted icons, making it a terrible sight to behold. Occasionally a juggernaut is constructed with an interior hiding space that can accommodate up to two Medium-size creatures safely.

COMBAT

A juggernaut attacks by rolling slowly forward, crushing all in its path to dust. Those who avoid this attack find themselves targeted by the construct's powerful fists, which try to force them under its rollers. A juggernaut targets escaping foes with spell-like abilities that hinder or block movement, and then changes direction to roll over immobile creatures. It stops only when changing direction or when blocked by some insurmountable obstacle. A juggernaut uses *wall of force* not only to block fleeing opponents, but also to make bridges over rivers and chasms so that it can pursue escaping targets.

Improved Grab (Ex): If a juggernaut hits an opponent that is at least one size category smaller than itself with a slam attack, it deals normal damage and attempts to start a grapple as a free action without provoking an attack of opportunity (grapple bonus +31). If it gets a hold, it can attempt to thrust the opponent under its rollers in the next round, dealing automatic squash damage. Alternatively, the juggernaut has the option to conduct the grapple normally, or simply use its hand to hold the opponent (–20 penalty on grapple check, but the juggernaut is not considered grappled). In either case, each successful grapple check it makes during successive rounds automatically deals slam damage.

Spell-Like Abilities: At will—*forcecage, grease, hold monster, magic missile, slow, wall of force, web.* Caster level 18th; save DC 13 + spell level.

Squash (Ex): As a standard action during its turn each round, a juggernaut can literally roll over opponents at least one size category smaller than itself. This attack deals 10d10+20 points of bludgeoning damage. A squashed opponent can attempt either an attack of opportunity at a –4 penalty or a Reflex save (DC 29) for half damage. A successful saving throw indicates that the target has been pushed back or aside (target's choice) as the juggernaut moves forward.

All-Around Vision (Ex): A juggernaut can see in all directions at once. Because of this ability, it gains a +4 racial bonus on Search and Spot checks, and it cannot be flanked.

Construct Traits: A juggernaut is immune to mind-affecting effects, poison, *sleep*, paralysis, stunning, disease, death effects, necromantic effects, and any effect that requires a Fortitude save unless it also works on objects. The creature is not subject to critical hits, subdual damage, ability

damage, ability drain, energy drain, or death from massive damage. It cannot heal itself but can be healed through repair. It cannot be raised or resurrected. A juggernaut has darkvision (60-foot range).

Fast Healing (Ex): A juggernaut regains lost hit points at the rate of 10 per round. Fast healing does not restore hit points lost from starvation, thirst, or suffocation, and it does not allow the juggernaut to regrow or reattach lost body parts.

Immunities (Ex): A juggernaut is immune to acid, electricity, and fire.

CONSTRUCTION

Since a juggernaut is constructed from massive blocks of granite and other dense stone, a typical specimen weighs at least 50,000 pounds. It costs 70,000 gp to create, including 5,000 gp for the body. Assembling the body requires a successful Craft (sculpting) or Profession (mason) check (DC 18). The creator must be 18th level and able to cast arcane spells. Completing the ritual drains 2,000 XP from the creator and requires the *bull's strength, geas/quest, limited wish, polymorph any object, forcecage, grease, hold monster, magic missile, slow, wall of force,* and *web* spells.

JULAJIMUS

Huge Aberration
Hit Dice: 16d8+80 (152 hp)
Initiative: +6
Speed: 50 ft.
AC: 22 (–2 size, +2 Dex, +12 natural), touch 10, flat-footed 20
Attacks: Bite +19 melee and 2 claws +14 melee
Damage: Bite 3d10+9, claw 3d8+4
Face/Reach: 10 ft. by 20 ft./10 ft.
Special Attacks: Fear aura, roar, stunning
Special Qualities: Darkvision 60 ft., DR 20/+2, enchantment immunity, polymorph self, fire resistance 20, sunlight vulnerability
Saves: Fort +10, Ref +7, Will +10
Abilities: Str 28, Dex 15, Con 20, Int 12, Wis 11, Cha 15
Skills: Climb +17, Disguise +12*, Intimidate +10, Jump +17, Listen +8, Spot +8
Feats: Cleave, Improved Initiative, Power Attack, Skill Focus (Disguise)

Climate/Terrain: Temperate forests
Organization: Solitary
Challenge Rating: 12
Treasure: Double standard
Alignment: Always neutral evil
Advancement: 17–32 HD (Gargantuan); 33–48 HD (Colossal)

Villagers often tell stories of the julajimus to their children. At some point in such a tale, the main character, a child, takes in a cute animal as a pet despite repeated warnings from his or her parents that there isn't enough food or space for the creature. The story ends with the rebellious child hiding the creature, only to have it turn into a julajimus one night and eat the child alive. In fact, the name "julajimus" is derived from an ancient phrase "julaji molus," or "eater of children." Ancient texts hint that the cult of an evil god created the first julajimuses from human prisoners.

A julajimus stands a bit more than 18 feet tall and looks somewhat like a massive baboon. Its arms are long and muscular, with four fully articulated joints each. The monster has dark blue or black fur covering its body, plus a long, blue, reptilian tail. The mouth of a julajimus is disproportionally large for the head and filled with razor-sharp teeth the size of scimitar blades.

Julajimuses are territorial, gathering in pairs only once per decade to mate. The presence of a julajimus in an area has a strange effect on nearby wildlife, causing animals to become more aggressive than normal. The monster is not afraid of civilization, and the lights of a village at night can attract a curious julajimus to investigate. Julajimuses speak Common.

COMBAT

The julajimus enjoys the sensation of gnawing on living creatures, so it always attacks with its bite first, then follows up with slashes from its two claws. Despite its size, the julajimus is fast and can easily outrun most prey.

Fear Aura (Su): A julajimus radiates a fear aura that can chill the blood of the bravest warrior. Any living creature within 20 feet of the monster must make a Will save (DC 20) or become frightened. Anyone who saves successfully is immune to this ability for 24 hours. Each round, a frightened subject gets a new saving throw at the same DC. This is a mind-affecting fear effect.

Roar (Su): Three times per day, a julajimus can loose an ear-splitting roar that can be heard for miles. Every creature within 60 feet must make a Fortitude save (DC 23) or become deafened for 3d6 hours and take 6d6 points of subdual damage.

Stunning (Su): If a julajimus successfully scores a critical hit with its claws, the opponent must make a Fortitude save

(DC 23) or be stunned for 1d4 rounds by the force of the blow. A stunned creature is unable to act and loses any positive Dexterity bonus to AC. Furthermore, any attacker gains a +2 bonus on attack rolls against it.

Enchantment Immunity (Ex): A julajimus is immune to all spells of the Enchantment school.

Polymorph Self (Su): At will, a julajimus can produce an effect like that of the *polymorph self* spell, except that the only forms it can assume are those of small, cuddly animals (such as a rabbit, chipmunk, or kitten), and reverting to its true form is a free action. This ability helps the julajimus lull its victim into a false sense of security before it shifts into its natural form to attack.

Sunlight Vulnerability (Ex): A julajimus becomes paralyzed when exposed to sunlight. Each round, it can make a Fortitude save (DC 20) to resist the paralysis. Once paralyzed, it is helpless, although its damage reduction and fire resistance still make it difficult to kill. The paralysis lasts for 1d4 rounds after the exposure to sunlight ends.

Skills: *A julajimus receives a +10 on Disguise checks when using its polymorph self ability.

KOPRU

Medium-Size Monstrous Humanoid (Aquatic)
Hit Dice: 8d8 (36 hp)
Initiative: +2
Speed: 5 ft., swim 40 ft.
AC: 15 (+2 Dex, +3 natural), touch 12, flat-footed 13
Attacks: Tail slap +10 melee and 2 claws +8 melee and bite +8 melee
Damage: Tail slap 1d6+2, claw 1d4+1, bite 1d4+1
Face/Reach: 5 ft. by 5 ft./5 ft.
Special Attacks: Constrict 3d6+3, dominate person, improved grab
Special Qualities: Darkvision 60 ft.
Saves: Fort +2, Ref +8, Will +9
Abilities: Str 15, Dex 14, Con 11, Int 11, Wis 12, Cha 10
Skills: Concentration +11, Escape Artist +11, Move Silently +10, Search +8, Swim +10
Feats: Iron Will, Multiattack

Climate/Terrain: Warm aquatic and marsh
Organization: Solitary, pair, patrol (3–5), or colony (6–24)
Challenge Rating: 6
Treasure: Standard coins (gold and platinum only), standard goods (gems only), no items
Alignment: Always chaotic evil
Advancement: 9–10 HD (Medium-size); 11–12 HD (Large)

Many generations ago, the koprus built a large and mysterious civilization under the sea. For unknown reasons their society declined, becoming ever more decrepit and degenerate, until now almost none of its former glory remains.

A kopru resembles no known creature, but it combines several familiar features into one monstrous whole. Its body is vaguely eellike but ends in three long, flexible, barbed tails. Its chest is nearly human, and the hands on its two arms end in vicious webbed claws. Its head grows directly from its trunk, like a fish's, and has large, unblinking eyes. The mouth is surrounded by four tentacles—an oddity that has led some scholars to propose that the koprus may somehow be related to mind flayers.

Koprus speak Common and Aquan.

COMBAT

Out of the water, a kopru is nearly helpless. On land, it cannot attack with its claws because it needs its arms to drag itself across the ground or prop its body up. A kopru in water, however, is a ferocious opponent in melee combat. Along with its claws and teeth, it lashes out with its tails, all three of which strike as one.

Constrict (Ex): With a successful grapple check, a kopru can constrict a grabbed opponent, dealing 3d6+3 points of bludgeoning damage.

Dominate Person (Su): Once per day, a kopru can produce an effect like that of a *dominate person* spell (caster level 10th; Will save DC 14), except that the range is 180 feet and the duration is eight days.

Improved Grab (Ex): If a kopru hits an opponent that is its own size or smaller with a tail attack, it deals normal damage

and attempts to start a grapple as a free action without provoking an attack of opportunity (grapple bonus +17, including a +7 racial bonus on grapple checks). If it gets a hold, it also constricts in the same round. Thereafter, the kopru has the option to conduct the grapple normally, or simply use its tails to hold the opponent (–20 penalty on grapple check, but the kopru is not considered grappled). In either case, each successful grapple check it makes during successive rounds automatically deals tail and constrict damage.

KOPRU SOCIETY

Kopru society is matriarchal and savage. The monsters live in underwater caves, often near the sites of their ancient, ruined cities. But these reminders of their former glory only serve to increase their bitterness.

LEECHWALKER

Medium-Size Vermin

Hit Dice: 13d8+39 (97 hp)

Initiative: +0

Speed: 30 ft., swim 20 ft.

AC: 12 (+2 natural), touch 10, flat-footed 12

Attacks: 2 tentacle rakes +13 melee

Damage: Tentacle rake 1d8+4 plus wounding

Face/Reach: 5 ft. by 5 ft./5 ft.

Special Attacks: Blood drink, improved grab, wounding

Special Qualities: All-around vision, immunities, vermin traits

Saves: Fort +11, Ref +4, Will +5

Abilities: Str 18, Dex 11, Con 16, Int —, Wis 13, Cha 7

Skills: Hide +3, Listen +5, Move Silently +5, Search +4, Spot +8, Swim +12

Climate/Terrain: Any marsh or underground

Organization: Solitary, pair, or gang (3–5)

Challenge Rating: 10

Treasure: None

Alignment: Always neutral

Advancement: 14–26 HD (Medium-size); 27–39 HD (Large)

The leechwalker is a thirsty vermin that can drain a creature of all its blood in a matter of moments. It usually lurks in swamps or damp underground areas.

A leechwalker appears to be a massive, 6-foot-tall humanoid covered with thousands of dark, writhing leeches.

Though it has a head, it possessses no recognizable facial features. Its body is slick, as if coated with a thin layer of clear slime, and it has an impossibly bloated stomach.

COMBAT

Leechwalkers are incapable of sizing up prey, so they fearlessly go straight for the kill, regardless of their opponents' capabilities. They usually try to grab their foes, hoping to drain blood through the thousands of mouths that make up their hides.

Blood Drink (Ex): A leechwalker can drink the blood from a grabbed victim with a successful grapple check. This attack deals 2d4 points of Constitution drain.

Improved Grab (Ex): If a leechwalker hits an opponent that is its own size or smaller with a tentacle rake attack, it deals normal damage and attempts to start a grapple as a free action without provoking an attack of opportunity (grapple bonus +13). If it gets a hold, it can use its blood drink ability in the same round. Thereafter, the leechwalker has the option to conduct the grapple normally, or simply use its tentacle to hold the opponent (–20 penalty on grapple check, but the leechwalker is not considered grappled). In either case, each successful grapple check it makes during successive rounds automatically deals tentacle rake and blood drink damage.

Wounding (Ex): A wound resulting from a leechwalker's tentacle rake attack bleeds for an additional 3 points of damage per round thereafter. Multiple wounds from such attacks result in cumulative bleeding loss (two wounds for 6 points of damage per round, and so on). The bleeding can be stopped only by a successful Heal check (DC 10) or the application of a *cure* spell or some other healing spell (*heal, healing circle,* or the like).

All-Around Vision (Ex): A leechwalker can see in all directions at once. Because of this ability, it gains a +4 racial bonus on Search and Spot checks, and it cannot be flanked.

Immunities: Because of the verminous covering of its body, a leechwalker takes half damage from bludgeoning weapons. It is not subject to subdual damage, ability damage, ability drain, or death from massive damage.

Vermin Traits: A leechwalker is immune to all mind-affecting effects (charms, compulsions, phantasms, patterns, and morale effects). It also has darkvision (60-foot range).

LEGENDARY ANIMALS

Throughout the world, legends describe extraordinary animals of incredible strength, speed, and power. Such an animal may have saved a village, fended off a pack of predators to protect the young, aided some legendary hero on a divine quest, or guided a lost child to safety. These are legendary animals.

According to some theories, such creatures have been imbued with power beyond that of all other animals so that they can serve as nature's defenders. In fact, they do not exist at all until a need for them arises. Legendary animals are created from normal animals of their kind through the power of nature (or a deity) whenever a character of appropriate level needs such a companion. Thus, they are rarely encountered outside the presence of a high-level druid or some other advanced character.

COMBAT

Legendary animals are no larger than normal animals of the same kind, but they are considerably more dangerous in combat.

Saving Throws: A legendary animal has all good saves.

LEGENDARY EAGLE

With its feathers of bright white and brilliant yellow, the legendary eagle is considered an omen of good weather and good times to come.

Combat

Like all birds of prey, the legendary eagle is a carnivore that hunts other birds, as well as small reptiles, snakes, and mammals. It attacks from the air with its claws and beak.

Skills: *A legendary eagle receives a +12 racial bonus on Spot checks made in daylight.

LEGENDARY APE

This ape appears little different from the common gorilla in its markings, but even the casual observer can tell that it is stronger, faster, and tougher than others of its kind.

Combat

Legendary apes are aggressive and territorial. They drop on opponents from trees to rend flesh with their powerful claws and teeth.

Rend (Ex): If a legendary ape hits a single target with both claws, it latches onto the opponent's body and tears the flesh. This attack deals 2d8+15 points of damage.

Scent (Ex): A legendary ape can detect approaching enemies, sniff out hidden foes, and track by sense of smell.

LEGENDARY WOLF

A fierce-looking wolf with black, white, or gray fur, this animal is generally not aggressive toward humanoids, though extreme hunger may make it attack.

Combat

A legendary wolf encountered singly may fight, or may retreat to assemble the pack. Whenever possible, legendary wolves live, move, and hunt in packs.

Trip (Ex): A legendary wolf that hits with a bite attack can attempt to trip the opponent as a free action (see Trip in Chapter 8 of the *Player's Handbook*) without making a touch attack or provoking an attack of opportunity. If the attempt fails, the opponent cannot react to trip the legendary wolf.

Scent (Ex): A legendary wolf can detect approaching enemies, sniff out hidden foes, and track by sense of smell.

Skills: A legendary wolf receives a +2 racial bonus on Listen, Move Silently, and Spot checks, and a +4 racial bonus on Hide checks. *It also receives a +8 racial bonus on Wilderness Lore checks when tracking by scent.

LEGENDARY SNAKE

A strong constrictor with a potent venomous bite, the legendary snake is found in underwater lakes, rivers, and streams. It attacks only when threatened.

Combat

Constrict (Ex): With a successful grapple check, a legendary snake can constrict a grabbed opponent, dealing 1d8+12 points of bludgeoning damage.

Improved Grab (Ex): If a legendary snake hits a Large or smaller opponent with a bite attack, it deals normal damage and attempts to start a grapple as a free action without provoking an attack of opportunity (grapple bonus +24). If it gets a hold, it can constrict in the same round. Thereafter, the legendary snake has the option to conduct the grapple normally, or simply use its coils to hold the opponent (−20 penalty on grapple check, but the legendary snake is not considered grappled). In either case, each successful grapple check it makes during successive rounds automatically deals bite and constrict damage.

Poison (Ex): A legendary snake delivers its poison (Fortitude save DC 25) with each successful bite attack. The initial and secondary damage is the same (1d8 points of Constitution damage).

	Legendary Eagle Small Animal	Legendary Ape Medium-Size Animal	Legendary Wolf Medium-Size Animal
Hit Dice:	12d8+36 (90 hp)	13d8+39 (97 hp)	14d8+70 (133 hp)
Initiative:	+10	+3	+9
Speed:	10 ft., fly 100 ft. (average)	40 ft., climb 20 ft.	60 ft.
AC:	25 (+1 size, +10 Dex, +4 natural), touch 21, flat-footed 15	19 (+3 Dex, +6 natural), touch 13, flat-footed 16	24 (+9 Dex, +5 natural), touch 19, flat-footed 15
Attacks:	2 claws +20 melee and bite +15 melee	2 claws +19 melee and bite + 14 melee	Bite +19 melee
Damage:	Claw 1d6+2, bite 1d8+1	Claw 1d8+10, bite 2d6+5	Bite 2d6 +10
Face/Reach:	5 ft. by 5 ft./5 ft.	5 ft. by 5 ft./5 ft.	5 ft. by 5 ft./5 ft.
Special Attacks:	—	Rend 2d8+15	Trip
Special Qualities:	Low-light vision	Low-light vision, scent	Low-light vision, scent
Saves:	Fort +11, Ref +18, Will +11	Fort +11, Ref +11, Will +11	Fort +14, Ref +18, Will +11
Abilities:	Str 15, Dex 30, Con 17, Int 2, Wis 16, Cha 13	Str 30, Dex 17, Con 16, Int 2, Wis 17, Cha 11	Str 25, Dex 28, Con 21, Int 2, Wis 15, Cha 10
Skills:	Listen +10, Spot +10*	Climb +19, Move Silently +11, Spot +9	Hide +13, Listen +10, Move Silently +12, Spot +10, Wilderness Lore +4*
Feats:	Weapon Finesse (bite) (B), Weapon Finesse (claw) (B)	—	Weapon Finesse (bite) (B)
Climate/Terrain:	Any forest, hills, plains, and mountains	Warm forest and mountains, and underground	Any forest, hills, mountains, plains, and underground
Organization:	Solitary or pair	Solitary, pair, or company (3–5)	Solitary or herd (5–8)
Challenge Rating:	6	7	7
Treasure:	None	None	None
Alignment:	Always neutral	Always neutral	Always neutral
Advancement:	13–24 HD (Small)	14–26 HD (Medium-size)	15–30 HD (Medium-size)

Scent (Ex): A legendary snake can detect approaching enemies, sniff out hidden foes, and track by sense of smell.

Skills: A legendary snake receives a +8 racial bonus on Hide, Listen, and Spot checks, and a +16 racial bonus on Balance checks. It can use its Strength or Dexterity modifier (whichever is better) for Climb checks.

LEGENDARY HORSE

Legendary horses can never be domesticated, only befriended. Ancient stories tell of heroes riding these creatures, but even the tales have become very rare.

Combat

A legendary horse can fight while carrying a rider, but the rider cannot also attack unless he or she succeeds at a Ride check (DC 10).

Scent (Ex): A legendary horse can detect approaching enemies, sniff out hidden foes, and track by sense of smell.

Carrying Capacity: A light load for a legendary horse is 0–1,200 pounds, a medium load is 1,201–2,400 pounds, and a heavy load is 2,401–3,600 pounds. A legendary horse can drag 18,000 pounds.

LEGENDARY BEAR

The legendary bear doesn't usually attack humans. Its diet consists primarily of plants and fish.

Combat

Improved Grab (Ex): If a legendary bear hits a Medium-size or smaller opponent with a claw attack, it deals normal damage and attempts to start a grapple as a free action without provoking an attack of opportunity (grapple bonus +32). Thereafter, the legendary bear has the option to conduct the grapple normally, or simply use its claw to hold the opponent (–20 penalty on grapple check, but the legendary bear is not considered grappled). In either case, each successful grapple check it makes during successive rounds automatically deals claw damage.

LEGENDARY TIGER

The legendary tiger is the fiercest and most dangerous land predator in the animal kingdom. It measures 8–10 feet long and weighs up to 600 pounds.

Combat

A legendary tiger prefers to attack from ambush, pouncing on its prey.

	Legendary Snake Large Animal	Legendary Horse Large Animal	Legendary Bear Large Animal
Hit Dice:	16d8+112 (184 hp)	18d8+144 (225 hp)	20d8+140 (230 hp)
Initiative:	+7	+2	+2
Speed:	30 ft., climb 30 ft., swim 30 ft.	80 ft.	50 ft.
AC:	22 (–1 size, +7 Dex, +6 natural), touch 16, flat-footed 15	19 (–1 size, +2 Dex, +8 natural), touch 11, flat-footed 17	21 (–1 size, +2 Dex, +10 natural), touch 11, flat-footed 19
Attacks:	Bite +19 melee	2 hooves +21 melee and bite +16 melee	2 claws +27 melee and bite +22 melee
Damage:	Bite 1d8+12 plus poison	Hoof 2d6+9, bite 1d6+4	Claw 2d6+13, bite 4d6+6
Face/Reach:	5 ft. by 10 ft. (coiled)/10 ft.	5 ft. by 10 ft./5 ft.	5 ft. by 10 ft./5 ft.
Special Attacks:	Constrict 1d8+12, improved grab, poison	—	Improved grab
Special Qualities:	Low-light vision, scent	Low-light vision, scent	Low-light vision, scent
Saves:	Fort +17, Ref +17, Will +12	Fort +19, Ref +13, Will +13	Fort +19, Ref +14, Will +15
Abilities:	Str 27, Dex 24, Con 24, Int 1, Wis 14, Cha 7	Str 29, Dex 14, Con 27, Int 2, Wis 15, Cha 10	Str 36, Dex 15, Con 25, Int 2, Wis 16, Cha 13
Skills:	Balance +24, Climb +22, Hide +14, Listen +12, Spot +12, Swim +16	Listen +9, Spot +9	Listen +8, Spot +8, Swim +18
Climate/Terrain:	Temperate and warm land, aquatic, and underground	Any land	Any forest, hills, mountains, plains, or underground
Organization:	Solitary	Solitary or herd (6–30)	Solitary or pair
Challenge Rating:	8	8	9
Treasure:	None	None	None
Alignment:	Always neutral	Always neutral	Always neutral
Advancement:	17–32 HD (Large)	19–36 HD (Large)	21–40 HD (Large)

	Legendary Tiger Large Animal	Legendary Shark Huge Animal (Aquatic)
Hit Dice:	26d8+182 (299 hp)	30d8+210 (345 hp)
Initiative:	+4	+4
Speed:	50 ft.	Swim 100 ft.
AC:	23 (–1 size, +4 Dex, +10 natural), touch 13, flat-footed 19	22 (–2 size, +4 Dex, +10 natural), touch 12, flat-footed 18
Attacks:	2 claws +29 melee and bite +24 melee	Bite +29 melee
Damage:	Claw 2d6+11, bite 2d8+5	Bite 2d8+13
Face/Reach:	5 ft. by 10 ft./5 ft.	10 ft. by 20 ft./10 ft.
Special Attacks:	Improved grab, pounce, rake 2d6+5	Improved grab, swallow whole
Special Qualities:	Low-light vision, scent	Keen scent, low-light vision
Saves:	Fort +22, Ref +19, Will +17	Fort +24, Ref +21, Will +19
Abilities:	Str 33, Dex 18, Con 24, Int 2, Wis 15, Cha 11	Str 28, Dex 19, Con 24, Int 1, Wis 14, Cha 7
Skills:	Hide +8*, Jump +15, Listen +5, Move Silently +12, Spot +7, Swim +14	Listen +9, Spot +9, Swim +17
Climate/Terrain:	Any forest, hill, mountains, plains, and underground	Any aquatic
Organization:	Solitary or pair	Solitary, pair, or school (3–5)
Challenge Rating:	10	10
Treasure:	None	None
Alignment:	Always neutral	Always neutral
Advancement:	27–48 HD (Large)	31–60 HD (Huge)

Improved Grab (Ex): If a legendary tiger hits a Medium-size or smaller opponent with a bite attack, it deals normal damage and attempts to start a grapple as a free action without provoking an attack of opportunity (grapple bonus +34). If it gets a hold, it can attempt to rake in the same round. Thereafter, the legendary tiger has the

option to conduct the grapple normally, or simply use its jaws to hold the opponent (–20 penalty on grapple check, but the legendary tiger is not considered grappled). In either case, each successful grapple check it makes during successive rounds automatically deals bite damage.

Pounce (Ex): If a legendary tiger charges, it can make a full attack (including a rake attempt, see below) even though it has moved.

Rake (Ex): In any round that a legendary tiger has a hold on an opponent (see Improved Grab, above), it can make two rake attacks (+29 melee) with its hind legs for 2d6+5 points of damage each. The legendary tiger can also attempt to rake when it pounces on an opponent.

Scent (Ex): A legendary tiger can detect approaching enemies, sniff out hidden foes, and track by sense of smell.

Skills: A legendary tiger receives a +8 racial bonus on both Hide and Move Silently checks. *In areas of tall grasses or heavy undergrowth, the Hide bonus improves to +16.

LEGENDARY SHARK

The legendary shark hunts anything it finds in the sea.

Combat

Improved Grab (Ex): If a legendary shark hits a Large or smaller opponent with a bite attack, it deals normal damage and attempts to start a grapple as a free action without provoking an attack of opportunity (grapple bonus +39). If it gets a hold, it can try to swallow in the next round. Alternatively, the legendary shark has the option to conduct the grapple normally, or simply use its mouth to hold the opponent (–20 penalty on grapple check, but the legendary shark is not considered grappled). In either case, each successful grapple check it makes during successive rounds automatically deals bite damage.

Swallow Whole (Ex): A legendary shark can swallow a Large or smaller creature by making a successful grapple check (grapple bonus +39), provided it already has that opponent in its maw (see Improved Grab, above). Once inside the legendary shark, the opponent takes 2d8+13 points of bludgeoning damage plus 1d8+4 points of acid damage per round from the shark's stomach. A successful grapple check allows the swallowed creature to climb out of the stomach and return to the legendary shark's mouth, where another successful grapple check is needed to get free. Alternatively, a swallowed creature can try to cut its way out with either claws or a light piercing or slashing weapon. Dealing at least 50 points of damage to the stomach (AC 18) in this way creates an opening large enough to permit escape. Once a single swallowed creature exits, muscular action closes the hole; thus, another swallowed opponent must cut its own way out. A legendary shark's stomach can hold up to 2 Large, 8 Medium-size, 32 Small, or 128 Tiny or smaller opponents.

Keen Scent (Ex): A legendary shark notices creatures by scent in a 180-foot radius and detects blood in the water at a range of up to 1 mile.

LEVIATHAN

Colossal Magical Beast (Aquatic)
Hit Dice: 32d10 +320 (496 hp)
Initiative: –2
Speed: Swim 90 ft.
AC: 22 (–8 size, –2 Dex, +22 natural), touch 0, flat-footed 22
Attacks: Bite +39 melee, or 2 tail slams +39 melee
Damage: Bite 4d6+15 and gulp, tail slam 2d6+15
Face/Reach: 50 ft. by 200 ft./15 ft.
Special Attacks: Gulp, ramming, swamping
Special Qualities: Darkvision 60 ft., DR 10/–, low-light vision, SR 36
Saves: Fort +28, Ref +16, Will +13
Abilities: Str 40, Dex 7, Con 30, Int 4, Wis 13, Cha 5
Skills: Listen +5, Spot +5, Swim +23
Feats: Iron Will

Climate/Terrain: Any aquatic
Organization: Solitary
Challenge Rating: 25
Treasure: None (see text)
Alignment: Usually neutral
Advancement: 33–48 HD (Colossal)

The leviathan is an immense sea creature that takes up residence in a stretch of water, usually a very deep strait, and terrorizes shipping through that zone for years. It sinks some ships and lets others pass without interference, according to its own unfathomable whims. Decades

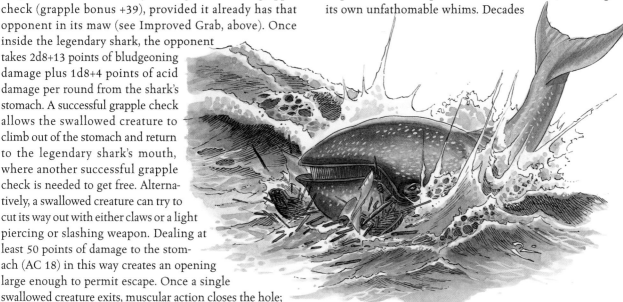

may pass without a sighting; then, for no apparent reason, the attacks resume, usually in a new location. Whether this is the same beast awakened from hibernation, the same beast somehow reborn, or an entirely new creature is unknown.

The leviathan is an immense whale of almost unimaginable proportions. Some have seen its head, others have seen its tail, but those who have seen enough of the monster to determine its actual size and appearance are dead.

Wherever the leviathan goes, other sea predators follow, because a sinking ship produces a rich feeding ground for sharks, barracudas, many varieties of giant fish, dark rays, and even sahuagin and locathah. Although the leviathan itself has no interest in treasure, the sea bed beneath its hunting ground becomes a graveyard for the contents of sunken ships. Many of these hulks are laden with treasure and valuable cargo.

COMBAT

Obviously, a creature such as the leviathan has no natural enemies. Everything in the ocean is its prey, but ships seem to be the only things that catch its attention. Once it breaches or swamps a ship, the leviathan circles back and begins scooping the bodies of both the living and the dead into its 20-foot-wide mouth. Its tactics imply a level of anger and a desire to spread destruction that contradict its low Intelligence score.

Gulp (Ex): A leviathan can swallow a Huge or smaller creature by making a successful bite attack. The monster's interior contains a mass of surging water. Each swallowed creature must make a Swim check (DC 15) every round. Success means the swallowed creature takes 1d3 points of subdual damage but can attack the leviathan from inside with any weapon other than a bow or crossbow. Failure means the swallowed creature takes 1d6 points of subdual damage and must immediately make a second Swim check (DC 15) to avoid going underwater and starting to drown. Anyone attacking the leviathan from the inside hits automatically. If the leviathan takes 50 points of damage from the inside, it disgorges the entire contents of its stomach.

Ramming (Ex): Once every 12 rounds, a leviathan can move at up to 720 feet and ram a Large or smaller creature or any sort of ship. To ram, the leviathan must end its movement in the target's space. If the target is a ship, the creature always precedes this attack with a long surface approach so everyone aboard can see what's coming. This attack deals 8d6+22 points of damage. If the target is a creature, it can attempt either an attack of opportunity or a Reflex save (DC 31) for half damage.

Upon ramming a ship, the leviathan can make a Strength check to breach its hull, which causes it to sink in 1d10 minutes. The break DC varies with the type of vessel rammed, as follows: rowboat DC 20, keelboat DC 23, sailing ship or longship DC 25, warship DC 27, or galley DC 30. (See Chapter 5 of the DUNGEON MASTER'S GUIDE for information about ships.) Regardless of the check result, every creature aboard must attempt a Reflex saving throw (DC 15). Success means the creature takes 1d10 points of damage from being thrown about by the impact; failure means the creature is hurled overboard.

Swamping (Ex): Once every 12 rounds, a leviathan can create waves up to 40 feet high by rising from the water and then slamming its enormous tail flukes or head against the surface. This causes any sailing vessel within 300 feet to capsize if the character steering it fails a Profession (sailor) check (DC 15). A modifier applies to this check based on the type of ship, as follows: rowboat –2, warship +0, galley or keelboat +3, sailing ship +5, longship +7. Any creature flung into the water by a capsizing ship must succeed at a Swim check (DC 15) or immediately begin drowning.

LINNORM

Linnorms are truly primeval creatures thought to be offshoots of dragons. No young ones have been sighted for centuries, so it is possible that these monsters are dying out. At any rate, by dragon accounting, the youngest known linnorms are ancient, and the more powerful individuals are even older than that.

A linnorm is easily distinguished from its more numerous draconic cousins by its lack of wings and rear legs. A linnorm has an immense, serpentine body, and it moves through a combination of walking with its forelegs and snakelike slithering.

No good or lawful linnorms are known to exist; these creatures are universally hateful, spiteful, and cruel. None of the three varieties is known for keeping its word or for honoring bargains. About the best that can be said of linnorms is that not all of them are avaricious.

Linnorms speak Draconic and Abyssal.

COMBAT

Linnorms rely on their breath weapons and prodigious strength in battle. They are also brilliant tacticians and strategists, so they usually delay attacking until conditions are to their advantage. Once battle is joined, they quickly single out the most dangerous foes for swift elimination.

Breath Weapon (Su): Using a breath weapon is a standard action. Once a linnorm breathes, it must wait 1d4 rounds before using a breath weapon again, no matter how many kinds it has. A blast from a breath weapon always starts at the linnorm's mouth and extends in a direction of its choice, with an area as noted in the description. At the time of use, the linnorm can choose to shape its breath weapon into either a line or a cone. The exact dimensions vary with the variety of linnorm (see the individual descriptions), but lines are always 5 feet high and 5 feet wide, and cones are as high and wide as they are long. If the breath weapon deals damage, each creature caught in the area can attempt a Reflex save (see individual descriptions for DCs) to take half damage. Saves against nondamaging breath weapons use the same DC, but the types vary as noted.

Crush (Ex): A flying linnorm can land on opponents three or more size categories smaller than itself as a standard action. A crush attack affects as many creatures as can fit under the linnorm's body. Each creature in the affected area must succeed

	Gray Linnorm Huge Dragon	Dread Linnorm Colossal Dragon	Corpse Tearer Gargantuan Dragon
Hit Dice:	13d12+65 (149 hp)	20d12+200 (330 hp)	28d12+224 (406 hp)
Initiative:	+0	−1	−1
Speed:	30 ft., fly 90 ft. (good), swim 30 ft.	50 ft., fly 90 ft. (good), swim 30 ft.	60 ft., burrow 50 ft., fly 90 ft. (good), swim 50 ft.
AC:	27 (−2 size, +19 natural), touch 8, flat-footed 27	31 (−8 size, −1 Dex, +30 natural), touch 1, flat-footed 31	33 (−4 size, −1 Dex, +28 natural), touch 5, flat-footed 33
Attacks:	Bite +18 melee and 2 claws +16 melee and tail slap +16 melee	2 bites +27 melee and 2 claws +25 melee and tail slap +25 melee	Bite +37 melee and 2 claws +35 melee and tail slap +35 melee
Damage:	Bite 2d6+7, claw 2d8+3, tail slap 2d6+10 plus poison	Bite 4d8+15 plus energy drain, claw 4d6+7, tail slap 4d6+22	Bite 4d6+13 plus energy drain, claw 2d8+6, tail slap 2d8+19
Face/Reach:	10 ft. by 30 ft./10 ft.	40 ft. by 120 ft./15 ft.	20 ft. by 80 ft./15 ft.
Special Attacks:	Breath weapon, crush 2d8+10, poison, spell-like abilities, spells	Breath weapons, crush 4d8+22, energy drain, spell-like abilities, spells, tail sweep 2d8+22	Breath weapon, crush 4d6+19, energy drain, spell-like abilities, spells, tail sweep 2d6+19
Special Qualities:	Blindsight 120 ft., DR 15/+1, immunities, keen senses, SR 31	Blindsight 120 ft., DR 20/+2, immunities, keen senses, SR 36	Blindsight 120 ft., DR 30/+3, immunities, keen senses, SR 39
Saves:	Fort +13, Ref +8, Will +10	Fort +22, Ref +11, Will +18	Fort +24, Ref +15, Will +21
Abilities:	Str 24, Dex 11, Con 20, Int 14, Wis 19, Cha 17	Str 40, Dex 8, Con 31, Int 15, Wis 22, Cha 21	Str 36, Dex 9, Con 26, Int 17, Wis 20, Cha 19
Skills:	Bluff +11, Concentration +20, Diplomacy +7, Intimidate +5, Knowledge (arcana) +16, Listen +17, Scry +16, Search +14, Sense Motive +12, Spellcraft +13, Spot +17, Swim +15	Bluff +24, Concentration +30, Diplomacy +7, Intimidate +7, Knowledge (arcana) +24, Listen +26, Scry +24, Search +24, Spellcraft +21, Spot +26, Swim +23	Bluff +28, Concentration +30, Diplomacy +10, Hide +15, Intimidate +6, Knowledge (arcana) +30, Listen +32, Scry +25, Search +30, Sense Motive +32, Spellcraft +28, Spot +32, Swim +21
Feats:	Alertness, Flyby Attack, Multiattack, Snatch	Alertness, Flyby Attack, Multiattack, Power Attack, Quicken Spell-Like Ability, Snatch	Alertness, Cleave, Enlarge Spell, Flyby Attack, Multiattack, Power Attack, Quicken Spell-Like Ability, Snatch
Climate/Terrain:	Any hills or mountains	Any land	Any land
Organization:	Solitary	Solitary	Solitary
Challenge Rating:	20	25	28
Treasure:	Standard	Standard	Double standard
Alignment:	Usually chaotic evil	Always chaotic evil	Always neutral evil
Advancement:	14–18 HD (Huge)	21–26 HD (Colossal)	29–34 HD (Gargantuan)

at a Reflex save (DC equal to that for the linnorm's breath weapon) or be pinned, automatically taking the given amount of bludgeoning damage. Thereafter, if the linnorm chooses to maintain the pin, treat it as a normal grapple attack. While pinned, the opponent takes crush damage each round.

Tail Sweep: A linnorm can sweep with its tail as a standard action. The sweep affects creatures four or more size categories smaller than the linnorm within a 20-foot-radius half-circle centered on the linnorm's rear. Each affected creature that fails a Reflex save (DC equal to that for the linnorm's breath weapon) takes the given amount of damage; a successful save halves the damage.

Blindsight (Ex): A linnorm can ascertain its surroundings by nonvisual means (mostly hearing and scent, but also by noticing vibration and other environmental clues). This ability enables it to discern objects and creatures within 120 feet. A linnorm usually does not need to make Spot or Listen checks to notice creatures within range of its blindsight.

Immunities: A linnorm is immune to sleep and paralysis effects.

Keen Senses (Ex): A linnorm sees four times as well a human in low-light conditions and twice as well in normal light. It also has darkvision with a range of 120 feet.

GRAY LINNORM

These creatures are the smallest of the linnorms. They are also the meanest and most aggressive.

The body of a gray linnorm is long, sleek, and very snakelike. It never uses its two arms to drag or support itself; instead it moves entirely as a snake, keeping the front portion of its body raised upright at all times. Its scales form a subtle pattern of variegated gray.

A gray linnorm lays claim to all that it can see, so it always seeks out a natural cave in a high place with a commanding view. By extension, any other creature it sees is a trespasser, and it never tolerates trespassers in its territory. As soon as it spots intruders, it moves to attack, usually via either magical flight or wind walking. A gray linnorm does not pause to study its foes or lay a careful trap; instead, it relies on speed, terror, and overwhelming offense.

Combat

A gray linnorm casts as many spells as possible while closing in on enemies, but it prefers fighting tooth and claw to standing off and pelting foes with magic. On the other hand, it prefers casting spells to taking a beating, so it always errs on the side of survival. In dire straits, a gray linnorm typically uses *meld into stone* to hide, and then *wind walk* or some other spell to leave the area.

Acid Breath (Su): A gray linnorm can breathe caustic slime in either a 50-foot cone or a 100-foot line. This attack deals 6d8 points of acid damage, or half that amount on a successful Reflex save (DC 21). On a failed save, the slime also eats away the target's nonmagical metal weapons and armor, making them useless in 1d6+5 rounds.

Poison (Ex): The tip of a gray linnorm's tail carries a venomous stinger that delivers its poison (Fortitude save DC 21) with each successful tail slap attack. The initial

damage is 1d6 points of Constitution damage, and the secondary damage is 2d6 points of Constitution damage.

Spell-Like Abilities: At will—*fly, protection from arrows;* 3/day—*contagion, meld into stone, shapechange, wind walk.* Caster level 17th; save DC 13 + spell level.

Spells: A gray linnorm can cast divine spells as a 17th-level cleric. It has access to spells from the Destruction and Evil domains (spells/day 6/6/6/6/6/4/4/3/2/1; save DC 14 + spell level).

Feats: A creature that is flung by a gray linnorm after being snatched travels 70 feet and takes 7d6 points of damage. If the gray linnorm is flying, the creature takes this damage or the appropriate falling damage, whichever is greater.

DREAD LINNORM

The dread linnorm is the largest of the linnorms. These creatures are aggressively territorial, defending their vast lairs vigorously against intruders.

A dread linnorm can grow to an immense length. Two shaggy, draconic heads, each at the end of its own long, serpentine neck, top its mammoth body. A dread linnorm's scales are primarily charcoal black, but they shimmer and flicker from black to gray as if lit from within.

This creature prefers to lair in a cave located in some remote, desolate place. Few natural caverns are big enough to house a dread linnorm comfortably, so it usually devotes considerable energy over the course of several centuries to excavating its home. Eventually, its lair becomes a tremendous subterranean labyrinth of twisting corridors, plunging shafts, lakes, hot springs, and fabulous natural grottoes, which can stretch for miles below the surface. Invaders could wander for weeks through a dread linnorm's lair without ever encountering the monster. The creature also fits out its lair with deadly traps to capture, bewilder, or kill intruders. These obstacles are often built around natural perils, such as scalding geysers, and sometimes they include triggers for hazards, such as massive rockfalls that can seal passages.

Treasure is not as important to a dread linnorm as it is to a dragon. A typical dread linnorm accumulates immense wealth over its long life but

cares little for it. Most of its treasure lies forgotten wherever it was dropped after a brief examination. Given the extensiveness of the creature's lair and the casual way it leaves valuables strewn about, it might seem easy to sneak in, scoop up a few bags of gold and silver, and slip away unseen. In fact, however, such an act unfailingly brings severe retribution. A dread linnorm doesn't care whether a thief stole a sack of gems, an ancient magic rod, or a bucket of rocks; it cares only that the sanctity of its lair was violated and its possessions stolen. Should this occur, it does all in its power to recover the stolen items and punish the thieves. Failing that, it vents its rage on its surroundings, laying waste to the countryside, leveling villages, burning crops, and devouring livestock.

Dread linnorms are always surly and uncommunicative.

Combat

A dread linnorm relies primarily on its twin breath weapons and its spells in combat. Once its opponents are severely damaged, it switches to melee attacks.

Breath Weapon (Su): As a standard action, a dread linnorm can breathe either with one head or with both heads simultaneously. It can produce two different breath weapons, cold or fire, each as either a 70-foot cone or a 140-foot line. Each head can use a different breath weapon, shape its breath weapon differently, or both. Whatever the shape, the cold breath deals 12d6 points of cold damage and the fire breath deals 12d6 points of fire damage. A successful Reflex save (DC 30) halves the damage from either attack. A creature caught in both breath weapons is affected by both and must save against each one separately.

Energy Drain (Su): Any living creature bitten by either head of a dread linnorm gains one negative level. For each negative level bestowed, the dread linnorm heals 5 points of damage. If the amount of healing is more than the damage the creature has taken, it gains any excess as temporary hit points. If the negative level has not been removed (with a spell such as *restoration*) before 24 hours have passed, the afflicted opponent must succeed at a Fortitude save (DC 25) to remove it. Failure means the opponent's level (or Hit Dice) is reduced by one.

Spell-Like Abilities: At will—*fly, telekinesis;* 4/day—*move earth;* 3/day—*power word stun;* 2/day—*antipathy, sympathy.* Caster level 18th; save DC 15 + spell level.

Spells: A dread linnorm can cast arcane spells as an 18th-level sorcerer (spells known 9/5/5/4/4/4/3/3/2/1; spells/day 6/8/7/7/7/7/6/6/5/3; save DC 15 + spell level).

Immunities (Ex): In addition to sleep and paralysis effects, a dread linnorm is immune to all spells of the Enchantment school.

Feats: A creature that is flung by a dread linnorm after being snatched travels 120 feet and takes 12d6 points of damage. If the dread linnorm is flying, the creature takes this damage or the appropriate falling damage, whichever is greater.

CORPSE TEARER

This hideous beast is generally considered to be the worst of a very bad lot. Characters who are lucky enough to encounter the creature in one of its rare, agreeable moods discover that it is knowledgeable about many ancient, magical mysteries. Whatever its initial mood, however, no meeting with it is likely to end without bloodshed unless the intruders pay a staggering duty—and even that is no guarantee of safety.

A corpse tearer's immense body is only a little shorter than that of a dread linnorm, but it usually keeps itself in a compact shape. Its scales are covered with slime, fungus, moss, lichen, and tufts of branching cilia. When it is lying still, a corpse tearer resembles an enormous, ancient, fallen tree.

Corpse tearers adjust easily to any climate or terrain, but they always make their homes beneath ancient burial grounds. Their lairs are usually guarded by their undead servants—everything from skeletons to very powerful undead such as vampires and banshees. These creatures are often the remains of adventurers who came looking for treasure, or just unlucky travelers who wandered too near the creature's territory. When not on guard duty, these undead tunnel into the ancient graves above the corpse tearer's lair in search of more gold, gems, and other treasures to increase its hoard.

Combat

A corpse tearer seldom fights in its lair becuase it prefers that intruders never find its home. Instead, when a threat draws near, it sends out undead minions to delay the strangers and learn their weaknesses. Then, when it feels that it has enough information about its foes, it takes to the sky and attacks with its breath weapons and spells, crushing or clawing paralyzed characters as the opportunity arises. It falls back on teeth and claws only as a last resort.

Breath Weapon (Su): As a standard action, a corpse tearer can breathe either paralysis or disease, each as either a 60-foot cone or a 120-foot line. The paralysis breath forces each living creature caught in its area to succeed at a Fortitude saving throw (DC 32) or be paralyzed for 1d6+12 rounds. Every living creature caught in the area of the corpse tearer's disease breath must succeed at a Fortitude save (DC 32) or contract linnorm fever. The incubation period is 12 hours, and the disease deals 1d6 points of Strength damage and 1d3 points of Constitution damage (see Disease in Chapter 3 of the DUNGEON MASTER's Guide).

Energy Drain (Su): Any living creature hit by a corpse tearer's claw gains one negative level. For each negative level bestowed, the corpse tearer heals 5 points of damage. If the amount of healing is more than the damage the creature has taken, it gains any excess as temporary hit points. If the negative level has not been removed (with a spell such as *restoration*) before 24 hours have passed, the

afflicted opponent must succeed at a Fortitude save (DC 28) to remove it. Failure means the opponent's level (or Hit Dice) is reduced by one.

Spell-Like Abilities: At will—*fly*; 1/day—*animate dead, control undead, darkness, dimension door, enervation, etherealness, polymorph self, protection from good, speak with dead, spectral hand, vampiric touch, water breathing.* Caster level 15th; save DC 14 + spell level.

Spells: A corpse tearer can cast divine spells as a 17th-level cleric. It has access to spells from the Destruction and Evil domains (spells/day 6/7/6/6/6/5/4/3/2/1; save DC 15 + spell level.)

Feats: A creature that is flung by a corpse tearer after being snatched travels 110 feet and takes 11d6 points of damage. If the corpse tearer is flying, the creature takes this damage or the appropriate falling damage, whichever is greater.

LOXO

Large Monstrous Humanoid

Hit Dice: 5d8+5 (27 hp)

Initiative: +1

Speed: 30 ft.

AC: 14 (–1 size, +1 Dex, +4 natural), touch 10, flat-footed 13

Attacks: Huge morningstar +8 melee and 2 slams +3 melee, or 2 slams +8 melee, or Large javelin +5 ranged

Damage: Huge morningstar 2d8+6, slam 1d6+2 (secondary) or 1d6+4 (primary), or Large javelin 1d8+4

Face/Reach: 5 ft. by 5 ft./10 ft.

Special Attacks: Berserk rage, trample 1d8+6

Special Qualities: Darkvision 60 ft.

Saves: Fort +2, Ref +5, Will +4

Abilities: Str 19, Dex 12, Con 13, Int 10, Wis 11, Cha 8

Skills: Climb +6, Listen +8, Spot +8, Wilderness Lore +8

Feats: Power Attack

Climate/Terrain: Warm plains

Organization: Solitary, pair, company (3–5), or herd (20–40 plus 20% noncombatants plus 1–4 2nd-level rangers, 1 2nd-level wizard, and 1 3rd–5th level ranger)

Challenge Rating: 2

Treasure: Standard

Alignment: Usually neutral

Advancement: By character class

Loxos are usually peaceful creatures, but they defend their territories and families with great tenacity. They are among the most dangerous of all desert dwellers to those who incur their wrath.

A loxo appears to be a humanoid elephant. Its skin is bluish-gray, wrinkled, and covered with rough, sparse hair. It has thick, round limbs, flat feet, short, stubby fingers, and large ears. Its most striking feature is the pair of trunks that grow from its face, framed by large tusks. Each trunk is about 2 feet long and has three fingerlike digits at the end. The typical loxo prefers simple, rustic clothing, particularly cut from cloth patterned with circles or diamonds.

Loxos speak their own language and Common.

COMBAT

Loxos prefer melee to ranged combat, and they use thrown weapons only when they can't close with enemies. If a herd is threatened, the adult male loxos charge intruders while the females move the young to a defensible location. Once the young are secure, the males make a fighting retreat toward the females, so that they too can join the melee.

Berserk Rage (Ex): A loxo that sees a clan member killed or incapacitated enters a berserk rage. For 6 rounds, the loxo gains a +4 bonus to Strength, a +4 bonus to Constitution, and a +2 morale bonus on Will saves, but

takes a −2 penalty to Armor Class. The following changes are in effect as long as the berserk rage lasts: HD 5d10+15 (37 hp); AC 12, touch 8, flat-footed 11; Atk +10 melee (2d8+9, Huge morningstar) and +5 melee (2d6+3, 2 slams), or +10 melee (1d6+6, 2 slams), or +5 melee (1d8+6, Large javelin); SA trample 1d8+9 (DC 18); SV Fort +4, Ref +5, Will +6; Str 23, Con 17; Climb +8. After the berserk rage ends, the loxo is fatigued (−2 penalty to Strength, −2 penalty to Constitution, can't charge or run) until the end of the encounter.

Trample (Ex): As a standard action during its turn each round, a loxo can trample Medium-size or smaller opponents. This attack deals 1d8+6 points of bludgeoning damage. A trampled opponent can attempt either an attack of opportunity at a −4 penalty or a Reflex save (DC 16) for half damage.

LOXO SOCIETY

Loxo herds are seminomadic. They move about, grazing and harvesting fruits and nuts from groves of trees they have planted. When they reach a grove or a good area for grazing, they build temporary huts to serve as shelter until it's time to move on. Loxos need massive amounts of grass and other vegetable material to fuel their big bodies. When not eating, these creatures create rustic works of art, which they barter for items or tools they need.

Loxo herds are divided into clans, and all members of a clan wear the same pattern of clothing. Each herd has a chief (called a lox-fithik, or herd-lieutenant), who is a ranger, and a tunnuk, who has at least two levels of wizard.

LOXO CHARACTERS

A loxo's preferred character class is ranger. Loxo rangers choose favored enemies from among the most common threats to their territories and habitats.

A loxo PC's effective character level (ECL) is equal to its class level + 7; thus, a 1st-level loxo ranger has an ECL of 8 and is the equivalent of an 8th-level character.

Medium-Size Outsider (Evil, Lawful)
Hit Dice: 7d8+7 (38 hp)
Initiative: +3
Speed: 30 ft., fly 70 ft. (good)
AC: 19 (+3 Dex, +6 natural), touch 13, flat-footed 16
Attacks: 2 claws +8 melee and bite +3 melee, or mighty composite longbow (+1 Str bonus) +10/+10 ranged
Damage: Claw 1d4+1, bite 1d6, mighty composite longbow (+1 Str bonus) 1d8+1/×3
Face/Reach: 5 ft. by 5 ft./5 ft.
Special Attacks: Disease, double bowfire, taklif arrow
Special Qualities: Outsider traits, protection from arrows, scent
Saves: Fort +6, Ref +8, Will +6
Abilities: Str 13, Dex 16, Con 13, Int 9, Wis 12, Cha 8
Skills: Balance +15, Jump +3, Listen +11, Search +8, Spot +11, Tumble +13
Feats: Dodge, Point Blank Shot
Climate/Terrain: Warm jungle and desert
Organization: Solitary, pair, or flight (3–6)
Challenge Rating: 5
Treasure: Standard plus 1 taklif arrow
Alignment: Always lawful evil
Advancement: 8–12 HD (Medium-size)

A marrash (plural marrashi) is a plague bearer that spreads disease through combat.

Physically, a marrash resembles a winged gnoll, except that it has birdlike talons on its hands and feet and double-jointed, birdlike legs. It stands about 5 feet tall and has a 10-foot wingspan. Occasionally wizards or sorcerers summon marrashi to the Material Plane to act as guards, assassins, or instruments of terror or revenge.

Every marrash carries a longbow and a quiver of arrows. About a third of its arrows are vectors for disease; the rest are normal except for one—a magic taklif arrow. Any creature hit by this arrow contracts a disease similar to the marrash variant of filth fever (see Disease, below), except that the spirit of a new marrash is generated within the victim's body. When the infected creature dies, the marrash spirit devours its soul over the next 1d6 days. Upon completing that process, the

newborn marrash rises in the victim's reconstituted corpse, which assumes the form of a marrash.

Like most outer-planar beings, marrashi are not willing servants for summoners. A marrash bound to serve a mortal tries to use its taklif arrow on its master without the latter's knowledge, in the hope that the newborn marrash will release its parent from bondage.

Marrashi speak Common and Infernal.

COMBAT

Marrashi consider themselves weak and vulnerable on the ground, so they take to the air whenever possible.

Disease (Ex): Any creature hit by a marrash's disease arrow must succeed at a Fortitude save (DC 14) or contract a more virulent outer-planar version of filth fever. The incubation period is 1d3 days, and the disease deals 1d3 points of Dexterity damage and 1d3 points of Constitution damage (see Disease in Chapter 3 of the DUNGEON MASTER's Guide). Each day thereafter that the disease lasts, the infected creature must also succeed at a second Fortitude save (DC 14), or 1 point each of that day's Dexterity and Constitution damage becomes Constitution drain instead.

Double Bowfire (Ex): In battle, a flying marrash grips its longbow with its taloned feet and draws the string with both hands. This unusual technique allows it to fire two arrows nearly simultaneously at its highest attack bonus as a full attack action.

Taklif Arrow: Any creature hit by a taklif arrow must succeed at a Fortitude save (DC 14) or contract a disease similar to the marrash variant of filth fever (see Disease, above). The incubation period is 1 day, and the disease deals 1d3 points of Dexterity damage and 1d3 points of Constitution damage (see Disease in Chapter 3 of the DUNGEON MASTER's Guide). However, a creature that fails any Fortitude saving throw after its initial infection dies instantly, and neither *raise dead* nor *resurrection* can restore it to life. The corpse rises as a new marrash 1d6 days later.

Protection from Arrows **(Sp):** A marrash can use *protection from arrows*, as the spell, at will. Caster level 10th.

Outsider Traits: A marrash has darkvision (60-foot range). It cannot be raised or resurrected.

Scent (Ex): A marrash can detect approaching enemies, sniff out hidden foes, and track by sense of smell.

Tiny Aberration
Hit Dice: 4d8 (18 hp)
Initiative: +1
Speed: 20 ft.
AC: 13 (+2 size, +1 Dex), touch 13, flat-footed 12
Attacks: 2 claws +3 melee
Damage: Claw 1d2–2
Face/Reach: 2 1/2 ft. by 2 1/2 ft./0 ft.
Special Attacks: Fear aura, meenlock transformation, paralysis, rend mind
Special Qualities: Darkvision 60 ft., dimension door, telepathy
Saves: Fort +1, Ref +2, Will +5
Abilities: Str 6, Dex 13, Con 10, Int 11, Wis 12, Cha 15
Skills: Hide +16, Listen +5, Move Silently +8, Spot +4, Wilderness Lore +8
Feats: Track (B)

Climate/Terrain: Any subterranean, temperate forest
Organization: Brood (3–5)
Challenge Rating: 3
Treasure: None
Alignment: Always lawful evil
Advancement: 5–6 HD (Tiny); 7–8 HD (Small)

These dreadful, pitiful creatures were once humans, dwarves, elves, gnomes, and halflings. Through indescribable tortures, they were transformed into the hideous creatures known as meenlocks. Now they themselves carry on their forebears' grisly work, kidnapping travelers and adventurers and inflicting the same nightmarish metamorphosis upon them.

A meenlock is a grotesque, twisted parody of a humanoid creature. It stands about 2 feet tall, but its body is stooped and deformed, causing it to drag the hooked claws that serve as its hands on the ground. Its hide is covered with shaggy spines and painful ulcers.

Meenlocks shun the light, so they excavate lairs deep beneath remote forests. They often create vast labyrinths of tunnels that connect subterranean caverns so that they can travel great distances without venturing

aboveground. The entrances to meenlock lairs are expertly camouflaged and sealed with flat stones. If the creatures discover that one of their entrances has been tampered with, they track down and capture the intruders to protect their secrets.

Meenlocks communicate entirely through telepathy. They can also grunt and click, but these sounds don't constitute a language. Occasionally the creatures act as if they are talking in order to conceal their telepathy ability from enemies.

COMBAT

Meenlocks fight if forced to do so, but they are weak combatants. They prefer to pick off members of a group one at a time over a long period. The first attack they usually launch against their selected target is a slow mental assault (see Rend Mind, below). Some meenlocks have been known to stalk and harass their victims in this way for days.

Fear Aura (Su): As a free action, a meenlock can produce a fear effect in a 30-foot-radius burst, centered on itself. Any creature within the area that fails a Will save (DC 14) becomes catatonic from fear for 1d4+4 rounds. During this time, it rolls into a ball, hugs its knees, or simply stands in place, shivering and staring. Any creature that makes a saving throw against the effect cannot be affected again by that meenlock's fear aura for 24 hours.

Meenlock Transformation (Su): Meenlocks drag their victims to their lairs and bind them to prevent their escape before starting the transformation. (A captured creature may be able to escape from its bonds and fight its way clear, but the odds are against it, especially since the height of the mazelike tunnels in a meenlock lair forces a Medium-size creature to crawl on hands and knees.) Then three or more of them gather around to touch each helpless humanoid or monstrous humanoid. After 1d6 hours of such physical contact with the meenlocks, all of the subject's ability scores fall to 1 (except for any already at 0), reducing him or her to a drooling, helpless state (no saving throw). A *heal* or *greater restoration* spell at this point restores the creature to normal. In another 1d6 hours, the transformation is complete; the subject becomes forever a meenlock, losing all of its previous classes and abilities. At this point, only a *wish* or *miracle* spell can restore the victim.

Paralysis (Ex): Any creature hit by a meenlock's claw must make a Fortitude save (DC 14) or be paralyzed for 3d6 rounds. The meenlocks use this time to bind the paralyzed creature. Once bound, a typical human can be carried by three meenlocks.

Rend Mind (Su): A meenlock can project thoughts and suggestions into the mind of a single creature within 300 feet. These thoughts are usually geared to cause paranoia—images of stalking monsters or peering eyes, and the sensation of being followed, watched, or sized up. The target of this mind-affecting phantasm must make a successful Will save (DC 14) or take 1d4 points of Wisdom damage. Once a meenlock uses this ability, it must wait 1d4 rounds before doing so again.

Dimension Door (Su): Once every 2 rounds, a meenlock can produce an effect like that of a *dimension door* spell, except that the range is only 60 feet and no additional weight can be transported.

Telepathy (Ex): A meenlock can communicate through telepathy with any other creature that has a language. This communication has a range of 300 feet.

MEGALODON

Gargantuan Beast (Aquatic)
Hit Dice: 24d10+168 (300 hp)
Initiative: +2
Speed: Swim 120 ft.
AC: 20 (−4 size, +2 Dex, +12 natural), touch 8, flat-footed 18
Attacks: Bite +24 melee
Damage: Bite 4d6+15
Face/Reach: 20 ft. by 40 ft./10 ft.
Special Attacks: Improved grab, swallow whole
Special Qualities: Darkvision 60 ft., keen scent, low-light vision
Saves: Fort +21, Ref +16, Will +9
Abilities: Str 31, Dex 15, Con 24, Int 1, Wis 12, Cha 10
Skills: Hide −10, Listen +6, Spot +6, Swim +18

Climate/Terrain: Any aquatic
Organization: Solitary or swarm (5–20)
Challenge Rating: 11
Treasure: None
Alignment: Always neutral
Advancement: 25–48 HD (Gargantuan); 49–72 HD (Colossal)

One of the largest predators in the world, a megalodon defers to dragons and little else. Large enough to devour an entire whale, the megalodon gives even hardened sailors nightmares.

A megalodon is normally 55 to 65 feet long, and it weighs between 10 to 60 tons. Rumors of individual megalodons reaching a length of 80 to 90 feet cannot be confirmed.

COMBAT

Megalodons attack anything they perceive to be edible—including each other. They can leap as high as 40 feet out of the water to snap at low-flying rocs and small dragons. They bite with their powerful jaws and can swallow smaller creatures.

Improved Grab (Ex): If a megalodon hits an opponent that is at least one size category smaller than itself with a bite attack, it deals normal damage and attempts to start a grapple as a free action without provoking an attack of opportunity (grapple bonus +40). If it gets a hold, it can try to swallow on the next round. Alternatively, the megalodon has the option to conduct the grapple normally, or simply use its jaws to hold the opponent (−20 penalty on grapple check, but the megalodon is not considered grappled). In either case, each successful grapple check it makes during successive rounds automatically deals bite damage.

Swallow Whole (Ex): A megalodon can swallow a single creature that is at least one size category smaller than itself by making a successful grapple check (grapple bonus +40), provided it already has that opponent in its mouth (see Improved Grab, above). Once inside the megalodon, the opponent takes 2d8+10 points of bludgeoning damage plus 1d8+4 points of acid damage per round from the megalodon's gullet. A successful grapple check allows the swallowed creature to climb out of the gullet and return to the monster's maw, where another successful grapple check is needed to get free. Alternatively, a swallowed creature can try to cut its way out with either claws or a light piercing or slashing weapon. Dealing at least 25 points of damage to the gullet (AC 20) in this way creates an opening large enough to permit escape. Once a single swallowed creature exits, muscular action closes the hole; thus, another swallowed opponent must cut its own way out. A Gargantuan megalodon's gullet can hold 2 Huge, 8 Large, 32 Medium-size, or 128 Small or smaller opponents.

Keen Scent (Ex): A megalodon notices creatures by scent within a 180-foot radius and detects blood in the water at a range of up to one mile.

MEGAPEDE

Colossal Vermin
Hit Dice: 32d8+256 (400 hp)
Initiative: −2
Speed: 80 ft., burrow 20 ft.
AC: 18 (−8 size, −2 Dex, +18 natural), touch 0, flat-footed 18
Attacks: 5 tentacle rakes +32 melee, or bite +32 melee
Damage: Tentacle rake 2d8+16, bite 4d6+16 plus poison
Face/Reach: 15 ft. by 100 ft./10 ft.
    Special Attacks: Poison
    Special Qualities: DR 25/+5, SR 31, tremorsense, vermin traits
Saves: Fort +26, Ref +8, Will +11
Abilities: Str 43, Dex 7, Con 27, Int —, Wis 12, Cha 4
Skills: Listen +10, Spot +7

Climate/Terrain: Warm desert
Organization: Solitary
Challenge Rating: 20
Treasure: None
Alignment: Always neutral
Advancement: 33–64 HD (Colossal)

True terrors of the desert, megapedes constantly hunt the dunes and sandy plains for food. The desert offers little refuge to creatures fleeing these enormous predators.

A megapede looks like an enormous centipede with a long, segmented body and hundreds of pairs of legs. Its tough, bulbous body is covered with dense orange and brown bristles. The creature's tremendous mandibles twitch involuntarily when it senses prey. A megapede can grow to more than 100 feet in length.

COMBAT

Megapedes lie in wait just under the sandy surface of the desert, lunging at creatures who wander too near. In a fight, a megapede usually rends its enemy with five vicious claw attacks per round. It reserves its poisonous bite for foes that prove especially daunting.

Poison (Ex): A megapede delivers its poison (Fortitude save DC 44) with each successful bite attack. The initial and secondary damage is the same (2d6 points of Constitution damage and 1d4 points of Dexterity drain).

Tremorsense (Ex): A megapede can automatically sense the location of anything within 120 feet that is in contact with the ground.

Vermin Traits: A megapede is immune to all mind-affecting effects (charms, compulsions, phantasms, patterns and morale effects). It also has darkvision (60-foot range).

MOONBEAST

Huge Aberration
Hit Dice: 18d8+90 (171 hp)
Initiative: +2
Speed: 30 ft., climb 10 ft.
AC: 17 (−2 size, +2 Dex, +7 natural), touch 10, flat-footed 15
Attacks: 10 tentacle rakes +21 melee
Damage: Tentacle rake 4d6+10
Face/Reach: 10 ft. by 10 ft./15 ft.
Special Attacks: Bite 4d8+10, constrict 3d10+15, fear aura, improved grab, spell-like abilities
Special Qualities: All-around vision, darkvision 60 ft., SR 22
Saves: Fort +11, Ref +8, Will +12
Abilities: Str 30, Dex 15, Con 21, Int 8, Wis 9, Cha 18
Skills: Climb +26, Listen +20, Search +3, Spot +18
Feats: Combat Reflexes, Iron Will, Power Attack

Climate/Terrain: Any land and underground
Organization: Solitary
Challenge Rating: 16
Treasure: 1/10th coins; 50% goods; 50% items plus 1 moonstone
Alignment: Always chaotic evil
Advancement: 19–27 HD (Huge); 28–36 HD (Gargantuan)

The moonbeast is a ferocious, tenacious, and thoroughly horrifying adversary. Simply seeing one can send strong adventurers fleeing for their lives, and actually fighting one is a challenge beyond the capabilities of all but the most powerful heroes. Unfortunately, because of the monster's ties to certain magic devices, some adventurers find themselves inadvertently (and often fatally) entangled with a moonbeast.

Since moonbeasts are active only at night and are usually invisible, eyewitness descriptions of them tend to be hazy. In reality, a moonbeast's body is a roughly cylindrical mass of squishy flesh, usually between 20 and 30 feet tall. Its height is variable; even a single beast sometimes changes in size from one appearance to the next. A moonbeast has no discernible head, no front or back, and no top or bottom—it is equally comfortable in any orientation. Its trunk is encircled at each end by a ring of tentacles. Each ring has a number of tentacles equal to 1 + 1/2 the moonbeast's Hit Dice, rounded down. (Advanced moonbeasts may have more tentacles, and thus more tentacle rake attacks, than the standard 18-HD variety.) These tentacles are lined with barbs and hooks to catch objects or prey, and they also serve as the moonbeast's means of locomotion. To move, the creature grabs fixed objects with its tentacles and drags itself forward. Its body is covered with a slick, oily substance. Four rings, each consisting of eight flexible, retractable, 1-foot-long eyestalks are placed above and below each ring of tentacles.

In spite of its immense size, a moonbeast can squeeze its soft body through an opening as small as a 5-by-5-foot square. Wherever it passes, it leaves a telltale trail of glistening slime. Moonbeasts are invisible most of the time, but their horrid smell and the noises they make almost constantly give away their presence to observant creatures.

COMBAT

A moonbeast uses its *improved invisibility* ability to remain invisible even in combat. In battle, a moonbeast prefers to strike, grab, and constrict. It can use as many as seven of its tentacles against a single target.

Bite (Ex): With a successful grapple check, a moonbeast can attempt to bite a grabbed opponent (+21 melee), dealing 4d8+5 points of slashing damage on a successful hit. A moonbeast cannot use its bite attack against a creature it has not already grabbed.

Constrict (Ex): With a successful grapple check, a moonbeast can crush a grabbed opponent, dealing 3d10+15 points of bludgeoning damage.

Fear Aura (Su): A moonbeast continually emanates a fear effect in a 60-foot-radius, centered on itself. Any creature within the area that fails a Will save (DC 23) is paralyzed with fear for 2d6 rounds. A new saving throw is required each time a potentially affected creature comes within range of the moonbeast.

Improved Grab (Ex): If a moonbeast hits an opponent that is at least one size category smaller than itself with a tentacle rake attack, it deals normal damage and attempts to start a grapple as a free action without provoking an attack of opportunity (grapple bonus +31). If it gets a hold, it automatically constricts and can attempt to bite the grabbed opponent in the same round. Thereafter, the moonbeast has the

option to conduct the grapple normally, or simply use a single tentacle to hold the opponent (–20 penalty on grapple check, but the moonbeast is not considered grappled). In either case, each successful grapple check it makes during successive rounds automatically deals tentacle rake and constrict damage and allows another bite attempt.

Spell-Like Abilities: At will—*dispel magic, fog cloud, improved invisibility, lightning bolt;* 1/day—*chain lightning, cloudkill, disintegrate, Evard's black tentacles, fireball, ice storm, mirror image, summon monster VI.* Caster level 18th; save DC 14 + spell level.

All-Around Vision (Ex): A moonbeast can see in all directions at once. Because of this ability, it gains a +4 racial bonus on Search and Spot checks, and it cannot be flanked.

MOONSTONES

In general, moonbeasts want nothing to do with the world. They are content to hide in their remote lairs, dreaming of their native homes (wherever those may be) and venturing out only occasionally to catch a meal. But each of these creatures is inseparably linked to a item called a moonstone—a rare and unusual gem that resembles a pearl. Magic items and very expensive pieces of jewelry occasionally contain moonstones.

Once in a creature's possession, a moonstone slowly and insidiously works its way into its owner's psyche. After 1d6+3 weeks, the owner must succeed at a Will save (DC 30) or become so attached to the item containing the moonstone that he or she would refuse to relinquish it under any circumstances. In the course of a campaign, this obsession can go unrecognized for quite a long time, and the owner may not be consciously aware of it until a situation arises that would require separation from the item.

At some point, however, the moonbeast that is linked to that moonstone awakens, leaves its lair, and begins tracking down the gem. Its ultimate goal is to recover the moonstone, slay the owner, and then return to its lair. Oddly, the monster seems to care nothing for the moonstone itself; it desires only that absolutely no one else possess it. In fact, the moonbeast is quite likely to abandon the recovered moonstone item somewhere during its return trip. The object may then lie forgotten for years before another unlucky adventurer discovers it anew and begins the horrid cycle all over again.

MOONCALF

Large Magical Beast
Hit Dice: 15d10+108 (190 hp)
Initiative: +7
Speed: 40 ft., fly 150 ft. (poor)
AC: 25 (–1 size, +3 Dex, +13 natural), touch 12, flat-footed 22
Attacks: 2 tentacle rakes +18 melee and 6 tentacle-arms +13 melee
Damage: Tentacle rake 2d6+4/19–20, tentacle-arm 1d6+2
Face/Reach: 5 ft. by 10 ft./10 ft. (30 ft. with tentacle rake)
Special Attacks: Bite 2d8+6, improved grab, spell-like abilities
Special Qualities: Blindsight 100 ft., DR 10/+1, keen senses
Saves: Fort +16, Ref +14, Will +12
Abilities: Str 18, Dex 16, Con 24, Int 21, Wis 21, Cha 11
Skills: Concentration +16, Hide +15, Knowledge (arcana) +10, Knowledge (history) +10, Listen +15, Spot +19
Feats: Alertness, Blind-Fight, Expertise, Improved Critical (tentacle rake), Improved Initiative, Improved Trip, Iron Will, Lightning Reflexes, Toughness

Climate/Terrain: Any hills or mountains
Organization: Solitary
Challenge Rating: 10
Treasure: Double standard
Alignment: Always neutral evil
Advancement: 19–27 HD (Huge); 28–60 HD (Gargantuan)

Mooncalves are otherworldly monstrosities that, according to rumor, flew down to earth from the dark side of the moon. When these creatures "come to ground," they never venture farther down than mountaintops, the tips of tall hills, and other high, lonely, desolate places.

A mooncalf combines the body of an immense cephalopod with the wings of a bat. It has six short tentacle-arms that it uses for close combat and two long tentacles that it uses to attack at a distance because of their 30-foot reach. The creature's beak-like mouth is located where the tentacles meet.

Mooncalves do not speak, but they can communicate telepathically with any other creature within a 100-foot radius that has a language.

MD

COMBAT

Mooncalves prefer to fly high above their targets, striking at foes from a distance with their spell-like abilities. In melee, they may grab and crush opponents with their tentacles, or drag foes into their slavering beaks, or command the elements to electrocute an enemy.

Bite (Ex): With each successful grapple check, a mooncalf automatically hits a grabbed opponent with its bite attack, dealing 2d8+6 points of slashing damage.

Improved Grab (Ex): If a mooncalf hits an opponent that is its own size or smaller with a tentacle rake attack, it deals normal damage and attempts to start a grapple as a free action without provoking an attack of opportunity (grapple bonus +23). If it gets a hold, it automatically hits with its bite attack on the same round. Thereafter, the mooncalf has the option to conduct the grapple normally, or simply use its tentacle to hold the opponent (−20 penalty on grapple check, but the mooncalf is not considered grappled). In either case, each successful grapple check it makes during successive rounds automatically deals tentacle rake and bite damage.

Spell-Like Abilities: 1/day—*call lightning, control weather, control winds, dominate animal, greater magic fang, protection from elements, quench, resist elements.* Caster level 9th; save DC 10 + spell level.

Blindsight (Ex): A mooncalf can ascertain its surroundings by nonvisual means (mostly hearing and scent, but also by noticing vibration and other environmental clues). This ability enables it to discern objects and creatures within 100 feet. The mooncalf usually does not need to make Spot or Listen checks to notice creatures within range of its blindsight.

Keen Senses (Ex): A mooncalf sees four times as well a human in low-light conditions and twice as well in normal light. It also has darkvision (100-foot range).

MOONRAT

Tiny Magical Beast

Hit Dice: 1/4 d10 (1 hp)
Initiative: +2
Speed: 15 ft., climb 15 ft.
AC: 14 (+2 size, +2 Dex), touch 14, flat-footed 14
Attacks: Bite +4 melee
Damage: Bite 1d3–4
Face/Reach: 2 1/2 ft. by 2 1/2 ft./0 ft.
Special Qualities: Darkvision 60 ft., low-light vision, lunar mind, scent, uncanny dodge
Saves: Fort +2, Ref +4, Will +3
Abilities: Str 2, Dex 15, Con 11, Int 2, Wis 13, Cha 2
Skills: Balance +10, Climb +10, Hide +16, Move Silently +8
Feats: Iron Will, Weapon Finesse (bite) (B)

Climate/Terrain: Any land and underground
Organization: Swarm (10–100)
Challenge Rating: 1/4
Treasure: None
Alignment: Always evil
Advancement: —

Moonrats are indistinguishable from normal rats except in moonlight. Lunar light has an insidious effect on these creatures, making them smarter, stronger, and more ferocious than any rat ought to be. On nights when the moon shines, moonrats pour out of their darkened lairs to soak up the pallid rays and spread terror throughout humanoid settlements.

COMBAT

Moonrats fight just like normal rats do, biting and tearing with their teeth. Under the influence of lunar light, moonrats also gain the ability to organize, converse with one another, formulate complex plans, and operate complicated devices. Their leaders remember things done and learned nights or even months before. When the moon's light is at its peak, moonrats are capable of making and acting on long-range plans that may require dozens of full-moon nights to complete. These schemes are often so subtle and involved that casual observers do not connect incidents relating to a long-range moonrat plan until it is too late to stop it.

Lunar Mind (Ex): A lunar modifier applies to a moonrat's Strength and Intelligence scores while under the influence of moonlight. The size of this modifier depends on the amount of moonlight that reaches the moonrat, according to the table below. On a clear night, the moonlight equivalent is the same as the actual phase of the moon. On a night when clouds or heavy mist obscure the moon, the moonlight equivalent is one or two steps (DM's choice) lower on the table than the actual moon phase. On worlds with multiple moons, either choose only one moon

to influence the moonrats, or estimate the moonlight equivalent of both moons on any given night, using the new moon and full moon entries as the minimum and maximum values, respectively, for that world.

Moonlight Equivalent	Lunar Modifier
New Moon	+0
Crescent	+1
Quarter	+2
Half	+4
Gibbous	+6
Full	+8

For every 2 points of Strength increase, a moonrat gains a +1 bonus on attack and damage rolls. The effect of the Intelligence boost is open to considerable DM interpretation. Use the Intelligence scores for the following creatures as benchmarks to determine the moonrats' increased intellectual capacity: Int 3 (minimum for a human), Int 6 (average for a gargoyle), Int 8 (average for a centaur or gnoll), Int 9 (average for an orc), Int 10 (average for a goblin). No extra skill points are gained for a lunar Intelligence boost.

Scent (Ex): A moonrat can detect approaching enemies, sniff out hidden foes, and track by sense of smell.

Uncanny Dodge (Ex): Because of its extraordinary sense of smell, a moonrat retains its Dexterity bonus to AC even when flat-footed, and it cannot be flanked.

Skills: A moonrat receives a +4 racial bonus on Hide and Move Silently checks and a +8 racial bonus on Balance checks. It uses its Dexterity modifier for Climb checks.

MORKOTH

Medium-Size Aberration (Aquatic)
Hit Dice: 7d8+7 (38 hp)
Initiative: +6
Speed: Swim 50 ft.
AC: 18 (+2 Dex, +6 natural), touch 12, flat-footed 16
Attacks: Bite +4 melee
Damage: Bite 1d8–1
Face/Reach: 5 ft. by 5 ft./5 ft.
Special Attacks: Hypnosis
Special Qualities: Darkvision 60 ft., spell reflection
Saves: Fort +3, Ref +4, Will +8
Abilities: Str 8, Dex 14, Con 13, Int 16, Wis 17, Cha 13
Skills: Hide +14, Knowledge (arcana) +10, Listen +13, Spellcraft +10, Spot +13, Swim +7
Feats: Blind-Fight, Dodge, Improved Initiative, Skill Focus (Hide)

Climate/Terrain: Any aquatic
Organization: Solitary
Challenge Rating: 5
Treasure: Standard
Alignment: Always chaotic evil
Advancement: 8–14 HD (Medium-size); 15–21 HD (Large)

Few creatures of the deep enjoy reputations for cruelty and hatred as extensive as that of the morkoth.

The top half of a morkoth resembles a deep-sea fish with bulging eyes, protruding teeth and a saillike fin along its back. Its lower body resembles that of an octopus in that it has eight tentacles, but the creature also sports limbs like the legs of a crustacean. Occasionally a morkoth has a squidlike beak instead of a mouth, but the typical version just has a maw like that of a fish.

A morkoth lives a solitary existence, spending most of its days inside a maze of tunnels constructed of rock or coral at the bottom of the sea. The outer part of a morkoth's lair usually consists of six tunnels, all spiraling outward, crisscrossing and interconnecting with one another in a bewildering pattern. The creature's actual home is at the center of this maze.

A morkoth uses a variety of lures to draw prey into its clutches. It may dangle treasure as a prize, but its hypnosis ability is the most powerful lure at its disposal. Once in a morkoth's clutches, a victim doesn't usually survive for long, since these creatures are interested in capturing only food, not slaves or captives. A morkoth has little interest in treasure except as a lure for prospective victims.

COMBAT

A morkoth's bite is its only offensive weapon. Normally it uses its hypnosis ability to lure a passing creature through its

maze, then devours its prey alive. The morkoth is a cautious monster, so it chooses its victims carefully. Typically, it tries to lure the last in a group of passing creatures into its tunnel, hoping that the others won't notice that one's absence until it is too late.

Hypnosis (Su): Any creature passing within 20 feet of the entrance to a morkoth's lair must make a successful Will saving throw (DC 14) or be hypnotized. A hypnotized creature moves unerringly through the maze at its usual speed. Once in center of the lair, the affected creature floats quietly in a trance, waiting to be devoured at the morkoth's leisure. A hypnotized creature is helpless against the morkoth's attacks but may attempt a new saving throw at the same DC each round that the morkoth attacks it.

A morkoth can hypnotize any number of creatures at one time. When it is outside its lair, this ability has a range of 20 feet. Hypnosis is a mind-affecting compulsion effect.

Spell Reflection (Su): The morkoth has a special type of spell resistance that causes the effect of any spell, spell-like ability, or magic item that it successfully resists (even those that affect areas) to bounce off and reflect back at the caster. If the caster of a spell or the user of a spell-like ability or magic item fails a caster level check (DC 15), he or she becomes either the spell's target or the point of origin for the spell's effect, as appropriate. If the morkoth is the subject of a *dispel magic* spell that is not reflected, its spell reflection ability is suppressed for 1 round.

MORKOTH TUNNELS

A creature that has successfully resisted the morkoth's hypnosis ability might try to rescue a friend who was drawn into the tunnels. The passages of a morkoth's lair are so narrow that only one Medium-size character can swim through any 5-foot section at a time. An ambitious DM could map out the mazelike tunnel system and allow the characters to try to work their way through it.

Alternatively, the DM could handle penetration of the lair abstractly as follows: Roll 2d6 to determine the number of intersections between the tunnel's entrance and the morkoth's lair, allowing 10 to 40 feet between intersections. At each intersection, have the lead character make an Intuit Direction check (DC 15) to discern the correct path. Each correct choice brings the group one intersection closer to the lair; each incorrect choice adds 1d6 intersections to the route and an equal number of rounds to the time needed to complete the trip.

It is always possible to navigate any labyrinth by simply choosing one wall and following wherever it goes. A creature using this method can eventually find the morkoth's chamber without error, but this route is usually not the shortest possible path. Roll 1d6+6 for the number of intersections the rescuers must traverse using this method.

MUDMAW

Large Magical Beast
Hit Dice: 8d10+24 (68 hp)
Initiative: +5
Speed: 20 ft., swim 30 ft.
AC: 17 (–1 size, +1 Dex, +7 natural), touch 10, flat-footed 16
Attacks: 2 tentacle rakes +11 melee and bite +6 melee
Damage: Tentacle rake 1d6+4, bite 1d8+2
Face/Reach: 5 ft. by 10 ft./10 ft.
Special Attacks: Constrict 2d8+6, improved grab, spell-like abilities, trample 2d6+6
Special Qualities: Darkvision 60 ft., DR 10/+1, low-light vision, scent, SR 18
Saves: Fort +9, Ref +7, Will +5
Abilities: Str 19, Dex 12, Con 17, Int 3, Wis 12, Cha 16
Skills: Hide +7*, Swim +12, Wilderness Lore +3
Feats: Improved Initiative, Iron Will

Climate/Terrain: Warm marsh
Organization: Solitary or pair
Challenge Rating: 7
Treasure: None
Alignment: Always neutral
Advancement: 9–16 HD (Large); 17–24 HD (Huge)

Mudmaws wait just below the surface of the water in swamps, slow rivers, and lakes for potential prey to come down to the water and drink. In this state, this carnivorous ambush predator resembles a floating log—a fact that many an unwary adventurer has discovered.

This fearsome swamp predator resembles a crocodile with a rubbery green tentacle growing from each corner of its mouth. Its immense maw is filled with needle-sharp teeth.

Mudmaws are intensely territorial; they have been known to attack even other mudmaws that intrude on the areas they claim. If some disaster makes more meat available than any one of them could eat, they allow others of their kind to share the bounty and then leave again. If two mudmaws are encountered, they are peacefully courting and preparing to mate.

COMBAT

A mudmaw typically tries to grab creatures two or more size categories smaller than itself with its tentacles and drag them under the water to drown. Against larger creatures within 40 feet, it uses *slow*, then lunges from the water at a full charge, trampling its prey before grabbing it and returning to the water. A mudmaw doesn't attack if it can't reach its prey with its tentacles or with a single 40-foot charge. Larger creatures, or those that prove to be a threat, find pursuing the monster difficult because it uses *soften earth and stone* to turn the edge of the water into a quagmire, then swims away or uses *water walk* to cross it.

Constrict (Ex): With a successful grapple check, a mudmaw can crush a grabbed opponent, dealing 2d8+6 points of bludgeoning damage.

Improved Grab (Ex): If a mudmaw hits an opponent that is at least one size category smaller than itself with a tentacle rake attack, it deals normal damage and attempts to start a grapple as a free action without provoking an attack of opportunity (grapple bonus +24, including +8 racial bonus on grapple checks). If it gets a hold, it also constricts in the same round. Thereafter, the mudmaw has the option to conduct the grapple normally, or simply use its tentacle to hold the opponent (–20 penalty on grapple check, but the mudmaw is not considered grappled). In either case, each successful grapple check it makes during successive rounds automatically deals tentacle rake damage.

Spell-Like Abilities: At will—*slow, soften earth and stone, water walk*. Caster level 5th; save DC 13 + spell level.

Trample (Ex): As a standard action during its turn each round, a mudmaw can trample opponents at least one size category smaller than itself. This attack deals 2d6+6 points of bludgeoning damage. A trampled opponent can attempt either an attack of opportunity at a –4 penalty or a Reflex save (DC 18) for half damage.

Scent (Ex): A mudmaw can detect approaching enemies, sniff out hidden foes, and track by sense of smell.

Skills: *A mudmaw receives a +20 bonus on Hide checks when in water.

These intelligent, mobile mushrooms are among the more unusual creatures that live deep below ground. Myconids (also called fungus ones) are gentle, quiet, shy, and thoughtful. They always view outsiders with distrust because they assume that all strangers are destructive and violent. To ensure that they can live in peace, they usually make their homes far from the more commonly traveled subterranean paths.

A myconid can be from 2 to 12 feet tall. The primary physical characteristics that distinguish it from other giant toadstools are its limbs—the lower half of its trunk is split in half to form two legs, and two arms depend from just below its "cap." It also has two eyes in the cap, which are perfectly concealed when it closes them. Its hands seem to have random numbers of fingers and thumbs. Occasionally, an individual with more than two arms or legs pops up.

A myconid has a life span of about twenty-four years. When first spawned, an infant resembles a giant toadstool. At the age of four, it reaches adulthood and becomes mobile. Thereafter, its appearance changes very little as it ages.

COMBAT

The fungus ones hide from strangers and fight only as a last resort. When forced into combat, a myconid releases spores as a ranged attack or uses its slams in melee.

Spores (Ex): As a standard action, a myconid can release a cloud of spores. These spores come in several different varieties, as described below. As it enters each new stage of life (increasing its Hit Dice by 1), a myconid gains a new variety of spore but does not lose access to the previous varieties. Each type of spore can be used a number of times per day equal to the myconid's Hit Dice. A 3-HD myconid, for example, has the first three spores (distress, reproduction, and rapport), and it can use each variety three times per day. Spores can be released either in a 120-foot spread or as a 40-foot ray against a single target, as noted in the individual spore descriptions.

Distress: These spores alert all other myconids within the area that danger is near. They are released in a 120-foot spread.

Reproduction: These spores eventually germinate into new infant myconids. They are released as a 120-foot spread and have no detrimental effects on nonmyconids.

Rapport: Myconids do not speak, but these spores enable them to establish telepathic communication with each other and with outsiders. A successful Fortitude saving throw (DC varies; see individual descriptions) negates the effect, but it is harmless. Rapport lasts for 30 to 60 minutes

MC

	Myconid Junior Worker Tiny Plant	Myconid Average Worker Small Plant	Myconid Elder Worker Medium-Size Plant
Hit Dice:	1d8 (4 hp)	2d8+2 (11 hp)	3d8+3 (16 hp)
Initiative:	+2	+2	+1
Speed:	20 ft.	20 ft.	20 ft.
AC:	14 (+2 size, +2 Dex), touch 14, flat-footed 12	13 (+1 size, +2 Dex), touch 13, flat-footed 11	12 (+1 Dex, +1 natural), touch 11, flat-footed 11
Attacks:	2 slams +1 melee	2 slams +2 melee	2 slams +3 melee, or spores +3 ranged touch
Damage:	Slam 1d3–1	Slam 1d4	Slam 1d6+1
Face/Reach:	2 1/2 ft. by 2 1/2 ft./0 ft.	5 ft. by 5 ft./5 ft.	5 ft. by 5 ft./5 ft.
Special Attacks:	—	—	Spores
Special Qualities:	Plant traits, spores	Plant traits, spores	Plant traits, spores
Saves:	Fort +2, Ref +2, Will +1	Fort +4, Ref +2, Will +1	Fort +4, Ref +2, Will +3
Abilities:	Str 8, Dex 15, Con 11, Int 9, Wis 12, Cha 12	Str 11, Dex 14, Con 12, Int 10, Wis 13, Cha 13	Str 12, Dex 13, Con 13, Int 10, Wis 15, Cha 14
Skills:	Craft (any one) +2, Hide +13, Knowledge (nature) +2, Listen +6, Move Silently +5, Profession (farmer) +4, Sense Motive +4, Spot +6, Wilderness Lore +4	Craft (any one) +4, Hide +10, Knowledge (nature) +4, Listen +6, Move Silently +5, Profession (farmer) +5, Sense Motive +4, Spot +6, Wilderness Lore +5	Craft (any one) +4, Hide +5, Knowledge (nature) +4, Listen +8, Move Silently +4, Profession (farmer) +6, Sense Motive +5, Spot +8, Wilderness Lore +6
Feats:	Alertness	Alertness	Alertness
Climate/Terrain:	Underground	Underground	Underground
Organization:	Solitary, pair, or gang (3–5)	Solitary, pair, or gang (3–5)	Solitary, pair, or gang (3–5)
Challenge Rating:	1/2	1	2
Treasure:	None	None	None
Alignment:	Usually lawful neutral	Usually lawful neutral	Usually lawful neutral
Advancement:	—	—	—

with outsiders, but for 8 hours with other myconids. Rapport spores can be released as either a 120-foot spread or a 40-foot ray. Regardless of the release area, the communication range is 120 feet once rapport is established.

Pacification: These spores are released as a 40-foot ray. The target must make a Fortitude saving throw (DC varies; see individual descriptions) or become passive for 1 minute. Being passive is similar to being dazed, except that the target can take partial actions that don't involve attacking. This is a mind-affecting compulsion effect.

Hallucination: These spores are released as a 40-foot ray. The target must make a Fortitude saving throw (DC varies; see individual descriptions) or suffer powerful hallucinations that duplicate the effects of a *confusion* spell for 1 hour.

Animation: Only the myconid sovereign has access to these spores. When released over a dead body, animation spores begin a process that covers the corpse with purple fungus. After 1d4 days, the corpse reanimates as a servant. A servant has all the characteristics of a zombie of the same size, except that it retains its previous creature type and it cannot be turned or otherwise affected as an undead. Over the course of 1d6 weeks, a myconid-animated corpse slowly decays. At the end of that period it simply disintegrates into dust.

Plant Traits (Ex): A myconid is immune to poison, *sleep*, paralysis, stunning, and polymorphing. It is not subject to critical hits or mind-affecting effects. The creature also has low-light vision.

Skills and Feats: A myconid gains skills and feats as though it were a fey. A myconid of any kind has EHD as though it were a Tiny plant.

JUNIOR WORKERS

These youngsters are four to eight years old. They assist their elders with daily chores and serve as a circle's first line of defense.

Combat

Junior workers are ineffective fighters. They release their spores at the first sign of danger and hide or retreat if threatened. If forced to fight, they tend to rush a single opponent as a group. Because a junior worker has a reach of 0 feet, it must enter an opponent's space to make melee attacks.

Spores (Ex): Junior workers have access only to distress spores.

AVERAGE WORKER

These myconids are eight to twelve years old. They are the backbone of the community, and they can perform a wide variety of tasks.

	Myconid Guard Medium-Size Plant	Myconid Circle Leader Large Plant	Myconid Sovereign Large Plant
Hit Dice:	4d8+8 (26 hp)	5d8+15 (37 hp)	6d8+21 (48 hp)
Initiative:	+1	+1	+1
Speed:	20 ft.	20 ft.	20 ft.
AC:	12 (+1 Dex, +1 natural), touch 11, flat-footed 11	12 (−1 size, +1 Dex, +2 natural), touch 10, flat-footed 11	12 (−1 size, +1 Dex, +2 natural), touch 10, flat-footed 11
Attacks:	2 slams +5 melee, or spores +5 ranged touch	2 slams +5 melee, or spores +6 ranged touch	2 slams +7 melee, or spores +8 ranged touch
Damage:	Slam 1d6+2	Slam 1d8+3	Slam 1d8+4
Face/Reach:	5 ft. by 5 ft./5 ft.	5 ft. by 5 ft./10 ft.	5 ft. by 5 ft./10 ft.
Special Attacks:	Spores	Spores	Spores
Special Qualities:	Plant traits, spores	Plant traits, spores	Plant traits, potion making, spores
Saves:	Fort +6, Ref +2, Will +3	Fort +7, Ref +2, Will +4	Fort +8, Ref +3, Will +5
Abilities:	Str 14, Dex 12, Con 15, Int 11, Wis 15, Cha 14	Str 16, Dex 12, Con 17, Int 11, Wis 16, Cha 15	Str 18, Dex 12, Con 17, Int 12, Wis 17, Cha 17
Skills:	Craft (any one) +4, Hide +5, Intimidate +6, Knowledge (nature) +4, Listen +8, Move Silently +4, Profession (farmer) +6, Sense Motive +6, Spot +8, Wilderness Lore +6	Craft (any one) +4, Diplomacy +4, Hide +1, Intimidate +6, Knowledge (nature) +4, Listen +9, Move Silently +4, Profession (farmer) +8, Sense Motive +8, Spot +9, Wilderness Lore +7	Craft (any one) +5, Diplomacy +5, Hide +1, Intimidate +8, Knowledge (nature) +5, Listen +9, Move Silently +4, Profession (farmer) +8, Profession (herbalist) +7, Sense Motive +8, Spot +9, Wilderness Lore +7
Feats:	Alertness	Alertness, Weapon Focus (spores)	Alertness, Brew Potion (B), Toughness, Weapon Focus (spores)
Climate/Terrain:	Underground	Underground	Underground
Organization:	Solitary, pair, patrol (3–5), or work gang (3–5 plus 3–5 workers)	Solitary, pair, patrol (3–5), work gang (3–5 plus 3–5 workers), or circle (4 junior workers plus average workers, elder workers, guards, and elder guards, for a total of 20)	Tribe (3–10 circles, plus 1 king and 5–10 zombie servants)
Challenge Rating:	4	6	7
Treasure:	None	None	No coins, no goods, standard items (potions only)
Alignment:	Usually lawful neutral	Usually lawful neutral	Usually lawful neutral
Advancement:	—	—	7–12 HD (Large); 13–18 HD (Huge)

Combat

Average workers are fairly proficient fighters. If alerted to danger, they usually try to hide and then either attack from ambush or wait until more capable myconids arrive on the scene. If such reinforcements are available, the average workers use the aid another action to assist their superiors in combat.

Spores (Ex): Average workers have access to both distress and reproduction spores.

ELDER WORKER

These myconids are twelve to sixteen years old. They serve as supervisors for other workers and as shock troops in combat.

Combat

Elder workers usually spray intruders with rapport spores rather than hiding, as more junior myconids do. They are quite willing to communicate rather than take aggressive action. If forced to fight, they try to eliminate the most formidable-looking foes first. If more capable myconids join the battle, elder workers use much the same tactics that average workers do.

Spores (Ex): Elder workers have access to distress, reproduction, and rapport spores (save DC 12 where applicable).

GUARD

These myconids are sixteen to twenty years old. They are charged with the defense of the circle.

Combat

Guards are fairly aggressive in combat, at least by myconid standards. Their preferred attack is their pacification spores, though they can use their slam attacks if forced into melee.

Spores (Ex): Guards have access to distress, reproduction, rapport, and pacification spores (save DC 14 where applicable).

CIRCLE LEADER

These myconids are twenty to twenty-four years old. As the name suggests, they lead and administer their circles.

Combat

Circle leaders join battle only if doing so seems necessary to keep their underlings from being slaughtered. In combat, they use their hallucination spores at the first opportunity. Like other myconids, they prefer to avoid melee combat altogether but can use their slams if they must.

Spores (Ex): Circle leaders have access to distress, reproduction, rapport, pacification, and hallucination spores (save DC 15 where applicable).

SOVEREIGN

A myconid sovereign is usually at least twenty-four years old. It rules over a tribe, advised by the oldest of the circle leaders. Sovereigns in neighboring areas try to ensure regular communication between their tribes, and they occasionally meet to discuss issues that affect multiple tribes.

Combat

Sovereigns use the same tactics as circle leaders, except that they also usually have a few myconid-animated zombies, or servants, to order into combat. If they join combat at all, sovereigns tend to advance on the enemy behind a rank of servants or circle leaders or both.

Spores (Ex): A myconid sovereign has access to distress, reproduction, rapport, pacification, hallucination, and animation spores (save DC 15 where applicable).

Potion Making (Su): Though it is not a spellcaster, a myconid sovereign can create various potions that mimic cleric and druid spells. It can duplicate the following effects, each once per day (but only for the purpose of brewing potions): *bull's strength, cure light wounds, cure moderate wounds, cure serious wounds, delay poison, endurance, endure elements, greater magic fang, invisibility to animals, lesser restoration, magic fang, negative energy protection, neutralize poison, protection from elements, remove blindness/deafness, remove disease, remove paralysis, resist elements.* Caster level 6th; save DC 12 + spell level.

MYCONID SOCIETY

A circle of myconids contains equal numbers of 1-HD, 2-HD, 3-HD, 4-HD, and 5-HD individuals. Each day is rigidly structured into 8 hours of rest, 8 hours of work (tending fungus farms), and 8 hours of melding into a transcendental, hallucinogenic, group-mind state. A melding can be broken only by myconid distress spores.

Myconids grow fungus for food. A tribe usually maintains several fungus farms, which the workers tend with an almost religious zeal. These creatures know everything there is to know about fungus, including the optimum conditions for growing each type, and how large a crop a given area might be expected to produce. Myconids also know how to make various items from fungus. Most of these, however, are useful only to myconids.

Myconid tribes consist of several circles living in close proximity. The circles in a tribe usually arrange themselves so that the distress spores from neighboring circles can reach at least one member of another circle in the tribe.

A myconid encountered away from its circle is performing some mission for its superiors. Such missions usually consist of keeping a lookout for intruders or scavenging for refuse to fertilize the fungus beds. Should a wandering myconid chance upon a humanoid body suitable for animation, it takes that back to its circle.

The sovereign is the only 6-HD myconid in a tribe. This creature organizes the circles, watches over the tribe, protects it from outside influences, animates guardians, and brews potions. When it dies, the oldest surviving circle leader in that tribe becomes the new sovereign.

NEEDLEFOLK

Medium-Size Plant
Hit Dice: 3d8+3 (16 hp)
Initiative: +0
Speed: 30 ft.
AC: 14 (+4 natural), touch 10, flat-footed 14
Attacks: Needles +2 ranged, or 2 claws +3 melee
Damage: Needles 1d12+1, claw 1d4+1
Face/Reach: 5 ft. by 5 ft./5 ft.
Special Qualities: Plant traits
Saves: Fort +4, Ref +1, Will +3
Abilities: Str 12, Dex 10, Con 13, Int 6, Wis 15, Cha 5
Skills: Hide +0*

Climate/Terrain: Any forest
Organization: Solitary or grove (5–50)
Challenge Rating: 2
Treasure: Standard
Alignment: Always neutral
Advancement: 4–9 HD (Medium-size)

Though needlefolk superficially resemble humanoids, they are in fact mobile plants. Because they lack roots, needlefolk must take in water and nutrients through a structure that resembles a mouth.

Under most circumstances a needlefolk's movements are slow and stately. When faced with danger, however, it can be nearly as quick and agile as a human.

A needlefolk is a green, hairless bipedal creature whose body is covered with short, stiff bristles (actually needlelike thorns). In human terms, its body is quite thin, even emaciated-looking. Its arms end in "hands" that sport vicious-looking claws (actually large, sturdy thorns). The coloration of the small leaves that cover the monster's body mirrors that of the foliage around them: green in spring and summer, red and yellow in autumn, and brown in winter. Needlefolk are deciduous, so they drop their leaves and become dormant through the cold season. A dormant needlefolk resembles a tree with two branches and a faint outline of a face in the bark atop its body.

Needlefolk have no appreciable society or culture. They live in the forest with no more social organization than trees or shrubs would have. Their dietary needs are all satisfied by absorbing light and by eating dirt, decaying leaves, and the occasional small, dead forest animal. They reproduce by seeds, which each needlefolk produces in the autumn. The seed pods are brown and covered with spiny thorns. Because they fall close to the parent plant, groves of needlefolk tend to spring up wherever one has chosen to spend a season.

The only thing that excites needlefolk is elves—they hate elves passionately. Needlefolk can sense the presence of an elf within 1,500 feet, and they always move to attack when one is detected. However, the monsters do possess enough intelligence and cunning not to commit suicide if they can see

that the odds are strongly against them. If badly outnumbered, a needlefolk may shadow the target elves until it can see that enough additional needlefolk have gathered in the area to shift the balance against the enemies. Needlefolk speak Sylvan.

COMBAT

Needlefolk are not tremendous fighters at close range; their preferred weapon is the small needles that cover their bodies. Each round, a needlefolk can launch a cluster of needles from its body (range increment 20 feet, maximum range 200 feet). The precise number of needles launched doesn't matter; either they all hit a single target as a cluster and deal 1d12+1 points of damage, or they all miss. If forced into melee, a needlefolk attacks with its claws.

Groups of needlefolk attack as individuals without any sort of plan or direction. Each one is cunning enough to determine where its own attacks might be best targeted, but it cares nothing for what the rest of its kind do in a fight.

Plant Traits (Ex): Needlefolk are immune to poison, *sleep*, paralysis, stunning, and polymorphing. They are not subject to critical hits or mind-affecting effects. The creatures also have low-light vision.

Skills: *A needlefolk's coloration and needles give it excellent camouflage in the forest. While there it has a +16 racial bonus on Hide checks when stationary. This bonus drops to +8 if it moves at up to half-speed.

NEOGI

Neogis are vicious, spiderlike scavengers, raiders, and slavers. They fit right into any setting where creepy creatures abound.

A neogi's eight-legged body is covered with stiff hair which makes it look something like a giant wolf spider. Instead of a spider's head, however, the neogi has a long flexible neck that extends upward and backward, then turns toward the front again in a large S-curve. Atop that sleek neck sits a small, narrow head, like that of an eel. Its jaws are lined with tiny, needle-sharp teeth, and small, black eyes are pushed well forward on the face. An occasional individual has a narrow beard growing from the front edge of its chin. The typical neogi dyes its naturally tan fur in one of many different hues and patterns. Some of these patterns signify family or rank; others are just for decoration. A neogi usually wears simple articles of decorative clothing and a belt or bandoleer with pouches for carrying its valuables.

Neogi lairs are usually laced with pits, chasms, narrow bridges, and precarious ledges. With their excellent balance and jumping skills and their ability to dash around enemies, neogis can move through these hazardous areas more quickly and safely than most attackers can.

	Neogi Spawn Tiny Aberration	Adult Neogi Small Aberration	Great Old Master Neogi Huge Vermin
Hit Dice:	1/4 d8–1 (1 hp)	5d8–5 (18 hp)	5d8+25 (47 hp)
Initiative:	+3	+3	–1
Speed:	20 ft., climb 20 ft.	30 ft., climb 20 ft.	20 ft.
AC:	15 (+2 size, +3 Dex), touch 15, flat-footed 12	17 (+1 size, +3 Dex, +3 natural), touch 14, flat-footed 14	10 (–2 size, –1 Dex, +3 natural), touch 7, flat-footed 10
Attacks:	Bite +5 melee	Bite +7 melee and 2 claws –3 melee, or light crossbow +7 ranged	Bite +1 melee
Damage:	Bite 1d3–4 plus poison	Bite 1d6–2 , claw 1d3–2, light crossbow 1d8/19–20	Bite 1d6
Face/Reach:	2 /2 ft by 2 1/2 ft./0 ft.	5 ft. by 5 ft./5 ft.	10 ft. by 10 ft./10 ft.
Special Attacks:	Poison	Enslave, poison	Poison, spit spawn
Special Qualities:	Darkvision 60 ft., immune to mind-affecting effects	Darkvision 60 ft., immune to mind-affecting effects	Vermin traits
Saves:	Fort –1, Ref +3, Will +2	Fort +0, Ref +4, Will +6	Fort +9, Ref +0, Will +3
Abilities:	Str 3, Dex 17, Con 9 Int 2, Wis 10, Cha 2	Str 6, Dex 17, Con 9 Int 15, Wis 14, Cha 16	Str 11, Dex 8, Con 20 Int —, Wis 15, Cha 1
Skills:	Balance +4, Climb +11, Jump +4, Move Silently +5	Balance +11, Climb +11, Disable Device +10, Intimidate +9, Jump +11, Move Silently +11	Balance +3, Move Silently +7
Feats:	Weapon Finesse (bite) (B)	Dodge, Mobility, Simple Weapon Proficiency, Weapon Finesse (bite) (B)	—
Climate/Terrain:	Any temperate or warm land and underground	Any temperate or warm land and underground	Any temperate or warm land and underground
Organization:	Swarm (10–40) or tribe (10–60 plus 10–60 adult neogi, 10–60 umber hulk slaves, and 1 great old master)	Nest (3–8 plus 3–8 umber hulk slaves)	Tribe (1 plus 10–60 spawn, 10–60 adult neogi, and 10–60 umber hulk slaves)
Challenge Rating:	1/4	4	6
Treasure:	None	Double standard	None
Alignment:	Usually lawful evil	Usually lawful evil	Always neutral
Advancement:	—	By character class	—

All neogis speak Common and Undercommon, and a large number of them also speak Terran.

COMBAT

The tactics of these monsters vary according to the kind of neogi involved. No neogi is particularly brave, but all of them are ruthless. They all share the following abilities.

Poison (Ex): Neogi poison is exceptionally virulent, considering that the creature itself is so frail. A neogi delivers its poison (Fortitude save DC 14 for all neogis) with each successful bite attack. The initial and secondary damage is the same (1d4 points of Wisdom damage).

Immune to Mind-Affecting Effects: Neogis are immune to all mind-affecting effects.

Skills: A neogi uses its Dexterity score instead of its Strength score for Climb and Jump checks.

SPAWN

These foul and dangerous pests usually are found only in the vicinity of a great old master. Sometimes, however, adult neogis let large numbers of spawn loose on the outskirts of their community and leave them to fend for themselves.

Combat

Neogi spawn usually prey on each other, but if they notice other prey, they charge toward it. In combat, they swarm over a single creature, biting until it succumbs to their poison. Thereafter, these little horrors devour their prey.

ADULT NEOGI

Adult neogis are the backbone of the community. They spend most of their time trying to acquire as much wealth and power as possible.

Combat

Adult neogis are not tremendous fighters, and they know it. Wherever possible, they have their umber hulk slaves (see Neogi Society, below) fight for them while they linger nearby looking for opportunities to use their enslave ability. Adult neogis often try to make foes more vulnerable to

enslavement by using their poison first, usually delivered via a crossbow bolt (see below). These creatures are nimble and difficult to corner.

Poison (Ex): As a standard action, an adult neogi can coat a weapon with poison from its fangs. The poison remains active for 1 minute after application and functions as it does when delivered by means of a bite.

Enslave (Su): Three times a day, a neogi can attempt to enslave any one living creature within 30 feet. This ability functions similarly to a *dominate monster* spell (caster level 16th; Will save DC 15). An enslaved creature obeys the neogi's telepathic commands to the letter. The subject can attempt a new Will save (DC 15) every 24 hours to break free. Otherwise, the neogi's control is broken only by the death of either the neogi or the enslaved creature, or by a *remove curse* or *dispel magic* effect, or if the neogi travels more than 1 mile from the enslaved creature.

This ability is not needed for neogis to subdue or control their umber hulk slaves (see Neogi Society, below).

GREAT OLD MASTER

A neogi that has grown old and senile is used as an incubator for infant neogi. In preparation for this event, adult neogis exude a fluid and inject it into the subject. This fluid causes the subject's body to swell into a 10-foot-diameter, bloated sack. Upon becoming a great old master, a neogi loses its intellect, memories, feats, magical abilities, and most skills. Its type changes to vermin. When the transformation is complete, adult neogis lay their eggs in the great old master's abdomen. Thereafter, the adult neogis provide the great old master with food—usually alive but immobilized—to sustain it and nourish the embryos that are devouring their host from the inside out. Eventually, twenty to forty neogi spawn chew their way out of the dying master. Most of these are in turn eaten by their voracious, newborn brothers and sisters, but a few survive to become the next generation of adult neogis.

Combat

A great old master can do little in combat except lurch about, biting and spewing forth spawn.

Spit Spawn (Ex): As a standard action, a great old master can spit out 2d4 spawn, which can attack the moment they land. The great old master can place the spawn anywhere within a range of 100 feet, but no two spawn can land more than 30 feet apart.

Also, when a great old master takes damage, it can release 2d4 spawn. This version of the spit spawn ability is usable once per round as a free action.

Vermin Traits: A great old master is immune to all mind-affecting effects (charms, compulsions, phantasms, patterns, and morale effects). It also has darkvision (60-foot range).

NEOGI SOCIETY

There's nothing to admire about neogi culture. These creatures are vicious murderers, plunderers, and slavers. Perhaps they kill to eat and enslave whatever is left over, or maybe they fill their chain gangs with slaves and eat whatever is left over. Either way, their rapacity has made them the enemies of every thinking race in the world. Only the mind flayers are known to have dealings with neogis, usually over the buying and selling of slaves.

Of all the races that neogis enslave, umber hulks are their favorites. Every neogi possesses at least one umber hulk, raised from birth to a life of slavery and conditioned to accept that situation as the natural order. These umber hulk slaves take orders from any neogi without question or thought. Umber hulk guards keep less compliant slaves (those under the effect of the neogi's enalave ability) under control and also act as soldiers in neogi armies and slave raids.

In the neogis' worldview, ownership is what fuels the universe. Everything belongs to the neogis as a whole—if not now, then it did in the past or it will in the future. Even a neogi can be owned as a slave by another neogi, and the slaves can own property and slaves, and those slaves can own property and other slaves, and so on.

NEOGI CHARACTERS

Many neogis become wizards or sorcerers. A neogi's favored class is sorcerer.

A neogi PC's effective character level (ECL) is equal to its class level + 8. Thus, a 1st-level neogi sorcerer has an ECL of 9 and is the equivalent of a 9th-level character.

NETHERSIGHT MASTIFF

Large Magical Beast
Hit Dice: 10d10+30 (85 hp)
Initiative: +5
Speed: 50 ft.
AC: 15 (−1 size, +1 Dex, +5 natural), touch 10, flat-footed 14
Attacks: Bite +13 melee
Damage: Bite 2d6+6
Face/Reach: 5 ft. by 10 ft./5 ft.
Special Attacks: Improved grab, wrenching attack
Special Qualities: Darkvision 60 ft., ethereal bite, low-light vision, scent, true sight

Saves: Fort +10, Ref +8, Will +6
Abilities: Str 19, Dex 13, Con 17, Int 6, Wis 12, Cha 12
Skills: Jump +9, Listen +9, Spot +8*, Wilderness Lore +5
Feats: Alertness, Improved Initiative, Iron Will

Climate/Terrain: Any cold or temperate land
Organization: Solitary or pack (5–20)
Challenge Rating: 8
Treasure: None
Alignment: Usually neutral
Advancement: 11–15 HD (Large); 16–30 HD (Huge)

Nethersight mastiffs are fierce predators native to arctic and subarctic areas of the Material Plane. These imposing, muscular canines have a taste for ethereal flesh, and they pursue it zealously, often passing over easier Material Plane prey in favor of a hunt on the Ethereal Plane.

A nethersight mastiff resembles a tremendous dire wolf with a black, shaggy coat and huge paws. It has a broad head with a short, wide muzzle, and its teeth glow with a pearly blue light. The typical nethersight mastiff is 8 feet in length and weighs 700 pounds.

Nethersight mastiffs speak Common.

COMBAT

Nethersight mastiffs are bold, aggressive carnivores that usually hunt in large packs, surrounding their prey to prevent escape, and then closing in for the kill. Because ethereal prey is more difficult to catch than Material Plane creatures, mastiffs always attack quickly and hold on with their jaws.

Improved Grab (Ex): If a nethersight mastiff hits an opponent that is at least one size category smaller than itself with a bite attack, it deals normal damage and attempts to start a grapple as a free action without provoking an attack of opportunity

(grapple bonus +18). If it gets a hold on an ethereal creature, it can attempt a wrenching attack on the next round. Alternatively, the nethersight mastiff has the option to conduct the grapple normally, or simply use its jaws to hold the opponent (–20 penalty on grapple check, but the nethersight mastiff is not considered grappled). In either case, each successful grapple check it makes during successive rounds automatically deals bite damage.

Wrenching Attack (Su): A nethersight mastiff can wrench a grabbed ethereal opponent onto the Material Plane by making a successful grapple check (grapple bonus +18). A wrenched opponent is then trapped on the Material Plane unless it has the means to return to the Ethereal Plane.

Ethereal Bite (Su): A nethersight mastiff's teeth have abilities similar to those of a ghost touch weapon, allowing it to bite ethereal creatures and negating the usual miss chance on any attack against an incorporeal creature.

Scent (Ex): A nethersight mastiff can detect approaching enemies, sniff out hidden foes, and track by sense of smell.

True Seeing (Su): This ability functions like the *true seeing* spell (caster level 16th), except that it is continuously active.

Skills: *A nethersight mastiff receives a +5 racial bonus on Spot checks when hunting creatures that are on the Ethereal Plane.

NIGHTMARE BEAST

Huge Magical Beast
Hit Dice: 15d10+105 (187 hp)
Initiative: +1
Speed: 30 ft.
AC: 21 (–2 size, +1 Dex, +12 natural), touch 9, flat-footed 20
Attacks: 2 tusks +22 melee and 2 claws +20 melee and bite +20 melee
Damage: Tusk 4d6+9/18–20, claw 2d4+4/19–20, bite 4d6+4/19–20
Face/Reach: 20 ft. by 30 ft./15 ft.
Special Attacks: Nightmares, spell-like abilities, trample 4d6+13
Special Qualities: Augmented critical, darkvision 60 ft., DR 15/+1, low-light vision, SR 20
Saves: Fort +16, Ref +10, Will +6
Abilities: Str 28, Dex 13, Con 24, Int 8, Wis 13, Cha 11
Skills: Jump +24, Spot +13
Feats: Improved Critical (tusk), Multiattack, Power Attack

Climate/Terrain: Any land
Organization: Solitary
Challenge Rating: 15
Treasure: 1/10th coins; 50% goods; 50% items
Alignment: Always chaotic evil
Advancement: 16–30 HD (Huge); 31–45 HD (Gargantuan)

With a disposition as bad as its reputation, it's no wonder that a nightmare beast spreads terror wherever it goes.

A nightmare beast stands at least 20 feet tall on its four legs. Each of its digits is tipped with a 3-foot-long claw. Its jaws are filled with 1-foot-long teeth and flanked by curved tusks the size of cavalry lances. A nightmare beast's thick, tough hide is typically dark gray with dark blue, purple, or brown splotches in between patches of bony material. Its red eyes, each the size of a man's head, glow in the dark.

The nightmare beast prefers to lair in a remote cave. It spends most of its time in search of food, and it tends to hunt in one area until the food supply is exhausted. At that point, it usually hibernates for up to one year, then awakens again in a ravenous state.

This monster has no interest in treasure, nor does it often bring any prey back to its lair, unless the kill is so large that it cannot be consumed all at once. A nightmare beast often inadvertently eats treasures along with their owners, so occasionally items of value turn up in the creature's lair at a later time.

Nightmare beasts speak Abyssal.

Combat

Few monsters aside from dragons are as dangerous as a nightmare beast. The creature attacks anything that looks like food with its teeth, tusks, and claws, dealing massive amounts of damage by means of its augmented critical ability. And in spite of all that damage potential, its most dangerous weapons are its spell-like abilities.

Nightmares (Su): Perhaps the nightmare beast's most powerful weapon is the one from which its name is derived. Every intelligent creature that falls asleep within 10 miles of a nightmare beast must succeed at a Will save (DC 17) or suffer from horrid, vivid nightmares of being stalked and killed by monsters, demons, cruel enemies, or whatever else it fears. The effect is otherwise the same as that of a *nightmare* spell (caster level 15th; Will save DC 17), except that a *dispel evil* spell cast on a victim does not stun the nightmare beast. A *remove curse* or a successful *dispel magic* negates the effect. Once a creature has either been affected by this ability or made a successful save, it cannot be affected by that nightmare beast's nightmare power again for 24 hours.

Spell-Like Abilities: 2/day—*chain lightning, cloudkill, dimension door* (1,000 ft. range), *disintegrate, dispel magic, fireball, heat metal, incendiary cloud, lightning bolt, monster summoning V, wall of fire.* Caster level 10th; save DC 10 + spell level.

Trample (Ex): As a standard action during its turn each round, a nightmare beast can trample opponents at least one size category smaller than itself by making a running jump from up to 35 feet away. This attack deals 4d6+13 points of bludgeoning damage. A trampled opponent can attempt either an attack of opportunity at a –4 penalty or a Reflex save (DC 26) for half damage.

Augmented Critical (Ex): A nightmare beast threatens a critical hit on a natural attack roll of 19–20 with any of its natural weapons.

NIMBLEWRIGHT

Medium-Size Construct
Hit Dice: 10d10 (55 hp)
Initiative: +7
Speed: 40 ft.
AC: 24 (+7 Dex, +7 natural), touch 17, flat-footed 17
Attacks: 2 rapier-hands +11 melee
Damage: Rapier-hand 2d6+4/12–20
Face/Reach: 5 ft. by 5 ft./5 ft.
Special Attacks: Spell-like abilities, tripping thrust
Special Qualities: Augmented critical, construct traits, SR 27, vulnerabilities
Saves: Fort +3, Ref +10, Will +6
Abilities: Str 19, Dex 24, Con —, Int 10, Wis 17, Cha 19
Feats: Combat Reflexes (B), Dodge (B), Expertise (B), Improved Disarm (B), Mobility (B), Spring Attack (B)

Climate/Terrain: Any land or underground
Organization: Solitary
Challenge Rating: 7
Treasure: Standard
Alignment: Always chaotic
Advancement: 11–15 HD (Medium-size); 16–30 HD (Large)

Nimblewrights are rapier-wielding constructs that disguise themselves as living humanoids. They often serve as hired bodyguards, but many are employed to infiltrate organizations and secret societies or spy on individuals. Unlike most constructs, a nimblewright is created with intelligence and

a distinct personality that allows for intuitive thinking and responsiveness. Like a golem, a nimblewright is a powerful creation that combines awesome magic with elemental forces. Its animating force is a spirit from the Elemental Plane of Water. The process of creating a nimblewright binds the unwilling spirit to the artificial body and subjects it to the will of the creator.

An undisguised nimblewright appears as a nondescript, steel-colored, mechanical human. When disguised, it wears clothes and uses spells to hide its true nature. In this way, it can appear as almost any Medium-size humanoid it wishes to become.

Nimblewrights speak Common, Elven, and Dwarven.

COMBAT

A nimblewright is an extremely dexterous combatant. In battle, it brings to bear all of its special fighting skills to deprive opponents of their weapons before running them through. If a nimblewright has ample warning of a fight, it enhances its combat skills with *cat's grace* and *haste* before joining melee.

The monster fights with two rapiers that are actually parts of its body. These rapiers are treated as natural weapons. When not in use, the weapons fold into its forearms. A nimblewright can fully deploy both rapiers as a free action.

Spell-Like Abilities: At will—*alter self, cat's grace, entropic shield, feather fall, haste.* Caster level 10th; save DC 14 + spell level.

Tripping Thrust (Ex): A nimblewright's rapier-hand attacks are powerful enough to push over creatures its own size or smaller. An opponent who is the target of a successful critical hit from a nimblewright must make a Reflex save (DC 19) or be knocked prone as if tripped.

Augmented Critical (Ex): A nimblewright threatens a critical hit on a natural attack roll of 12–20. On a successful critical hit, its foe is subject to a tripping thrust attack (see above).

Construct Traits: A nimblewright is immune to mind-affecting effects, poison, *sleep*, paralysis, stunning, disease, death effects, necromantic effects, and any effect that requires a Fortitude save unless it also works on objects. The creature is not subject to critical hits, subdual damage, ability damage, ability drain, energy drain, or death from massive damage. It cannot heal itself but can be healed through repair. It cannot be raised or resurrected. A nimblewright has darkvision (60-foot range).

Vulnerabilities: A cold effect slows a nimblewright for 3 rounds, and a fire effect stuns it for 1 round.

CONSTRUCTION

A nimblewright's body is a hollow humanoid shell made of flexible precious metal alloys weighing 500 pounds. It costs 35,000 gp to create, which includes 15,000 gp for the body. Assembling the body requires a successful Craft (sculpting) or Profession (mason) check (DC 16). The creator must be 18th level and able to cast arcane spells. Completing the ritual drains 1,600 XP from the creator and requires the *geas/quest, haste, limited wish,* and *polymorph any object* spells.

OCEAN STRIDER

Huge Fey (Aquatic)
Hit Dice: 30d6+60 (165 hp)
Initiative: +5
Speed: 50 ft., swim 60 ft.
AC: 19 (–2 size, +1 Dex, +10 natural), touch 9, flat-footed 18
Attacks: Gargantuan masterwork falchion +18/+13/+8 melee and tail slap +12 melee, or Gargantuan masterwork trident +18/+13/+8 melee and tail slap +12 melee, or tail slap +17 melee
Damage: Gargantuan masterwork falchion 2d8+6/18–20, Gargantuan masterwork trident 4d6+6, tail slap 1d6+2 (secondary) or 1d6+6 (primary)
Face/Reach: 10 ft. by 5 ft./15 ft.
Special Attacks: Frightful presence, ramming, spell-like abilities
Special Qualities: DR 30/+3, low-light vision, SR 28, water breathing, water walk
Saves: Fort +12, Ref +18, Will +23
Abilities: Str 19, Dex 13, Con 15, Int 16, Wis 22, Cha 14
Skills: Hide +12, Intimidate +23, Intuit Direction +16, Jump +13, Listen +26, Spot +26, Swim +12, Wilderness Lore +16
Feats: Alertness, Blind-Fight, Cleave, Dodge, Expertise, Improved Initiative, Mobility, Power Attack, Spring Attack, Sunder

Climate/Terrain: Any aquatic
Organization: Solitary
Challenge Rating: 18
Treasure: Standard
Alignment: Always chaotic neutral
Advancement: By character class

Ocean striders live to protect the seas and oceans from those who sail upon them. These immense fey consider themselves defenders of natural waterways, and they dislike anyone who would plunder the depths for personal gain.

An ocean strider resembles a 20-foot-tall cross between an elf and a killer whale. Like an orca, it has a mouth full of pointed teeth, rubbery skin, black and white markings on its body, and a stubby, fluked tail. Like an elf, it has two arms, two legs, and a humanoid face. The typical ocean strider wears mithral scale mail and carries a masterwork falchion or trident sized for its convenient use.

Because of its water walk ability, an ocean strider can move at its land speed over the surface of the ocean as well as the bottom. Its name is derived from the majestic picture it makes striding over the wave tops, its weapon raised in defiance.

Once an ocean strider claims a particular stretch of water, it considers all creatures not native to those waters, or to the skies above, to be intruders. It begins by approaching ships that enter its realm and ordering them to turn back or face destruction. Usually, an ocean strider is content to allow ships' crews to reverse course, or even to negotiate if they wish. Those who promise to travel carefully, without dumping their trash overboard or killing more fish than they can eat, can sometimes negotiate safe passage with an ocean strider. Only when an intruder attempts to sail past without parleying or attacks does the ocean strider become openly aggressive. But woe to those who behave properly only until they believe themselves out of danger, because ocean striders have been known to follow ships for many miles if they have doubts about a crew's commitment to proper use of the ocean's gifts. Many a ship's captain has tried to persuade an ocean strider to reveal the limits of its demesne, but these canny sea-dwellers prefer to not to let intruders know the true extent of their ability to observe and punish wrongdoers.

Ocean striders speak Common, Elven, and Aquan.

COMBAT

In battle, an ocean strider first uses its powerful spell-like abilities to confuse, disorient, and soften up opponents. Then it uses the Spring Attack feat to enter combat with its weapon.

Frightful Presence (Ex): The mere presence of an ocean strider inspires terror in all creatures within 100 feet of it that have fewer Hit Dice or levels than it has. Each potentially affected opponent must succeed at a Will save (DC 32) or become shaken—a condition that lasts until the opponent is out of range. A successful save leaves that opponent immune to that ocean strider's frightful presence for 24 hours.

Ramming (Ex): As a standard action during its turn each round, an ocean strider can swim at up to quadruple speed (240 feet) and ram a waterborne target (such as a ship or another creature). To ram, the ocean strider must end its movement in the target's space. This attack deals 2d8+6 points of damage. If the target is a creature, it can attempt either an attack of opportunity or a Reflex save (DC 29) for half damage. Upon ramming a ship, the ocean strider can make a Strength check to breach its hull, which causes the ship to sink in 1d10 minutes. The break DC varies with the type of vessel rammed, as follows: rowboat DC 20, keelboat DC 23, sailing ship or longship DC 25, warship DC 27, or galley DC 30. (See Chapter 5 of the *Dungeon Master's Guide* for information about ships.) Regardless of the check result, every creature aboard must attempt a Reflex saving throw (DC 15). Success means the creature takes 1d10 points of damage from being thrown about by the impact; failure means the creature is hurled overboard.

Spell-Like Abilities: 6/day— *control water, fog cloud, ice storm, obscuring mist*; 5/day— *acid fog, cone of cold, elemental swarm* (water only), *horrid wilting, summon nature's ally IX* (water or aquatic creatures only). Caster level 20th; save DC 17 + spell level.

Water Breathing (Ex): An ocean strider has gills as well as lungs, so it can breathe water as well as it can air.

Water Walk (Su): An ocean strider continuously produces an effect like that of a *water walk* spell (caster level 20th).

OCEAN STRIDER CHARACTERS

An ocean strider's preferred class is ranger, though many choose to become clerics. Ocean strider clerics worship Deep Sashelas and may choose any two of the following domains: Chaos, Protection, and Water. Claims by sea captains that they have encountered shadowdancer ocean striders remain unconfirmed.

An ocean strider PC's effective character level (ECL) is equal to its class level + 35. Thus, a 1st-level ocean strider ranger has an ECL of 36 and is the equivalent of a 36th-level character.

ORCWORT

An orcwort is a walking, blood-thirsty terror that prefers to make its home on the fringe of a populated area. This giant plant wanders by night until it finds an appropriate spot to settle, then sinks some of its roots into the ground, making it seem that an immense tree has grown up in the spot overnight. Over the course of the next week, the orcwort produces five to twenty pods that, when mature, break open to release mobile fruits called wortlings. The parent plant then sends out its wortlings in hunting parties to bring back warm-blooded sustenance—usually livestock and humanoids.

An orcwort is capable of devouring the entire population of a small village in a single feeding. Once it has stripped an area of warm-blooded animal life, it moves on in search of other population centers.

COMBAT

Both the orcwort and its wortlings are effective combatants. They share the following qualities.

Partial Immunity to Piercing (Ex): Piercing weapons deal only half damage to orcworts and wortlings. The minimum damage per hit with such a weapon is 1 point.

Plant Traits (Ex): An orcwort or wortling is immune to poison, *sleep*, paralysis, stunning, and polymorphing. It is not subject to critical hits or mind-affecting effects.

Woodsense (Ex): An orcwort or wortling can automatically sense the location of anything within 60 feet that is in contact with vegetation, even objects or creatures that are not in contact with the same vegetation as itself.

Skills and Feats: Orcworts and wortlings gain skills and feats as though they were fey.

	Wortling Small Plant	Orcwort Colossal Plant
Hit Dice:	3d8 (13 hp)	32d8+288 (432 hp)
Initiative:	+6	+2
Speed:	30 ft., climb 15 ft.	10 ft.
AC:	16 (+1 size, +2 Dex, +3 natural), touch 13, flat-footed 14	12 (–8 size, –2 Dex, +12 natural), touch 0, flat-footed 12
Attacks:	2 claws +5 melee	6 slams +30 melee
Damage:	Claw 1d3+2 plus poison	Slam 4d6+14
Face/Reach:	5 ft. by 5 ft./5 ft.	40 ft. by 40 ft./25 ft.
Special Attacks:	Poison, swarming	Entangling roots, improved grab, paralysis, swallow whole
Special Qualities:	Partial immunity to piercing, plantmind, plant traits, woodsense	DR 5/–, partial immunity to piercing, plant traits, telepathy, woodsense
Saves:	Fort +3, Ref +3, Will +1	Fort +27, Ref +8, Will +13
Abilities:	Str 15, Dex 14, Con 11, Int 2, Wis 11, Cha 6	Str 39, Dex 7, Con 29, Int 10, Wis 16, Cha 8
Skills:	Climb +10, Hide +11, Move Silently +7	Hide –3, Move Silently +13
Feats:	Improved Initiative	Improved Initiative
Climate/Terrain:	Temperate or warm plains, hills, and marsh	Temperate or warm plains, hills, and marsh
Organization:	Band (5–20)	Crop (1 orcwort plus 5–20 wortlings)
Challenge Rating:	3	20
Treasure:	None	None
Alignment:	Always neutral	Always neutral
Advancement:	4–9 HD (Medium-size)	33–64 HD (Colossal)

WORTLING

Wortlings are the mature fruits of the orcwort plant. When one of the orcwort's pods ripens, it falls to the ground and breaks open to release a wortling.

When first "hatched," a wortling resembles a small, wrinkled, purple orc. Its body seems portly, and its arms and legs are somewhat lumpy compared with those of a real humanoid. Although its face resembles that of a humanoid, a wortling is blind and cannot speak, hear, or smell—its apparent sensory organs are merely blobs of plant tissue with no actual function.

A hungry orcwort dispatches up to twenty of its "ripe" wortlings at a time to hunt food and bring it back. The wortlings navigate terrain using their woodsense. When on the prowl, wortlings seek out Medium-size or smaller prey because such creatures are easier to transport back to the parent plant than larger creatures.

The average life span of a wortling is 1d4+1 days. If any wortlings are left alive when the parent plant is ready to move on, the orcwort commands them to arrange themselves well apart from each other at the extreme range of its telepathy and root themselves. If left undisturbed for one year, each of these wortlings grows into a new orcwort, which pulls up its roots and begins looking for food. During its maturation period, a rooted wortling is immobile and helpless.

Combat

Wortlings use very simple tactics—overwhelm, subdue, and return with the food. In melee, they prefer to gang up on one foe rather than attack separate enemies. They fight with a great sense of urgency, and when they do manage to bring down a foe, a few of them immediately carry off their prize to feed the orcwort, leaving any remaining wortlings to continue the hunt. They never willingly enter areas without natural vegetation because they are effectively blind in such places.

Poison (Ex): A wortling delivers its poison (Fortitude save DC 11) with each successful claw attack. The initial damage is *sleep* for 1 minute, and the secondary damage is *sleep* for 1d10 minutes. Both of these *sleep* effects work only against living creatures but otherwise function as the spell of the same name.

Swarming (Ex): Wortlings can swarm over and around each other with ease, so up to three of them can occupy the same 5-foot-by-5-foot space. They are likewise adept at attacking as a group; for every wortling that is grappling a foe (grapple bonus +0), every wortling gets a +1 competence bonus on attack rolls against that foe.

Plantmind (Ex): All wortlings within fifteen miles of their orcwort parent are in constant communication. If one is aware of a particular danger, they all are. If one in a particular group is not flat-footed, none of them are. No wortling in such a group is considered flanked unless they all are.

ORCWORT

An orcwort looks like a gigantic, woody pitcher plant draped in thick creeper vines. It is crowned with a canopy of bramblelike branches and green, bushy foliage. Dormant wortling pods hang from the orcwort's branches, resembling round, oversized prunes.

Combat

In combat, an orcwort reaches out with its vines to entwine nearby prey. It then uses other tendrils to pick out choice victims one at a time and drop them into its open maw. An orcwort recalls any wortling raiding parties it has sent out whenever it is under attack.

Entangling Roots (Ex): As a free action, an orcwort can twist its roots around all creatures within 15 feet of it, holding them fast. This effect otherwise functions like an *entangle* spell (caster level 10th; save DC 24).

Improved Grab (Ex): If an orcwort hits a Gargantuan or smaller opponent with a slam attack, it deals normal damage and attempts to start a grapple as a free action without provoking an attack of opportunity (grapple bonus +54). If it gets a hold, it can transfer the opponent to its maw in the next round. Alternatively, the orcwort has the option to conduct the grapple normally, or simply use one tendril to hold the opponent (–20 penalty on grapple check, but the orcwort is not considered grappled). In either case, each successful grapple check it makes during successive rounds automatically deals slam damage.

Paralysis (Ex): An orcwort secretes digestive juices that can paralyze creatures in contact with it. Any creature swallowed by an orcwort must succeed at a Fortitude save (DC 35) or be paralyzed for 2d4 rounds.

Swallow Whole (Ex): An orcwort can swallow a Huge or smaller creature by making a successful grapple check (grapple bonus +54), provided it already has that opponent in its maw (see Improved Grab, above). Once inside the orcwort's pitcher, the opponent takes 2d8+8 points of acid damage per round and is subject to the paralyzing effect of its digestive juices (see Paralysis, above). A successful grapple check allows a swallowed creature to climb out of the pitcher (assuming it is not paralyzed) and return to the orcwort's maw, where another successful grapple check is needed to get free. Alternatively, a swallowed creature can try to cut its way out with either claws or a light piercing or slashing weapon. Dealing at least 20 points of damage to the pitcher (AC 18) in this way creates an opening large enough to permit escape. Once a single swallowed creature exits, muscular action closes the hole; thus, another swallowed opponent must cut its own way out. The orcwort's pitcher can hold 2 Huge, 8 Large, 32 Medium-size, or 128 Small or smaller creatures.

Telepathy (Su): An orcwort can communicate telepathically with any of its wortlings within fifteen miles.

ORMYRR

Huge Monstrous Humanoid

Hit Dice: 7d8+21 (52 hp)

Initiative: +2

Speed: 20 ft., swim 40 ft.

AC: 17 (–2 size, +2 Dex, +7 natural), touch 10, flat-footed 15

Attacks: 4 claws +13 melee and bite +8 melee, or weapon +13/+8 melee and 3 light weapons +13 melee and bite +8 melee, or weapon +11/+6 melee and 3 weapons (at least one of which is not light) +11 melee and bite +8 melee, or 4 stones +5 ranged

Damage: Claw 2d4+8, by weapon (damage bonus +8 for primary hand and +4 for each off hand), bite 1d8+4, stone 1d6+8 (primary hand) or 1d6+4 (off hand)

Face/Reach: 10 ft. by 25 ft./10 ft.

Special Attacks: Constrict 1d8+12, improved grab

Special Qualities: Darkvision 60 ft., enhanced multiweapon fighting, weapon use

Saves: Fort +5, Ref +7, Will +6

Abilities: Str 26, Dex 15, Con 16, Int 11, Wis 12, Cha 13

Skills: Knowledge (arcana) +9, Listen +11, Spellcraft +9, Swim +16

Feats: Multidexterity, Multiweapon Fighting (B)

Climate/Terrain: Temperate and warm aquatic (rivers, lakes, and the shores of both)

Organization: Solitary, pair, or tribe (6–12)

Challenge Rating: 6

Treasure: Standard

Alignment: Usually lawful neutral

Advancement: 8–14 HD (Huge); 15–21 HD (Gargantuan)

Ormyrrs are intelligent, seminomadic creatures that live in small settlements along muddy river banks and lake shores. For the most part, they keep to themselves, except while hunting or feeding their passion for acquiring magic items.

An ormyrr has an enormous, grublike body that can measure as much as 25 feet long. At the top of the body is a froglike head that appears impossibly large and heavy. Below the head, four short but powerful arms extend out from the body. Thick, bony ridges above the eyes and a wide mouth filled with serrated teeth complete the beast's monstrous appearance.

Hunting parties of ormyrrs can roam as far as 40 miles from their homes. They travel by river as much as possible during their forays, then come ashore for the actual hunt.

Ormyrrs have no magical ability at all, but magic fascinates them; in fact, their goal as a race is to develop a unique ormyrr magic. They covet magic and magic items, and the chance to take possession of a magic item, scroll, or book is the one thing that can make one of these normally reasonable creatures lie, steal, or attack without provocation.

Needless to say, this tendency can draw them into conflict with adventurers. Since they are innately lawful, however, those seeking to recover magic items that ormyrrs have stolen can sometimes get farther by appealing to the creatures' sense of right and wrong than by attacking, hurling accusations, or trying to steal the items back.

Ormyrrs speak Common.

COMBAT

Most often, ormyrrs fight with weapons rather than with their claws. The typical ormyrr possesses at least one magic weapon, usually with a +1 or +2 enhancement bonus, and fights with more than one weapon at once to take advantage of its enhanced multiweapon fighting special quality.

A preferred tactic among ormyrrs is to hide along a river bank and ambush enemies with a hail of hurled stones, sling stones, axes, and nets. If the situation looks promising, the ormyrrs close in with drawn weapons. If not, they simply slip into the river and swim away from danger.

Constrict (Ex): With a successful grapple check, an ormyrr can crush a grabbed opponent, dealing 1d8+12 points of bludgeoning damage.

Improved Grab (Ex): If an ormyrr hits an opponent that is at least one size category smaller than itself with two claw attacks, it deals normal damage and attempts to start a grapple as a free action without provoking an attack of opportunity (grapple bonus +23). If it gets a hold, it also constricts on the same round. Thereafter, the ormyrr has the option to conduct the grapple normally, or simply use its claws to hold the opponent (–20 penalty on grapple check, but the ormyrr is not considered grappled). In either case, each successful grapple check it makes during successive rounds automatically deals damage for two claw attacks.

Enhanced Multiweapon Fighting (Ex): This ability lessens the penalty for off-hand weapon use by 2 for both primary and off hands. Thus, when combined with the creature's Multidexterity and Multiweapon Fighting feats, it allows the use of one or more light off-hand weapons with no penalty on the attack rolls.

Weapon Use (Ex): An ormyrr is proficient with all simple and martial weapons.

PHASE WASP

Tiny Magical Beast
Hit Dice: 2d10 (11 hp)
Initiative: +4
Speed: 10 ft., fly 60 ft. (perfect)
AC: 17 (+2 size, +4 Dex, +1 natural), touch 16, flat-footed 13
Attacks: Sting +0 melee
Damage: Sting 1d4–4
Face/Reach: 2 1/2 ft. by 2 1/2 ft./0 ft.
Special Attacks: *Magic missile*
Special Qualities: Darkvision 60 ft., low-light vision, *see invisibility*
Saves: Fort +3, Ref +7, Will +2
Abilities: Str 3, Dex 19, Con 10, Int 2, Wis 15, Cha 6
Skills: Listen +6, Spot +6, Wilderness Lore +3
Feats: Alertness

Climate/Terrain: Any temperate or warm land
Organization: Swarm (5–20)
Challenge Rating: 2
Treasure: None
Alignment: Always neutral
Advancement: 3–4 HD (Tiny); 5–6 HD (Small)

Phase wasps are 18-inch-long insects that can see and attack invisible and ethereal creatures (in the latter case, without crossing the planar boundary). They rarely attack creatures three or more size categories larger than themselves unless provoked.

Like ordinary wasps, these creatures live in large colonies. Each colony builds a nest about 10 feet in diameter out of "paper" that its members

have made from chewed-up wood or paper and their own saliva. Because such a nest requires a tremendous amount of paper, many wizards and libraries offer bounties for the destruction of nearby phase wasp nests.

Though they do not speak, phase wasps utilize an elaborate signaling system to communicate within their hives. Their "signal language" seems to be based on a system of subtle smells, body postures, and flight patterns.

COMBAT

Normally, phase wasps attack only to defend themselves or their nests. They converge on intruders in swarms, fire their *magic missiles*, and then swoop in to sting until they can use their missiles again.

Magic Missile (Sp): A phase wasp can produce an effect that functions like a *magic missile* spell (caster level 3rd). Once it has used this ability, it must wait 1d4 rounds before it can do so again.

See Invisibility (Sp): A phase wasp produces an effect like that of a *see invisibility* spell (caster level 3rd), except that is always active.

PHOENIX

Large Magical Beast
Hit Dice: 20d10+40 (150 hp)
Initiative: +7
Speed: 15 ft., fly 200 ft. (average)
AC: 23 (–1 size, +3 Dex, +6 natural, +5 deflection), touch 17, flat-footed 23
Attacks: 2 claws +23 melee, or bite +23 melee
Damage: Claw 1d8+4/19–20, bite 2d6+4
Face/Reach: 10 ft. by 15 ft./5 ft.
Special Attacks: Shriek, spell-like abilities
Special Qualities: Darkvision 60 ft., *defensive aura*, DR 20/+3, immolation, low-light vision, planar travel, spell-like metamagic, SR 35, telepathy, uncanny dodge
Saves: Fort +14, Ref +15, Will +11
Abilities: Str 18, Dex 16, Con 15, Int 18, Wis 17, Cha 21
Skills: Knowledge (arcana) +20, Knowledge (history) +20, Spot +25
Feats: Empower Spell, Enlarge Spell, Extend Spell, Flyby Attack, Heighten Spell, Improved Critical (claw), Improved Initiative, Iron Will, Maximize Spell

Climate/Terrain: Any land
Organization: Solitary
Challenge Rating: 24
Treasure: None
Alignment: Always neutral good
Advancement: —

The phoenix, or firebird, is a creature of tremendous power and potent omen. Many intelligent races look upon it as a god, or at least as a god's messenger.

Physically, a phoenix resembles an immense bird of prey. It measures between 10 and 15 feet from beak to tail, but its wingspan can be as wide as 40 feet. By far its most striking feature, however, is its plumage. All of its feathers are the colors of fire—primarily scarlet, crimson, and orange. In flight or at rest, a phoenix looks like a bird made of flame.

When a phoenix reaches the end of its natural life, or when it finds itself in an extreme, life-threatening situation, it immolates itself with intense fire. After its death, a new phoenix arises from the ashes.

Because of its traditional association with renewal and rebirth, most cultures ascribe some symbolic meaning to the sighting of a phoenix. Some consider it a positive omen—a sign of the gods' favor and a promise of renewed life and increased prosperity in the coming years. Others (usually those with a darker outlook on life) see the firebird as a sign of approaching death and destruction—an ordeal that only the strongest will survive. Whatever meaning a particular culture associates with this creature, there's no doubt that it is on the side of good. A phoenix doesn't involve itself in worldly affairs or join in mundane conflicts, but neither does it shy away from attacking evil.

COMBAT

In battle, a phoenix usually begins by shrieking to soften up its enemies before joining melee with its claws and beak. It has no fear of fighting to the death, since its immolation ability ensures its later rebirth.

Shriek (Ex): Once per minute, a phoenix can utter a war shriek that forces every opponent within 30 feet to succeed at a Will save (DC 22) or be slowed (as the *slow* spell) for 1 round. This is a sonic, mind-affecting effect.

Spell-Like Abilities: Always active—*detect evil, detect magic, protection from evil*; at will—*blindness, blink, blur, color spray, cure light wounds, dancing lights, find the path, find traps, fire seeds* (using drops of its own blood rather than holly berries as a material component; no acorn grenades), *heal, invisibility, misdirection, negative energy protection, neutralize poison, polymorph self, produce flame, remove fear, remove curse, see invisibility*; 1/day—*incendiary cloud, reincarnate, pyrotechnics, summon nature's ally IX, veil, wall of fire*. Caster level 20th; save DC 15 + spell level.

After 10 rounds of ritual and preparation—*dismissal, dispel evil, dispel magic*. Caster level 40th; save DC 15 + spell level.

Defensive Aura (Sp): A phoenix has a +5 deflection bonus to Armor Class. This ability is always in effect.

Immolation (Su): When it knows that death is near, a phoenix immolates itself as a full-round action. This produces a cloud of flame in a 20-foot-high, 15-foot-radius spread. Each creature in the area takes 40d6 points of damage (Reflex DC 22 half). Half of this damage is fire; the rest results directly from divine power and is therefore not subject to reduction by *protection from elements (fire), fire shield (chill shield)*, or similar magic. This action kills the original phoenix and produces a new one, fully grown and unharmed, from the ashes. This new bird arrives at the end of the round.

Planar Travel (Su): A phoenix can enter and exit the Astral Plane or the Ethereal Plane at will and navigate through these planes without error or risk.

Spell-Like Metamagic (Ex): A phoenix can apply any one of its metamagic feats (Empower Spell, Enlarge Spell, Extend Spell, Heighten Spell, Maximize Spell) to a spell-like ability by using that ability as a full-round action.

Telepathy (Su): A phoenix can communicate telepathically with any nonavian creature within 60 feet. It can also speak normally with any avians.

Uncanny Dodge (Ex): A phoenix retains its Dexterity bonus to AC even when flat-footed, and it cannot be flanked. Even if it fails a Spot check, it still knows that something is in the area; it merely lacks any details as to its exact location or description.

PLANETOUCHED

"Planetouched" is a term used to describe a creature that can trace its bloodline back to an outsider. The effects of an outsider's bloodline can manifest in its descendants for many generations. Though not as dramatically altered as half-fiends or half-celestials, the planetouched still have some special qualities because of their unusual ancestors.

The planetouched discussed here are exceedingly rare. Chaonds are humans with slaadi blood, while zenythris are descended from mysterious beings of law whose identity is only guessed at.

There are no "typical" chaonds and zenythris. These creatures neither form their own cultures nor belong to homogenous societies. Instead, they adopt the standards and the beliefs of the cultures they are born into.

Combat

Chaonds and zenythris fight with weapons as humanoids do.

Outsider Traits: A planetouched has darkvision (60-foot range). It cannot be raised or resurrected.

CHAOND

Infused with primal forces, chaonds are living embodiments of the force of chaos in the universe. Though their slaadi ancestry may be several generations removed, these beings still fit only marginally into civilized societies.

A chaond resembles a human but seems much cruder, both in form and in temperament. Its brutish appearance is usually marked by wild, unkempt hair, blocky facial features, and a stocky torso and limbs.

Its true nonhuman nature is given away by the slow, shifting colors of its eyes, hair, or skin. The typical chaond has a gravelly voice that tends to come out like a croak when the creature is excited.

Most chaonds are chaotically aligned, which has earned them a reputation as wily and whimsical beings. They often exist on the fringe of a society because they refuse to succumb to the rule of law. Chaonds wishing to explore their primal sides usually take on professions that involve adventuring in the natural wilderness or harnessing elemental forces.

Chaonds speak Common.

Combat

Considering their heritage, it should be no surprise that most chaonds fight dirty, with little regard for rules or fairness. They often conceal small, poisoned weapons on their persons. But while chaonds enjoy a good brawl, there are few issues that they consider worthy of a fight to the death.

Shatter (**Sp**): Once per day, a chaond can use *shatter* (caster level 1st or the chaond's character level, whichever is higher; save DC 11).

MD

	Chaond Medium-Size Outsider	Zenythri Medium-Size Outsider
Hit Dice:	1d8+1 (5 hp)	1d8 (4 hp)
Initiative:	+2	+1
Speed:	30 ft.	30 ft.
AC:	12 (+2 Dex), touch 12, flat-footed 10	11 (+1 Dex), touch 11, flat-footed 10
Attacks:	Sickle +1 melee, or dart +3 ranged	Scimitar +3 melee, or light crossbow +2 ranged
Damage:	Sickle 1d6, dart 1d4	Scimitar 1d6+1/18–20, light crossbow 1d8/19–20
Face/Reach:	5 ft. by 5 ft./5 ft.	5 ft. by 5 ft./5 ft.
Special Attacks:	*Shatter*	*True strike*
Special Qualities:	Acid resistance 5, cold resistance 5, outsider traits, sonic resistance 5	Electricity resistance 5, fire resistance 5, outsider traits, sonic resistance 5
Saves:	Fort +3, Ref +4, Will +2	Fort +2, Ref +3, Will+3
Abilities:	Str 11, Dex 14, Con 12, Int 10, Wis 11, Cha 9	Str 13, Dex 12, Con 10, Int 10, Wis 13, Cha 9
Skills:	Escape Artist +5, Jump +4, Move Silently +4, Tumble +5	Balance +6, Intuit Direction +4, Search +4
Feats:	Dodge	Weapon Focus (scimitar)
Climate/Terrain:	Any land and underground	Any land and underground
Organization:	Solitary or twins	Solitary
Challenge Rating:	1	1
Treasure:	Standard	Standard
Alignment:	Usually chaotic	Usually lawful
Advancement:	By character class	By character class

Skills: A chaond receives a +2 racial bonus on Escape Artist and Tumble checks.

haond Characters

The first class taken by a chaond character becomes that character's favored class. Once chosen, it cannot be changed.

A chaond PC's effective character level (ECL) is equal to its class level + 1. Thus, a 1st-level chaond wizard has an ECL of 2 and is the equivalent of a 2nd-level character.

ENYTHRI

Zenythris are often viewed as contemplative beings who strive for personal perfection in every action they take. Many feel the need to impose their own brand of order on the world about them. Some even travel to lawless regions for the express purpose of creating order there. From a zenythri's viewpoint, such exercises serve to illuminate the underlying purpose and structure that lies dormant in all things.

A zenythri appears as a perfect version of a human. Its skin is flawlessly smooth, and its muscles are well defined and taut. Even its hair falls effortlessly into place around its handsomely chiseled face. A zenythri could almost blend unnoticed among humans were it not for the slightly blue or purple tint of its skin and hair.

Most zenythris feel compelled to contribute to the societies in which they dwell. As such, they actively work toward positions of responsibility, which often bring with them significant social status. Zenythris are natural leaders and consummate strategists, and they gladly accept leadership roles. These planetouched seem to have no interest in good or evil so long as they accomplish their goals. Such a disposition lends itself as readily to tyrannical methods as benign ones.

Zenythris speak Common. A zenythri that acquires additional languages speaks them perfectly, without any sort of accent.

ombat

Zenythris fight instinctively, sizing up opponents for strengths and weaknesses during melee. They relish in executing difficult combat moves and work hard to develop complex fighting styles.

True Strike (Sp): Once per day, a zenythri can use *true strike* (caster level 1st or the zenythri's character level, whichever is higher).

Skills: A zenythri receives a +2 racial bonus on Balance and Intuit Direction checks.

enythri Characters

A zenythri's favored class is monk.

A zenythri PC's effective character level (ECL) is equal to its class level + 1. Thus, a 1st-level zenythri monk has an ECL of 2 and is the equivalent of a 2nd-level character.

PSURLON

Psurlons are wormlike creatures with formidable mental powers. The resemblance between psurlons and worms is likely more than coincidence; perhaps the monsters were magically created from earthworms, or an earthworm is a radically degenerate form of psurlon.

A psurlon has a long, tubular, pinkish body marked with faint rings, just like an earthworm's. It also has two arms and two legs, each of which also looks like a giant earthworm. The psurlon's head is little more than a blunt end to its tubular body. Its only facial feature is a circular maw filled with gnashing teeth that serves as a mouth. It has visual organs (for darkvision) spaced evenly around the head. The typical psurlon wears a decorative or utilitarian belt fitted with straps and hooks to carry items, but no other clothing or armor.

Psurlons often choose to live solitary lives, or to live only with their mates. Sometimes, however, psurlons form small communities called clusters for the purpose of claiming territory or working toward a common cause.

Psurlons speak Undercommon.

COMBAT

Psurlons never use melee weapons. They can fight with their bare claws and teeth, but this does not make them very formidable opponents in physical combat. The real danger a psurlon presents is in its ability to cloud, numb, and control the minds of others.

Blindsight (Ex): A psurlon can ascertain its surroundings by sensing sound, scent, heat, and vibration. This ability enables it to discern objects and creatures within 60 feet. The psurlon usually does not need to make Spot or Listen checks to notice creatures within range of its blindsight.

Immunities (Ex): Psurlons are immune to *sleep*, charm, and hold effects.

Telepathy (Su): A psurlon can communicate telepathically with any creature within 250 feet that has a language.

AVERAGE PSURLON

Average psurlons perform all day-to-day tasks related to keeping a cluster running smoothly. Of all psurlons, it is these that most often strike out to live on their own.

	Average Psurlon Medium-Size Aberration	Elder Psurlon Medium-Size Aberration	Giant Psurlon Large Aberration
Hit Dice:	7d8+7 (38 hp)	12d8+12 (66 hp)	18d8+36 (117 hp)
Initiative:	+6	+6	+5
Speed:	30 ft.	30 ft.	40 ft.
AC:	12 (+2 Dex), touch 12, flat-footed 10	12 (+2 Dex), touch 12, flat-footed 10	10 (−1 size, +1 Dex), touch 10, flat-footed 9
Attacks:	2 claws +6 melee and bite +4 melee	2 claws +11 melee and bite +9 melee	2 claws +16 melee and bite +14 melee
Damage:	Claw 1d4+1, bite 2d4	Claw 1d4+2, bite 2d4+1	Claw 1d6+4, bite 2d6+2
Face/Reach:	5 ft. by 10 ft./5 ft.	5 ft. by 10 ft./5 ft.	10 ft. by 20 ft./10 ft.
Special Attacks:	Spell-like abilities	Spell-like abilities	Spell-like abilities
Special Qualities:	Blindsight 60 ft., darkvision 120 ft., DR 15/+1, immunities, SR 14, telepathy	Blindsight 60 ft., darkvision 120 ft., DR 15/+1, immunities, SR 16, telepathy	Blindsight 60 ft., darkvision 120 ft., DR 15/+1, immunities, SR 16, telepathy
Saves:	Fort +3, Ref +4, Will +7	Fort +5, Ref +6, Will +13	Fort +10, Ref +9, Will +17
Abilities:	Str 13, Dex 14, Con 12, Int 18, Wis 11, Cha 17	Str 14, Dex 15, Con 12, Int 20, Wis 17, Cha 17	Str 18, Dex 12, Con 15, Int 17, Wis 18, Cha 17
Skills:	Balance +12, Concentration +11, Escape Artist +10, Heal +10, Spellcraft +14	Balance +15, Concentration +16, Escape Artist +10, Heal +16, Spellcraft +18	Balance +12, Concentration +20, Escape Artist +10, Heal +18, Spellcraft +19
Feats:	Combat Casting, Dodge, Improved Initiative, Iron Will, Multiattack	Combat Casting, Dodge, Expertise, Improved Initiative, Iron Will, Mobility, Multiattack	Combat Casting, Expertise, Great Fortitude, Improved Initiative, Iron Will, Lightning Reflexes, Multiattack
Climate/Terrain:	Underground	Underground	Underground
Organization:	Solitary, pair, team (3–6 plus 1 elder psurlon), cluster (8–14 plus 1 elder psurlon), or strike team (3–6 plus 1 elder psurlon and 1 giant psurlon)	Solitary, cluster (1 plus 8–14 average psurlons), or strike team (1 plus 1 giant psurlon and 3–6 average psurlons)	Solitary or strike team (1 plus 1 elder psurlon and 3–6 average psurlons)
Challenge Rating:	5	9	15
Treasure:	Standard	Standard	Standard
Alignment:	Usually lawful evil	Usually lawful evil	Always neutral evil
Advancement:	8–14 HD (Medium-size)	13–24 HD (Medium-size)	19–36 HD (Large)

An average psurlon stands about 5 feet tall and weighs about 130 pounds.

Combat

Although they do not relish combat, average psurlons are naturally suspicious and bad-tempered. They usually unleash their spell-like abilities against anything that approaches too closely. They usually begin with *mind fog* and then, if menaced by a whole group, follow up with *dominate person* to make physically powerful foes turn on their allies.

Spell-Like Abilities: At will—*detect thoughts, dominate person, hold monster, mind fog, sleep;* 1/day—*stoneskin.* Caster level 10th; save DC 13 + spell level.

ELDER PSURLON

Elder psurlons are leaders within their communities. They are respected for their experience, resourcefulness, and superior mental abilities.

An elder psurlon stands about 5 feet tall and weighs about 130 pounds.

Combat

Elder psurlons use much the same tactics as average psurlons do, but they are more likely to direct the battle from the rear while their underlings bear the brunt of the fighting.

Spell-Like Abilities: At will—*detect thoughts, dominate person, hold monster, mass suggestion, mind fog, sleep;* 1/day—*stoneskin.* Caster level 12th; save DC 13 + spell level.

GIANT PSURLON

Giant psurlons are bred for combat. Like all psurlons, however, their mental powers are more formidable than their physical abilities.

A giant psurlon stands 12 feet tall and weighs about 600 pounds.

ombat

Giant psurlons prefer to attack from afar. After softening up the opposition with *mind fog*, a giant psurlon follows up with *disintegrate* against the most dangerous opponent.

Spell-Like Abilities: At will—*detect thoughts, dominate person, hold monster, mass suggestion, mind fog, sleep;* 1/day—*disintegrate, stoneskin.* Caster level 18th; save DC 13 + spell level.

RAGEWIND

Large Undead
Hit Dice: 31d12 (201 hp)
Initiative: +5
Speed: Fly 120 ft. (perfect)
AC: 22 (–1 size, +5 Dex, +8 deflection), touch 22, flat-footed 17
Attacks: 6 longswords +17/+12/+7 melee
Damage: Longsword 1d8+3/19–20
Face/Reach: 5 ft. by 5 ft./10 ft.
Special Attacks: Blade fury, whirlwind
Special Qualities: DR 20/+3, invisibility, see invisibility, SR 30, superior multiweapon fighting, undead traits, weapon proficiency
Saves: Fort +10, Ref +15, Will +18
Abilities: Str 17, Dex 20, Con —, Int 13, Wis 13, Cha 12
Skills: Balance +7, Hide +16, Intuit Direction +6, Jump +5, Listen +21, Search +22, Spot +22, Tumble +20
Feats: Blind-Fight, Combat Reflexes, Dodge, Expertise, Flyby Attack, Improved Disarm, Mobility, Spring Attack, Whirlwind Attack

Climate/Terrain: Any land and underground
Organization: Solitary, pair, or cluster (3–5)
Challenge Rating: 19
Treasure: None (but see below)
Alignment: Usually chaotic evil
Advancement: 32–48 HD (Large); 49–64 HD (Huge)

Also called sword spirits, ragewinds are the embodied wrath of dead warriors who perished in useless battles. They are usually found in the most volatile and violent of the Outer Planes, but a few sometimes escape to wander the Material Plane as well. On rare occasions, ragewinds

form on the Material Plane at the sites of massive battles with heavy casualties.

A ragewind normally appears as a churning whirlwind, within which dozens of suspended weapons dance and clash. Its true form is a vaguely humanoid, semisolid cloud of white or gray fog. It has no treasure other than the weapons it carries.

A ragewind can speak Common in a shrill voice that sounds like the howling of an autumn wind, but it seldom bothers to do so.

COMBAT

Though longswords are specified in the statistics given above, a ragewind may incorporate and utilize any sort of melee weapon, as long as each is at least one size category smaller than the monster. Some of these weapons may have magical properties, at the DM's option. No matter how many weapons are incorporated into the ragewind's form, it can bring no more than six of them to bear at a time.

A ragewind attacks with the weapons that are held aloft in its swirling winds. Each of these weapons functions independently, as though wielded by a different individual. The ragewind delights in disarming its opponents and using their own weapons against them. If overmatched, it uses its invisibility to escape.

Blade Fury (Su): Three times per day, a ragewind can expand itself outward into a 15-foot-radius spread, filling that entire space with its whirling weapons. This attack deals 20d6 points of slashing damage to every creature within that area (Reflex DC 26 half). Immediately after this attack, the ragewind reverts to its normal size and shape. Once it has used its blade fury attack, it must wait 1d4+1 rounds before it can do so again. A ragewind cannot benefit from both blade fury and whirlwind at the same time.

Whirlwind (Su): A ragewind can intensify the swirling air that composes its usual form to the strength of a whirlwind as a free action. When it does so, it transforms into a whirling mass of air and weapons 5 feet wide and 20 feet high. Each creature that is at least two size categories smaller than the ragewind and in contact with it must succeed at a Reflex save (DC 26) or take 3d6 points of damage. Whether or not this save is successful, an affected creature must immediately make a second Reflex save against the same DC. Failure indicates that the affected creature is picked up by

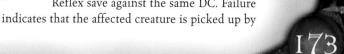

the winds and takes an additional 1d8 points of damage that round and each round thereafter that it remains suspended in the winds. (The ragewind may also direct weapon attacks at creatures caught within its whirlwind if desired, though it gains no special bonuses for doing so.) A flying creature may leave the whirlwind with a successful Reflex save, though it still takes damage for the round in which it does so.

A ragewind may also cause its whirlwind to touch the ground, kicking up a swirling cloud of debris with a 10-foot radius. This cloud obscures all vision, including darkvision, beyond 5 feet. Creatures at a distance of 5 feet have one-half concealment, and those farther away have total concealment. A creature caught in this dust cloud must succeed at a Concentration check (DC 20) to cast a spell.

Invisibility (Su): At will, a ragewind can suppress its whirlwind to become invisible. This ability otherwise functions like the *invisibility* spell (caster level 20th).

See Invisibility (Su): This ability functions like the *see invisibility* spell (caster level 20th), except that it is always active.

Superior Multiweapon Fighting (Ex): A ragewind fights with six weapons at once. Because the creature is an amalgam of many dead warriors, a separate intelligence controls each weapon. Thus, the ragewind has no penalty on attack rolls for attacking with multiple weapons, and the number of attacks and the damage bonus for each weapon are calculated as though the weapon were held in a primary hand.

Undead Traits: A ragewind is immune to mind-affecting effects, poison, *sleep*, paralysis, stunning, disease, death effects, necromantic effects, and any effect that requires a Fortitude save unless it also works on objects. It is not subject to critical hits, subdual damage, ability damage, ability drain, energy drain, or death from massive damage. A ragewind cannot be raised, and resurrection works only if it is willing. The creature has darkvision (60-foot range).

Weapon Proficiency: A ragewind is proficient with all simple and martial weapons.

RAGGAMOFFYN

Raggamoffyns are mysterious constructs composed of animated scraps and bits of cloth, metal, or other refuse from civilized societies—particularly those where magic is common. Raggamoffyns tend to cluster together, operating as much in secret as possible, taking control of selected hosts to further their agendas.

Unlike other constructs, a raggamoffyn is not the result of any deliberate act of creation. Rather, it is formed when leftover magical energy interacts with inanimate objects. The exact process is not well understood, but it always results in one of four types of raggamoffyn.

A raggamoffyn appears as an animated, ragtag assortment of odds and ends, roughly humanoid in shape. The four types differ both in the kinds of refuse that form their bodies and the powers they possess.

COMBAT

Above all, a raggamoffyn seeks to acquire a host that it can dominate. The creatures refrain from harming potential hosts as long as possible, so they work quickly by rushing in with touch attacks. A foe that is successfully dominated is wrapped by the raggamoffyn, which then uses its host to defend itself and other raggamoffyns. Raggamoffyns unleash their full melee attack capabilities against foes that are resistant to their mind controlling powers, fearing rightfully that an escaped foe will warn others of the raggamoffyn's existence.

Control Host (Su): A raggamoffyn can attempt to take control of any creature it has wrapped (see below). This ability functions like the *dominate monster* spell (caster level 18th; save DC varies; see individual descriptions). As a free action, the monster may relinquish control over its host by physically and mentally disengaging itself from the latter's body. Use the captured one template (see the appendix) for a creature under the control of a raggamoffyn.

Improved Grab (Ex): If a raggamoffyn hits an opponent that is its own size or smaller with a slam attack, it deals normal damage and attempts to start a grapple as a free action without provoking an attack of opportunity (grapple bonus varies; see individual descriptions). If it gets a hold, it can attempt to wrap (see below) in the next round. Alternatively, the raggamoffyn has the option to conduct the grapple normally, or simply use its appendage to hold the opponent (–20 penalty on grapple check, but the raggamoffyn is not considered grappled). In either case, each successful grapple check it makes during successive rounds automatically deals slam damage.

Wrap (Ex): With a successful grapple check, a raggamoffyn can wrap itself around any foe it has already grabbed with another successful grapple check. The monster forms a skintight layer around the wrapped creature, covering it from head to toe but leaving enough space for the creature to breathe through its mouth and nose. Attacks on such a target deal half their damage to the monster and half to the wrapped creature. An affected creature can extract itself by making a successful grapple check. Once it has wrapped a creature, the raggamoffyn can attempt to control it on its next action.

Construct Traits: A raggamoffyn is immune to mind-affecting effects, poison, *sleep*, paralysis, stunning, disease, death effects, necromantic effects, and any effect that requires

	Tatterdemanimal Small Construct	Common Raggamoffyn Medium-Size Construct
Hit Dice:	1d10 (5 hp)	3d10 (16 hp)
Initiative:	+5	+2
Speed:	40 ft., fly 40 ft. (clumsy)	30 ft., fly 30 ft. (clumsy)
AC:	16 (+1 size, +5 Dex), touch 16, flat-footed 11	17 (+2 Dex, +5 natural), touch 12, flat-footed 15
Attacks:	Slam +1 melee	Slam +4 melee
Damage:	Slam 1d4	Slam 1d6+3
Face/Reach:	5 ft. by 5 ft./5 ft.	5 ft. by 5 ft./5 ft.
Special Attacks:	Control host, improved grab, wrap	Control host, improved grab, suffocate, wrap
Special Qualities:	Construct traits, immunity to blunt weapons	Construct traits
Saves:	Fort +0, Ref +5, Will +4	Fort +1, Ref +3, Will +3
Abilities:	Str 10, Dex 21, Con —, Int 10, Wis 19, Cha 15	Str 14, Dex 15, Con —, Int 10, Wis 15, Cha 17
Climate/Terrain:	Any	Any
Organization:	Solitary, pair, or gang (3–6)	Solitary, pair, or gang (3–4)
Challenge Rating:	1	3
Treasure:	None	None
Alignment:	Usually chaotic neutral	Always neutral
Advancement:	2–3 HD (Small)	4 HD (Medium-size); 5–9 HD (Large)

	Guttersnipe Medium-Size Construct	Shrapnyl Large Construct
Hit Dice:	8d10 (44 hp)	12d10 (66 hp)
Initiative:	+1	+0
Speed:	20 ft., fly 20 ft. (clumsy)	20 ft., fly 10 ft. (clumsy)
AC:	21 (+1 Dex, +10 natural), touch 11, flat-footed 20	24 (–1 size, +15 natural), touch 9, flat-footed 24
Attacks:	Slam +7 melee	Slam +12 melee, or gore +12 melee
Damage:	Slam 1d6+1	Slam 1d8+4, gore 1d8+4
Face/Reach:	5 ft. by 5 ft./5 ft.	5 ft. by 5 ft./10 ft.
Special Attacks:	Control host, *glitterdust*, improved grab, wrap	Cloud of steel, control host, improved grab, wrap
Special Qualities:	Construct traits, immunities	Construct traits, vulnerability to *shatter*
Saves:	Fort +2, Ref +3, Will +5	Fort +4, Ref +4, Will +8
Abilities:	Str 13, Dex 13, Con —, Int 10, Wis 16, Cha 17	Str 18, Dex 11, Con —, Int 10, Wis 19, Cha 17
Climate/Terrain:	Any	Any
Organization:	Solitary, pair, or gang (3–4)	Solitary or pair
Challenge Rating:	5	7
Treasure:	None	None
Alignment:	Always neutral	Always neutral
Advancement:	9–16 HD (Medium-size); 17–24 HD (Large)	13–18 HD (Large); 19–36 HD (Huge)

a Fortitude save unless it also works on objects. The creature is not subject to critical hits, subdual damage, ability damage, ability drain, energy drain, or death from massive damage. It cannot heal itself but can be healed through repair. It cannot be raised or resurrected. A raggamoffyn has darkvision (60-foot range).

ATTERDEMANIMAL

Tatterdemanimals are the least powerful of the raggamoffyns. They often lurk around rubbish mounds and other places where refuse is heaped.

A tatterdemanimal appears as a swirling heap of small, dirty, tattered rags and other scraps of cloth.

Combat

Tatterdemanimals often take animals as hosts because they are the easier to capture.

Control Host (Su): The tatterdemanimal's control host ability has a Will save DC of 12.

Improved Grab (Ex): A tatterdemanimal's grapple bonus is +1.

Common   *Shrapnyl*   *Guttersnipe*   *Tatterdemanimal*

Immunity to Blunt Weapons (Ex): A tatterdemanimal takes no damage from bludgeoning weapons.

COMMON

Scholars theorize that common raggamoffyns form from enchanted gloves, robes, hats, and other magic clothing that was lost or discarded by its owners. They are usually found near cemeteries and places where magical battles have recently transpired.

A common raggamoffyn looks like a suit of mismatched clothing with no wearer. The clothing appears to be in good repair, and it would probably still be usable if it could be separated from the construct.

Combat

A common raggamoffyn directs its host creature in combat. It suffocates the host when it has either lost control over the creature or has no further use for it.

Control Host (Su): The common raggamoffyn's control host ability has a Will save DC of 14.

Improved Grab (Ex): A common raggamoffyn's grapple bonus is +4.

Suffocate (Ex): A common raggamoffyn can asphyxiate a wrapped creature by drawing the air from its lungs. This attack automatically deals 1d4 points of damage per round.

GUTTERSNIPE

Guttersnipes are most prevalent around settlements of dwarves, gnomes, and halflings. They form from worn-out and discarded adventuring and construction gear.

A guttersnipe appears as a whirling mound of frayed rope, worn leather pieces, strings, belts, and swatches of cloth. Within this mass of material is a core made of small gems, bits of glass, and glitter.

Combat

Guttersnipes are content to lie in wait for suitable hosts. They save their *glitterdust* ability to dazzle foes when they need to escape.

Control Host (Su): The guttersnipe's control host ability has a Will save DC of 17.

Glitterdust (Sp): Once per day, a guttersnipe can use *glitterdust* (caster level 5th; save DC 15).

Improved Grab (Ex): A guttersnipe's grapple bonus is +7.

Immunities (Ex): Guttersnipes are immune to spell effects that produce light or darkness.

SHRAPNYL

Shrapnyls are the only raggamoffyns made entirely of metal. They lurk near battlegrounds as well as forges.

A shrapnyl consists of bits of metal in every size. Its appearance can vary greatly—one might consist of swords, shields, and cooking gear, while another could contain a helm, coins, chains, and keys.

COMBAT

Shrapnyls are the most aggressive of the raggamoffyns. They do not hesitate to use their cloud of steel attack when faced with an overwhelming situation.

Cloud of Steel (Ex): Once per day, a shrapnyl can explode into a deadly cloud of flying, sharp debris. Every creature within a 10-foot spread centered on the shrapnyl takes 4d10 points of damage (Reflex DC 16 half). This attack instantly frees a creature wrapped by the shrapnyl from its control, and the wrapped creature takes no damage from that cloud of steel attack.

Control Host (Su): A shrapnyl's control host ability has a Will save DC of 19.

Improved Grab (Ex): A shrapnyl's grapple bonus is +17.

Vulnerability to *Shatter*: The *shatter* spell deals 3d6 points of damage to a shrapnyl.

RAMPAGER

Large Beast
Hit Dice: 14d10+70 (147 hp)
Initiative: +2
Speed: 50 ft.
AC: 23 (–1 size, +2 Dex, +12 natural), touch 11, flat-footed 21
Attacks: 2 claws +14 melee and bite +9 melee
Damage: Claw 1d6+5 plus 1d6 acid, bite 2d6+2 plus poison
Face/Reach: 5 ft. by 10 ft./5 ft.
Special Attacks: Acid, armor damage, fear aura, poison
Special Qualities: Darkvision 60-ft., low-light vision, scent
Saves: Fort +14, Ref +11, Will +6
Abilities: Str 20, Dex 15, Con 21, Int 2, Wis 15, Cha 10
Skills: Spot +12

Climate/Terrain: Temperate and warm deserts, plains, and hills
Organization: Solitary
Challenge Rating: 12
Treasure: None
Alignment: Always chaotic evil
Advancement: 15–25 HD (Large); 26–35 HD (Huge)

Rampagers (sometimes called "so-ut," their goblin name) are vicious, nocturnal predators that live only to destroy and kill. Oddly, their armor, weaponry, and aggressiveness go far beyond the levels necessary to bring down food. In fact, rampagers enjoy killing, and they usually kill far more than they can eat. In fact, as long as prey is available, a rampager doesn't even stop killing long enough to feed.

A rampager stands taller than a man (8 to 10 feet high). Its body, a solid knot of muscle, is covered with an extremely tough, scaly hide. The monster has no head as such; its face juts out from the forward edge of its body. Two bone-white eyes peer out from the scaly mass above the gaping, fang-filled mouth. From behind the face jut two muscular arms, each of which ends in two long, hooked claws. The four thick, stumplike legs are similar to those of an elephant, and a triangular, muscular tail drags behind the monster. A rampager has very poor hearing, but its scent ability makes up for that lack.

COMBAT

Something about metal drives a rampager mad. It attacks creatures wearing metal armor before anyone or anything else. Once all such targets are dead, it turns its attention to those wielding metal weapons. After all the metal nearby is demolished, the rampager starts on the largest structures in the area, ignoring even creatures that are attacking it in favor of demolishing a building (though it does defend itself once it has lost more than half of its original hit points). Only after all nearby built-up structures have been leveled does it finally turn against unarmored heroes or townspeople.

Acid (Ex): The acid that coats a rampager's claws not only deals extra damage on successful attacks, it also dissolves an opponent's armor and clothing, making those items useless in 1 round unless the wearer succeeds at a Reflex save (DC 22). Success indicates that the affected equipment can be saved by washing it within 1 minute. Washing requires a full-round action and at least 1 pint of water.

Armor Damage (Ex): A rampager's teeth can catch and tear an opponent's armor. If the opponent has both armor and a shield, roll 1d6: A roll of 1–4 affects the armor and a roll of 5–6 affects the shield. Make a grapple check (grapple bonus +19) whenever the rampager hits with a bite attack, adding to the opponent's roll any bonus for the armor or shield because of magic. If the rampager wins, the affected armor or shield is torn away and ruined.

Fear Aura (Ex): Each creature that is the target of a rampager's attack or is within 30 feet of such a target must succeed at a Will saving throw (DC 17) or become shaken. A shaken creature that is still within 30 feet of the rampager on its next turn must make a second Will saving throw (DC 17) to avoid becoming frightened (same penalties as shaken; must flee until beyond the 30-foot radius of the effect).

Poison (Ex): A rampager's acidic saliva acts as a weak poison (Fortitude DC 22) with each successful bite attack. The initial damage is 1 point of Strength damage, and the secondary damage is 1d4 points of Strength damage.

Scent (Ex): A rampager can detect approaching enemies, sniff out hidden foes, and track by sense of smell.

REASON STEALER

Medium-Size Ooze
Hit Dice: 5d10+15 (42 hp)
Initiative: −5
Speed: 10 ft., climb 10 ft.
AC: 5 (−5 Dex), touch 5, flat-footed 5
Attacks: Slam +5 melee, or weapon +5 melee and slam +0 melee
Damage: Slam 1d6+3 (primary), by weapon +3, slam 1d6+1 (secondary)
Face/Reach: 5 ft. by 5 ft./5 ft.
Special Attacks: Devour mind, improved grab
Special Qualities: Blindsight 60 ft., DR 20/+1, grotesque form, ooze traits
Saves: Fort +2, Ref −4, Will −4
Abilities: Str 14, Dex 1, Con 12, Int —, Wis 1, Cha 1

Climate/Terrain: Any underground
Organization: Solitary
Challenge Rating: 5
Treasure: None
Alignment: Always neutral
Advancement: 6–10 HD (Medium-size); 11–15 HD (Large)

The reason stealer is a relentless, subterranean killer that murders other creatures to steal their intelligence. Reason stealers live below ground but make their way to the surface to hunt.

In its normal form, a reason stealer is a 4-foot-diameter puddle of grainy, brownish-yellow slime. If it has recently fed upon a creature possessing some form of intelligence, it can roughly mimic its victim's shape. Such an assumed form is misshapen and blobby, and it only vaguely resembles the creature that the reason stealer killed.

A reason stealer doesn't speak any language. When it steals a creature's mind, it randomly mumbles words in that creature's language.

COMBAT

A reason stealer lashes out at prey with a sticky pseudopod. Upon delivering the death blow to a foe with its pseudopod, it steals the opponent's intellect. Once a reason stealer gains a modicum of sentience, it becomes a far deadlier opponent because it can use all the skills, feats, and spells it has absorbed from its prey. Sentient reason stealers ceaselessly search for new prey because they are desperate to avoid returning to their previous mindless state.

Devour Mind (Su): A reason stealer transfers an opponent's Intelligence score to itself upon dealing it a killing blow with a slam attack. This process also heals the monster of 5 points of damage per point of Intelligence gained. Upon devouring a mind, the reason stealer has access to any of the dead opponent's other ability scores, skill ranks, base attack bonus, and base save bonuses, and it can use any of these characteristics that are higher than its own. It also gains the use of the opponent's feats and any prepared arcane spells. The reason stealer understands that it must remove spell components from a victim's body to cast spells. All these acquired features last for 24 hours. If a reason stealer devours the mind of a victim while it still has the abilities of a previous one, it uses the higher of the two (the new victim's or its current value) for ability scores, base attack bonus, base save bonuses, and skill ranks. It also gains any feats and spells possessed by the new victim that it did not already have.

Improved Grab (Ex): If a reason stealer hits an opponent that is its own size or smaller with a slam attack, it deals normal damage and attempts to start a grapple as a free action without provoking an attack of opportunity (grapple bonus +9, including a +4 racial bonus on grapple attacks from the sticky substance that covers its pseudopod). If it gets a hold, it has the option to conduct the grapple normally, or simply use its pseudopod to hold the opponent (−20 penalty on grapple check, but the reason stealer is not considered grappled). In either case, each successful grapple check it makes during successive rounds automatically deals slam damage.

Blindsight (Ex): A reason stealer is blind, but its entire body is a primitive sensory organ that can ascertain prey by scent and vibration. This ability enables it to discern objects and creatures within 60 feet. A reason stealer usually does not need to make Spot or Listen checks to notice creatures within range of its blindsight.

Grotesque Form (Su): A reason stealer that has devoured the mind of a creature with an Intelligence score of 1 or higher can shape its body into a bizarre reflection of that creature. If the reason stealer has abilities gained from more than one creature, it assumes a form similar to the last one it killed. A reason stealer with a humanoid form can wield weapons, using the fighting skills of any victims it devoured. It always retains one pseudopod with which to attack. A reason stealer can maintain a grotesque form as long as it has an Intelligence score.

Ooze Traits: A reason stealer is immune to mind-affecting effects, poison, *sleep*, paralysis, stunning, and polymorphing. It is not subject to critical hits or flanking.

RED SUNDEW

Huge Plant
Hit Dice: 15d8+75 (142 hp)
Initiative: –1
Speed: 20 ft.
AC: 11 (–2 size, –1 Dex, +4 natural), touch 7, flat-footed 11
Attacks: 4 slams +18 melee
Damage: Slam 2d6+9 plus acid
Face/Reach: 10 ft. by 10 ft./15 ft.
Special Attacks: Improved grab, sticky acid
Special Qualities: Immunities, plant traits, woodsense
Saves: Fort +14, Ref +4, Will +6
Abilities: Str 29, Dex 8, Con 21, Int 2, Wis 13, Cha 8

Climate/Terrain: Temperate and warm forests
Organization: Solitary or patch (2–5)
Challenge Rating: 13
Treasure: None
Alignment: Always neutral
Advancement: 16–28 HD (Huge); 29–45 HD (Gargantuan)

Red sundews are vicious, migratory predators that roam forested areas hunting for unwary prey. Unlike many carnivorous plants, the red sundew is highly nomadic, so it rarely remains in one geographic area for long. Though they are found primarily in coastal forests and hot jungles, red sundews can also inhabit cooler woodlands far from these wet areas.

A red sundew measures almost 20 feet high and 10 feet across. Its body looks like a wide mound of tangled, ropy rags in red, green, and rust colors. These "rags" are actually ropelike vines coated with a sweet-smelling goo, which gives the plant a slick, wet appearance. Underneath the mass of vines, a red sundew has a single stem that measures about 12 feet high and 5 feet across. This stem is supported by two leglike appendages.

A red sundew begins digesting its prey during combat, smearing the sticky acid that coats its entire body over its opponent. Once the opponent dies, the red sundew uses its tentacles to draw the corpse inside its body mass, where it continues the digestion process.

COMBAT

Red sundews are aggressive hunters. They attack with their tentacles, wrapping them firmly around prey to prevent escape while the sticky acid that coats their tentacles begins the digestion process. Multiple red sundews often travel together and combine their efforts while hunting. These carnivorous plants flee when more than half their number has been slain.

Improved Grab (Ex): If a red sundew hits an opponent that is at least one size category smaller than itself with a slam attack, it deals normal damage and attempts to start a grapple as a free action without provoking an attack of opportunity (grapple bonus +28). If it gets a hold, it has the option to conduct the grapple normally, or simply use its tentacle to hold the opponent (–20 penalty on grapple check, but the red sundew is not considered grappled). In either case, each successful grapple check it makes during successive rounds automatically deals slam damage.

Sticky Acid (Ex): A red sundew is coated with a thick, acidic goo. Any creature or object that makes physical contact with the monster is smeared with this sticky acid, which deals 1d6 points of acid damage per round until removed. Thus, any successful hit from or against the red sundew automatically deals acid damage to the opponent or the opponent's weapon, depending upon the point of contact. Sticky acid remains on a creature or object for 1d4+1 rounds. It cannot be scraped off, but it can be washed off with a full-round action and at least 1 gallon of water.

Immunities (Ex): Red sundews are immune to fire and acid.

Plant Traits (Ex): A red sundew is immune to poison, *sleep*, paralysis, stunning, and polymorphing. It is not subject to critical hits or mind-affecting effects. The creature also has low-light vision.

Woodsense (Ex): A red sundew can automatically sense the location of anything within 60 feet that is in contact with vegetation, even objects or creatures that are not in contact with the same vegetation as itself.

ROGUE EIDOLON

Large Construct
Hit Dice: 9d10 (49 hp)
Initiative: +0
Speed: 30 ft. (can't run)
AC: 21 (–1 size, +12 natural), touch 9, flat-footed 21
Attacks: 2 slams +10 melee
Damage: Slam 2d6+5
Face/Reach: 5 ft. by 5 ft./10 ft.
Special Attacks: Blood spray, *confusion*
Special Qualities: Construct traits, DR 20/+2, SR 19
Saves: Fort +3, Ref +3, Will +1
Abilities: Str 21, Dex 11, Con —, Int 2, Wis 6, Cha 13

Climate/Terrain: Any
Organization: Solitary
Challenge Rating: 9
Treasure: None
Alignment: Always chaotic neutral
Advancement: 10–18 HD (Large); 19–27 HD (Huge)

Many centuries ago, hidden cults of various dark gods created large statues in the images of their leaders. The faces of these statues were left blank, except for the symbols of their deities, to indicate each god's mastery over its followers. These statues were placed at honored locations in temples where they presided over countless sacrifices.

A dark deity that was especially pleased with a particular cult cell sometimes sent the tiniest shred of its power across the dimensions to infuse that cult's statue, granting it minimal sentience. Over the years, these divinely powered constructs went insane, becoming rogue eidolons consumed with murderous rage. Most of them destroyed the cults over which they presided, down to the last member, then went on to find other victims.

A rogue eidolon is typically 12 to 14 feet tall and usually has a humanoid shape. It is always constructed of purple stone (often magically treated to achieve that distinctive color), and its hands are pitch black. Its face is blank except for a crude symbol or rune (the symbol of an evil deity) carved into the otherwise featureless visage. This symbol leaks a thick, viscous fluid that looks like blood and has a sharp, metallic odor. Drops of this disgusting fluid evaporate within minutes of falling to the ground, leaving vivid red stains where they fell. Beyond that, one rogue eidolon differs wildly from the next in appearance, though most are badly weathered and possess monstrous deformities, such as horns, a hunched back, tumorous lumps, or misshapen limbs.

COMBAT

A rogue eidolon usually attacks any living creature it encounters, but the nature of its insanity makes it completely unpredictable. Occasionally a rogue eidolon simply ignores intruders, perhaps believing them to be loyal cult members or simply animals unworthy of its attention. At other times, it may attack and even pursue the same group, believing its members to be infidels and enemies.

The monster attacks by smashing victims with its stony fists. Tactics mean little to it, and its attacks are so single-minded that it often ignores easier targets once it has selected a victim.

Blood Spray (Su): As a free action, a rogue eidolon can spew a gout of thick blood from the seeping symbol in its face at a single target within 30 feet. Any creature struck by this blood must make a Will save (DC 15) or be afflicted with a terrible madness that causes it to see all its friends as hated enemies. An affected creature immediately attacks its closest ally, using the best tactics and items at its disposal. This murderous frenzy prevents spellcasting but not the activation of magic items that require spell completion, and it lasts for 3d6 rounds. Once a rogue eidolon has used its blood spray, it must wait 1d4 rounds before it can do so again.

Confusion (Sp): Any creature struck by a rogue eidolon must make a Will save (DC 15) or become confused. This condition is permanent; only a *greater restoration, limited wish, miracle,* or *wish* spell can restore the subject to normal. The effect is otherwise identical with that of a *confusion* spell (caster level 10th).

Construct Traits: A rogue eidolon is immune to mind-affecting effects, poison, *sleep,* paralysis, stunning, disease, death effects, necromantic effects, and any effect that requires a Fortitude save unless it also works on objects. The creature is not subject to critical hits, subdual damage, ability damage, ability drain, energy drain, or death from massive damage. It cannot heal itself but can be healed through repair. It cannot be raised or resurrected. A rogue eidolon has darkvision (60-foot range).

RUKARAZYLL

Large Outsider (Earth, Evil)

Hit Dice: 12d8+48 (102 hp)

Initiative: +8

Speed: 70 ft., climb 50 ft.

AC: 23 (−1 size, +8 Dex, +3 natural, +3 profane), touch 20, flat-footed 12

Attacks: 3 tendrils +19 melee and bite +4 melee, or spit ooze +19 ranged

Damage: Tendril 1d6−2, bite 1d6−2 plus 2d4 acid

Face/Reach: 5 ft. by 5 ft./10 ft.

Special Attacks: Fungus, spell-like abilities, spit ooze

Special Qualities: DR 20/+2, evasion, outsider traits, profane alacrity, SR 23

Saves: Fort +12, Ref +16, Will +11

Abilities: Str 6, Dex 27, Con 19, Int 18, Wis 17, Cha 18

Skills: Balance +22, Bluff +19, Climb +6, Concentration +14, Diplomacy +8, Disguise +19, Escape Artist +16, Forgery +9, Hide +14, Intimidate +19, Jump +0, Knowledge (religion) +12, Search +9, Sense Motive +18, Spellcraft +12, Spot +8, Tumble +23

Feats: Expertise, Improved Disarm, Improved Trip, Weapon Finesse (tendril)

Climate/Terrain: Any

Organization: Solitary, pair, or cell (3–12)

Challenge Rating: 14

Treasure: Double standard

Alignment: Always chaotic evil

Advancement: 13–24 HD (Large); 25–36 HD (Huge)

Rukarazylls are consummate deceivers and tricksters. When summoned to the Material Plane (usually from the Elemental Plane of Earth), they delight in masquerading as charismatic men or women. In such guises, they often attempt to convince locals to establish cults dedicated to apparently benign (but altogether fabricated) minor deities. Over time, the rukarazyll slowly perverts the followers of such cults to the worship of an evil deity. When it doesn't have the time or resources to seed cults, a rukarazyll contents itself with selling cursed items that it passes off as beneficial, or posing as a priest and inflicting diseases on those seeking healing, or pursuing other underhanded and cruel tricks.

In its true form, a rukarazyll is a loathsome creature. Its body is a bulbous mass of seething fungoid matter, studded with eyes and gasping orifices that leak stinking, black drool. It has six long, hook-studded tendrils that extrude from various random points on its body. Three of these tendrils serve as legs; the other three serve as hands. Extending from the top of the body is a long scaly tentacle, atop which sits a head that resembles a ram's skull, complete with horns. Great fangs stud the rukarazyll's lipless mouth, from which bubbling acidic froth constantly dribbles. Writhing nests of pale fungal filaments fill its eye sockets, and more of these filaments grow out of other random spots all over its body. The monster's natural voice is thick and gurgling, as if its throat were partially clogged with mud, but it can disguise its voice as well as its body when it adopts another form.

COMBAT

The rukarazyll is physically weak, but it makes up for its lack of strength with speed and accuracy granted by the unholy energy it channels. It enjoys melee combat so much that it often forgoes its spell-like abilities if a chance to fight presents itself.

Combat with a rukarazyll is both disorienting and terrifying. As a full attack action, the monster can strike with three of its tendrils and bite with its acidic jaws. It takes full advantage of its feats, using Expertise to best effect and Improved Trip and Improved Disarm as opportunities arise. It also relies on its Tumble skill to avoid drawing attacks of opportunity as it weaves about.

Fungus (Su): Any living creature struck by a rukarazyll's melee attack must make a Fortitude saving throw (DC 20) or become infested with the fecund fungus that grows on the monster's body. Infestation requires 1 round for a Small or smaller creature or 1d4 rounds for a Medium-size creature. Each size category larger than Medium-size adds an extra 1d4 rounds to the infestation time. An affected creature can free itself of the fungus before infestation is complete with either a *remove disease* spell or by taking 10 points of fire or cold damage.

Once infestation is complete, the fibrous white filaments begin to seethe and twist in the host's body, actively trying to resist any actions the host attempts. Because of this, the host incurs a –2 penalty on all attack rolls, Dexterity-based skill checks, and Reflex saving throws. In addition, the fungus continues to grow in the host's body (albeit at a much slower rate), dealing 1 point of Charisma drain per day. A host whose Charisma reaches 0 becomes unconscious, and within 1 hour his or her body transforms into an immobile heap of fungus that lives for 3d6 weeks before perishing. Any creature that comes into contact with one of these transformed bodies must make a successful Fortitude saving throw (DC 20) or become infested, with the same onset time and effects as infestation from the rukarazyll itself. A *remove disease* spell given after infestation is complete destroys the fungus but does not restore lost Charisma.

Spell-Like Abilities: At will—*alter self, blur, cat's grace, darkness, desecrate, detect good, detect magic, entangle, mirror image, plant growth, protection from good, snare, telekinesis, teleport without error* (self plus 50 pounds of objects only), *undetectable alignment*; 3/day—*polymorph self, unhallow, unholy blight*; 1/day—*command plants, contagion, heal, wall of thorns.* Caster level 12th; save DC 14 + spell level.

Spit Ooze (Su): Once every 10 minutes, a rukarazyll can expel a Medium-size gray ooze (see the *Monster Manual*) from its mouth as a grenadelike weapon with a 10-foot range increment. If it hits a target, the gray ooze can immediately attempt to use its improved grab ability and constrict if it gets a hold. If the attack misses, determine miss distance and direction normally. The ooze then moves to attack in the next round. Gray oozes created in this manner live only 2d4 rounds, dissolving into pools of gray goo when that duration expires.

Evasion (Ex): If exposed to any effect that normally allows a Reflex save for half damage, a rukarazyll takes no damage on a successful save.

Outsider Traits: A rukarazyll has darkvision (60-foot range). It cannot be raised or resurrected.

Profane Alacrity (Su): A rukarazyll is infused with an unholy energy that grants it improved reflexes and speed. This energy gives the monster a +3 profane bonus to AC and allows it to take 10 on Balance, Escape Artist, and Tumble checks in any circumstance. Once per hour, a rukarazyll can call upon its profane alacrity ability to gain a temporary boost to its movement, doubling both its speed and the profane bonus to its AC for 1 minute. Afterward, the rukarazyll's profane energy is depleted for 1 hour. During this period, it has no profane bonus to AC and cannot take 10 on Balance, Escape Artist, or Tumble checks except in circumstances that would ordinarily allow it.

Large Construct
Hit Dice: 17d10 (93 hp)
Initiative: +1
Speed: 30 ft.
AC: 28 (–1 size, +1 Dex, +18 natural), touch 10, flat-footed 27
Attacks: Slam +18/+13/+8 melee
Damage: Slam 2d8+10 plus stunning strike
Face/Reach: 5 ft. by 5 ft./10 ft.
Special Attacks: Runic spells, stunning strike
Special Qualities: Construct traits, DR 30/+3, fast healing 10, find master, guard, *shield master, teleport without error*
Saves: Fort +5, Ref +6, Will +5
Abilities: Str 24, Dex 13, Con —, Int —, Wis 11, Cha 1

Climate/Terrain: Any land or underground
Organization: Solitary
Challenge Rating: 10
Treasure: None
Alignment: Always neutral
Advancement: 18–25 HD (Large); 26–51 HD (Huge)

Runic guardians are constructs similar to shield guardians (see the *Monster Manual*), but with far superior physical and magical capabilities. Runic guardians are especially popular among dwarves and giants, though spellcasters of all races find them useful.

A runic guardian is a massive, human-shaped figure made of stone, steel, and lead. Its hands and arms are constructed of hollow stone and filled with lead for a more deadly punch. Carved, magic runes inlaid with precious metals adorn its head, limbs and torso. Whenever a runic guardian casts a spell, these runes flare up into a variety of brilliant colors.

A runic guardian serves one master that is designated at the time of its creation, and no other. The construct is keyed to a specific, unique piece of jewelry (normally a ring or amulet) worn by its master and made at the time of its creation. The master can use this piece of jewelry to call the runic guardian to his or her side from any distance, or even from another plane. A runic guardian knows whether or not the bearer of its jewelry is really its master, and it slays any pretenders outright.

COMBAT

In battle, a runic guardian protects its master by casting predetermined defensive spells upon him or her, then pounding away at foes with its leaden fists. Runic guardians equipped with offensive spells use them only when directly commanded to do so. A runic guardian is instantly aware of its master's death, whether or not it was present at the time. When the master's death

occurs, the construct immediately goes on a rampage, attacking all creatures within sight. Possession of its jewelry in such a circumstance gains the bearer neither control over the construct nor safety from its attacks. The runic guardian does not stop until destroyed.

Runic Spells (Sp): A runic guardian can hold up to six spells. These spells must be cast into its body when it is created. One spell can be placed on the runic guardian's head, one on each limb, and one on its torso. The table below gives the maximum level of spell that each of its body parts can hold. Alternatively, the entire guardian can accommodate a single inscribed spell of 6th or 7th level, but this covers its whole body.

Body Part	Highest Spell Level
Head	1st
Each arm	2nd
Each leg	3rd
Torso	5th

Each of these spells is usable once per day as a spell-like ability. The runic guardian discharges a spell either when directly commanded to do so or when a predetermined situation arises.

Stunning Strike (Ex): Any creature hit by a runic guardian's slam attack must make a successful Fortitude saving throw (DC 25) or be stunned (unable to act, loses any Dexterity bonus to AC, and an attacker gets a +2 bonus on attack rolls against it) for 1 round, in addition to taking the normal damage from the blow. Constructs, oozes, plants, undead, incorporeal creatures, and creatures immune to critical hits cannot be stunned.

Construct Traits: A runic guardian is immune to mind-affecting effects, poison, *sleep*, paralysis, stunning, disease, death effects, necromantic effects, and any effect that requires a Fortitude save unless it also works on objects. The creature is not subject to critical hits, subdual damage, ability damage, ability drain, energy drain, or death from massive damage. It cannot heal itself but can be healed through repair. It cannot be raised or resurrected. A runic guardian has darkvision (60-foot range).

Fast Healing (Ex): A runic guardian regains lost hit points at the rate of 10 per round. Fast healing does not restore hit points lost from starvation, thirst, or suffocation, and it does not allow the runic guardian to regrow or reattach lost body parts.

Find Master (Su): No matter the distance, a runic guardian can find the piece of jewelry that connects it with its master, and it teleports to that spot when called. (Should the master call the construct and then remove the jewelry, the runic guardian finds only the jewelry upon its arrival.) This ability functions even across planar boundaries.

Guard (Ex): The runic guardian blocks blows, granting its master a +4 deflection bonus to AC. This power functions only when the runic guardian is within 5 feet of its master.

Shield Master (Sp): A runic guardian's master, when in possession of the keyed piece of jewelry, can activate this defensive ability when within 150 feet of the construct. *Shield master* transfers three-fourths of the damage that would otherwise be dealt to the master to the runic guardian instead. This ability otherwise functions like the *shield other* spell (caster level 25th), except that it provides no AC or saving throw bonuses.

Teleport without Error (Sp): Once per day, a runic guardian can use *teleport without error* (caster level 18th). It normally uses this ability to answer a call from its master, teleporting unerringly to his or her side.

CONSTRUCTION

The process for creating a runic guardian is nearly identical with that for creating a shield guardian. A runic guardian costs 200,000 gp to create. This price includes the construct's physical body, the keyed piece of jewelry, and all the materials and spell components that are consumed or become a permanent part of the guardian.

Creating the body requires a successful Profession (engineer) or Craft (sculpting) check (DC 20). The creation of the keyed jewelry item requires a successful Craft (metalworking) check (DC 15). This jewelry is always made of the same metals and other materials as the guardian's runes.

After the body and jewelry are constructed, the creature must be animated through magical rites that require one month to complete. The creator must be at least 16th level and have the Craft Wondrous Item feat. The creator must cast any spells he or she wishes to place on the runic guardian personally at this time, though they may come from an outside source such as a scroll. The creator must labor for at least 8 hours per day in a specially prepared workroom or laboratory that costs 2,000 gp to establish.

SHADOW SPIDER

Huge Magical Beast
Hit Dice: 13d10+65 (136 hp)
Initiative: +5
Speed: 50 ft., climb 30 ft.
AC: 13 (−2 size, +1 Dex, +4 natural), touch 9, flat-footed 12
Attacks: 4 claws +19 melee and bite +17 melee
Damage: 4 claws 2d4+8, bite 2d6+4 plus paralysis
Face/Reach: 15 ft. by 15 ft./10 ft.
Special Attacks: Improved grab, paralysis, silk slick
Special Qualities: Darkvision 60 ft., DR 15/+1, low-light vision, *shadow walk*, SR 23
Saves: Fort +13, Ref +11, Will +5
Abilities: Str 26, Dex 13, Con 20, Int 5, Wis 13, Cha 8
Skills: Climb +21, Hide −2*, Listen +5, Spot +6
Feats: Improved Initiative, Lightning Reflexes, Multiattack

Climate/Terrain: Any underground
Organization: Solitary
Challenge Rating: 12
Treasure: Standard
Alignment: Always neutral
Advancement: 14–26 HD (Huge); 27–39 HD (Gargantuan)

Shadow spiders are carnivorous ambush predators from the Plane of Shadow that prefer to hunt on the Material Plane. They possess frightening intelligence and cunning.

A shadow spider is a huge, shadowy arachnid. It has a 5-foot-diameter body and stands roughly 2 1/2 feet tall. Its eight eyes are such a deep red color that they appear black.

A shadow spider maintains a larder (actually a pocket in the Plane of Shadow) stacked with the desiccated corpses of its prey. The monster never carries treasure; it simply leaves its victims' possessions on the corpses. When its larder becomes overfilled, the shadow spider abandons it and finds a new one to fill with food.

Shadow spiders speak Common.

COMBAT

A shadow spider prepares elaborate traps for its victims in dungeons and caverns. It uses its silk slick ability to make a slope or stair slippery, then waits in the shadows at the bottom. When a creature falls, the shadow spider steps out of the shadows and attempts to grab its prey with its four foreclaws. If successful, the monster uses *shadow walk* to carry the victim to its larder in the Plane of Shadow. Once there, the shadow spider paralyzes and abandons that creature, then returns to its trap for more prey. Only when there are no more

creatures, or it is in danger of dying, does a shadow spider return to its larder and begin eating. Shadow spiders never clean up their traps, so adventurers occasionally get forewarning of one from the dropped items (belongings of past victims) that litter the area.

Improved Grab (Ex): If a shadow spider hits an opponent that is at least one size category smaller than itself with two claw attacks, it deals normal damage and attempts to start a grapple as a free action without provoking an attack of opportunity (grapple bonus +29). If it gets a hold, it has the option to conduct the grapple normally, or simply use two claws to hold the opponent (−20 penalty on grapple check, but the shadow spider is not considered grappled). In either case, each successful grapple check it makes during successive rounds automatically deals damage for two claw attacks.

Paralysis (Ex): A shadow spider's teeth are coated with a paralyzing fluid. Any creature hit by its bite must make a successful Fortitude save (DC 21) or be paralyzed for 4 rounds.

Silk Slick (Su): As a full-round action, a shadow spider can spray a layer of spider silk over any solid surface. It can cover up to 100 square feet with this substance, which dries and evaporates in 13 rounds. The slick silk functions in all other respects like a *grease* spell (caster level 13th; Reflex save DC 21).

Shadow Walk **(Sp):** At will, a shadow spider can use *shadow walk* (caster level 10th; Will save DC 16).

Skills: *A shadow spider gets a +20 circumstance bonus on Hide checks when in shadows.

SIRINE

Medium-Size Fey (Aquatic)
Hit Dice: 4d6 (14 hp)
Initiative: +4
Speed: 30 ft., swim 60 ft.
AC: 17 (+4 Dex, +3 deflection), touch 17, flat-footed 13
Attacks: Short sword +2 melee, or touch +2 melee touch
Damage: Short sword 1d6/19–20, touch 1d4 Int
Face/Reach: 5 ft. by 5 ft./5 ft.
Special Attacks: *Charming song,* Intelligence damage, spell-like abilities
Special Qualities: Deflection, low-light vision, soothing touch
Saves: Fort +1, Ref +8, Will +7
Abilities: Str 10, Dex 18, Con 11, Int 13, Wis 16, Cha 17
Skills: Animal Empathy +10, Concentration +7, Heal +10, Hide +11, Perform (dancing, singing, plus one other) +14, Swim +15, Wilderness Lore +10
Feats: Dodge, Expertise

Climate/Terrain: Temperate or warm aquatic
Organization: Solitary or family (3–8)
Challenge Rating: 5
Treasure: Standard
Alignment: Usually chaotic neutral
Advancement: 5–8 HD (Medium-size)

Sirines are playful, gregarious creatures that love to sing, swim, dance, and laugh. They frequently draw strangers into their games and parties, but they rarely grant such visitors more than a few hours of their time.

A sirine appears to be a normal human woman in most respects, although its skin often has a noticeable yellow or green tinge. The hair can be any normal, human hair color, or it can be lustrous silver or dark green. A sirine wears only lightweight clothing while on land and often nothing at all while in the water. The typical sirine carries a short sword or dagger at all times.

Although sirines are always happy to have fun with strangers, they are extremely reclusive about their communities. They take care to seek camaraderie only when away from their homes, and then only for a short while. Any creature that follows a sirine home, or stumbles upon that location accidentally, is likely to come under attack.

After a few hours, most sirines have had enough of the companionship of other creatures, so they slip away, usually by diving underwater. For a stranger, and particularly a male, earning the trust of a sirine is nearly impossible. These creatures trust no one except other sirines, though in time of need they do accept any offered aid. Such assistance does not earn the giver any more of a sirine's company than would otherwise have been bestowed, however, nor does the creature feel obligated to reward its benefactor in any way. Occasionally a sirine bestows a gift, usually a small gem, seashell, or other trinket, on an admirer who has been particularly charming company.

COMBAT

Sirines are not especially tough in a stand-up fight, but they excel at evading and escaping from enemies. They rarely let themselves get drawn into battle unless their homes are threatened. Instead, they use their spell-like abilities and special attacks to slip away, or use a combination of singing and Intelligence drain to incapacitate foes and then dump them far away where they can cause no harm.

Approxmiately one-third of all sirines are proficient with bows, javelins, or slings. About one in ten sirines has a magic weapon, usually a *javelin of lightning.*

Charming Song (Sp): At will, a sirine can sing a special song that functions like a *charm person* spell (caster level 2nd; save DC 14), except that it lasts for 11 hours and affects every creature that hears it.

Intelligence Damage (Su): Any creature hit by a sirine's touch attack takes 1d4 points of Intelligence damage (or 2d4 points on a critical hit).

Spell-Like Abilities: 1/day—*fog cloud, improved invisibility, polymorph self.* Caster level 11th; save DC 13 + spell level.

Deflection (Su): A sirine is surrounded by an aura that grants it a deflection bonus to AC equal to its Charisma bonus.

Soothing Touch (Su): A sirine, if it desires, can use its touch to restore 1d6 points of Intelligence damage caused by any sirine.

Skills: A sirine receives a +8 racial bonus on Perform checks.

COMBAT

Medium-Size Undead

Hit Dice: 4d12+3 (29 hp)

Initiative: −1

Speed: 30 ft.

AC: 11 (−1 Dex, +2 natural), touch 9, flat-footed 11

Attacks: Slam +6 melee, or touch +6 melee touch, or Kyuss's gift +1 ranged touch

Damage: Slam 1d6+6 and Kyuss's gift

Special Attacks: Create spawn, fear aura, Kyuss's gift

Special Qualities: Curative transformation, fast healing 5, turn resistance +2, undead traits

Saves: Fort +1, Ref +0, Will +4

Abilities: Str 18, Dex 9, Con —, Int 6, Wis 11, Cha 15

Skills: Hide +5, Jump +10, Move Silently +5, Spot +6

Feats: Toughness

Climate/Terrain: Any land and underground

Organization: Solitary, pair, shamble (3–4), or horde (3–4 plus 1–6 Huge or larger zombies)

Challenge Rating: 5

Treasure: None

Alignment: Always chaotic evil

Advancement: 5–8 HD (Medium-size); 9–12 HD (Large)

Spawn of Kyuss are disgusting undead creatures created by Kyuss, a powerful evil cleric turned demigod. Completely mad, the spawn of Kyuss wander caverns, crypts, and sometimes the open countryside searching for victims.

A spawn of Kyuss looks like a well-rotted zombie. Only once the monster is within 20 feet do the writhing, green worms crawling in and out of its skull orifices become apparent. A spawn of Kyuss is usually clad in rotted clothing, though a rare few wear decaying pieces of armor.

A cleric of 16th level or higher may use a *create greater undead* spell to create new spawn of Kyuss. This process requires maggots from the corpse of a diseased creature in addition to the normal material components.

Spawn of Kyuss split into multiple smaller groups when creating their own spawn, and it is rare to encounter more than three of them together. Occasionally a larger creature falls under the curse of a spawn of Kyuss and follows it as a normal zombie (see below).

Unlike zombies, spawn of Kyuss are not limited to partial actions, and they are intelligent enough to pretend that they have restricted movement until ready to attack. They normally use their fear auras to scatter victims, then gang up on individuals until they have caught all opponents.

Create Spawn (Su): Once per round as a free action, a spawn of Kyuss can transfer a worm from its own body to that of an opponent. It can do this whenever it hits with a slam attack, but it can also make the transfer by means of a successful melee touch attack or a ranged touch attack, hurling a worm at a foe from a distance of up to 10 feet.

Each worm is a Fine vermin with AC 10 and 1 hit point. It can be killed with normal damage or by the touch of silver. On the spawn's next action, the worm burrows into its host's flesh. (A creature with a natural armor bonus of +5 or higher is immune to this burrowing effect.) The worm makes its way toward the host's brain, dealing 1 point of damage per round for 1d4+1 rounds. At the end of that period, it reaches the brain. While the worm is inside a victim, a *remove curse* or *remove disease* effect destroys it, and a *dispel evil* or *neutralize poison* effect delays its progress for 10d6 minutes. A successful Heal check (DC 20) extracts the worm and kills it.

Once the worm reaches the brain, it deals 1d2 points of Intelligence damage per round until it either is killed (by *remove curse* or *remove disease*) or slays its host (death occurs at 0 Intelligence). A Small, Medium-size, or Large creature slain by a worm rises as a new spawn of Kyuss 1d6+4 rounds later; a Tiny or smaller creature quickly putrefies; and a Huge or larger creature becomes a normal zombie of the appropriate size. Newly created spawn are not under the control of their parent, but they usually follow whatever spawn of Kyuss created them.

Fear Aura (Su): A spawn of Kyuss continuously radiates a fear effect. This ability functions like a *fear* spell (caster level 7th; Will save DC 14), except that it affects all creatures within a 40-foot radius. Any creature that makes a successful saving throw against the effect cannot be affected again by the fear aura of that spawn of Kyuss for 24 hours.

Kyuss's Gift (Su): Any creature hit by a spawn of Kyuss's slam attack must succeed at a Fortitude save (DC 12) or contract this supernatural disease. The incubation period is 1 day, and the disease deals 1d6 points of Constitution damage and 1d4 points of Wisdom damage (see Disease in Chapter 3 of the *Dungeon Master's Guide*).

These effects manifest as rotting flesh and dementia. An affected creature gets only half the benefits of natural and magical healing, though a *cure disease* effect removes the affliction.

Curative Transformation (Ex): Any *remove curse* or *remove disease* effect, or a more powerful version of either of these effects, transforms a spawn of Kyuss into a normal zombie.

Fast Healing (Ex): A spawn of Kyuss regains lost hit points at the rate of 5 per round. Fast healing does not restore hit points lost from starvation, thirst, or suffocation, and it does not allow the spawn of Kyuss to regrow or reattach lost body parts.

Turn Resistance (Ex): A spawn of Kyuss is treated as an undead with 6 Hit Dice for the purpose of turn, rebuke, command, and bolster attempts.

Undead Traits: A spawn of Kyuss is immune to mind-affecting effects, poison, *sleep*, paralysis, stunning, disease, death effects, necromantic effects, and any effect that requires a Fortitude save unless it also works on objects. It is not subject to critical hits, subdual damage, ability damage, ability drain, energy drain, or death from massive damage. A spawn of Kyuss cannot be raised, and resurrection works only if it is willing. The creature has darkvision (60-foot range).

SPELL WEAVER

Medium-Size Monstrous Humanoid
Hit Dice: 10d8–10 (36 hp)
Initiative: +3
Speed: 30 ft.
AC: 18 (+3 Dex, +5 natural), touch 13, flat-footed 15
Attacks: 2 slams +9
Damage: Slam 1d3–1
Face/Reach: 5 ft. by 5 ft./5 ft.
Special Attacks: Spell-like abilities, spells
Special Qualities: Chromatic disk, darkvision 60 ft., immunity to mind effects, shielded mind, spell weaving, SR 21, telepathy
Saves: Fort +2, Ref +10, Will +10
Abilities: Str 9, Dex 16, Con 9, Int 18, Wis 17, Cha 16
Skills: Knowledge (arcana) +13, Scry +14, Spellcraft +17, Spot +12, Use Magic Device +15
Feats: Empower Spell, Enlarge Spell, Extend Spell, Heighten Spell, Spell Focus (Abjuration), Spell Focus (Evocation), Spell Penetration

Climate/Terrain: Any land
Organization: Solitary or raid (3–6)
Challenge Rating: 10
Treasure: Double items (magic items only)
Alignment: Usually neutral
Advancement: 11–30 HD (Medium-size)

These creatures are enigmatic in the extreme. Outside of the fact that they covet magic items, little is known about them. Most encounters with spell weavers occur when they attempt to purloin magic items from other creatures.

A spell weaver is a scrawny, hairless, six-armed creaure about 5 feet tall. It is humanoid in shape, with a vaguely birdlike face and large, dark eyes. A long neck allows it to twist and turn its face in any direction.

Usually only one spell weaver is encountered at a time, but occasionally these monsters organize themselves into a raiding party to seize a particular item. Such a raid is extremely well planned and is usually the result of months of investigation conducted through a combination of scrying and simple spying—an activity made easier by the spell weaver's *invisibility* power. Spell weavers do not communicate with anyone except their own kind. This means, of course, that no one has ever had a meaningful conversation with a spell weaver, so nothing is known about the background, motivations, or society of these creatures other than what their actions reveal. Occasionally, for reasons that no one else understands, a spell weaver leaves a written note where a humanoid can find it. Such messages are invariably rambling and often completely incoherent, so they usually raise more questions than they answer.

Spell weavers do not speak, but they can communicate with one another telepathically across a distance of 1,000 miles.

COMBAT

A spell weaver is pathetically weak in melee but powerful in magic. Its ability to cast multiple spells simultaneously makes it a dangerous opponent indeed. A spell weaver usually remains invisible until it is ready to attack, then uses *plane shift* to escape, hopefully in possession of the magic item for which it came.

Spell-Like Abilities: Always active—*see invisiblity*; at will—*detect magic, invisibility*; 1/day—*plane shift*. Caster level equals spell weaver's effective sorcerer level; save DC 13 + spell level.

Spells: A spell weaver casts spells as a sorcerer two levels higher than its Hit Dice. (That is, a spell weaver with 10 Hit Dice casts spells as a 12th-level sorcerer; spells known 9/5/5/4/3/2/1; spells/day 6/7/7/7/6/5/3; save DC 13 + spell level, or 15 + spell level for Abjuration and Evocation spells.) A spell weaver prefers combinations of spells that focus on attacks, defense, and transportation.

Chromatic Disk: A spell weaver is never without its chromatic disk. This 6-inch-diameter indestructible disk glows with colors that slowly shift through the spectrum. This object stores ten additional spell levels of energy that the creature can tap and use as it wishes—the spell weaver could, for example, cast two extra 5th-level spells in a day, or three 3rd-level spells and one 1st-level spell, or any other combination of extra spell levels that adds up to ten, so long as no single spell is higher than 5th level. (For this purpose, two 0-level spells are equivalent to one 1st-level spell.) To tap this spell energy, a spell weaver must hold the chromatic disk in at least one of its hands. The disk automatically recharges itself to full power every night, at midnight. A spell powered by the disk is cast as though the caster had the Spell Focus feat for the spell in question.

Only a spell weaver can utilize a chromatic disk. Should any other creature pick one up and try to tap its energy (by employing the Use Magic Device skill, for instance), it explodes, dealing 4d10 points of damage to everything within a 30-foot radius.

Immunity to Mind-Affecting Effects: Because its alien mind functions differently than those of other creatures, a spell weaver is immune to all mind-affecting spells and effects.

Shielded Mind (Ex): Attempts by creatures of other races to communicate telepathically with a spell weaver, or to read its mind, always fail. A creature making such an attempt must succeed at a Will save (DC 17) or be affected as if by a *confusion* spell (caster level equals spell weaver's effective sorcerer level) for 1d6 days. This effect can be dispelled or removed with a *heal* effect.

Spell Weaving (Ex): These monsters are infamous for their ability to cast more than one spell at a

time. Casting a spell occupies a number of the spell weaver's arms equal to the spell's level (maximum 6th). A spell weaver can cast more than one spell simultaneously, as long as the sum of the spell levels is six or less. It could, for example, cast one 6th-level spell, one 4th-level and one 2nd-level spell, one 3rd-level and three 1st-level spells, six 1st-level spells, or any combination of spells whose levels add up to six or less. (A single 0-level spell occupies one arm.)

Telepathy (Su): Spell weavers can communicate with each other telepathically at a range of up to 1,000 miles.

SPELLGAUNT

Large Magical Beast
Hit Dice: 16d10+48 (136 hp)
Initiative: +2
Speed: 40 ft., climb 20 ft.
AC: 18 (–1 size, +2 Dex, +7 natural), touch 11, flat-footed 16
Attacks: Bite +24 melee and 2 claws +17 melee
Damage: Bite 1d8+8, claw 1d6+2
Face/Reach: 5 ft. by 10 ft./5 ft.
Special Attacks: Disjunctive bite, enhanced bite, force web, snatch item
Special Qualities: Darkvision 60 ft., DR 40/+4, detect magic, low-light vision, quick leap, SR 35
Saves: Fort +13, Ref +12, Will +5
Abilities: Str 18, Dex 14, Con 16, Int 13, Wis 11, Cha 21
Skills: Balance +10, Climb +11, Hide +14, Jump +19, Spot +21
Feats: Expertise, Improved Disarm, Improved Trip, Multiattack, Weapon Focus (bite)

Climate/Terrain: Any forest, mountains or underground
Organization: Solitary, pair, or nest (10–40)
Challenge Rating: 12
Treasure: None
Alignment: Always neutral
Advancement: 17–30 HD (Large); 31–45 HD (Huge)

Spellgaunts feast upon the arcane energy stored within magic items and creatures that use spells, draining the magic from them in the process.

A spellgaunt appears as a bizarre, elongated arachnid. Its spindly legs are 10 feet long, and its flat, golden body is covered with hairy, chitinous plates. The monster has tremendous, saw-edged fangs that end in fine, razor-sharp points. Sparkling saliva drips continuously from its maw.

COMBAT

A spellgaunt senses magic items and attacks any creature that carries one. It usually tries to immobilize foes with its force web first, then moves in to feed, drinking up the strongest magic first. Foes that evade its webs are bitten and clawed. If outnumbered, a spellgaunt moves quickly to snatch any visibly displayed magic items, then flees to its lair to feed in peace.

Disjunctive Bite (Su): A magic item bitten by a spellgaunt (see Attacking an Object in Chapter 8 of the *Player's Handbook*) must make a successful Will save (DC 23) or instantly become a nonmagical object. A spellgaunt feeding on an artifact has a 33% chance of destroying the item. If it destroys the item, it must make a successful Fortitude save (DC 25) or die instantly from an overwhelming ingestion of magical energy.

A spellcaster or a creature with supernatural or spell-like abilities that is bitten by a spellgaunt must make a Fortitude save (DC 23) or lose the ability to cast spells or use its magical abilities for 1d2 rounds.

Enhanced Bite (Ex): A spellgaunt's fangs function as +4 weapons.

Force Web (Su): A spellgaunt can spray flexible strands of sticky, invisible force at a single Medium-size or smaller target up to 20 feet away. A successful Reflex save (DC 23) lets the target avoid the webs; failure means the creature is stuck and entangled (–2 penalty on attack rolls and –4 penalty to Dexterity). A force web is immune to damage of all kinds from most spells, including *dispel magic*. However, *disintegrate* immediately destroys a force web, and it is also vulnerable to the effects of a *sphere of annihilation* or a *rod of cancellation*. Since force webs extend into the Ethereal Plane, they also affect ethereal creatures. A force web dissolves after 1d4 hours.

Snatch Item (Ex): A spellgaunt can take an openly displayed magic item away from an opponent with a successful disarm attempt, whether or not the item is actually a weapon. It cannot remove armor or other items that are attached at multiple locations, but it can snatch forcefully enough to break a single strap or other such attachment—the strap holding a wand to an opponent's belt, for example.

Detect Magic (Su): A spellgaunt can see magical auras in its line of sight to a range of 120 feet. It immediately senses the aura strength of each magic item and magical effect it detects.

Quick Leap (Ex): A spellgaunt can make a standing jump as a free action.

Skills: A spellgaunt receives a +4 racial bonus on Hide checks, a +6 racial bonus on Jump checks, and a +12 racial bonus on Spot checks.

Huge Fey (Incorporeal)
Hit Dice: 20d6+200 (270 hp)
Initiative: +1
Speed: Fly 60 ft. (perfect)
AC: 16 (–2 size, +1 Dex, +7 deflection), touch 16, flat-footed 15
Attacks: None
Damage: None
Face/Reach: 10 ft. by 10 ft./15 ft.
Special Attacks: Spell-like abilities
Special Qualities: All-around vision, elemental manifestation, fast healing 10, incorporeal subtype, low-light vision, natural invisibility, telepathy, SR 34
Saves: Fort +16, Ref +13, Will +16
Abilities: Str —, Dex 13, Con 30, Int 20, Wis 19, Cha 25
Skills: Animal Empathy +14, Concentration +23, Diplomacy +9, Knowledge (nature) +16, Listen +15, Search +9, Sense Motive +18, Spellcraft +18, Spot +17, Wilderness Lore +18
Feats: Cleave*, Dodge, Expertise, Great Cleave*, Improved Bull Rush*, Improved Disarm, Improved Trip*, Mobility, Power Attack*, Sunder*

Climate/Terrain: Any
Organization: Solitary
Challenge Rating: 23
Treasure: None
Alignment: Always neutral
Advancement: 21–30 HD (Huge); 31–60 HD (Gargantuan)

A spirit of the land is a powerful force of nature that lies dormant until the area it guards is threatened. Each inhabits a particular geographical area, existing as a living part of the land. A spirit of the land usually assumes dominion over a small valley, a river, a desert, or some other bounded geographical feature. These creatures dwell in all regions of the world, and more than one can exist within the same area, each concerned with a particular aspect of the terrain.

In its natural form, a spirit of the land is an invisible and intangible force. It appears as a shapeless mist to creatures that can see invisible things. When it wishes to manifest a physical form, a spirit of the land can assume the shape of a humanoid, animal, or elemental of its own size composed of one particular element—air, earth, fire, or water.

Spirits of the land are always aware of what transpires in their territories, and they punish all who would ravage or defile them. They get along well with druids as well as with races that respect the land.

Spirits of the land speak Common, Elven, Dwarven, and most goblinoid languages. They can also communicate telepathically with speakers of other languages.

COMBAT

In combat, a spirit of the land prefers to strike invisibly, using its command over weather, nature, and the elements to destroy its enemies. Opponents may find themselves

confronted by an earthquake, followed by a rain of lightning bolts accompanied by hurricane-force winds. A spirit attacks relentlessly, coordinating its actions to keep foes off balance while remaining unseen. To fight in melee, a spirit of the land must manifest an elemental form. In this shape, it usually focuses on destroying one foe before moving on to the next.

Spell-Like Abilities: At will—*chain lightning, chill metal, cone of cold, control water, control weather, control winds, create water, earthquake, fire storm, fog cloud, heat metal, ice storm, incendiary cloud, lightning bolt, move earth, produce flame, quench, sleet storm, solid fog, soften earth and stone, spike stones, stone shape, wall of fire, wall of ice, wall of stone, whirlwind, wind wall.* Caster level 20th; save DC 17 + spell level.

All-Around Vision (Ex): A spirit of the land is a part of all the terrain that surrounds it, so it sees from all directions at once. Because of this ability, it gains a +4 racial bonus on Search and Spot checks, and it cannot be flanked, regardless of its form.

Elemental Manifestation (Su): Once per day, a spirit of the land can assume a form composed of elemental material (air, earth, fire, or water), so long as that element exists in some form on its terrain. In elemental form, a spirit of the land is no longer invisible or incorporeal. It gains the element-specific qualities noted in the appropriate manifestation section below and loses the benefits of the incorporeal subtype. Should a spirit of the land's elemental manifestation be destroyed, the monster dissipates but is not slain. A dissipated spirit of the land must wait 24 hours before it can use any of its abilities again.

While a spirit of the land is manifested, the following changes to its statistics are in effect: AC 19, touch 9, flat-footed 18; Atk +14 melee (2d8+6, 2 slams); SQ DR 30/+3; Str 23.

Incorporeal Subtype: In its incorporeal form, a spirit of the land can be harmed only by other incorporeal creatures, +1 or better magic weapons, spells, spell-like abilities, and supernatural abilities. The creature has a 50% chance to ignore any damage from a corporeal source, except for force effects or attacks made with ghost touch weapons. An incorporeal spirit of the land can pass through solid objects, but not force effects, at will. Its attacks ignore natural armor, armor, and shields, but deflection bonuses and force effects work normally against them. An incorporeal spirit of the land always moves silently and cannot be heard with Listen checks if it doesn't wish to be.

Natural Invisibility (Su): An incorporeal spirit of the land remains invisible even when it attacks. This ability is always active, but the monster can suppress or resume it as a free action.

Telepathy (Su): A spirit of the land can communicate telepathically with any creature within 5 miles that has a language.

Feats: *A spirit of the land has access to the feats marked with an asterisk only while it is manifested.

AIR MANIFESTATION

To manifest as air, a spirit of the land must have a windy valley, breezy seashore, or the like in its terrain. In this form, it gains the following abilities.

Air Mastery (Ex): Any airborne creature takes a –1 penalty on attack and damage rolls made against a spirit of the land manifested as air.

Flight (Ex): A spirit of the land manifested as air is naturally buoyant. At will as a free action, it can produce an effect like that of the *fly* spell (caster level 5th), except that the effect applies only to itself. This ability gives it a fly speed of 120 feet (perfect).

EARTH MANIFESTATION

An earth manifestation simply requires any type of land. In this form, a spirit of the land gains the following ability.

Earth Mastery (Ex): A spirit of the land manifested as earth gains a +1 bonus on attack and damage rolls if its foe is touching the ground.

FIRE MANIFESTATION

A fire manifestation requires a volcanic region, hot spring, or the like on the spirit of the land's terrain. In this form, it gains the following abilities.

Burn (Ex): Any creature that is hit by the slam attack of a spirit of the land manifested as fire, or that hits the monster with a natural weapon or an unarmed attack, must succeed at a Reflex save (DC 30) or catch on fire. The fire burns for 1d4 rounds.

Fire Subtype (Ex): A spirit of the land manifested as fire is immune to fire damage but takes double damage from cold unless a saving throw for half damage is allowed. In that case, the creature takes half damage on a success and double damage on a failure.

WATER MANIFESTATION

To manifest as water, a spirit of the land must have a river, lake, pond, or other waterway in its terrain. In this form, it gains the following abilities.

Swim (Ex): A spirit of the land manifested as water can swim at a speed of 60 feet.

Water Mastery (Ex): A spirit of the land manifested as water gains a +1 bonus on its attack and damage rolls if its opponent is touching water.

STONE SPIKE

Medium-Size Elemental (Earth)

Hit Dice: 3d8+12 (25 hp)

Initiative: –1

Speed: 20 ft.

AC: 18 (+8 natural), touch 10, flat-footed 18

Attacks: 2 slams +6 melee

Damage: Slam 1d8+4

Face/Reach: 5 ft. by 5 ft./5 ft.

Special Qualities: Elemental traits

Saves: Fort +7, Ref +1, Will +1

Abilities: Str 18, Dex 8, Con 19, Int 4, Wis 11, Cha 11

Skills: Listen +6, Spot +4

Feats: Power Attack

Climate/Terrain: Any land and underground

Organization: Solitary, pair, or gang (3–5)

Challenge Rating: 2

Treasure: None

Alignment: Always neutral

Advancement: 4–9 HD (Large)

The stone spike is a cousin of the earth elemental. Dwarf spellcasters often summon and bind stone spikes to serve as guards and to assist

with tunnel construction. They are slow but untiring fighters and workers.

A stone spike resembles a roughly sculpted column of stone with four or more crystal-tipped arms. Sharp, stony protrusions cover its body.

Stone spikes seem to like dwarves, and they usually serve such masters without complaint. Sages speculate that the monsters think of dwarves as kindred spirits—hard-working, rugged, and indomitable.

Stone spikes speak Terran and Dwarven.

COMBAT

Stone spikes lack the coordination to employ more than two of their arms at once. These creatures prefer to plod resolutely forward in combat, battering any foe that comes within reach.

Elemental Traits (Ex): A stone spike is immune to poison, *sleep*, paralysis, and stunning. It is not subject to critical hits or flanking, and it cannot be raised or resurrected. The creature also has darkvision (60-foot range).

SWAMPLIGHT LYNX

Large Magical Beast

Hit Dice: 10d10+30 (85 hp)

Initiative: +5

Speed: 50 ft.

AC: 15 (–1 size, +1 Dex, +5 natural), touch 10, flat-footed 14

Attacks: 2 claws +14 melee and bite +9 melee

Damage: Claw 1d6+5, bite 1d8+2

Face/Reach: 5 ft. by 10 ft./5 ft.

Special Attacks: Improved grab, pounce, rake 1d3+2, spell-like abilities

Special Qualities: Darkvision 60 ft., low-light vision, marsh move

Saves: Fort +10, Ref +8, Will +5

Abilities: Str 20, Dex 13, Con 17, Int 10, Wis 15, Cha 14

Skills: Hide +5*, Jump +6, Listen +7, Move Silently +9, Spot +8

Feats: Dodge, Improved Initiative, Run

Climate/Terrain: Any marsh

Organization: Solitary, pair, or pride (5–10)

Challenge Rating: 7

Treasure: None

Alignment: Usually neutral

Advancement: 11–15 HD (Large); 16–30 HD (Huge)

Swamplight lynxes are sleek, nocturnal hunters that prowl marshes and wet lowlands. They are fond of humanoid prey, and they especially enjoy the taste of elven flesh.

A swamplight lynx is a sturdy animal, 9 to 10 feet long, with a sleek, lithe, feline body. It has large paws, a small head, and a short tail. Its coat can be any shade from dark yellow to olive, and this coloration allows it to blend in easily with its swampy surroundings.

A swamplight lynx cannot speak, but it can be trained to understand any one language.

COMBAT

Swamplight lynxes are cunning foes, whether stalking their prey over long distances or waiting patiently in ambush. They often use their *light* ability to surprise, distract and confuse their prey before pouncing with bared claws. Swamplight lynxes are solitary animals, but they do engage in cooperative hunting.

Pounce (Ex): If a swamplight lynx charges, it can make a full attack (including a rake attempt; see below) even though it has moved.

Improved Grab (Ex): If a swamplight lynx hits an opponent that is at least one size category smaller than itself with a bite attack, it deals normal damage and attempts to start a grapple as a free action without provoking an attack of opportunity (grapple bonus +19). If it gets a hold, it can also rake on the same round. Thereafter, it has the option to conduct the grapple normally, or simply use its jaws to hold the opponent (–20 penalty on grapple check, but the swamplight lynx is not considered grappled). In either case, each successful grapple check it makes during successive rounds automatically deals bite damage.

Rake (Ex): On any round that a swamplight lynx has a hold on an opponent (see Improved Grab, above), it can make two rake attacks (+14 melee) with its hind legs for 1d3+2 points of damage each. The swamplight lynx can also attempt to rake when it pounces on an opponent.

Spell-Like Abilities: At will—*blur, daze, faerie fire, light.* Caster level 6th; save DC 12 + spell level.

Marsh Move (Ex): Swamplight lynxes take no movement penalties for moving in marshes or mud.

Skills: *A swamplight lynx receives a +4 bonus on Hide checks when in marshlands.

SYLPH

Small Outsider (Air)
Hit Dice: 3d8–3 (10 hp)
Initiative: +1
Speed: 30 ft., fly 90 ft. (good)
AC: 12 (+1 size, +1 Dex), touch 12, flat-footed 11
Attacks: Unarmed strike +3 melee
Damage: Unarmed strike 1d2–1 subdual
Face/Reach: 5 ft. by 5 ft./5 ft.
Special Attacks: Spells
Special Qualities: *Improved invisibility*, outsider traits, spells, SR 14, *summon elemental*
Saves: Fort +2, Ref +4, Will +6
Abilities: Str 8, Dex 13, Con 8, Int 15, Wis 16, Cha 17
Skills: Animal Empathy +9, Concentration +5, Escape Artist +7, Hide +11, Move Silently +7
Feats: Empower Spell

Climate/Terrain: Temperate and warm mountains
Organization: Solitary
Challenge Rating: 5
Treasure: Standard (gems and magic items only)
Alignment: Usually neutral
Advancement: 4–9 HD (Small)

Sylphs are native to the Elemental Plane of Air, but they have a liking for the scenery of the Material Plane. They often maintain homes high in the mountains, but since they love to travel, they are rarely found near their homes.

A sylph appears as a small, beautiful woman with translucent, brightly colored wings. The typical sylph prefers filmy clothing and brightly colored jewelry.

Sylphs always become invisible at the approach of strangers and remain so until they know whether there is any danger. The mere presence of danger, however, doesn't necessarily cause them to flee; they are so naturally curious that they may linger in dangerous situations just to watch. They are generally friendly, especially to human males.

Sylphs speak Auran and Common.

COMBAT

Sylphs seldom engage in physical combat and usually do not carry any weapons. They depend on their spells and special abilities to protect themselves. When threatened, they often summon elementals to defend them.

Spells: A sylph can cast arcane spells as a sorcerer. Caster level = sylph's Hit Dice + 4; spells known 7/5/3/2; spells/day 6/7/7/5; save DC 13 + spell level.

Improved Invisibility (**Sp**): At will, a sylph can use *improved invisibility* (self only).

Outsider Traits: A sylph has darkvision (60-foot range). It cannot be raised or resurrected.

Summon Elemental (**Sp**): Once per day, a sylph can use *summon monster VI* (caster level 12th) to summon a Large air, earth, fire, or water elemental.

TEMPEST

Gargantuan Elemental (Air, Earth, Fire, Water)

Hit Dice: 24d8+216 (324 hp)

Initiative: –2

Speed: Fly 60 ft. (good)

AC: 24 (–4 size, –2 Dex, +10 natural, +10 deflection), touch 14, flat-footed 24

Attacks: Slam +23/+18/+13/+8 melee

Damage: Slam 2d8+13

Face/Reach: 40 ft. by 40 ft./10 ft.

Special Attacks: Burn, drench, spell-like abilities, whirlwind

Special Qualities: *Defensive aura*, DR 15/+2, elemental mastery, elemental traits, fire subtype

Saves: Fort +23, Ref +12, Will +8

Abilities: Str 29, Dex 6, Con 28, Int 8, Wis 11, Cha 17

Skills: Concentration +18, Listen +11, Spot +12

Feats: Cleave, Power Attack

Climate/Terrain: Any land

Organization: Solitary

Challenge Rating: 16

Treasure: None

Alignment: Always chaotic neutral

Advancement: 25–48 HD (Gargantuan); 49–72 HD (Colossal)

Though it resembles a massive storm, a tempest is actually an intelligent, living creature related to both elementals and genies. All four elements coexist within its form: air in the wind, earth in the whirling sand and dirt, fire in the heat of the lightning, and water in the rain.

Tempests are uncommunicative for the most part. Very rarely, one of them may know a few dozen words in Common. Other than that, they speak only the languages of the elementals.

COMBAT

A tempest is seldom in a good mood, so most encounters with these creatures end in a battle.

Burn (Ex): Anyone hit by a tempest's slam attack must succeed at a Reflex save (DC 31) or catch fire. The flame burns for 1d4 rounds. A burning creature can take a move-equivalent action to put out the fire. Any creature hitting a tempest with a natural weapon or unarmed attack takes fire damage as though hit by its slam attack and also catches fire unless it succeeds at a Reflex save.

Drench (Ex): The tempest's touch puts out torches, campfires, exposed lanterns, and other open flames of nonmagical origin if these are of Huge size or smaller. The creature can dispel magical fire it touches as if by *dispel magic* (caster level equal to tempest's HD).

Spell-Like Abilities: At will—*chill touch, gust of wind, lightning bolt, wind wall.* Caster level 9th; save DC 13 + spell level.

Whirlwind (Su): A tempest can transform itself into a whirlwind (or vortex if underwater) once every 10 minutes and remain in that form for up to 1 round for every 2 HD it has. The whirlwind is 5 feet wide at the base, up to 30 feet wide at the top, and between 10 and 50 feet tall (tempest's choice). In this form, it can move through the air (or water, as a vortex) or along a surface at its fly speed.

Any creature one or more size categories smaller than the tempest that comes into contact with the whirlwind must make a successful Reflex save (DC 31) or take 4d6 points of damage. It must also succeed at a second Reflex save (DC 31) or be picked up bodily and held suspended in the powerful winds, automatically taking 4d6 points of damage per round. A creature that can fly is allowed a Reflex save at the same DC each round to escape the whirlwind. The creature still takes damage but can leave if the save is successful. The tempest can eject any carried creatures whenever it wishes, depositing them wherever it happens to be.

If the whirlwind's base touches the ground, it creates a swirling cloud of debris. This cloud is centered on the

tempest and has a diameter equal to half the whirlwind's height. The cloud obscures all vision, including darkvision, beyond 5 feet. Creatures 5 feet away have one-half concealment, while those farther away have total concealment. Anyone caught in the cloud must succeed at a Concentration check (DC 31) to cast a spell.

Defensive Aura (Sp): A tempest has a +10 deflection bonus to Armor Class. This ability is always in effect.

Elemental Mastery (Ex): A tempest gains a +1 bonus on attack and damage rolls if both it and its foe are in contact with any of the four elements (air, earth, fire, or water).

Elemental Traits (Ex): A tempest is immune to poison, *sleep*, paralysis, and stunning. It is not subject to critical hits or flanking, and it cannot be raised or resurrected. The creature also has darkvision (60-foot range).

Fire Subtype (Ex): A tempest is immune to fire damage but takes double damage from cold unless a saving throw for half damage is allowed. In that case, the creature takes half damage on a success and double damage on a failure.

TERATOMORPH

Gargantuan Ooze
Hit Dice: 28d10+170 (324 hp)
Initiative: –3
Speed: 30 ft., fly 50 ft. (poor), swim 90 ft.
AC: 3 (–4 size, –3 Dex), touch 3, flat-footed 3
Attacks: Slam +28 melee
Damage: Slam 4d6+16 plus entropic touch
Face/Reach: 30 ft. by 30 ft./15 ft.
Special Attacks: Entropic touch, portalwake, warp reality
Special Qualities: Blindsight 240 ft., detect law, dimensional instability, immunities, ooze traits, SR 32
Saves: Fort +14, Ref +6, Will +4
Abilities: Str 32, Dex 5, Con 20, Int —, Wis 1, Cha 1

Climate/Terrain: Any aquatic and underground
Organization: Solitary
Challenge Rating: 16
Treasure: Standard
Alignment: Always neutral
Advancement: 29–36 HD (Gargantuan); 37–84 HD (Colossal)

Teratomorphs lurk in the watery depths of the sea and in underground caverns. Normally, they spend most of their time floating on underwater currents, but sometimes these currents wash them ashore. Occasionally they come ashore of their own volition to search for food.

A teratomorph is a shapeless horror the size of a cottage. Its body consists primarily of thick, translucent, iridescent slime coating coils of opaque tissue that shift and move, as though constantly in a state of flux. Beneath its slimy hide, bursts of energy occasionally flash, lighting portions of its form momentarily. Sections of the ooze periodically emit beams of light or crackling energy, while other sections fade into smoke or vanish altogether.

A teratomorph gains nutrients by infesting living creatures with the force of chaos. The very act of transforming another creature with its entropic touch sustains and nurtures the ooze's growth. But a creature does not have to come in contact with a teratomorph to experience its entropic effects. In fact, the monster's very presence can unravel reality and tear holes in the fabric between planes. Unlucky creatures that pass too close to a teratomorph sometimes find themselves transported to other planes with no means of returning.

Powerful spellcasters have long sought ways to harness the powers of the teratomorph. Unfortunately, portions of the ooze that are separated from the main body do not last long, dissolving into nothingness after only a few hours. The otherworldly matter that makes up the body of a teratomorph remains unstable until enough of it is concentrated in one place that its mass defeats the internal forces working to tear it apart. This effect probably explains why teratomorphs smaller than Gargantuan are never encountered. When such a creature reaches 84 Hit Dice, it immediately splits into smaller oozes, each with 28 Hit Dice.

COMBAT

The teratomorph is a mindless creature. When it isn't eating, it is on the move looking for something to eat. It surges forth to attack any Small or larger creature that passes within range of its blindsight, but it ignores creatures smaller than this.

A teratomorph attacks by extruding a massive wave of chaotic protoplasm to smash its prey. Not only does this attack deal extensive bludgeoning damage, it also infuses the creature touched with raw chaos.

Entropic Touch (Su): The entropic energy that surges through a teratomorph's shapeless body causes horrible transformations in living creatures that come into contact with it. If a creature struck by a teratomorph's slam attack fails a Fortitude saving throw (DC 29), its body transforms in some way, causing one of the following effects:

1d20	Result
1–7	Physical Mutation. The touch of the teratomorph transforms the opponent's anatomy, resulting in 1d6 points of Strength drain or Dexterity drain (50% chance for each).
8–13	Tissue Annihilation. The touch of the ooze causes tiny portions of the opponent's anatomy to vanish, resulting in 2d4 points of Constitution drain.
14–18	Transformation. The opponent undergoes a transformation as though affected by a *polymorph any object* spell (caster level 20th). This painful process deals 5d20 points of subdual damage. The DM can randomly determine the subject's new form or choose a particular form.
19	Bonding. The ooze sticks to the target and automatically succeeds at a grapple check. Each round thereafter, the teratomorph can attempt a new grapple check (grapple bonus +44) to deal 4d6+16 points of bludgeoning damage. The opponent must succeed at a new Fortitude saving throw (DC 29) each round that the teratomorph deals damage to avoid further effects from the entropic touch. (If this result comes up more than once, roll again.)
20	Absorption. The opponent is entirely absorbed by the ooze. An absorbed creature dies instantly and leaves behind no trace of a body, so only a *miracle, true resurrection,* or *wish* spell can restore it to life. Absorbing a creature grants the ooze a new permanent Hit Die.

Portalwake (Su): The presence of a teratomorph places tremendous strain on the borders between the planes, causing tears and rips to appear nearby. Each round, one creature within a 120-foot radius of the teratomorph, chosen at random, must make a Reflex saving throw (DC 19) or be moved to a random plane as though by a *plane shift* spell.

Warp Reality (Su): The potent chaotic energy that surges through and out of a teratomorph's body can have amazing effects on the surrounding terrain. When the monster is at rest, this energy is calm, but when the monster moves or attacks, the energy lashes out in a 120-foot emanation. These ripples of chaos cause the surrounding terrain to warp and writhe, imposing a –4 circumstance penalty on attack rolls and Dexterity checks for all creatures in the area except the teratomorph.

Every round that this reality warp persists, there is a 10% chance that the chaotic energy manifests in a more dramatic manner. Such chaos manifestations duplicate spell effects. Roll 1d20 and refer to the appropriate line on the following table to determine the spells effects produced. All these effects function as the spells of the same names (caster level 20th; save DC 10 + spell level), except that they affect all the appropriate targets (except the teratomorph) within the warp reality area and last for 1 round.

Roll	Result
1–4	*Entangle* and *obscuring mist*
5–8	*Color spray* and *glitterdust*
9–12	*Stinking cloud* and *spike growth*
13–14	*Spike stones* and *cloudkill*
15–16	*Insect plague* and *mind fog*
17–18	*Acid fog* and *transmute rock to mud*
19	*Fire storm* and *reverse gravity*
20	*Earthquake* and *prismatic spray* (roll once for all affected creatures)

Blindsight (Ex): A teratomorph is blind, but its entire body is a primitive sensory organ that can ascertain prey by scent and vibration. This ability enables it to discern objects and creatures within 240 feet. A teratomorph usually does not need to make Spot or Listen checks to notice creatures within range of its blindsight.

Detect Law (Su): A teratomorph has a continual detect law ability (as the spell) with a range of 20 feet.

Dimensional Instability (Su): Each time an opponent strikes a teratomorph with a weapon, there is a chance that the portion of the creature's body struck simply doesn't exist at that instant. Any melee or ranged attack directed at the teratomorph has a 20% miss chance that cannot be avoided with spells such as *true seeing* or *true strike. Dimensional anchor* negates this ability, reducing the miss chance to 0% for the duration of the effect.

Immunities (Ex): A teratomorph is immune to lightning, acid, and all spells with the chaotic descriptor.

Ooze Traits: A teratomorph is immune to mind-affecting effects, poison, *sleep,* paralysis, stunning, and polymorphing. It is not subject to critical hits or flanking.

THRI-KREEN

Medium-Size Monstrous Humanoid

Hit Dice: 2d8 (9 hp)

Initiative: +2

Speed: 40 ft.

AC: 15 (+2 Dex, +3 natural), touch 12, flat-footed 13

Attacks: 4 claws +3 melee and bite –2 melee, or gythka +4 melee and bite –2 melee, or chatkcha +4 ranged

Damage: Claw 1d4+1, bite 1d4 plus poison, gythka 2d6+1, chatkcha 1d6+1

Special Attacks: Poison, psionics*

Special Qualities: Darkvision 60 ft., immunity to *sleep,* leap

Saves: Fort +0, Ref +5, Will +4

Abilities: Str 12, Dex 15, Con 11, Int 8, Wis 12, Cha 7

Skills: Balance +4, Climb +3, Hide +4*, Jump +35, Listen +6, Spot +4

Feats: Deflect Arrows (B), Weapon Focus (gythka)

Climate/Terrain: Temperate or warm desert

Organization: Solitary or pack (5–10)

Challenge Rating: 1

Treasure: None

Alignment: Usually chaotic neutral

Advancement: By character class

Thri-kreen, often called mantis warriors, are intelligent humanoids with insectlike features. They prefer deserts and savannas, where they maintain a nomadic lifestyle as hunters.

A thri-kreen looks like a bipedal praying mantis. Of the six limbs protruding from its midsection, two are used for walking, and each of the other four ends in a four-fingered

hand. A sandy yellow exoskeleton covers an adult thri-kreen's body. Two compound eyes, two antennae, and a complicated jaw structure that includes a pair of wicked mandibles give its head an insectlike appearance. The typical thri-kreen wears a harness, belt, and slings for holding its equipment, but no clothing or armor.

Thri-kreen are at home in arid, open landscapes where they can easily blend in with the windblown dunes and bare rock. Permanent thri-kreen communities are almost nonexistent; instead, packs of thri-kreen range widely over their own territories, foraging and hunting for daily sustenance. On rare occasions, two or more packs may come together to join their strength against especially dangerous intruders.

Thri-kreen speak a language made up of clicks and snaps of their mandibles. Most thri-kreen whose packs roam near humanoid civilizations also speak Common.

COMBAT

While hunting, thri-kreen use their natural camouflage to sneak up on potential prey. Thri-kreen can close to combat (and flee from it) more quickly than most of their foes because of their speed and their ability to leap. They can use the gythka and chatkcha (exotic weapons that are unique to mantis warriors), but they prefer to attack with their claws and their poisoned bites.

Poison (Ex): A thri-kreen delivers its poison (Fortitude save DC 11) with a successful bite attack. The initial and secondary damage is the same (paralysis for 2d6 minutes). A thri-kreen produces enough poison for one bite per day.

Psionics (Sp): *When using the *Psionics Handbook*, apply the following psionic abilities to a thri-kreen. At will—*chameleon, know direction*; 1/day—*displacement, lesser metaphysical weapon*. Manifester level 10th; save DC 8 + power level.

Attack/Defense Modes: ego whip, mind thrust/thought shield, empty mind. A thri-kreen manifests powers, and gains additional attack and defense modes, as if it were a psychic warrior or a psion with Psychometabolism as its primary discipline. (A psionic thri-kreen character's favored class is psychic warrior, though a few choose monk or psion with the primary discipline of Psychometabolism.)

Immunity to Sleep (Ex): Since thri-kreen do not sleep, they are immune to magic *sleep* effects. A thri-kreen spellcaster still requires 8 hours of rest before preparing spells.

Leap (Ex): A thri-kreen is a natural jumper. It gains a +30

competence bonus on all Jump checks, and its maximum jumping distance is not limited by height.

Skills: *The exoskeleton of a thri-kreen blends in well with desert terrain, granting it a +4 racial bonus on Hide checks in sandy or arid settings.

THRI-KREEN CHARACTERS

A thri-kreen character's preferred class is ranger, but a few prefer the path of the cleric or druid. A thri-kreen character begins play with Hit Dice 2d8, which gives it a +2 base attack bonus; base saves Fort +0, Ref +3, Will +3; Deflect Arrows, Exotic Weapon Proficiency [gythka], and Exotic Weapon Proficiency [chatkcha] as bonus feats; one additional feat of choice; and skill points equal to twice its Intelligence score. Its class skills as a thri-kreen are Balance, Climb, Hide, Jump, Listen, and Spot. Many thri-kreen also qualify for the monstrous feats Multiattack, Multidexterity, and Multiweapon Fighting and choose these in preference over other feats.

A nonpsionic thri-kreen PC's effective character level (ECL) is equal to its class level + 3. Thus, a 1st-level nonpsionic thri-kreen ranger has an ECL of 4 and is the equivalent of a 4th-level character.

A psionic thri-kreen PC's effective character level (ECL) is equal to its class level +5. Thus, a 1st-level psionic thri-kreen ranger has an ECL of 6 and is the equivalent of a 6th-level character.

THRI-KREEN EQUIPMENT

Thri-kreen warriors have invented two exotic weapons that are unique to their race—the gythka and the chatkcha. These are described below.

Gythka: This Large exotic melee double weapon is a polearm with a blade at each end. The wielder can fight with it as if fighting with two weapons, but doing so incurs all the normal attack penalties associated with fighting with two weapons, as if the wielder had a one-handed weapon and a light weapon (see Attacking with Two Weapons in Chapter 8 of the *Player's Handbook*). A thri-kreen who has the Multiweapon Fighting feat can wield two gythkas at once as double weapons because of its four arms.

Each end of a gythka deals 2d6 points of damage. Each end is a slashing weapon that deals double damage on a critical hit and threatens a critical hit on an attack roll of 20. *Cost:* 60 gp; *Weight:* 25 lb.

Chatkcha: This Medium-size exotic ranged weapon is a crystalline throwing wedge. Its sheer weight makes it unwieldy in the hands of those not proficient with it.

A chatkcha deals 1d6 points of piercing damage and has a range increment of 20 feet. It deals double damage on a critical hit and threatens a critical hit on an attack roll of 20. *Cost:* 1 gp; *Weight:* 3 lb.

TWIG BLIGHT

Small Plant
Hit Dice: 1d8+1 (5 hp)
Initiative: +1
Speed: 20 ft.
AC: 15 (+1 size, +1 Dex, +3 natural), touch 12, flat-footed 14
Attacks: 2 claws +0 melee
Damage: Claw 1d3–1 plus poison
Face/Reach: 5 ft. by 5 ft./5 ft.
Special Attacks: Poison
Special Qualities: Partial immunity to piercing weapons, plant traits
Saves: Fort +3, Ref +1, Will +0
Abilities: Str 8, Dex 13, Con 12, Int 5, Wis 11, Cha 4
Skills: Hide +10, Listen +4, Move Silently +5, Spot +4
Feats: Skill Focus (Hide)

Climate/Terrain: Any temperate land and underground
Organization: Solitary
Challenge Rating: 1/3
Treasure: None
Alignment: Always chaotic evil
Advancement: 2–3 HD (Small)

Twig blights are tree-like creatures of evil disposition. They can root themselves in normal soil and draw nutrients like normal plants, and they look much like woody shrubs in this mode. But these monsters have a special taste for blood, and they greatly prefer that to making food through photosynthesis. Indeed, a twig blight that lives underground must subsist on blood, since it gets no sunlight.

A twig blight normally stands about 3 1/2 feet tall. Its leafless branches interlock to create a humanoid shape.

Sages believe that the first twig blights grew from seeds of the Gulthias Tree, which sprouted from a wooden stake used to slay an ancient vampire. Instead of producing fruit, twig blights reproduce through their root systems, like aspen trees.

Twig blights speak Sylvan.

COMBAT

Twig blights usually huddle together in a group, trying to blend in with an area's natural vegetation (or with piles of debris or firewood) until suitable prey comes along. They particularly enjoy lurking near campsites or waterholes, where they can often catch prey unawares.

Poison (Ex): A twig blight delivers its poison (Fortitude save DC 11) with each successful claw attack. The initial damage is 1 point of Strength damage; there is no secondary damage.

Plant Traits (Ex): A twig blight is immune to poison, *sleep*, paralysis, stunning, and polymorphing. It is not subject to critical hits or mind-affecting effects. The creature also has low-light vision.

Skills and Feats: A twig blight gains skills and feats as a fey.

VAPORIGHU

Medium-Size Outsider (Evil)
Hit Dice: 10d8+30 (75 hp)
Initiative: –1
Speed: 30 ft.
AC: 20 (–1 Dex, +11 natural), touch 9, flat-footed 20
Attacks: 2 slams +12 melee
Damage: Slam 1d6+2/19–20 plus corrosive slime
Face/Reach: 5 ft. by 5 ft./5 ft.
Special Attacks: Corrosive slime, fear aura, poison breath, spell-like abilities
Special Qualities: DR 20/silver, outsider traits, SR 17, *summon night hag*, uncanny dodge
Saves: Fort +10, Ref +6, Will +6
Abilities: Str 15, Dex 9, Con 16, Int 13, Wis 8, Cha 10
Skills: Balance +12, Concentration +16, Intimidate +13, Knowledge (the planes) +14, Listen +12, Spellcraft +13, Spot +12
Feats: Improved Bull Rush, Improved Critical (slam), Power Attack

Climate/Terrain: Any land and underground
Organization: Solitary
Challenge Rating: 9
Treasure: Standard
Alignment: Always neutral evil
Advancement: 11–18 HD (Medium-size); 19–30 HD (Large)

Vaporighus are native to the plane of Gehenna. In all respects they are petty, sadistic, and voracious. The only force that motivates them is the gnawing pain of hunger that they can never satiate.

A vaporighu is a hideous, bloated, waddling blob of hairy flesh, vaguely humanoid in shape. Its skin is the color of

throw (DC 15) or become frightened for 2d4 rounds. An opponent who succeeds at the saving throw is immune to that vaporighu's fear aura for 24 hours. This is a mind-affecting fear effect.

Poison Breath (Ex): Once every 1d4 rounds, a vaporighu can exhale poison breath as a standard action. This creates a 15-foot cone of toxic and corrosive green vapor. Every creature in the area takes 1d10 points of acid damage (no saving throw). The vapor is poisonous (Fortitude save DC 18). The primary damage is paralysis (3d6 rounds); the secondary damage is 3d6 Con. The vapor lingers for 2d6 rounds, dealing acid damage and requiring a new saving throw each round a creature remains within it or touches it. Vaporighus are immune to their own poison breath and to that of others of their kind.

Spell-Like Abilities: At will—*animate objects, enlarge, fly, light, mislead, produce flame, sleep.* Caster level 10th; save DC 10 + spell level.

Outsider Traits: A vaporighu has darkvision (60-foot range). It cannot be raised or resurrected.

Summon Night Hag (Sp): Once per day, a vaporighu can summon one night hag. This ability functions like a *summon monster VII* spell (caster level 10th).

Uncanny Dodge (Ex): Because of its unusual talent for detecting prey, a vaporighu retains its Dexterity bonus to AC (if any) even when flat-footed, and it cannot be flanked.

WINDGHOST

Huge Aberration
Hit Dice: 18d8+72 (153 hp)
Initiative: +10
Speed: Fly 30 ft. (good)
AC: 21 (−2 size, +6 Dex, +7 natural), touch 14, flat-footed 15
Attacks: Bite +21 melee
Damage: Bite 2d8+13
Face/Reach: 5 ft. by 5 ft./5 ft.
Special Attacks: Darkvision 60 ft., improved grab, spell-like abilities, swallow whole, windsong
Special Qualities: Fast healing 3, flight, immunities, SR 25, true seeing
Saves: Fort +10, Ref +14, Will +13
Abilities: Str 28, Dex 23, Con 18, Int 15, Wis 14, Cha 19
Skills: Hide +12, Knowledge (arcana) +15, Listen +17, Spot +18
Feats: Combat Reflexes, Flyby Attack, Improved Initiative, Lightning Reflexes, Weapon Focus (bite)

Climate/Terrain: Any temperate or warm
Organization: Solirary, pair, brood (3–5), or swarm (6–10)
Challenge Rating: 15
Treasure: None
Alignment: Usually lawful
Advancement: 19–32 HD (Huge); 33–54 HD (Gargantuan)

gangrenous rot and drips with poisonous slime. Long, tangled, and matted fur hangs in shaggy layers from its forearms, back, belly, and stumplike legs, and its head is topped with a pair of small horns. Where its mottled skin is visible, veins of pulsing bile can be seen just beneath the surface. Its breath comes and goes in enormous, wheezing gurgles, punctuated by an occasional explosion of mucus. A vaporighu reeks of all the decay and sulphurous stench of Gehenna.

Vaporighus seem to perform no specific function in Gehenna other than to waylay whatever is unfortunate enough to cross their paths. They often pick out likely hiding places near portals or the rare watering holes in Gehenna and wait for victims to approach.

Vaporighus speak Abyssal and Infernal, but they usually do not communicate.

COMBAT

Vaporighus are tenacious opponents. They fight without subtlety or art, and they fight to the death.

Corrosive Slime (Ex): Vaporighus constantly exude a mucuslike slime that contains a corrosive substance. A vaporighu's slam attack leaves behind a smear of slime. An opponent's armor and clothing dissolve and become useless in 1 round unless the wearer succeeds at a Reflex save (DC 18). Any weapon that strikes a vaporighu dissolves in 1 round unless the wielder succeeds at a Reflex save (DC 18). Even on a failed save, armor, clothing, or weapons can be saved by washing, which requires a full-round action and at least 1 pint of water or weak acid (such as wine) per item.

Fear Aura (Su): Anyone (except other vaporighus) who sees a vaporighu within 30 feet must make a Will saving

opportunity (grapple bonus +30). If it gets a hold, it can try to swallow in the next round. Alternatively, the windghost has the option to conduct the grapple normally, or simply use its jaws to hold the opponent (–20 penalty on grapple check, but the windghost is not considered grappled). In either case, each successful grapple check it makes during successive rounds automatically deals bite damage.

Spell-Like Abilities: At will—*antimagic field, dispel magic, spell turning.* Caster level 16th; save DC 14 + spell level.

Swallow Whole (Ex): A windghost can swallow a single creature that is at least two size categories smaller than itself by making a successful grapple check (grapple bonus +30), provided it already has that opponent in its mouth (see Improved Grab, above). Once inside the windghost, the opponent takes 1d8+4 points of bludgeoning damage and 1d6+2 points of acid damage per round from the monster's stomach. A successful grapple check allows the swallowed creature to climb out of the stomach and return to the windghost's mouth, where another successful grapple check is needed to get free. Alternatively, a swallowed creature can try to cut its way out with either claws or a light piercing or slashing weapon. Dealing at least 25 points of damage to the stomach (AC 20) in this way creates an opening large enough to permit escape. Once a single swallowed creature exits, muscular action closes the hole; thus, another swallowed opponent must cut its own way out. A Huge windghost's stomach can hold 1 Medium-size, 4 Small, 16 Tiny, or 64 Diminutive or smaller opponents.

Windsong (Su): Two or more windghosts within 90 feet of each other can emit a harmonizing sonic drone that throws off the equilibrium of any creature that hears it. The sound causes any creature within 120 feet (except windghosts) that fails a Will save (DC 23) to take a –6 circumstance penalty on Concentration checks, a –8 enhancement penalty to Dexterity, and move at half normal speed. These penalties remain as long as the windghosts continue to sing. A successful save renders a creature immune to that particular pair of windghosts' windsong for 24 hours. Windghosts can end a windsong at will.

Fast Healing (Ex): A windghost regains lost hit points at the rate of 3 per round. Fast healing does not restore hit points lost from starvation, thirst, or suffocation, and it does not allow the windghost to regrow or reattach lost body parts.

Flight (Ex): A windghost is naturally buoyant and can fly (as the spell) as a free action at a speed of 30 feet.

Immunities (Ex): Windghosts are immune to air and mind-affecting effects.

True Seeing (Su): A windghost sees all things as if affected by *true seeing* (arcane version).

Mysterious observers that float casually through the skies, windghosts are unfathomable creatures that inspire curiosity, puzzlement, and sometimes fear.

The body of a windghost is conical. From top to base, it measures 24 feet. At its base is a gaping, circular mouth, 8 feet across and lined with rows of teeth. Its body tapers up to a rounded cap. A windghost's rough and mottled hide is purplish gray in color, and it has milk-white eyes. The windghost has two 20-foot tentacles dangling from either side of its base. These appendages primarily serve to carry items. A windghost's body and eyes sparkle with ripples of blue and violet light. This light is strong enough to illuminate the creature's form but makes it appear ghostly, hence its name.

Windghosts may appear frightening, but they are not aggressive creatures. Nonetheless, their unexpected arrivals and strange appearance often lead to unprovoked attacks from frightened ground-dwellers.

Windghosts speak Auran.

COMBAT

Windghosts never attack without provocation. When threatened, they surround themselves with magical protections before swooping down to physically attack. If facing overpowering opponents, windghosts flee, flying straight up until they are out of sight.

Improved Grab (Ex): If a windghost hits an opponent that is at least one size category smaller than itself with a bite attack, it deals normal damage and attempts to start a grapple as a free action without provoking an attack of

WYSTE

Huge Aberration

Hit Dice: 5d8+25 (47 hp)

Initiative: +1

Speed: 10 ft., swim 40 ft.

AC: 18 (−2 size, +1 Dex, +9 natural), touch 9, flat-footed 17

Attacks: 7 tentacle rakes +7 melee

Damage: Tentacle rake 1d4+6

Face/Reach: 5 ft. by 20 ft./10 ft.

Special Attacks: Bite, improved grab

Special Qualities: Acid immunity, blindsight 120 ft.

Saves: Fort +6, Ref +2, Will +4

Abilities: Str 22, Dex 13, Con 20, Int 1, Wis 11, Cha 8

Skills: Listen +4, Spot +4, Swim +14

Feats: Alertness (B)

Climate/Terrain: Any underground

Organization: Solitary, pair or school (3–8)

Challenge Rating: 5

Treasure: None

Alignment: Always neutral

Advancement: 6–15 HD (Huge)

The wyste (pronounced "wist") is an alien creature much like a giant worm that inhabits fetid pools of alien slime.

A typical specimen is 2 feet in diameter and 25 feet long. A wyste's skin is translucent, showing strange, twisted strands of pulsing organs underneath. The creature has no face, just a large sucker hole fringed by long, claw-tipped tentacles. The tentacles allow the wyste to feed and defend itself, and they also serve as sensory organs. So far as is known, a wyste operates only by instinct and lives to feed.

COMBAT

A wyste lunges up to 15 feet out of its slimy pools to attack creatures that approach. Wystes in an area often attack as a group; others nearby might be attracted by the commotion, too. When a wyste kills a victim, it drags its prey away to be consumed at leisure.

Bite (Ex): When a wyste grapples an opponent, its tentacles draw the victim to its toothed sucker hole. On the round after the wyste grabs, it makes a regular attack with its bite (in lieu of any claw attacks), gaining a +4 bonus on the attack roll (+11 melee). If the bite attack misses, the wyste drops the character, who falls prone in front of the creature. If the bite attack is successful, the victim takes 1d6+9 points of damage. The wyste can then deal bite damage automatically every round. The victim can escape by winning an opposed grapple check against the wyste, making a successful Escape Artist check against the wyste's grapple check result, or by killing the wyste.

Improved Grab (Ex): If a wyste hits a Large or smaller opponent with one or more tentacle attacks, it deals normal damage and attempts to start a grapple as a free action without provoking an attack of opportunity (grapple bonus +17, plus a +2 bonus for each tentacle that hit beyond the first). The wyste can make only one grapple attack per round, no matter how many tentacles it devotes to the effort. If it gets a hold, it has the option to conduct the grapple normally, or simply use its tentacles to hold the opponent (−20 penalty on grapple check, but the wyste is not considered grappled). In either case, each successful grapple check it makes during successive rounds automatically deals damage for all the tentacles used to hold the opponent.

Blindsight (Ex): A wyste is blind, but its tentacles are sensory organs that can ascertain prey by scent and vibration. This ability enables it to discern objects and creatures within 120 feet. A wyste usually does not need to make Spot or Listen checks to notice creatures within range of its blindsight.

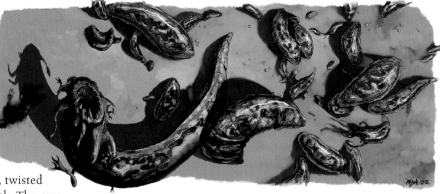

YAK FOLK

Large Monstrous Humanoid

Hit Dice: 5d8+10 (32 hp)

Initiative: +4

Speed: 30 ft.

AC: 16 (−1 size, +7 natural), touch 9, flat-footed 16

Attacks: Quarterstaff +9 melee, or falchion +8 melee

Damage: Quarterstaff 1d6+6, falchion 2d4+6/18–20

Face/Reach: 5 ft. by 5 ft./10 ft.

Special Attacks: *Body meld*

Special Qualities: Command genie, darkvision 60 ft., use staff

Saves: Fort +3, Ref +4, Will +6

Abilities: Str 18, Dex 11, Con 15, Int 14, Wis 15, Cha 14

Skills: Disguise +10*, Heal +6, Innuendo +8, Knowledge (arcana) +10, Use Magic Device +10

Feats: Improved Initiative, Power Attack, Weapon Focus (quarterstaff)

Climate/Terrain: Any mountains

Organization: Solitary, pair, or herd (3–12 plus 1 leader of 1st–5th level and 1–2 humanoid or giant slaves per yak folk), or tribe (11–20 plus 1 leader of 5th–12th level, 1–2 lieutenants of 1st–5th level, 1–2 humanoid or giant slaves per yak folk, and a force of 10–40 fighting slaves)

Challenge Rating: 4
Treasure: Standard plus staff (see below)
Alignment: Usually neutral evil
Advancement: By character class

Yak folk are humanoid yaks who walk about on their hind legs, dress in fine clothing, and dabble in magic. They are slightly smaller than minotaurs, but aside from a vague resemblance they have little in common with those creatures. Their shaggy fur is generally well groomed, and their horns are often decorated with tassels or silver tips. Jewelry is common, and they wear fine clothing of wool and silk. All adult yak folk carry staffs that are often magical, and most also arm themselves with falchions.

Yak folk live among remote mountain peaks and valleys, inaccessible to all but the hardiest travelers and explorers.

Yak folk speak Common.

COMBAT

Most yak folk use their falchions or staffs, magical or otherwise, in combat.

Body Meld (Sp): Once per day a yak folk can merge its body with that of a humanoid or giant of Small to Large size. Except where noted here, this power functions like a *magic jar* spell heightened to 9th level (caster level 20th; Will save DC 21 negates). To use this ability, the yak folk must touch the intended target for 20 minutes without interruption (yak folk usually restrain their victims while using this ability). At the end of this period, the target must make a Will save to remain conscious. On a failed save, the host's mind becomes unconscious, and the yak folk assumes control. There is no *magic jar* per se—the yak folk physically merges its body with the victim's body without the use of an intermediate vessel. *Body meld* lasts until dispelled or dismissed.

The process works only on humans, elves, dwarves, half-orcs, and any creature of the giant type. The yak folk shares all the victim's knowledge, memories, skills, feats, and extraordinary abilities, but none of its spell-like or supernatural abilities. The yak folk retains all of its own supernatural and spell-like abilities. The merging does not shed a magical aura (so a *detect magic* spell does not reveal it), but a *true seeing* spell reveals the victim's dual nature.

If the host body is slain, the yak folk dies with it. Separating the two bodies takes half as long as melding (10 minutes). The host regains consciousness 1d6 minutes after the separation is complete.

Only characters who know the victim personally have any chance to realize that something is wrong, by making a Spot check opposed by the yak folk's Disguise check (which in this case represents how well the yak folk impersonates its host).

Command Genie (Su): Once per day, a yak folk can summon and command a janni of evil alignment, but it can never have more than one janni under its control at one time. The janni is a slave bound to serve until the second sunrise after the summoning. The yak folk are greatly disliked by all genies, but for reasons lost in antiquity, no genie can attack a yak folk. Genies sometimes work to thwart the yak folk's plans or disrupt their lives in other, indirect ways, but even this is done cautiously because the genies know that if they antagonize the yak folk too much, the lives of enslaved jann will only become worse and their tasks more onerous.

Use Staff (Ex): A yak folk can use any magic staff. This ability is similar to the Use Magic Device skill except that it applies only to magic staffs and the yak folk does not require a skill check. The chance that any particular yak folk possesses a magic staff is equal to its Hit Dice × 5%.

YAK FOLK SOCIETY

Yak folk settle in secluded mountain valleys, creating realms that are sheltered from the worst of nature's abuse—havens of greenery and life in the midst of barren, snow-covered peaks. In these seemingly idyllic hideaways, the yak folk rule over their human, elf, or dwarf subjects with iron fists.

The yak folk, for all their learning and culture, are enormously evil overlords. They care for their hapless subjects only to the extent that a live serf is better than a dead one, and keeping a serf alive is easier than working oneself.

Outsiders stumbling into an enclave of yak folk are usually surprised and pleased to find what appears to be a utopia hidden in the mountains, and the yak folk do all in their power to foster that image until the strangers can be disarmed and enslaved.

Their cities consist of several thousand yak folk plus five or six times as many enslaved minions. A city is surrounded by smaller enclaves and tribal outposts.

YAK FOLK CHARACTERS

A yak folk's favored class is sorcerer. Most yak folk leaders are sorcerers or sorcerer/clerics. Yak folk clerics tend to venerate chaotic and evil gods and often have access to the Evil and Trickery domains.

A yak folk PC's effective character level (ECL) is equal to its class level + 7. Thus, a 1st-level yak folk sorcerer has an ECL of 8 and is the equivalent of an 8th-level character.

YUGOLOTH

Possibly the greediest, most selfish beings in the Outer Planes, yugoloths reign supreme among the evil outsiders of the plane of Gehenna.

Yugoloths often act as mercenaries for demons, devils, and other planar powers. They are enthusiastic bodyguards and soldiers because they take such glee in hurting others, but they turn on their masters if the enemy makes them a better offer. They also make good torturers, because they delight in misery.

The yugoloths are led by a yugoloth of surpassing power known as the General of Gehenna, who rules with an iron fist—exactly as far as his reach extends. There is no widespread or organized opposition to his rule, but yugoloths outside his immediate sphere of influence have little hesitation about acting independently. The General rules from the Crawling City, a great metropolis supported by thousands of grafted-together legs that slowly wanders the volcanic Gehennan landscape.

Whatever their form, yugoloths tend to have the smell of brimstone around them. In their native form, they leave a faint trail of ash unless they consciously choose not to.

Yugoloths speak Abyssal, Draconic, and Infernal.

COMBAT

In general, yugoloths are focused combatants. They choose one opponent out of a group and attack until it falls, then move on to the next foe. They fight at a frantic pace, using their best attacks and spell-like abilities right away, even if they're not sure what they're facing.

All yugoloths have the following special abilities in common.

Outsider Traits: A yugoloth has darkvision (60-foot range). It cannot be raised or resurrected.

Summon Yugoloth **(Sp):** Most yugoloths can summon others of their kind as though casting a *summon monster* spell, but they have only a limited chance of success. Roll d%: On a failure, no yugoloths answer the summons. Summoned creatures remain for 1 hour, then return whence they came. A yugoloth that is itself summoned cannot use its own summon ability for 1 hour.

Yugoloth Traits: A yugoloth is immune to poison and acid. It has cold, fire, and electricity resistance 20. Yugoloths can communicate telepathically with any creature within 100 feet that has a language.

MARRAENOLOTH

The marraenoloths serve a specialized function, possibly the most specialized of any of the yugoloths. They are the ferrymen on the River Styx, somberly poling their ghastly crafts along that sepulchral river and through all the horrid planes it visits.

These pallid humanoids are little more than skeletons clothed in rotted robes and grave wrappings. Only their red-glowing eyes show signs of life. Like all natives of Gehenna, they are pitiless and mercenary. They can speak any language, but they communicate with other marraenoloths telepathically.

Only by remaining scrupulously neutral in their dealings with all others do the marraenoloths retain the ability to move freely throughout the evil-aligned Outer Planes. They can move away from the River Styx, but

	Marraenoloth Medium-Size Outsider (Evil)	Arcanaloth Medium-Size Outsider (Evil)	Yagnoloth Large Outsider (Evil)
Hit Dice:	10d8 (45 hp)	12d8 (54 hp)	10d8+40 (85 hp)
Initiative:	+2	+7	+2
Speed:	50 ft.	30 ft., fly 50 ft. (poor)	50 ft.
AC:	21 (+2 Dex, +9 natural), touch 12, flat-footed 19	28 (+3 Dex, +15 natural), touch 13, flat-footed 25	21 (–1 size, +2 Dex, +10 natural), touch 11, flat-footed 19
Attacks:	Bite +11 melee	2 claws +12 melee and bite +7 melee	Greatsword +9/+4 melee and claw +20 melee, or greataxe +9/+4 melee and claw +20 melee
Damage:	Bite 1d6+1	Claw 1d4 plus poison, bite 1d6	Greatsword 2d6/19–20, greataxe 1d12/×3, claw 1d6+10 plus stunning blow
Face/Reach:	5 ft. by 5 ft./5 ft.	5 ft. by 5 ft./5 ft.	5 ft. by 5 ft./10 ft.
Special Attacks:	Fear gaze, spell-like abilities	Poison, spell-like abilities, spells	Breath weapon, energy drain, *shocking grasp*, stunning blow
Special Qualities:	Outsider traits, SR 21, yugoloth traits	DR 15/+3, outsider traits, partial immunity to spells, SR 24, yugoloth traits	DR 15/+1, outsider traits, SR 25, muscular arm, yugoloth traits
Saves:	Fort +7, Ref +9, Will +9	Fort +8, Ref +11, Will +14	Fort +11, Ref +9, Will +9
Abilities:	Str 13, Dex 15, Con 10, Int 13, Wis 14, Cha 10	Str 11, Dex 16, Con 11, Int 20, Wis 18, Cha 17	Str 30, Dex 14, Con 19, Int 15, Wis 15, Cha 16
Skills:	Appraise +14, Balance +15, Bluff +13, Diplomacy +2, Intimidate +2, Intuit Direction +15, Knowledge (the planes) +14, Listen +4, Profession (boater) +13, Spot +4, Swim +13	Bluff +17, Concentration +14, Diplomacy +19, Gather Information +18, Innuendo +19, Intimidate +20, Knowledge (arcana) +19, Knowledge (the planes) +19, Profession (scribe) +19, Sense Motive +19, Spellcraft +20	Climb +22, Concentration +17, Diplomacy +5, Intimidate +16, Jump +20, Knowledge (the planes) +15, Listen +15, Sense Motive +15, Spot +15
Feats:	Alertness, Combat Casting, Dodge	Empower Spell, Improved Initiative, Iron Will, Spell Focus (Abjuration)	Cleave, Power Attack, Weapon Focus (claw)
Climate/Terrain:	Any aquatic	Any land and underground	Any land and underground
Organization:	Solitary	Solitary, pair, or embassy (3–4)	Solitary
Challenge Rating:	10	17	10
Treasure:	Standard (coins only)	Standard	Standard
Alignment:	Always neutral evil	Always neutral evil	Always neutral evil
Advancement:	11–20 HD (Medium-size)	13–24 HD (Medium-size)	11–30 HD (Large)

their skiffs cannot, and a marraenoloth seldom goes anywhere its boat can't take it.

Marraenoloths never carry cargo, only passengers. Payment must be made in advance and must be at least 100 gp per passenger. Although marraenoloths seldom, if ever, get lost on the labyrinthine channels of the Styx, there is a 15% chance on any chartered journey that the boatman delivers the passengers into an ambush, arranged and paid for by a third party. Each additional 100 gp paid per passenger reduces the chance by 5%.

Combat

Marraenoloths rely almost exclusively on their spell-like abilities for offense and defense.

Fear Gaze (Su): When a marraenoloth stares at a creature, the latter must succeed at a Will saving throw (DC 15) or become shaken for 1d4 rounds. This is a mind-affecting fear effect.

Spell-Like Abilities: At will—*alter self, animate dead, charm person, phantasmal killer, poison, produce flame, teleport without error.* Caster level 10th; save DC 10 + spell level.

Summon Yugoloth (Sp): Once per day, a marraenoloth can summon another marraenoloth with a 75% chance of success.

ARCANALOTH

Arcanaloths are the scribes, record-keepers, negotiators, and deal-makers for the yugoloths of Gehenna. As such, they are

grasping, wheedling manipulators, but at least they're generally true to their word.

An arcanaloth has humanoid form but the head of a jackal or dog. It dresses finely but is businesslike and abrupt, if not downright surly.

Arcanaloths can speak and write any language.

Combat

Arcanaloths are weak in melee, but they are powerful spellcasters. In addition to all the usual powers of yugoloths, arcanaloths have the following special abilities.

Partial Immunity to Spells: Mind-affecting spells have no effect on arcanaloths.

Poison (Ex): An arcanaloth's claws are coated with poison. It delivers this poison (Fortitude save DC 16) with each successful claw attack. The initial and secondary damage is the same (1 point of Strength damage).

Spell-Like Abilities: At will—*darkness, fly, heat metal, invisibility* (self only), *magic missile, shapechange, telekinesis, warp wood*; 1/day—*fear, major image*. Caster level 12th; save DC 13 + spell level.

Spells: An arcanaloth can cast arcane spells as a 12th-level sorcerer (spells known 9/5/5/4/3/2/1; spells/day 6/7/7/7/6/5/3; save DC 13 + spell level, or 15 + spell level for Abjuration spells).

Summon Yugoloth (Sp): Once per day, an arcanaloth can summon another arcanaloth with a 40% chance of success.

YAGNOLOTH

In the simplistic feudal hierarchy of Gehenna, yagnoloths are minor lords. Each rules over a territory, with vassal yugoloths at its beck and call. The rationale behind this arrangement is not clear, since yagnoloths are neither stronger nor brighter than many of their subjects. Whatever the reason, the ruling powers of Gehenna enforce the existing order, and the yagnoloths profit from it.

In fact, the yagnoloths squeeze every advantage possible from their positions, up to and including sanctioning executions of yugoloths that are considerably more physically and magically powerful than themselves, but lower in the hierarchy. Such actions are little different from what any yugoloth would do if given the opportunity. Nonetheless, the fact that the yagnoloths' authority exceeds their personal power has earned them a special sort of resentment. No other yugoloth can pass up an opportunity to betray its yagnoloth overlord—for the right price.

As a secondary effect of their despised status, yagnoloths cannot summon other yugoloths.

A yagnoloth is humanoid and stands 10 to 15 feet tall. Its hide is red and scaly; its head is small and skeletal and topped by ears resembling bats' wings. A yagnoloth's favored arm is enormous, thickly knotted with muscles, and long enough to drag on the ground. It uses this arm for its claw attack. The other arm appears small in comparison and is about the size of a normal human arm. This arm is always the one it uses to wield a weapon. The weapon may be a magic item but is never a specific weapon or one with a special ability. A yagnoloth that possessed such a weapon would be assassinated in short order by its underlings.

Combat

A yagnoloth always attacks with both arms in melee. It wields a greataxe or greatsword with its smaller arm, but that arm is fairly weak (Str 10) and the yagnoloth does not receive any Strength bonus when using it.

Breath Weapon (Su): As a standard action, a yagnoloth can exhale a cloud of acid every 1d4 rounds. This cloud affects a single 5-foot cone for 1 round. A character in that space must make a Reflex saving throw (DC 19); failure means the character takes 2d6 points of acid damage and is stunned for an equal number of rounds.

Energy Drain (Su): The truly horrific power of the yagnoloth is its ability to drain life force. The victim must be unconscious or stunned. The yagnoloth places its head against the victim's flesh. For each full round the yagnoloth remains in contact, the victim gains 1d4 negative levels. The Fortitude save DC to remove each negative level is 18.

Shocking Grasp (Sp): A yagnoloth can use this ability three times per day, causing 1d8+10 points of electricity damage each time. Caster level 10th.

Stunning Blow (Ex): Any character struck by a yagnoloth's massive arm must make a Fortitude saving (DC 25) to avoid being stunned for a number of rounds equal to the points of damage dealt by the blow.

Muscular Arm (Ex): A yagnoloth's larger arm functions as a primary natural weapon, even when it is used to make secondary attacks. This ability negates any secondary attack penalty and allows the yagnaloth its full Strength bonus with its claw, whether the attack is primary or secondary.

APPENDIX: TEMPLATES

A templated creature is created by adding a template to an existing creature. The following rules set out the procedures for building a templated creature, such as a death knight.

Sometimes a template changes a creature's type. In such a case, the creature gains the vulnerabilities and immunities of the new type. All other characteristics, including Hit Die size, base attack bonus, base saves, feats, and skills, remain unchanged unless otherwise indicated in the template description.

The ability score adjustments associated with a template cannot reduce any of a creature's ability scores below 1, unless otherwise noted.

CAPTURED ONE

A captured one is a living creature that is under the control of a raggamoffyn. The raggamoffyn has access to its host's memories and draws on its host's experiences. The captured

one eats, speaks, and lives all under the direction of its raggamoffyn master.

Captured ones speak Common and whatever languages the base creature speaks.

CREATING A CAPTURED ONE

"Captured one" is a template that can be added to a giant, humanoid, monstrous humanoid, animal, beast, or vermin (hereafter known as the "base creature") that is the same size as or smaller than the dominating raggamoffyn. The creature's type changes to construct. Both the raggamoffyn's and the base creature's statistics and special abilities are modified as noted here.

Hit Dice: A captured one maintains separate hit point totals for each of its two parts.

Initiative: Same as raggamoffyn.

Speed: Same as base creature.

Armor Class: Use either the raggamoffyn's natural armor bonus or the base creature's natural armor bonus (if any), whichever is higher.

Attacks: Same as base creature, modified by new ability modifiers.

Damage: Same as base creature.

Special Attacks: The raggamoffyn gains control over all special attacks that the base creature possesses, including spells and spell-like abilities. The raggamoffyn's wrap and improved grab special attacks are unavailable while it controls the host.

Special Qualities: Both the raggamoffyn and the base creature retain any special qualities they had previously.

Construct Traits: A captured one is immune to mind-affecting effects, poison, *sleep*, paralysis, stunning, disease, death effects, necromantic effects, and any effect that requires a Fortitude save unless it also works on objects. The creature is not subject to critical hits, subdual damage, ability damage, ability drain, energy drain, or death from massive damage. The raggamoffyn portion cannot heal itself but can be healed through repair; the base creature portion heals normally. It cannot be raised or resurrected. A captured one has darkvision (60-foot range).

Senses (Ex): The raggamoffyn sees and hears everything that the base creature is able to.

Shared Damage (Ex): An attack on a captured one deals half its damage to the raggamoffyn and half to the dominated creature.

Saves: A captured one uses the raggamoffyn's base Fortitude, Reflex, and Will saves.

Abilities: A captured one uses the Constitution, Intelligence, and Charisma scores of the base creature and the Strength, Dexterity, and Wisdom scores of the raggamoffyn.

Skills: Same as base creature.

Feats: Same as base creature.

Climate/Terrain: Same as raggamoffyn.

Organization: Solitary, pair, or gang (3–4).

Challenge Rating: Same as base creature +2.

Treasure: Standard.

Alignment: Same as raggamoffyn.

Advancement: Same as base creature.

SAMPLE CAPTURED ONE

Here is a sample captured one using a bugbear as the base creature along with a common raggamoffyn.

**Captured Bugbear/
Common Raggamoffyn
(Goblinoid)
Medium-Size
Construct
Hit Dice:** Ragga-moffyn 3d10 (16 hp) and bugbear 3d8+3 (16 hp)

Initiative: +2

Speed: 30 ft.

AC: 20 (+2 Dex, +5 natural, +2 leather, +1 small wooden shield), touch 12, flat-footed 18

Attacks: Morningstar +4 melee, or javelin +4 ranged

Damage: Morningstar 1d8+2, javelin 1d6+2

Face/Reach: 5 ft. by 5 ft./5 ft.

Special Qualities: Darkvision 60 ft., construct traits, senses, shared damage

Saves: Fort +2, Ref +3, Will +3

Abilities: Str 14, Dex 15, Con 13, Int 10, Wis 15, Cha 9

Skills: Climb +2, Hide +4, Listen +5, Move Silently +7, Spot +5

Feats: Alertness

Climate/Terrain: Any

Organization: Solitary, pair, or gang (3–4)

Challenge Rating: 4

Treasure: Standard

Alignment: Always neutral

Advancement: By character class

Construct Traits: A captured one bugbear is immune to mind-affecting effects, poison, *sleep*, paralysis, stunning, disease, death effects, necromantic effects, and any effect that requires a Fortitude save unless it also works on objects. The creature is not subject to critical hits, subdual damage, ability damage, ability drain, energy drain, or death from massive damage. The common raggamoffyn component cannot heal

itself but can be healed through repair; the bugbear component heals normally. It cannot be raised or resurrected. A captured one bugbear has darkvision (60-foot range).

Senses: Both components of the captured one bugbear see and hear everything the bugbear can.

Shared Damage (Ex): An attack on a captured one bugbear deals half its damage (rounded down) to the raggamoffyn and half (rounded up) to the bugbear.

CHIMERIC CREATURE

Chimeric creatures are hybrids that combine the traits of a monstrous goat and a chromatic dragon with those of a third creature, which must be an animal, beast, or vermin.

A chimeric creature has at least three heads. The goat head sits to the right of the other heads. It has glowing amber eyes and long ochre horns. The scaly dragon head sits to the left and has black eyes. The dragon scales of a chimeric creature may be black, blue, green, red, or white. The central head of a chimeric creature is the head of the third creature. A chimeric creature has the hindquarters of a black goat, the wings of a dragon, and the forequarters of the third creature. The *Monster Manual* describes one chimeric creature, the chimera.

Chimeric creatures speak Draconic.

CREATING A CHIMERIC CREATURE

"Chimeric" is a template that can be added to any Medium-size, Large, or Huge animal, beast, or vermin (referred to hereafter as the base creature). The creature's type changes to magical beast. It uses all the base creature's statistics and special abilities except as noted here. Adding the chimeric template to a lion results in a chimera as described in the *Monster Manual*. (That monster is considered to already have the chimeric template.)

Hit Dice: Increased to d10. Use the base creature's Hit Dice or 9 Hit Dice, whichever is higher.

Speed: Same as base creature, but chimeric creatures gain wings and can fly at a speed of 50 feet (poor).

AC: Base creature's natural armor bonus improves by +6.

Attacks and Damage: A chimeric creature retains all the attacks of the base creature and also gains a bite attack for 2d6 points of damage from its dragon head and a butt attack for 1d8 points of damage from its goat head.

Whichever natural weapon has the highest base damage becomes its primary attack. If two natural weapons have the same base damage, the one that also delivers a special attack (such as poison) is primary. If a tie still exists, choose one of the tied attacks to be primary for that creature.

Special Attacks: A chimeric creature retains all the special attacks of the base creature and also gains a breath weapon based on its dragon variety.

Breath Weapon (Su): Every 1d4 rounds, a chimeric creature's dragon head can use a breath weapon that deals 3d8 points of damage. Anyone in the area can make a Reflex save for half (DC 10 + 1/2 chimeric creature's Hit Dice + chimeric creature's Constitution modifier). Use all rules for dragon breath (see the Dragon entry in this book), except as specified in the table below.

To determine the head color and breath weapon randomly, roll 1d10 and consult the table below.

1d10	Head Color	Breath Weapon
1–2	Black	Line of acid*
3–4	Blue	Line of lightning*
5–6	Green	Cone of gas**
7–8	Red	Cone of fire**
9–10	White	Cone of cold**

* The line is always 5 feet high, 5 feet wide, and 40 feet long.
** The cone is always 20 feet long.

Special Qualities: Same as base creature, plus scent.

Saves: Same base saves as base creature.

Abilities: Increased from the base creature as follows: Str +4, Dex +1, Con +4, Int +2, Wis +0, Cha +0.

Skills: A chimeric creature's three heads give it a +2 racial bonus on Listen and Spot checks.

Feats: A chimeric creature gains Multiattack as a bonus feat.

Climate/Terrain: Any land or underground.

Organization: Same as base creature.

Challenge Rating: 9 or same as base creature +1, whichever is higher.

Treasure: Standard.

Alignment: Always same as dragon component.

Advancement: Same as base creature if it originally had 9 or more Hit Dice; otherwise 10–18 (same size category); 19–27 (one size category larger).

Sample Chimeric Creature

Here is a sample chimeric creature using an ankheg as the base creature and a white dragon head.

Chimeric Ankheg
Large Magical Beast

Hit Dice: 9d10+45 (94 hp)

Initiative: +0

Speed: 30 ft., burrow 20 ft., fly 50 ft. (poor)

AC: 24 (–1 size, +15 natural), touch 9, flat-footed 24

Attacks: Bite +12 melee and bite +10 melee and butt +10 melee

Damage: Bite 2d6+7 (ankheg), bite 2d6+3 (dragon), butt 1d8+3

Face/Reach: 5 ft. by 10 ft./5 ft.

Special Attacks: Acid, breath weapon, improved grab, spit acid

Special Qualities: Darkvision 60 ft., low-light vision, scent, tremorsense

Saves: Fort +11, Ref +6, Will +4

Abilities: Str 25, Dex 11, Con 21, Int 3, Wis 13, Cha 6

Skills: Climb +11, Listen +9, Spot +3

Feats: Multiattack (B)

Climate/Terrain: Temperate and warm forest, plains, and underground

Organization: Solitary, pair, or cluster (3–4)

Challenge Rating: 9

Treasure: None

Alignment: Always chaotic evil

Advancement: 10–18 HD (Large); 19–27 HD (Huge)

Acid (Ex): Acidic enzymes drip from the mouth of the ankheg head each round it maintains a hold on a grabbed creature. The acid automatically deals 1d4 points of acid damage each round.

Breath Weapon (Su): A chimeric ankheg's dragon head can emit a 20-foot cone of cold that deals 3d8 points of cold damage (Reflex DC 19 half).

Improved Grab (Ex): If a chimeric ankheg hits an opponent that is at least one size category smaller than itself with its ankheg bite attack, it deals normal damage and attempts to start a grapple as a free action without provoking an attack of opportunity (grapple bonus +17). If it gets a hold, it has the option to conduct the grapple normally, or simply use its jaws to hold the opponent (–20 penalty on grapple check, but the chimeric ankheg is not considered grappled). In either case, each successful grapple check it makes during successive rounds automatically deals bite and acid damage. If the chimeric ankheg is damaged after grabbing its prey, it retreats backward down its tunnel at its burrow speed, dragging the victim with it.

Scent (Ex): A chimeric ankheg can detect approaching enemies, sniff out hidden foes, and track by sense of smell.

Spit Acid (Ex): A chimeric ankheg can spit a line of acid 5 feet high, 5 feet wide, and 30 feet long. Any creature hit by this attack takes 4d4 points of acid damage (Reflex DC 19 half). One such attack depletes the chimeric ankheg's acid supply for 6 hours. It cannot spit acid or deal acid damage with its bite

during this time. Chimeric ankhegs do not use this ability unless they are desperate or frustrated. They most often spit acid when reduced to fewer than half of their hit points or when they have not successfully grabbed an opponent.

Tremorsense (Ex): A chimeric ankheg can automatically sense the location of anything within 60 feet that is in contact with the ground.

DEATH KNIGHT

Gods of death create death knights. They are martial champions of evil. These horrible undead are most commonly raised from the ranks of blackguards, fighters, rangers, and barbarians; but a paladin who falls from grace near the moment of death may also become a death knight. Paladins who become death knights are subject to the same modifications as are presented for the blackguard in Chapter 2 of the DUNGEON MASTER's Guide.

A death knight's physical form is that of its decayed body. The face is a blackened skull covered with patches of rotting flesh, with two pinpoints of orange light in the eye sockets. The voice of a death knight is chilling, seeming to echo from deep within. Death knights were powerful people in life, and so they often wear expensive or magic clothing and armor. They are quite fond of wearing flowing capes to mark them as figures of importance.

Death knights speak the languages they knew in life.

CREATING A DEATH KNIGHT

"Death knight" is a template that can be added to any evil humanoid creature of 6th level or higher (referred to hereafter as the character). The character's type changes to undead. It uses all the character's statistics and special abilities except as noted here.

Hit Dice: All the character's Hit Dice (current and future) become d12s.

Speed: Same as the character.

AC: The death knight has +5 natural armor, or the character's natural armor, whichever is better.

Attacks: Death knights usually fight with martial weapons, but if disarmed they will use a touch attack.

Damage: The death knight's touch attack uses negative energy to deal damage equal to 1d8 + the death knight's Charisma bonus to living creatures. Each successful touch attack also deals 1 point of Constitution damage. A Will save (DC 10 + 1/2 death knight's HD + death knight's Charisma modifier) reduces the damage by half and negates the Constitution damage. Characters with natural attacks can use their natural weaponry or use the touch attack, as they prefer.

Special Attacks: A death knight retains all the character's special attacks and gains those described below.

Abyssal Blast (Su): Once per day, a death knight can unleash a blast of eldritch fire. The blast fills a 20-foot-radius spread anywhere within a range of 400 feet + 40 feet per HD of the death knight. The blast deals 1d6 points of damage per HD of

the death knight (maximum 20d6). Half of the damage is fire damage, but the rest results directly from divine power and is therefore not subject to being reduced by *protection from elements* (*fire*), *fire shield* (*chill shield*), or similar magic. A Reflex save (DC 10 + 1/2 death knight's HD + death knight's Charisma modifier) reduces the damage by half.

Fear Aura (*Su*): Death knights are shrouded in a dreadful aura of death and evil. Creatures of less than 5 HD within 15 feet of a death knight must succeed at a Will save (DC 10 + 1/2 death knight's HD + death knight's Charisma modifier) or be affected as though by a *fear* spell cast by a sorcerer of the death knight's level.

Undead Followers: A death knight attracts lesser undead creatures that happen to exist within a 200-mile radius. It may have up to twice its levels in Hit Dice of followers. The followers arrive monthly in the following increments: 1d6 ghouls, 1d4 ghasts, 1d12 medium skeletons, 1d4 wights, or 1d8 medium zombies once per week. These creatures remain in the service of the death knight until destroyed. These creatures are in addition to any undead creatures the death knight might be able to command or rebuke as a class ability.

Spells: A death knight can cast any spells it could while alive, unless alignment restrictions prohibit the casting of a particular spell.

Special Qualities: A death knight retains all the character's special qualities and gains those described below.

Damage Reduction (*Su*): A death knight's undead body is tough, giving the creature damage reduction 15/+1.

Immunities (*Ex*): Death knights are immune to cold, electricity, and polymorph in addition to those immunities possessed by undead (see undead traits, below).

Spell Resistance (*Su*): A death knight gains spell resistance 20 +1 per character's level beyond 10th.

Summon Mount (*Su*): A death knight has the ability to summon a mount, typically a nightmare, though it may be of any other species normally used as a mount. The mount may have no more Hit Dice than half the death knight's levels. If the mount is lost or killed, the death knight may summon another one after a year and a day.

Turn Immunity (*Ex*): A death knight cannot be turned. It can be banished with *holy word*, however, just as if it were an evil outsider. (The banished death knight returns to the plane of the evil god it serves.)

Undead Traits: A death knight is immune to mind-affecting effects, poison, *sleep*, paralysis, stunning, disease, death effects, necromantic effects, and any effect that requires a Fortitude save unless it also works on objects. It is not subject to critical hits, subdual damage, ability damage, ability drain, energy drain, or death from massive damage. A death knight cannot be raised, and resurrection works only if it is willing. The creature has darkvision (60-foot range).

Saves: Same as character.

Abilities: A death knight gains +4 to Strength and +2 to both Wisdom and Charisma. Being undead, it has no Constitution score.

Skills: Same as character.

Feats: Same as character.

Climate/Terrain: Any land and underground.

Organization: Solitary or troupe (see undead followers, above).

Challenge Rating: Same as character +3.

Treasure: Double standard.

Alignment: Same as character (always evil).

Advancement: Death knights continue to advance in level as per their original class.

DEATH KNIGHT CHARACTERS

A death knight PC's effective character level (ECL) is equal to the creature's character level +5; thus, a 7th-level fighter/3rd-level blackguard death knight has an ECL of 15 and is the equivalent of a 15th-level character.

A character with the ability to spontaneously cast *cure* spells who becomes a death knight loses that ability, but gains the ability to spontaneously cast *inflict* spells.

SAMPLE DEATH KNIGHT

Here is a sample death knight that uses a human fighter/blackguard as the character.

7th-level Fighter/3rd-level Blackguard
Medium-Size Undead
Hit Dice: 10d12 (65 hp)
Initiative: +5
Speed: 20 ft. (full plate armor)
AC: 26 (+1 Dex, +8 full plate, +2 enhancement, +5 natural), touch 11, flat-footed 25
Attacks: Touch +15 melee, or +3 greatsword +19/+14 melee, or heavy crossbow +11 ranged
Damage: Touch 1d8 plus 1 point Con, +3 greatsword 2d6+12/19–20, heavy crossbow 1d10/19–20
Special Attacks: Abyssal blast, Constitution damage, fear aura 15 ft., smite good 1/day, command undead 3/day

Special Qualities: Aura of despair, dark blessing, *detect good*, DR 15/+1, immunities, poison use, SR 20, summon mount, undead followers, undead traits

Saves: Fort +8, Ref +4, Will +5

Abilities: Str 21, Dex 13, Con —, Int 10, Wis 14, Cha 10

Skills: Climb +3, Diplomacy +5, Handle Animal +3, Hide +1, Intimidate +4, Jump +3, Knowledge (religion) +2, Listen +3, Ride (horse) +6

Feats: Cleave, Dodge, Great Cleave, Improved Initiative, Mobility, Power Attack , Sunder, Weapon Focus (greatsword), Weapon Specialization (greatsword)

Climate/Terrain: Any land and underground
Organization: Solitary or troupe
Challenge Rating: 13
Treasure: Double standard
Alignment: Usually lawful evil
Advancement: By character class

Abyssal Blast (Su): Reflex save DC 15.

Fear Aura (Su): Will save DC 15.

Smite Good (Su): 1/day, +3 to one damage roll against a good opponent.

Immunities: Death knights are immune to turning, cold, electricity, and polymorph.

Undead Traits: A death knight is immune to mind-affecting effects, poison, *sleep*, paralysis, stunning, disease, death effects, necromantic effects, and any effect that requires a Fortitude save unless it also works on objects. It is not subject to critical hits, subdual damage, ability damage, ability drain, energy drain, or death from massive damage. A death knight cannot be raised, and resurrection works only if it is willing. The creature has darkvision (60-foot range).

Spells Prepared: 1st–*doom*, *inflict light wounds*; 2nd— *bull's strength*. Save DC 12 + spell level.

Possessions: +2 full plate armor, +3 greatsword.

Constitution Damage (Su): Will save DC 15.

HALF-GOLEM

Half-golems are the results of good-intentioned actions taken too far. While the application of a poultice infused with curative herbs or the casting of a spell can save the life of an injured or diseased person, only powerful magic can replace a missing limb. Such magic is often beyond the reach of the ordinary person working in a quarry or a mill, or scything a field of grain, who suffers the loss of one or more limbs.

Arcane artisans applied their knowledge of golem construction to come up with a way to restore such a person to wholeness. While the initial results were promising, there was a limit to the effectiveness of the technique—many people who received one or more new limbs through this process proved unable to withstand the trauma of the transformation and became permanently evil as a result. Individuals of evil intent now exploit this limitation, purposely

creating ravening, unholy crosses between living beings and golems.

CONSTRUCTION

There are two steps to making a half-golem. The first is constructing the limbs, and the second is attaching the limbs.

Molding a limb from clay, preparing one made of flesh, carving it from stone, or forging it from iron requires an appropriate skill (see the specific half-golem descriptions for details) and can be done by anyone. Infusing a formed limb with magic requires the Craft Wondrous Item and Craft Magic Arms and Armor feats. It takes one month to complete the magical rituals. The creator must labor for at least 8 hours each day in a specially prepared laboratory or workroom. The chamber is similar to an alchemist's laboratory and costs 500 gp to establish.

When not working on the rituals, the creator must rest and can perform no other activities, just as if he or she were creating a golem. As with a golem, if the creator is personally constructing the limbs, he or she can perform the building and the rituals together.

Once created, the limbs are treated as spell completion items. Any character capable of casting the appropriate level of spell (see specific descriptions) can attach a limb. All that's left to do is perform the final gestures and speak the words needed to imbue the limb with magic. All the limbs to be attached to a particular body must be of the same type—it's not possible, for instance, to attach a limb made of iron to a half-golem that already has a new limb made of stone. Any such attempt automatically fails, leaving the second type of limb unattached.

The Danger

Each time a limb is attached to his or her body, the recipient makes a Will save. The DC of the save varies according to the number of new limbs the character has received.

	Save DC
First new limb	15
Second new limb	19
Third new limb	25
Fourth new limb	33
Fifth new limb	43
Sixth new limb	55

A character who succeeds at all the saves he or she is required to make takes on the attributes of a half-golem as described below—except that the character retains his or her alignment, gains a +4 bonus to Constitution, and does not change type or gain construct traits. As soon as the character fails one of these required saves, he or she becomes a half-golem of neutral evil alignment. The character then has no Constitution score and the character's type changes to construct, granting him or her construct traits. A neutral evil half-golem retains the memories and knowledge of its former life, but its personality becomes murderous and cruel. It demonstrates

the hatred of flesh creatures common to elementals, and it seeks methods appropriate to its class to slaughter as many flesh creatures as possible.

CREATING A HALF-GOLEM

"Half-golem" is a template that can be added to any animal, beast, giant, humanoid creature, magical beast, or monstrous humanoid (referred to hereafter as the character). There is no minimum level or Hit Dice requirement to become a half-golem. The character's type changes to construct once a Will save is failed. Each half-golem takes on the characteristics of a particular type of golem (flesh, clay, stone, or iron) as described later in this section.

A half-golem's abilities are primarily those of the character, with the following exceptions.

Hit Dice: Same as character.
Initiative: Same as character –1, to account for the half-golem's reduced Dexterity (see Abilities, below).
Speed: Same as character, but a half-golem cannot run.
AC: A half-golem replaces any natural armor bonus it may have had with a new natural armor bonus that varies according to its type (see the table below). The change to Dexterity (see Abilities, below) also affects the half-golem's Armor Class.
Attacks: Same as character.
Damage: Same as character.
Face/Reach: Same as character.
Special Attacks: Same as character (and see the table below).
Special Qualities: Same as character; plus construct traits (upon a failed Will save), damage resistance (see table below), and others by type (see table below).
Saves: A half-golem gains a +2 racial bonus on Fortitude saves; otherwise same as character.
Abilities: Half-golems have –2 Dex, +4 Con (or no Con upon a failed Will save), –6 Int, +0 Wis, and –6 Cha. Strength varies by type (see the table below). The number of limbs attached does not alter a half-golem's Strength score.

Skills: Same as character, modified by new ability modifiers. The drop in Intelligence does not retroactively remove skill points spent.
Feats: Same as character.

Climate/Terrain: Same as character.
Organization: Solitary, pair, or squad (5–20).
Challenge Rating: Same as character +3.
Treasure: Standard.
Alignment: Same as character (if all Will saves succeed) or always neutral evil (if any Will save fails).
Advancement: By character class.

COMBAT

A half-golem fights as the character from which it is created. Half-golems are usually straightforward, unsubtle combatants that rely on their great strength to win the day. They rarely use teamwork or cooperation, even when banded together.

Construct Traits: A half-golem is immune to mind-affecting effects, poison, *sleep*, paralysis, stunning, disease, death effects, necromantic effects, and any effect that requires a Fortitude save unless it also works on objects. The creature is not subject to critical hits, subdual damage, ability damage, ability drain, energy drain, or death from massive damage. It cannot heal itself but can be healed through repair. It cannot be raised or resurrected. A half-golem has darkvision (60-foot range).

Magic Immunity (Ex): Half-golems completely resist all magical and supernatural effects, except as noted in the appropriate golem descriptions (see *Monster Manual*).

HALF-GOLEM CHARACTERS

Half-golem characters are shunned by society, so they either seek revenge against the world around them or retreat from it. Those who seek revenge generally become fighters or rogues. Those who retreat from it become barbarians, rangers, or druids. A rare few become, or remain, evil clerics.

COMMON HALF-GOLEMS

	Flesh	Clay	Stone	Iron
Natural armor	+5	+7	+9	+11
Special attacks		Wound	Slow	Breath weapon
Damage reduction	5/silver	10/silver	15/+1	25/+2
Special Qualities	Berserk	Berserk, haste, immune to piercing and slashing		Rust vulnerability
Strength	+6	+8	+10	+12
Magic immunity	As flesh golem	As clay golem	As stone golem	As iron golem

	Flesh Half-Golem Medium-Size Construct	Clay Half-Golem Medium-Size Construct
Hit Dice:	1d10 (5 hp)	1d10 (5 hp)
Initiative:	+0	+0
Speed:	30 ft. (can't run)	30 ft. (can't run)
AC:	19 (+5 natural, +3 masterwork studded leather armor, +1 masterwork small steel shield), touch 10, flat-footed 19	21 (+7 natural, +3 masterwork studded leather armor, +1 masterwork small steel shield), touch 10, flat-footed 21
Attacks:	Battleaxe +7 melee	Battleaxe +8 melee
Damage:	Battleaxe 1d8+5/×3	Battleaxe 1d8+6/×3
Special Attacks:	—	Wound
Special Qualities:	Berserk, construct traits, DR 5/silver, magic immunity	Berserk, construct traits, DR 10/silver, haste, immune to piercing and slashing weapons, magic immunity
Saves:	Fort +4, Ref +0, Will +0	Fort +4, Ref +0, Will +0
Abilities:	Str 21, Dex 10, Con —, Int 1, Wis 11, Cha 1	Str 23, Dex 10, Con —, Int 1, Wis 11, Cha 1
Skills:	Climb +7, Jump +7	Climb +8, Jump +8
Feats:	Power Attack, Weapon Focus (battleaxe)	Power Attack, Weapon Focus (battleaxe)

	Stone Half-Golem Medium-Size Construct	Iron Half-Golem Medium-Size Construct
Hit Dice:	1d10 (5 hp)	1d10 (5 hp)
Initiative:	+0	−1
Speed:	30 ft. (can't run)	30 ft. (can't run)
AC:	23 (+9 natural, +3 masterwork studded leather armor, +1 masterwork small steel shield), touch 10, flat-footed 23	25 (−1 Dex, +11 natural, +3 masterwork studded leather armor, +1 masterwork small steel shield), touch 10, flat-footed 25
Attacks:	Battleaxe +9 melee	Battleaxe +10 melee
Damage:	Battleaxe 1d8+7/×3	Battleaxe 1d8+8/×3
Special Attacks:	Slow	Breath weapon
Special Qualities:	Construct traits, DR 15/+1, magic immunity	Construct traits, DR 25/+2, magic immunity, rust vulnerability
Saves:	Fort +4, Ref +0, Will +0	Fort +4, Ref +0, Will +0
Abilities:	Str 25, Dex 10, Con —, Int 1, Wis 11, Cha 1	Str 27, Dex 10, Con —, Int 1, Wis 11, Cha 1
Skills:	Climb +9, Jump +9	Climb +10, Jump +10
Feats:	Power Attack, Weapon Focus (battleaxe)	Power Attack, Weapon Focus (battleaxe)

Climate/Terrain: Any land and underground

Organization: Solitary, pair, or squad (5–20)

Challenge Rating: 4

Treasure: Standard (the sample creatures all have masterwork studded leather armor, masterwork small steel shields, and battleaxes)

Alignment: Same as character (if all Will saves succeed) or always neutral evil (if any Will save fails)

Advancement: By character class (fighter)

SAMPLE HALF-GOLEMS

Examples of four half-golems, each using a 1st-level half-orc fighter who has failed a Will save (see The Danger) as the character, are provided here.

A half-golem looks like a bizarre and horrifying melding of a golem and the character it once was. The materials of its golem limbs twine and crawl across its flesh, like ivy growing across a building or tree. In many cases, a half-golem's flesh is horribly scarred and has the pale gray color of death. Half-golems speak whatever languages they spoke before their transformations, but their voices are harsh and strangled.

FLESH HALF-GOLEM

A flesh half-golem is a tortured soul whose replacement limbs were stolen from the dead. Flesh golems' replacement limbs are rudely stitched to their bodies and may have different skin color or texture from the rest of the character's skin.

Berserk (Ex): A flesh half-golem that takes damage in combat flies into a berserk rage the following round, attacking wildly until either it or its opponent is dead. It gains +4 Strength, +4 Constitution, and −2 AC. A flesh half-golem cannot end its berserk state voluntarily. If the flesh

half-golem is a barbarian, the bonuses and the penalty are cumulative with the barbarian rage class feature.

Construction

The pieces of a flesh golem must come from corpses of the same size and type as the recipient (for instance, a Medium-size humanoid character can not use Small animal limbs). The limbs must not have decayed significantly. "Construction" of the limb requires a successful Craft (leatherworking) or Heal check (DC 20). The rituals cost 10,000 gp and 200 XP and require *bull's strength* and *geas/quest*. Attaching the limb requires the ability to cast 6th-level arcane spells.

CLAY HALF-GOLEM

A clay half-golem has a grotesquely distorted musculature, such as an over-large chest, arms attached by thick knots of muscle at the shoulder, stubby fingers, or arms that hang almost to the ground. Its features often appear partially melted. Typically it drips bits of clay, and its slimy replacement "flesh" coats its weapons.

Berserk (Ex): A clay half-golem that takes damage in combat flies into a berserk rage the following round, attacking wildly until either it or its opponent is dead. It gains +4 Strength, +4 Constitution, and –2 AC. A clay half-golem cannot end its berserk state voluntarily. If the clay half-golem is a barbarian, the bonuses and the penalty are cumulative with the barbarian rage class feature.

Wound (Ex): The damage a clay half-golem deals doesn't heal naturally. Only a spell of 6th level or higher with the healing descriptor (such as *heal*) can repair it.

Haste (Su): After it has engaged in at least 1 round of combat on a given day, a clay half-golem can use *haste* upon itself once during that day as a free action. The effect lasts 3 rounds and is otherwise the same as the spell.

Immunity to Slashing and Piercing (Ex): Slashing and piercing weapons, whether normal or magical, deal no damage to a clay half-golem.

Construction

A clay limb must be sculpted from a single block of clay weighing at least 100 pounds. The sculpting requires a successful Craft (sculpting) or Profession (mason) check (DC 20). The rituals cost 12,000 gp and 240 XP and require *animate objects* and *geas/quest*. Attaching the limb requires the ability to cast 6th-level divine spells.

STONE HALF-GOLEM

A stone half-golem drags thick limbs of roughly chiseled stone, stylized to suit its creator. For example, one might appear armored, have a particular symbol carved on it, or have designs worked into it. The limbs may be of different types of stone.

Slow (Su): A stone golem can use *slow* as a free action once every 2 rounds. The effect has a range of 10 feet and a duration of 7 rounds, requiring a successful Will save (DC 13) to negate. The ability is otherwise the same as the spell.

Construction

A stone limb must be chiseled from a single block of stone weighing at least 300 pounds. The carving requires a successful Craft (stoneworking) check (DC 20). The rituals cost 16,000 gp and 320 XP and require *geas/quest* and *stone to flesh*. Attaching the limb requires the ability to cast 6th-level arcane spells.

IRON HALF-GOLEM

The limbs of an iron half-golem appear bolted or riveted to the flesh. Irregular and haphazard iron plates join flesh and metal limbs. The limbs can be fashioned in any manner, just like those of a stone half-golem, although they usually appear armored. They are much smoother than those of a stone half-golem.

Breath Weapon (Su): As a free action, an iron half-golem can emit a cloud of poisonous gas from its limbs in a 10-foot cone directly in front of it. The cloud lasts 1 round, and the limbs can emit another cloud every 1d4+1 rounds. The initial damage is 1d4 points of Constitution damage, and the secondary damage is death. A Fortitude save (DC 10+ 1/2 the iron half-golem's Hit Dice + the iron half-golem's Constitution modifier) negates both effects.

Rust Vulnerability (Ex): An iron half-golem is affected by rust attacks, such as that of a rust monster or a *rusting grasp* spell.

Construction

An iron limb is sculpted from 500 pounds of pure iron. The sculpting requires a successful Craft (armorsmithing) or Craft (weaponsmithing) check (DC 20). The rituals cost 20,000 gp and 400 XP and require *cloudkill* and *geas/quest*. Attaching the limb requires the ability to cast 6th-level arcane spells.

MONSTER OF LEGEND

A monster of legend is a creature chosen by a god to perform an appointed task. The creature is imbued with divine abilities and great strength to better accomplish its goal. A monster of legend is a unique creature and considered to be an archetype for creatures of the same kind. These divinely enhanced creatures are often set to guard artifacts or planar portals.

Monsters of legend are highly dangerous creatures. They are stronger, tougher, and fiercer than their normally encountered kin. Most have potent attack forms and special qualities that mark them as having been touched by divine forces. Monsters of legend are rarely encountered by chance. They leave their lairs only when on divine missions or when exacting revenge on those who threaten their divine missions.

CREATING A MONSTER OF LEGEND

"Monster of legend" is a template that can be added to any animal, beast, magical beast, or monstrous humanoid (hereafter referred to as the base creature). The creature's type changes to outsider, though the monster of legend's home plane is the Material Plane. It has all the base creature's attributes except as noted here.

Hit Dice: All the base creature's Hit Dice increase to d8s (if smaller than d8, otherwise same as base creature).

Speed: Same as base creature.

AC: Base creature's natural armor bonus improves by +5.

Attacks: Same as base creature.

Damage: Same as base creature or as indicated on the table below, whichever is greater.

Size	Slam	Bite	Claw	Gore
Fine	1	1	—	—
Diminutive	1d2	1d2	1	—
Tiny	1d3	1d3	1d2	1
Small	1d4	1d4	1d3	1d2
Medium-size	1d6	1d6	1d4	1d3
Large	1d8	1d8	1d6	1d4
Huge	2d6	2d6	2d4	1d6
Gargantuan	2d8	2d8	2d6	1d8
Colossal	4d6	4d6	2d8	2d6

Special Attacks: A monster of legend retains the base creature's extraordinary, supernatural, and spell-like abilities. In addition, it gains one of the following special attacks.

Breath Weapon (Su): Every 1d4 rounds, the monster of legend can use a breath weapon (15-foot cone, 3d6 damage). Choose one of the following energy types: acid, fire, lightning, or cold. A target can make a Reflex save (DC 10 + 1/2 monster of legend's Hit Dice + monster of legend's Constitution modifier) for half damage.

Frightful Presence (Ex): When a monster of legend makes a loud sound (a roar, growl, or other sound appropriate to its form), it inspires terror in all creatures within 20 feet that have fewer Hit Dice or levels than it has. Each potentially affected opponent must succeed at a Will save (DC 10 + 1/2 monster of legend's Hit Dice + monster of legend's Charisma modifier) or become shaken—a condition that lasts until the opponent is out of range. A successful save leaves that opponent immune to that monster of legend's frightful presence for 24 hours.

Poison (Ex): A monster of legend delivers its poison with each successful bite attack. A target that succeeds at a Fortitude save (DC 10 + 1/2 the monster of legend's Hit Dice + the monster of legend's Constitution modifier) does not take poison damage from that particular attack. The initial and secondary damage is the same: 1d6 points of Strength damage.

Raging Blood (Su): Choose whether the monster of legend has acid, fire, or electricity in its blood. Each time damage is dealt to the creature with a piercing or slashing attack, its blood sprays outward in a 5-foot cone, dealing 1d4 points of damage of the selected energy type to all within range (no saving throw). A monster of legend is not harmed by its own blood.

Spells: The monster of legend casts divine spells from the cleric list and from the Protection, Strength, and War domains as a 5th-level cleric (save DC 10 + spell level + the monster of legend's Wisdom modifier). It does not gain extra domain spell slots for these domains as a cleric would.

Special Qualities: A monster of legend retains the base creature's extraordinary, supernatural, and spell-like abilities. In addition, it gains two of the following special qualities.

Damage Reduction (Su): 10/+1.

Enhanced Attributes (Ex): The save DC for each of the monster of legend's special attacks, spells, and spell-like abilities increases by +4.

Fast Healing (Ex): A monster of legend regains lost hit points at the rate of 5 per round. Fast healing does not restore hit points lost from starvation, thirst, or suffocation, and it does not allow the monster of legend to regrow or reattach lost body parts.

Greater Damage (Ex): Damage dice for the creature's natural attacks are increased by one die type, as indicated on the table below.

Old Damage	New Damage
—	1
1	1d2
1d2	1d3
1d3	1d4
1d4	1d6
1d6	1d8
1d8	2d6

Haste (Su): The creature is supernaturally quick. It can take an extra partial action each round, as if affected by a *haste* spell.

Immunities (Ex): The creature is immune to two of the following effects: acid, electricity, fear, poison, polymorphing, or mind-affecting effects.

Reflective Hide (Su): The creature has a silvery sheen to its skin and is permanently protected by a *spell turning* effect.

Regrow Limbs (Ex): If the creature loses a limb, head, or body part, a new one grows in 1 round. A monster of legend with this ability cannot be slain by a vorpal weapon's head-severing ability.

See in Darkness (Su): The creature can see perfectly in darkness of any kind, even that created by *deeper darkness* spells.

Spell Resistance (Su): The creature has spell resistance equal to 10 + 1/2 monster of legend's Hit Dice.

Subtype (Ex): The creature has one of the following subtypes: cold or fire.

Saves: Each of the base creature's base saves increases by +3.

Abilities: Increase from the base creature as follows: Str +10, Dex +6, Con +10, Int +2, Wis +2, Cha +4.

Skills: A monster of legend has skill points as the base creature, adjusted for its increased Intelligence score. Its class skills are as the base creature.

Feats: A monster of legend gains Improved Initiative and Multiattack as bonus feats.

Climate/Terrain: Same as base creature.
Organization: Same as base creature.
Challenge Rating: Same as base creature +2.
Treasure: Same as base creature.
Alignment: Same as base creature.
Advancement: Same as base creature.

SAMPLE MONSTER OF LEGEND

Here is a sample monster of legend using a minotaur as the base creature.

Minotaur of Legend
Large Outsider
Hit Dice: 6d8+42 (69 hp)
Initiative: +7
Speed: 40 ft., fly 30 ft. (poor)
AC: 22 (–1 size, +3 Dex, +10 natural), touch 12, flat-footed 22
Attacks: Gore +14 melee, or Huge greataxe +14/+9 melee and gore +12 melee
Damage: Gore 1d8+13 (primary), Huge greataxe 2d8+13/×3, gore 1d8+4 (secondary)
Face/Reach: 5 ft. by 5 ft./10 ft.
Special Attacks: Breath weapon (15-ft. cone of fire), charge 4d6+13
Special Qualities: Darkvision 60 ft., DR 10/+1, immunities, natural cunning, outsider traits, scent
Saves: Fort +14, Ref +11, Will +9
Abilities: Str 29, Dex 16, Con 25, Int 9, Wis 12, Cha 10
Skills: Intimidate +6, Jump +13, Listen +11, Search +7, Spot +11
Feats: Great Fortitude, Improved Initiative (B), Multiattack (B), Power Attack

Climate/Terrain: Any underground
Organization: Solitary, pair, or gang (3–4)
Challenge Rating: 6
Treasure: Double standard
Alignment: Usually chaotic evil
Advancement: By character class

Breath Weapon (Su): Every 1d4 rounds, the minotaur of legend can breathe a 15-foot cone of fire that deals 3d6 points of fire damage (Reflex DC 20 half).

Charge (Ex): A minotaur of legend typically begins a battle by charging at an opponent, lowering its head to bring its mighty horns into play. In addition to the normal benefits and hazards of a charge, this allows the creature to make a single gore attack that deals 4d6+13 points of damage.

Immunities (Ex): A minotaur of legend is immune to acid and mind-affecting effects.

Natural Cunning (Ex): Although a minotaur of legend is not especially intelligent, it possesses innate cunning and logical ability. This makes it immune to *maze* spells, prevents it from ever becoming lost, and enables it to track enemies. Further, the creature is never caught flat-footed.

Outsider Traits: A minotaur of legend has darkvision (60-foot range). It cannot be raised or resurrected.

Scent (Ex): A minotaur of legend can detect approaching enemies, sniff out hidden foes, and track by sense of smell.

SPELLSTITCHED

Spellstitched creatures are undead creatures that have been powerfully enhanced and fortified by arcane means. The undead gain the ability to cast spells, can resist being turned, and become more difficult to attack in melee. The process benefits undead with intelligence far more than it helps those that are mindless, since intelligent undead can discharge their spells tactically.

The outward sign that an undead creature has been spellstitched is its rune-covered body. The runes are carved into the bones of skeletal undead or tattooed on the rotting flesh of other corporeal undead. These runes may not be immediately noticeable to an observer, appearing to be cracks in bones or wrinkles in the skin.

Spellstitched creatures can be created only by a wizard or sorcerer of sufficient level to cast the spells to be imbued in the undead's body. The process for creating a spellstitched creature requires the expenditure of 1,000 gp for carving or tattooing materials as well as 500 XP for every point of Wisdom that the undead creature possesses. Undead that are spellcasters can spellstitch themselves.

CREATING A SPELLSTITCHED CREATURE

"Spellstitched" is a template that can be added to any corporeal undead (referred to hereafter as the base creature). The template uses all the base creature's statistics and special abilities except as noted here.

Special Attacks: A spellstitched creature retains all the special attacks of the base creature and gains the following special attack.

Spell-Like Abilities: A spellstitched creature with a Wisdom score of 10 or higher can be imbued with spell-like abilities. All spells selected must be from the schools of Conjuration, Evocation, or Necromancy. These abilities are used as if the spells were cast by a sorcerer of the same level as the number of Hit Dice the spellstitched creature possesses.

Wisdom	Example Undead	Spells Known	Times/Day
10	Skeleton, zombie	2 1st-level	4
11–12	Bodak	plus 2 2nd-level	4/4
13–14	Ghast, ghoul, wight	plus 2 3rd-level	4/4/2
15–16	Devourer	plus 2 4th-level	4/4/2/2
17–18	Lich	plus 2 5th-level	4/4/2/2/2
19+	Nightshade	plus 1 6th-level	4/4/2/2/2/1

Spells Known is the number of different spells the creature has access to as spell-like abilities. A creature with a Wisdom score higher than 10 gains the spells from the row on the table corresponding to its Wisdom score, and the spells from all the rows above that row.

Times/Day is the number of times per day that the creature can use spell-like abilities of a given level. The creator of the creature must decide how to allocate the spells known. Once this determination has been made for a particular ability, it cannot be changed. For instance, the sample spellstitched creature has *magic missile* and *obscuring mist* as its 1st-level spell-like abilities. It can use *magic missile* three times per day and *obscuring mist* once per day. The creator cannot later change either the spells or the times per day each can be used.

Special Qualities: A spellstitched creature retains all the special qualities of the base creature and gains the following special qualities.

Damage Reduction: A spellstitched creature with 1–3 HD has no damage reduction. One with 4–7 HD has DR 5/+1; one with 8–11 HD has DR 5/+2; and one with 12 or more HD has DR 10/+3.

Spell Resistance: A spellstitched creature has spell resistance equal to 15 + base creature's Charisma bonus.

Turn Resistance (Ex): A spellstitched creature has +2 turn resistance. This value is added to the base creature's turn resistance (if any).

If the base creature already has one or more of these special qualities, use the better value.

Saves: Same as base creature +2.
Abilities: Same as base creature.
Skills: Same as base creature.
Feats: Same as base creature.

Climate/Terrain: Same as base creature.
Organization: Same as base creature.
Challenge Rating: Same as base creature +1.

Treasure: Same as base creature.

Alignment: Same as base creature.

Advancement: Same as base creature.

SAMPLE SPELLSTITCHED CREATURE

Spellstitched Ghast

Medium-Size Undead

Hit Dice: 4d12 (26 hp)

Initiative: +2

Speed: 30 ft.

AC: 16 (+2 Dex, +4 natural), touch 12, flat-footed 14

Attacks: Bite +4 melee and 2 claws +1 melee

Damage: Bite 1d8+1 plus paralysis, claw 1d4 plus paralysis

Face/Reach: 5 ft. by 5 ft./5 ft.

Special Attacks: Paralysis, stench, spell-like abilities

Special Qualities: Create spawn, DR 5/+1, SR 18, turn resistance +4, undead traits

Saves: Fort +3, Ref +5, Will +8

Abilities: Str 13, Dex 15, Con –, Int 13, Wis 14, Cha 16

Skills: Climb +6, Escape Artist +8, Hide +8, Intuit Direction +3, Jump +6, Listen +8, Move Silently +7, Search +6, Spot +8

Feats: Multiattack, Weapon Finesse (bite)

Climate/Terrain: Any land or underground

Organization: Solitary, pair, gang (3–4), or pack (3–4 plus 7–12 ghouls)

Challenge Rating: 4

Treasure: Standard

Alignment: Always chaotic evil

Advancement: 5–6 HD (Medium-size)

Paralysis (Ex): Anyone hit by a spellstitched ghast's bite or claw attack must succeed at a Fortitude save (DC 15) or be paralyzed for 1d6+4 minutes. Even elves are vulnerable to this paralysis.

Stench (Ex): The stink of death and corruption surrounding these creatures is sickening. Each creature within 10 feet must succeed at a Fortitude save (DC 15) or be wracked with nausea, taking a –2 circumstance penalty on all attack rolls, saves, and skill checks for 1d6+4 minutes.

Spell-Like Abilities: 3/day—*darkness, magic missile;* 1/day—*flame arrow, Melf's acid arrow, obscuring mist, vampiric touch.* Caster level 4th; save DC 17 + spell level.

Create Spawn (Su): Humanoid victims of a spellstitched ghast that are not devoured by the creature rise as ghasts (not spellstitched ghasts) in 1d4 days.

Turn Resistance (Ex): A spellstitched ghast is treated as an undead with 8 Hit Dice for the purpose of turn, rebuke, command, and bolster attempts.

Undead Traits: A spellstitched ghast is immune to mind-affecting effects, poison, *sleep,* paralysis, stunning, disease, death effects, necromantic effects, and any effect that requires a Fortitude save unless it also works on objects. It is not subject to critical hits, subdual damage, ability damage, ability drain, energy drain, or death from massive damage. A spellstitched ghast cannot be raised, and resurrection works only if it is willing. The creature has darkvision (60-foot range).

TAURIC

A tauric creature is a hybrid being possessing the head, arms, and upper torso of a humanoid, and the legs and lower body of an animal, beast, or vermin. Some are created as the result of magical experiments or as divine punishment for failing their deities. Tauric creatures of the same kind form a unique race with its own culture, language, and religion. Tauric creatures are not to be confused with two-legged humanoid/creature hybrids such as the minotaur or the satyr, which have different traits from their apparent component creatures.

Tauric creatures speak the languages of both of their component creatures, as well as any language they have developed as a people.

CREATING A TAURIC CREATURE

"Tauric" is a template that combines two creatures into one hybrid creature. The template can be added to any Small or Medium-size corporeal humanoid (referred to hereafter as the base humanoid) and any Medium-size or Large corporeal animal, beast, or vermin with at least four legs (referred to hereafter as the base creature). A tauric creature's type changes to monstrous humanoid. It otherwise uses all the base creature's attributes and special abilities except as noted below.

Size: Same as base creature.

Hit Dice: Add the base humanoid's and base creature's Hit Dice to get the tauric creature's Hit Dice, each of which changes to a d8. A humanoid that normally has a class instead of 1 Hit Die counts as a 1-HD creature.

AC: A tauric creature has the natural armor bonus of the base creature or the base humanoid, whichever is better.

Attacks and Damage: A tauric creature retains the natural weapons and base damage of the base humanoid and the base creature, provided that the tauric creature's physical form is capable of delivering those attacks. The absence of the base creature's head always results in the loss of the base creature's bite attack. If the creature loses its primary attack in this fashion, all of its remaining natural attacks are still secondary. A tauric creature has the base attack bonus of a monstrous humanoid of the tauric creature's total nonclass Hit Dice.

Special Attacks: A tauric creature retains the special attacks of the base humanoid and the base creature, provided that the tauric creature is capable of delivering the attack. The absence of the base creature's head always results in the loss of the base creature's breath weapon or gaze attack.

Special Qualities: A tauric creature retains the special qualities of the base humanoid and the base creature.

Saves: For each saving throw, use the base save for either the base creature or the base humanoid, whichever is higher.

Abilities: A tauric creature uses the base humanoid's Intelligence, Wisdom, and Charisma scores, and it uses the base creature's Strength, Dexterity, and Constitution scores.

Skills: A tauric creature gains skill points as a monstrous humanoid of its nonclass Hit Dice. Treat skills from both the base creature's list and the base humanoid's list as class skills. If the creature has a class, it gains skill points for class levels normally.

Feats: A tauric creature gains feats as a monstrous humanoid of its nonclass Hit Dice. It favors the feats of the base creature and the base humanoid.

Climate/Terrain: Same as either base humanoid or base creature, whichever is more restrictive.

Organization: Same as either base humanoid or base creature, whichever uses the smaller number ranges.

Challenge Rating: Same as base creature +1.

Treasure: Same as base humanoid.

Alignment: Same as base humanoid.

Advancement: By character class of base humanoid.

SAMPLE TAURIC CREATURE

Here is an example of a tauric creature using a griffon as the base creature and a 1st-level hobgoblin warrior as the base humanoid.

Tauric Hobgoblin-Griffon
Large Monstrous Humanoid
Hit Dice: 8d8+24 (60 hp)
Initiative: +2
Speed: 30 ft., fly 80 ft. (average)
AC: 18 (−1 size, +2 Dex, +6 natural, +1 small wooden shield), touch 11, flat-footed 16
Attacks: Longsword +11/+6 melee and 2 claws +6 melee, or javelin +9 ranged
Damage: Longsword 1d8+4/19–20, claw 2d6+2, javelin 1d6+4

Face/Reach: 5 ft. by 10 ft./5 ft.
Special Attacks: Pounce, rake 1d6+2
Special Qualities: Darkvision 60 ft., low-light vision, scent
Saves: Fort +11, Ref +8, Will +2
Abilities: Str 18, Dex 15, Con 16, Int 10, Wis 10, Cha 10
Skills: Intimidate +5, Jump +13, Listen +13, Move Silently +5, Spot +12*
Feats: Alertness, Great Fortitude

Climate/Terrain: Temperate and warm hills and mountains
Organization: Solitary, pair, or pride (6–10)
Challenge Rating: 5
Treasure: Standard
Alignment: Usually lawful evil
Advancement: By character class

Pounce (Ex): If a tauric hobgoblin-griffon charges, it can make a full attack (including a rake attempt; see below) even though it has moved.

Rake (Ex): A tauric hobgoblin-griffon that pounces on an opponent can make two rake attacks (+10 melee) with its hind legs for 1d6+2 points of damage each.

Skills: A tauric hobgoblin-griffon receives a +4 racial bonus on Jump and Move Silently checks. *It also receives a +4 racial bonus on Spot checks in daylight.

TITANIC

Titanic creatures are created as the result of powerful transformation magic as well as forces of nature gone awry. Because of a titanic creature's limited intelligence, it is incapable of perceiving itself as a Gargantuan being and has difficulty interacting with its much "smaller" surroundings. The transformation usually leaves a titanic creature confused or bewildered.

Except for their size, titanic creatures look identical to the smaller creatures they were. Titanic creatures tower over most living things, ranging between 32 and 64 feet in height (or length). They weigh anywhere from 32,000 to more than 200,000 pounds.

CREATING A TITANIC CREATURE

"Titanic" is a template than can be applied to any Medium-size or smaller animal or vermin (referred to hereafter as the base creature). It uses all the base creature's statistics and special abilities except as noted here.

Size: Increase to Gargantuan.

Hit Dice: Increase HD to 25.

Speed: Same as base creature or 20 feet, whichever is greater. A titanic creature with flight has clumsy maneuverability.

AC: A titanic creature's AC is equal to 10 + the creature's size modifier (always −4 for a Gargantuan creature) + the creature's Dexterity modifier + 20 (natural armor).

Attacks: A titanic creature's base attack bonus (with any attack it is capable of making) is 18 (25 Hit Dice × 3/4). If the base creature has no physical attack that deals damage,

JJ

assign one natural attack appropriate to the base creature.

Damage: Replace the base creature's damage values with the titanic damage values given below.

TITANIC DAMAGE VALUES

Bite	Claw	Gore	Slam
3d8	3d6	3d8	2d8

Face/Reach: A titanic creature's face/reach is 20 ft. by 20 ft/20 ft., or 10 ft. by 40 ft./10 ft., or 20 ft. by 40 ft./10 ft., depending on its body shape.

Special Attacks: A titanic creature retains the special attacks of the base creature and also gains the abilities and modifications described below.

Area Attacks (Ex): A titanic creature's area attacks (such as a spider's ability to generate webs) increase in size to gigantic proportions. Multiply the height, width, and length of the base creature's area attack by the area modifier given on the Titanic Modifiers table.

Increased Damage (Ex): Damage from a special attack other than poison or trample is tripled, if the attack deals hit point damage.

Poison Increase (Ex): If the base creature has a poison attack, increase the initial and secondary damage to 2d6. The save DC to avoid a titanic creature's poison is 22 + the creature's Constitution modifier.

Trample (Ex): As a standard action during its turn each round, a titanic creature can trample Huge or smaller opponents. This attack deals points of damage equal to 3d8 + 1 1/2 times the creature's Strength bonus. A trampled opponent can attempt either an attack of opportunity at a –4 penalty or a Reflex save (DC 22 + the titanic creature's Str bonus) for half damage.

Special Qualities: Same as base creature.

TITANIC MODIFIERS

Size of Base Creature	Str	Dex	Con	Area Modifier
Fine	+36	–12	+16	×12
Diminutive	+36	–10	+16	×10
Tiny	+34	–8	+16	×8
Small	+30	–6	+16	×6
Medium-size	+26	–4	+14	×4

Saves: A titanic creature has a base save bonus of +14 in each category (ability modifiers apply as normal).

Abilities: Strength, Dexterity, and Constitution change as indicated on the Titanic Modifiers table, but the Dexterity score can never be lower than 10. Intelligence, Wisdom, and Charisma are the same as the base creature.

Skills: Same as base creature, adjusted for size and ability score changes.

Feats: A titanic creature receives Great Fortitude as a bonus feat.

Climate/Terrain: Same as base creature.

Organization: Solitary, pair, or cluster (3–5).

Challenge Rating: 13 if base creature's CR is 1 or lower; same as base creature + 13 if base creature's CR is 2 or more.

Treasure: Same as base creature.

Alignment: Same as base creature.

Advancement: None

SAMPLE TITANIC CREATURE

Here is an example of a titanic creature using a toad as the base creature.

Titanic Toad
Gargantuan Animal
Hit Dice: 25d8+200 (312 hp)
Initiative: +0
Speed: 20 ft.
AC: 26 (–4 size, +20 natural), touch 6, flat-footed 26
Attacks: Bite +27 melee
Damage: Bite 3d8+19
Face/Reach: 20 ft. by 20 ft./20 ft.
Special Attacks: Trample 3d8+19
Special Qualities: Low-light vision
Saves: Fort +24, Ref +14, Will +16
Abilities: Str 37, Dex 10, Con 27, Int 1, Wis 14, Cha 4
Skills: Hide –4, Listen +5, Spot +5
Feats: Great Fortitude (B)

Climate/Terrain: Temperate and warm land and aquatic
Organization: Solitary
Challenge Rating: 13
Treasure: None
Alignment: Always neutral
Advancement: —

Trample (Ex): As a standard action during its turn each round, a titanic toad can trample a Huge or smaller opponent. This attack deals 3d8+19 points of bludgeoning damage. A trampled opponent can attempt either an attack of opportunity at a –4 penalty or a Reflex save (DC 35) for half damage.

WARBEAST

The warbeast is a creature born and raised to serve as a rider's mount. Bred for exceptional strength, aggression, and surefootedness, these creatures are powerfully built, strong-willed, and openly belligerent.

CREATING A WARBEAST

"Warbeast" is a template that can be added to any Medium-size or larger animal, beast, or vermin (referred to hereafter as the base creature). A warbeast uses all the base creature's attributes and special abilities except as noted here.

The *Monster Manual* describes a few "war creatures" that have qualities similar to those of a warbeast but differ from standard creatures of a given kind. These creatures are considered to already have a separate "war template" and cannot have the warbeast template added. For example, one cannot apply the warbeast template to a heavy warhorse.

Hit Dice: Same as base creature +1.

Speed: Same as base creature +10 feet.

AC: Same as base creature.

Attacks: Same as base creature (modified as appropriate for added Hit Die and Strength increase).

Damage: Same as base creature (modified as appropriate for Strength increase).

Special Qualities: A warbeast retains the special qualities of the base creature and gains the following special quality.

Combative Mount (Ex): A rider on a trained warbeast mount gets a +2 circumstance bonus on all Ride checks. A trained warbeast is proficient with light, medium, and heavy armor. A vermin warbeast, being mindless and therefore untrainable, cannot have this ability.

Saves: Same as base creature (modified as appropriate for the added Hit Die and ability score increases).

Abilities: Increase from base creature as follows: Str +3, Dex +0, Con +3, Int +0, Wis +2, Cha +0.

Skills: A warbeast receives a +1 racial bonus on Listen and Spot checks.

Climate/Terrain: Same as base creature.
Organization: Solitary.
Challenge Rating: Same as base creature +1.
Treasure: None.
Alignment: Same as base creature.
Advancement: Same as base creature.

TRAINING A WARBEAST

A warbeast can be reared and trained just as the base creature can. If the base creature is a domestic animal, the creature need not be specially reared, but it must be trained for two months (Handle Animal DC 20) to develop its abilities.

A warbeast based on a wild animal must be reared for one year (Handle Animal DC 15 + HD of the warbeast), then trained for 2 months (Handle Animal DC 20 + HD of the warbeast).

A warbeast based on a beast must be reared for one year (Handle Animal DC 20 + HD of the warbeast), then trained for 2 months (Handle Animal DC 25 + HD of the warbeast).

A warbeast based on a vermin, being mindless, is untrainable.

A trained warbeast is capable of carrying a rider into battle, and it gains the combative mount special quality (see above).

Market Price: The market price of a warbeast is a function of its Hit Dice: 50 gp/HD for a warbeast of 3 HD or less, or 100 gp + 75 gp/HD for one of 4 HD or more.

SAMPLE WARBEAST

Here is a sample warbeast using a rhinoceros as the base creature.

Warbeast Rhinoceros
Large Animal
Hit Dice: 9d8+63 (103 hp)
Initiative: +0
Speed: 30 ft. (base 40 ft.)
AC: 20 (–1 size, +7 natural, +4 scale barding), touch 9, flat-footed 20
Attacks: Gore +14 melee
Damage: Gore 2d6+13
Special Qualities: Combative mount, low-light vision
Face/Reach: 5 ft. by 10 ft./5 ft.
Saves: Fort +13, Ref +6, Will +5
Abilities: Str 29, Dex 10, Con 24, Int 2, Wis 15, Cha 2
Skills: Listen +13, Spot +3

Climate/Terrain: Warm plains
Organization: Solitary
Challenge Rating: 5
Treasure: None
Alignment: Always neutral
Advancement: 10–13 HD (Large); 14–27 HD (Huge)

The market price for a warbeast rhinoceros is 775 gp.

Combat

Combative Mount (Ex): A rider on a warbeast rhinoceros gets a +2 circumstance bonus on Ride checks. A warbeast rhinoceros is proficient with light, medium, and heavy armor.

RAZOR BOAR

Large Beast
Hit Dice: 15d10+45 (127 hp)
Initiative: +1
Speed: 50 ft.
AC: 27 (–1 size, +1 Dex, +17 natural), touch 10, flat-footed 26
Attacks: Gore +18 melee and 2 hooves +13 melee, or bite +18 melee
Damage: Gore 1d8+8, hoof 1d4+4, bite 1d8+8
Face/Reach: 5 ft. by 10 ft./5 ft.
Special Attacks: Trample 2d6+12, vorpal tusks
Special Qualities: Darkvision 60 ft., DR 20/+3, fast healing 10, low-light vision, scent, SR 21
Saves: Fort +12, Ref +10, Will +7
Abilities: Str 27, Dex 13, Con 17, Int 2, Wis 14, Cha 9
Skills: Listen +8, Spot +7, Wilderness Lore +6

Climate/Terrain:
   Temperate or warm forest or mountains
Organization:
   Solitary
Challenge Rating:
   10
Treasure: None
Alignment: Always neutral
Advancement:
   16–30 HD (Large);
   31–45 HD (Huge)

This enormous boar has a black-bristled hide marked by hundreds of old scars. Its eyes are wild and bloodshot, and its tusks are more than three feet long, gleaming like polished ivory and sharper than many swords.

COMBAT

A razor boar attacks intruders on its territory without provocation or warning. If attacking more than one target, it tramples one and slashes the other with its tusks and forehooves. The creature is swift for its size, and the thickness of its hide allows it to shrug off many blows. Razor boars have been known to recover from seemingly mortal wounds, track down their attackers, and exact revenge.

Trample (Ex): As a standard action during its turn each round, a razor boar can trample opponents at least one size category smaller than itself. This attack deals 2d6+12 points of bludgeoning damage. A trampled opponent can attempt either an attack of opportunity at a –4 penalty or a Reflex save (DC 25) for half damage.

Vorpal Tusks (Ex): On a successful critical hit against a creature of up to one size category larger than itself, the razor boar's gore attack severs the opponent's head (if it has one) from its body. Though some creatures,

The game text presented on pages 220 and 221 is considered Open Game Content. The artwork is property of Wizards of the Coast and cannot be reproduced without permission.

such as golems and undead other than vampires, are not affected by the loss of their heads, most creatures die when their heads are cut off.

Fast Healing (Ex): A razor boar regains lost hit points at the rate of 10 per round. Fast healing does not restore hit points lost from starvation, thirst, or suffocation, and it does not allow the razor boar to regrow or reattach lost body parts.

Scent (Ex): A razor boar can detect approaching enemies, sniff out hidden foes, and track by sense of smell.

SCORPIONFOLK

Large Monstrous Humanoid
Hit Dice: 12d8+12 (66 hp)
Initiative: +1
Speed: 40 ft.
AC: 16 (−1 size, +1 Dex, +6 natural), touch 10, flat-footed 15
Attacks: Sting +15 melee and 2 claws +13 melee, or Large heavy lance +11/+6/+1 melee and sting +13 melee and 2 claws +13 melee
Damage: Sting 1d8+4 plus poison (primary), claw 1d6+2, Large heavy lance 2d6+6/×3, sting 1d8+2 plus poison (secondary)
Face/Reach: 5 ft. by 10 ft./5 ft.
Special Attacks: Poison, spell-like abilities, trample 1d8+6
Special Qualities: Darkvision 60 ft., fire resistance 5, SR 18
Saves: Fort +5, Ref +9, Will +10
Abilities: Str 19, Dex 12, Con 13, Int 8, Wis 14, Cha 15
Skills: Diplomacy +4, Intimidate +11, Listen +13, Sense Motive +11, Spot +13
Feats: Alertness, Multiattack, Power Attack

Climate/Terrain: Warm desert, plains, and hills
Organization: Solitary, pair, company (3–5), patrol (6–20 plus 2–8 Medium-size monstrous scorpions plus 1 3rd–5th level ranger), or troop (21–40 plus 4–32 Medium-size monstrous scorpions and 1–4 Large monstrous scorpions plus 1 6th–8th level cleric plus 1 6th–8th level ranger)
Challenge Rating: 7
Treasure: Standard
Alignment: Usually lawful evil
Advancement: By character class

Scorpionfolk are nomadic creatures forced into desolate regions by other races.

From the waist up, a scorpionfolk appears to be a four-armed humanoid covered with black armor. From the waist down, it looks like an enormous scorpion. One pair of arms ends in vicious claws, while the other pair ends in humanoid hands. A scorpionfolk has waxy, gray skin, and its eyes are entirely black.

Scorpionfolk speak Common and Terran.

COMBAT

Scorpionfolk use *major image* to create illusions of small oases or wells, luring travelers into traps. They then charge their opponents, attacking with their lances. Any who survive the charge are trampled and attacked with stingers, claws, and any melee weapons carried by the creatures. In addition to their claws and sting, scorpionfolk may use falchions, spears, scimitars, short bows, or crossbows.

Poison (Ex): A scorpionfolk delivers its poison (Fortitude save DC 17) with each successful sting attack. The initial and secondary damage is 1d4 points of Dexterity damage.

Spell-Like Abilities: 1/day—*major image*; 2/day—*mirror image*. Caster level 10th; save DC 12 + spell level.

Trample (Ex): As a standard action during its turn each round, a scorpionfolk can trample opponents at least one size category smaller than itself. This attack deals 1d8+6 points of bludgeoning damage. A trampled opponent can attempt either an attack of opportunity at a −4 penalty or a Reflex save (DC 20) for half damage.

SCORPIONFOLK SOCIETY

Scorpionfolk are nomads that live austerely and move frequently. They carry their belongings with them, and use tents for shelter.

Companies and patrols are usually younger individuals out hunting or scouting in force. Scorpionfolk tribes tend to include more experienced—and less expendable—individuals. Scorpionfolk survive through a combination of hunting, foraging, and raiding. They sometimes barter with creatures powerful enough to withstand their attacks.

SCORPIONFOLK CHARACTERS

A scorpionfolk character's preferred class is ranger, with some few taking levels of barbarian. Scorpionfolk rarely become druids, preferring levels of cleric instead. Reports of scorpionfolk sorcerers have not been confirmed.

A scorpionfolk PC's effective character level (ECL) is equal to its class level + 16. Thus, a 1st-level scorpionfolk ranger has an ECL of 17 and is the equivalent of a 17th-level character.

The game text presented on pages 220 and 221 is considered Open Game Content. The artwork is property of Wizards of the Coast and cannot be reproduced without permission.

Moonrat 1/4
Neogi spawn 1/4

Twig blight 1/3

Corollax 1/2
Jermlaine 1/2
Myconid, junior worker 1/2

Ash rat 1
Average ixitxachitl 1
Bladeling 1
Bogun 1
Chaond 1
Ether scarab 1
Crested felldrake 1
Myconid, average worker 1
Tatterdemanimal 1
Thri-kreen 1
Zenythri 1

Abeil, vassal 2
Abyssal maw 2
Abyssal skulker 2
Cloaked ape 2
Dire hawk 2
Dread guard 2
Grimalkin 2
Loxo 2
Myconid, elder worker 2
Needlefolk 2
Phase wasp 2
Spitting felldrake 2
Stone spike 2

Advespa 3
Boggle 3
Cervidal 3
Cryptoclidus 3
Desmodu bat, guard bat 3
Desmodu bat, hunting bat 3
Dire toad 3
Fihyr 3
Fire bat 3
Grell 3
Hammerer 3
Horned felldrake 3
Meenlock 3
Pulverizer 3
Raggamoffyn, common 3
Vampiric ixitxachitl 3
Wortling 3

Asperi 4
Captured one bugbear 4
Clay half-golem 4
Dire horse 4
Electrum clockwork horror 4
Flesh half-golem 4
Iron half-golem 4
Myconid, guard 4
Neogi, adult 4
Spellstitched ghast 4
Stone half-golem 4
Yak folk 4

Abyssal ravager 5
Average psurlon 5
Chain golem 5
Desmodu bat, war bat 5
Dire snake 5
Gambol 5
Gold clockwork horror 5
Guttersnipe 5
Half-fiend, durzagon 5
Jovoc 5
Lupinal 5
Marrash 5
Morkoth 5
Reason stealer 5
Sirine 5
Spawn of Kyuss 5
Stained glass golem 5
Sylph 5
Tauric hobgoblin-griffon 5
Warbeast rhinoceros 5
Wyste 5

Abeil, soldier 6
Blood ape 6
Catoblepas 6
Hook horror 6
Kopru 6
Legendary eagle 6
Minotaur of legend 6
Myconid, circle leader 6
Neogi, great old master 6
Ormyrr 6

Allosaurus 7
Amnizu 7
Ankylosaurus 7
Breathdrinker 7
Darktentacles 7
Dire elk 7
Frost salamander 7
Legendary ape 7
Legendary wolf 7
Mudmaw 7
Myconid, sovereign 7
Nimblewright 7
Platinum clockwork horror 7
Scorpionfolk 7
Shrapnyl 7
Swamplight lynx 7

Glimmerskin 8
Gravorg 8
Legendary horse 8
Legendary snake 8
Nethersight mastiff 8
Palrethee 8
Quetzalcoatlus 8

Adamantine clockwork horror ...9
Braxat 9
Chimeric ankheg 9
Desmodu 9
Dune stalker 9
Elder psurlon 9
Galeb duhr 9

Immoth 9
Legendary bear 9
Malebranche 9
Rogue eidolon 9
Vaporighu 9
Zovvut 9

Avolakia 10
Brass golem 10
Bronze serpent 10
Dire elephant 10
Greenvise 10
Leechwalker 10
Legendary shark 10
Legendary tiger 10
Marraenoloth 10
Mooncalf 10
Razor boar 10
Runic guardian 10
Spell weaver 10
Yagnoloth 10

Bone naga 11
Crimson death 11
Fomorian 11
Forest giant 11
Forest sloth 11
Juggernaut 11
Megalodon 11

Abeil, queen 12
Air weird 12
Earth weird 12
Ethereal slayer 12
Firbolg 12
Fire weird 12
Julajimus 12
Rampager 12
Seismosaurus 12
Shadow spider 12
Spellgaunt 12
Sun giant 12
Water weird 12

Death knight (sample) 13
Dragonflesh golem 13
Grizzly mastodon 13
Jarilith 13
Red sundew 13
Spinosaurus 13

Titanic toad 13

Rukarazyll 14

Ethereal doppelganger 15
Giant psurlon 15
Great fihyr 15
Nightmare beast 15
Windghost 15

Cloud ray 16
Gravecrawler 16
Jahi 16
Moonbeast 16
Tempest 16
Teratomorph 16

Arcanaloth 17
Banshee 17
Deathbringer 17
Effigy 17

Kelvezu 18
Ocean strider 18

Corpse gatherer 19
Famine spirit 19
Flesh jelly 19
Ocean giant 19
Ragewind 19

Gray linnorm 20
Megapede 20
Orcwort 20

Bone ooze 21

Chaos roc 22

Phoenix 24

Dread linnorm 25
Leviathan 25

Hellfire wyrm 26
Mountain giant 26

Corpse tearer 28
Fiendwurm 28

DRAGON CRs BY AGE AND COLOR

Age	Amethyst	Crystal	Emerald	Sapphire	Topaz
Wyrmling	3	2	2	2	3
Very young	4	3	4	4	4
Young	6	4	6	6	6
Juvenile	8	7	8	8	9
Young adult	11	10	11	10	12
Adult	14	12	14	13	14
Mature adult	16	15	16	15	17
Old	18	17	18	18	19
Very old	19	18	19	19	20
Ancient	21	20	21	21	22
Wyrm	23	21	22	22	23
Great wyrm	25	23	24	24	25

FIND THE EDGE
YOU NEED TO SUCCEED

Whether you swing steel or sling spells, you want to make sure your character
has what it takes to walk out of every encounter with treasure and a tale to tell.
Inside *Complete Divine*, *Complete Adventurer*, and *Complete Warrior*,
you'll find the stuff of which legends are made.

Look for them at your favorite hobby shop or bookstore.

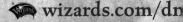
wizards.com/dn